SANGHA AND STATE IN BURMA

*A Study of Monastic
Sectarianism and Leadership*

Map of Burma indicating places mentioned in the text

SANGHA AND STATE IN BURMA

A Study of Monastic Sectarianism and Leadership

E. MICHAEL MENDELSON

edited by John P. Ferguson

Cornell University Press | ITHACA AND LONDON

Cornell University Press gratefully acknowledges
a grant from the Andrew J. Mellon Foundation
that aided in bringing this book to publication.

First published 1975 by Cornell University Press.
Published in the United Kingdom by Cornell University Press Ltd.,
2–4 Brook Street, London W1Y 1AA.

International Standard Book Number 0-8014-0875-X
Library of Congress Catalog Card Number 75-13398
Printed in the United States of America by York Composition Co., Inc.

to M.Y.N.E. and to P. A., who came with,
and to M., who came afterward:
kindred by blood

Contents

Appendixes

Editor's Preface

It has been a privilege to work with E. Michael Mendelson and to help to bring his long-awaited research to publication. Because Michael Mendelson left the field of anthropology some years ago, I feel it will be helpful for the reader to understand something of his background and to have some idea of why an editor was required for this book's publication.

Edward Michael Mendelson was born in France on June 30, 1928, and raised in France, Belgium, and England. After studying history and English literature as a scholar of King's College, Cambridge, he returned to France as a journalist. Through seeing a movie, he discovered the Musée de l'Homme and promptly enrolled as a student. His teachers over the next two years included Marcel Griaule and fellow workers among the Dogon and Bambara of the French Sudan; André Leroi-Gourhan, the prehistorian; Claude Lévi-Strauss; and the distinguished Southeast Asia scholar Paul Lévy. As a student at the Ecole des Hautes Etudes, Mendelson wrote a paper for Lévy entitled "Tiger Mythology among the Assam Nagas," which earned him a School Diploma. He also worked on the Naga collections at the Musée de l'Homme.

In 1951 he came to the United States as a Smith-Mundt-Fulbright Scholar. After a period of orientation at Yale, he worked at Chicago under Fred Eggan, Sol Tax, and, especially, Robert Redfield. With Claude Tardits, he was the first to lecture at Chicago on the work of Lévi-Strauss, Leenhardt, and Griaule. In 1952, as a research assistant to Redfield, he went to Cuba for a short survey trip inspired by William Bascom of Northwestern. Later in the year, he was sent by Redfield to Santiago Atitlan, Guatemala, for work on his dissertation, "Religion and World-View," in that village.

Returning to England in 1953, Mendelson worked at the London School of Economics under Raymond Firth, Isaac Schapira, and S. F. Nadel. He obtained his doctorate from Chicago in 1957 with a work which remained unpublished, because of Redfield's death, but was subsequently issued in Spanish by the Ministry of Education of the Guatemalan government. He became a teaching assistant at the London School of Economics and, in 1958, obtained a Rockefeller grant, mediated by the Royal Institute of International Affairs, to study religion and politics in Burma. During his stay in Burma, he was asked to join the School of Oriental and African Studies (where he had studied Burmese under Hla Pe and Anna Allott) as lecturer in Southeast Asian anthropology in Christoph von Furer Haimendorf's Anthropology Department. Mendelson taught in that department for some years, writing and publishing many papers and addressing many professional conferences. He also worked on the text which was to become the basis for this book.

In the summer of 1967, Mendelson resigned from SOAS as well as from a visiting professorship in the Southeast Asia Program at Cornell University which would have been taken up that fall. He has undertaken no further anthropological activities since that date.

His years of field work in Burma and ground-breaking research produced a lengthy and highly complex manuscript which had to be abandoned before completion, and my role as editor has been to edit the material in such a fashion that its length would meet present-day publishing exigencies, its complexity would be explicated and clarified for the reader not completely familiar with Burmese Buddhism, and its contribution to anthropological research would remain vital. The original manuscript assumed a rather complete knowledge of Burmese history, culture, and Buddhism. The editing process has therefore consisted mainly of weaving the original material into a narrative with historical continuity, explaining the necessary terminology, clarifying the relationship of ethnographic data to the book's major themes, and helping, through discussions with Michael Mendelson, to bring the major themes to a point of focus.

To aid me in the editing process, Michael Mendelson reached across a decade of separation from his manuscript (to say nothing of fifteen years of absence from Burma) to make available his complete field notes and his personal diary from the period, as well as the basic Burmese translations and records. Although he and I have discussed various major points involving the book's key issues, our understanding was that I would edit the main body of the manuscript quite definitely on my own, and basically I have done so. Whenever necessary, I have added to the book the insights of my own research and labeled these with "J.F." in the footnotes. If through my own studies I noted discrepancies in the original manuscript, I edited the original so that it is now as accurate as possible. A few references to recent scholarly works not included in the original have been added when particularly relevant. The final product therefore is one which seeks to be faithful to the original but which also has grown into a somewhat up-dated version, different in some ways from what it was a decade ago. Yet I must make it clear that, even with these changes, the present text presents, in the vast majority of the paragraphs, the author's original wording, and to the best of my ability I have tried to retain both the original content and meaning.

Despite these efforts, the book remains complex and detailed because the subject of Burmese Buddhism is intricate and complicated beyond belief. Michael Mendelson pioneered in an area for which there were few established trails or guides, and at such stages in human exploration all data garnered are precious to those who follow. To aid the reader to follow him, I have added a map on which are most of the place names mentioned in the text, a glossary that gives the major terms used and their derivation, many explanatory footnotes, subheadings, glosses for foreign words in the text itself, and a detailed index that can be used as a research tool to trace persons and themes throughout the book's narrative. With such, it should be possible for the readers and scholars of the future to share the excitement of Michael Mendelson's original explorations.

I wish to thank most sincerely the Cornell Southeast Asia Program for its generous grant which helped to defray the costs of editing this book. Most appreciated also is the invaluable help given to me by both U Myo Lwin, Burmese cataloger at the Wason Library at Cornell, and Raymond Khamkeo of Chiengmai, Thailand, in dealing with vital definitions and transcriptions of Burmese terms. My thanks also are tendered to A. Thomas Kirsch, who introduced me not only to the study of Theravada Buddhism but also to Michael Mendelson. To my wife Catherine, who patiently typed all the various versions of this manuscript and whose care for detail and consistency helped to clarify the data as well, my deepest gratitude is offered.

JOHN P. FERGUSON

Ithaca, New York

Author's Preface

I wish, in this Preface, to say something about the conditions under which this work came into being, conditions rendered that much stranger, perhaps, by the fact that its author left it unfinished. Those who are frustrated in their attempts to enter Burma today should not jump to the conclusion that entry was easy in the late fifties. My wife and I endured what seemed at the time an endless wait while various bureaucracies made up their minds whether or not we were going to be allowed in; we endured particularly trying negotiations in regard to the grant obtained; we had to perform miracles of high-wire ambiguity in obtaining vital materials (a car, an icebox, photo supplies, and so on) while yet ignorant of the fate of our visas and sailing dates. Nor did matters become any easier when, after many weeks on a ship of the Bibby Line, we finally entered the Promised Land. Had I, like many anthropologists, been able to settle in a pleasant village, our stay would undoubtedly have been of a very different nature. A study at the national level, however, required a good deal of moving about. Hence, we were at the mercy of one bureaucratic office or another for almost every single day of our stay. Of all this, I wish only to say what I felt at the time: Franz Kafka had never really seen any of it, having failed to visit Southeast Asia. I wish I could say that some help had been forthcoming from officials who my British nationality would have led me to believe might be helpful. That is not the case. Above all we felt we suffered, unlike American scholars for whom a "little man" from a foundation could always be found to run errands and act as buffer between anthropologist and bureaucrat, from a constant grinding down which very nearly led to severe illness toward the end of my stay. As it was, a substantial illness prevented my entry into the monkhood for a month; I have always regretted the frustration of that plan. This kind of thing is mentioned less for its own sake than for the light it may cast on the attitude I took toward data-collection in my chosen field. To say that life was obsessive is to speak but very mildly.

In other respects, I was undoubtedly fortunate. At this time it was still possible to get about in Burma. My wife and I spent some eight months in Rangoon (with side trips on my part to such places as Pegu and Prome) and went on a trip to Bangkok to attend the World Fellowship of Buddhists meeting. After that, we made our headquarters at Mandalay. During these months when based at Mandalay, we traveled in the Kachin States, all over the Shan States as far north as Muse and over to the Thai border, in central Burma around Mount Popa, Pagan, Pakokku, and other sites, and up the Chindwin River to Monywa. There was personal danger in this at the time; we were fortunate in escaping it. Living conditions in Rangoon, thanks to two very good friends, were virtually luxurious; elsewhere, they were abominable. The total time we spent in Burma between the summer of 1958 and the winter of 1959 was about eighteen months.

From the beginning, there was some conflict of intention regarding the basic plan of research. The Royal Institute of International Affairs, an early sponsor, was especially interested in the relations between the monkhood and the leading politicians of the regimes then in power. As an anthropologist, dissatisfied with theories of Burmese religion then current, I felt I would not be satisfied with less than a total view of Burmese religion. At the time this seemed to mean Theravada Buddhism on the one hand, spirit cults on the other. Some nine months into my stay I began to discover evidence of another, third, component, messianic Buddhism, which I came to consider my most original area of research and which I was rather frustrated in not being able to give my full attention to.

The evidence for the work done prior to this book on the third component of Buddhism has appeared in a number of articles listed in the Bibliography. The reader may gather from those that the kind of information I was looking for tended to be gathered more directly from the field in the case of animism and messianism, less directly in the case of Buddhism. Perhaps, if I had managed to concentrate more on the Sangha and politics, I would have devoted more field work to those two areas instead of record and document collection. As it was, it seemed to me that there was such an abominable paucity of documents, such a desperate need to find out if any existed, then to obtain them and to translate them, that I became somehow wary of the validity of my own observations and became obsessively concerned with objective documentation of the no man's land, the ghost patch, the misty country I was attempting to pin down. (It should also be said that I was influenced by my healthy respect for the Ecole Française d'Extrême Orient and its great insistence on documentation.) Once this search was begun, there was no end to it. Weeks were spent in visit after visit to this or that office to obtain complete runs of certain documents, magazines, reviews. Weeks were spent in Land Offices making copies of plans which might or might not prove useful. More weeks were spent hunting down copies of chronicles and monastic histories which might reveal the kind of facts needed in order to begin pinning down, *somewhere,* the elusive, faceless, monkhood of Burma. In all of this, I may have lost sight overmuch of the fact that my eyes could look at and record those faces. The texture of this book suffers from that fact.

In any event, this book represents not even one-third of the complete work I originally planned; in its original form, the manuscript came to something like half a million words. My aim was to produce one or more volumes on the Sangha, one on messianism, and one on animism. In effect, the volume this book grew out of took some ten years to write. In 1967, I had to abandon the project entirely and it was pretty clear to me even then that nothing short of a miraculous rescue job could save it. In the meantime, I watched while colleagues who had been in the field after me, Manning Nash, Melford Spiro, and others—not to forget the political scientists, of whom the most talented remains undoubtedly Donald Smith—published their results.

The material omitted from this book, however, will not be lost and will be preserved for possible future publication. A partial list of such material includes data on monastic population figures, lay Buddhist organizations, monastic landholdings, legal cases involving monks, Sangayana publication efforts, doctrinal debates involving political overtones such as the *Lu The Lu Pyit* book controversy, ritual giving to monks at *shinbyu, katthein, ahlu*s, and so on, and more material on the Institute of Advanced Buddhist Studies. Also of particular interest for possible future publication efforts is the partially completed research on Sarvastivadin influences, messianic *gaing*s, *nat* symbolism, cosmology, alchemy, astrology, Buddhist and animist rituals, all of which, of necessity, had to remain outside the realm of this present volume.

I was fortunate, indeed, to encounter John Ferguson, through the kind mediation of A. Thomas Kirsch of Cornell University. Desirous of embarking with Ferguson on the project, I was nevertheless, frankly, rather afraid of having to immerse myself again in subjects I had, over the years, acquired good reasons to forget. John Ferguson, a person of tremendous tact, was able to assure me very quickly that he had my material at his fingertips, and I found that his memory and fanatical attention to complex detail were even more noteworthy than mine had been while I was working on this book. He became, in effect, an alter ego, to whom most decisions could easily be left. I found his edited text a miracle of reduction: it has given me the least possible feeling of the "missing limbs" variety, and he has given me back the precious gift of some degree of pride in my own work which I thought I had irretrievably lost.

The editing procedure has had, I believe, one major effect on the work as a whole. My original text paid more attention to lay Buddhism than the edited version does—mostly for reasons of space. The major point lost owing to this, I think, is my argument that some lay Buddhists in power or near power during my stay appear to have been well satisfied with calling for a halt to progress in the education of monks, and for a limitation of same, in order to be able to take into their own hands certain powers previously held by monks. Ferguson and I, however, felt that so much was to be gained by concentrating on the task of explaining the Sangha that the loss of the lay data could be borne.

Since I had left the book unfinished, Ferguson—as the chapters went by—made a growing contribution to the clarification of certain issues, such as the ultimate relation between different kinds of lay and religious power. I think, in short, that my editor has contributed greatly to the book's improvement and for this—outside of the more mechanical tasks so well performed—my gratitude is due; the usual disclaimer regarding my own faults must be made: any defects this book may have are due strictly to me. It is also true that, in the course of his work, Ferguson came to certain conclusions which differ from mine and which we must look forward to hearing about as his own career progresses. At certain moments it was no longer possible to tell whether joint authorship had not set in, especially in the first and very last chapters. This book would not have been published but for his almost miraculous intervention.

Though I write this fifteen years after my return from Burma, I wish to try to remember some of the many, many people who helped along the way—knowing, alas, that a complete list is impossible.

To my masters in anthropology the gratitude of a novice is due: their names are recorded in the Editor's Preface. To Raymond Firth I owe a special debt of gratitude for intervening on my behalf during the grant negotiations; to Christoph von Furer Haimendorf and my other colleagues at the School of Oriental and African Studies—Anna Allott, Adrian Mayer, Frederick Bailey, Barbara Ward, Harry Shorto, and Hla Pe, especially—I am indebted for providing the context in which I did the preliminary work on this book. A number of scholars in many parts of the world, men such as Gordon Luce, Edmund Leach, John Furnivall, and D. G. E. Hall, also provided their expertise and friendship at various times. Among Burma men, I have had many friends. Two are not cited as often in this work as they have been in other works of mine, yet their conversation was always of the greatest value: I speak of Emmanuel Sarkisyanz and F. K. Lehman.

In daily life, a few individuals helped to keep my spirits alive while so many others did not: U Aung Chan Tha, Geoffrey and Kathleen Bates, Daw Hti Hti (Mrs. G. Luce), Sao Htun Hmat Win, U Kyaw Sein, Daw Mi Mi Khaing, Peter Murray, Taw Paya Nge, U San Pe, David and Kit Steinberg, Dr. Suvi, U Tha Gyaw, U Thein Han, U Thwe, U Thwe Sein, U Tun Hla Oung, David and Assia Wevill, and Maung Ye Myint.

Among the many monks who helped and befriended me in Burma I would like to record a special debt of gratitude and reverence to the Patthan Sayadaw and U Thetkyawuntha, both of Rangoon, the Anisekhan Sayadaw of Sagaing, and the Mahagandayon Sayadaw of Amarapura.

An individual who deserves my highest gratitude is U Ba Hla (H. Connar), who did a great deal of work for me in translating documents old and new and kept up a fascinating correspondence until this was no longer possible. In a very real sense he is one of the authors of this book; I hope he knows of that in due course.

Likewise, I wish to remember particularly U Ohn Ghine (the Australian Buddhist author David Maurice), who was a very special friend.

I thank the Rockefeller Foundation for the grant which enabled me to go to Burma. To the people of Cornell who very nearly welcomed me in 1967 and to those who again stepped forward to help in 1973, much thanks.

Finally, and most importantly: to Patricia Mendelson, who shared the journey, the travails, much of the labor and many of the rewards, the ever-affectionate memory of our youth.

E. MICHAEL MENDELSON

Warnerville, New York

SANGHA AND STATE IN BURMA

A Study of Monastic
Sectarianism and Leadership

Introduction

The Burmese Buddhist Sangha, one of the five leading orders of monks in Theravada Southeast Asia, is a body of some 100,000 men devoted to the ideals set forth by Gotama the Buddha about 2,500 years ago. Dressed in yellow robes, ranging from saffron to canary, they go bare-headed and shaved of all head hair, and are allowed to carry only a few requirements, such as a fan and a parasol. Their behavior is regulated by an enormously complex body of rules known as the Vinaya-Pitaka, or Book of Discipline, a third part of the Buddhist Pali scriptures (Tipitaka), the other parts of which deal with such subjects as psychology, ethics, and metaphysics. The Vinaya provides rules for correct behavior, deportment, schedules, dress, admissions, discipleship, eating, control of sexuality, celibacy, confession, travel, property, residence, conflict regulation, and schismaticism.

The monks live in "monasteries" (*kyaung*s), which can range from single-room huts to vast complexes including many buildings of various sizes (*kyaungtaik*s); they live either singly or in groups numbering from two or three to several hundred monks. Apart from these residences, which should normally belong to the Order as a whole and which are put up for them by lay supporters (*taga*s and *tagama*s), they, according to the Vinaya, own very little or no property. The primary basis for their subsistence is a simple donor relationship with lay supporters whereby food and other necessities are received regularly. Monks either go on food-collecting rounds from house to house, or the donors bring food to the monastery. Frequently, a senior layman will take up the task of being a lay steward (*kappiya*), serving as intermediary between lay donors and a monk who is prevented by the Vinaya from receiving certain gifts directly. Other legitimate monk requirements—medicine, household goods, books, and so on—are also provided by lay supporters. Fashions as to what articles may be given individually or in collective donations (*ahlus*), of a potlatch type, may vary. It can never be sufficiently stressed that Vinaya interdiction against banking any form of property and accumulating any kind of wealth or stores tends to work against the Sangha's becoming a "church" with an independent secular power base of its own. That such a situation is likely to lead to conservatism on the Sangha's part is only too obvious.

Monks, in the scriptures, are referred to as a "field of merit." Simply put, a monk does not thank a lay supporter for a gift: rather, it is the lay supporter who is grateful to the monk for affording him the opportunity of acquiring merit by his gift. With this important qualification, we may say that the traditional function of monks "in return" for support has been to educate the local children, to grace (rather than officiate at) life-cycle ceremonies by their presence,[1] and to act as advisers on a wide range of topics (the ritual of *shinbyu,* or the initiation into manhood and marriageability by means of a period spent by every male in the monkhood, somewhat transcends this list of functions). Medicine and other arts, including magic, have been known to be practiced by monks, but since ideally, at any rate, the Buddha is a human being to be imitated rather than a god to be adored, the monk does not serve as a mediating priest. The essential duty of the monk, outside of a concern for his lay supporter's welfare, is to devote himself to the improvement of his meditational practices and to hasten his liberation from all worldly attachments. Having left behind him parents and all family whatsoever, he is not expected to cling to any form of worldliness or to debase himself by dealing with politics. And yet, of course, a Burmese monk is a Burmese, as a Sinhalese monk a Sinhalese, or a Thai monk a Thai. While advising laymen, monks can hardly be expected to escape knowledge of local politics along with everything else in the local melting pot. Thus, a realistic view must be that such a large order of able-bodied and unusually gifted men must in some form or another have wielded some kind of political influence, the nature of which has to be very carefully determined.

It is the aim of this book first of all to achieve a clearer picture than heretofore of the sociological nature of the Sangha. Again and again

---

1. While the monk does not take as active a role in Buddhist ritual as does a Roman Catholic priest, he does, through his prestige and dignified manner, as well as by occasional chanting of Pali exorcisms (*paritta*), play a central role in such ritual occasions. It could be considered perhaps a passive type of officiation. J. F.

books have discussed the Sangha, but it has been faceless: with very few exceptions one never knew who these monks were, how many they were, exactly how organized, exactly how related (or not) among themselves, and so forth.[2] As with other Theravada Sanghas (except for those in Ceylon), a man can enter the Burmese Order and leave it at will with little bother, so that determining who is a fully committed monk and who is spending a little while in the Order for any one of a variety of reasons is very difficult. Likewise, since everyone wears the same yellow robe and there are no grade badges, it is hard to tell who is a venerable abbot, who is merely an old recluse, who is a full-fledged monk, who is merely a novice, and so forth.

In order to get at the sociology, I have not hesitated to go back into history and to challenge a number of views on the Sangha's evolution which have by now become almost canonical. The historical sources, however, are in great disarray. I must warn the reader, therefore, that unavoidably the first chapter or two will make for difficult reading. My editor and I had only a few pieces of a very valuable quilt, and at present there is little chance of finding others. Does one throw away the bits and pieces? We decided to keep them.

Investigation of the history of the Sangha from medieval times to the present has led me to argue that a number of important factors have been more or less constant through time. One such factor has been the splitting off of sectarian groups from the main body of the Sangha. Most frequently, these new groups justify the split, not in terms of a new doctrinal interpretation, but rather in terms of a redressal of laxity which creeps into the Sangha at large: a reassertion of Vinaya. The lay authority usually reacts to these new sects in one of two patterns. If the lay authority is *weak,* it may try to manipulate the sectarian break to its own advantage, thus dividing in order to rule. In the process, it may seem to be favoring and even creating a sect out of incipient dissatisfactions. If the authority is *strong,* it may attempt and even succeed in forcing the whole Sangha into one pattern, with one head, and simply defrock or disbar those monks who do not conform. Turning over the whole Sangha to a new form giving extra stress to Vinaya may be part of this unification process, which is often given the name of "purification." Purification has thus been both a laymen's task and an internal

2. Spiro 1970 is a significant exception to the above.

monastic concern since Buddhism began, and the rhetoric of purification is likely to be employed whether lay authority be strong or weak—a factor which does confuse our estimate of the relative strength of lay power. On the Sangha's side, cleaving to Vinaya (having less property and worldly influence) weakens the Sangha in one sense. Since it inspires the laymen by its religiosity, however, Vinaya purism is double-edged, and cleaving to Vinaya may eventually, in fact, bring it power and prestige. When a strong lay power decides to back internal monastic movements toward Vinaya purism, this Sangha influence may be at its height.

It has become apparent that, when an alien culture invades the Buddhist world and complicates the simple lay-donor–monk-receiver pattern, the Sangha's influence as a whole—its independence—may be at stake.[3] At such a time, monks may discover that one way of fighting this is regrouping into smaller orders, mini-Sanghas as it were, so as to overcome the overall Sangha tendency to amorphousness and to resist the encroachments of an unsympathetic lay power. The Vinaya rhetoric to support this is always at hand: let us regroup, let us be more disciplined, let us be less compromising. But of course this is only one way. The very amorphousness can also be, if rightly handled, an instrument of self-protection: it could be considered a kind of typical defense response throughout all Burmese bureaucracy, perhaps in *all* bureaucracy. The low degree of Sangha organization in most situations, however, gives this amorphousness special resistant powers. My argument is that the mini-Sanghas eventually led to a major irony in modern Burmese history. When the AFPFL[4] ruled an independent Burma, they wished to be again as the kings had been and to "purify" the Sangha. In the meantime, the Sangha had become extremely wary. The Buddhist Revival launched by Prime Minister U Nu, seen as a "purification" campaign, may be said to have run aground on this rock. The AFPFL under Nu did not behave as a really strong king; it did not, or could not, force a unified Order. The result is that it played fast and loose with the sects, and the sects, in turn, played fast and loose with it.

The Western concept of sectarianism tends to require a real doctrinal

---

3. The major alien invasion was, of course, the British colonization of Burma beginning in 1824.

4. The Burmese postwar political party of Aung San, Nu, Than Tun, and others.

difference for the definition of a sect. In Mahayana Buddhism, we find such differences. In Theravada, they are minimal. Fear of sectarianism (a splitting force in a vulnerable, propertyless Order dependent almost manically on correct transmission from the Therevada path of the Elders) and a lack of any deep doctrinal differences have conspired to cause Burmese to tell Westerners that sects are but minimally important among them, and so far our scholars have believed them. This book challenges that belief and finds that sectarian activity, shaped in the rhetoric of discipline rather than doctrine, is a prime moving force in the history of relations between Sangha and state in Burma.

There are two ways of using the word *sect* which pertain to two different disciplines. In Orientalism (or in the History of Religions) one concentrates on those things which Buddhism itself uses to distinguish a sect from the Sangha as a whole or from other sects. In anthropology, on the other hand, one might turn to the literature on factionalism for a source of useful concepts: a body of research which concentrates on the way in which differences between human groups develop, whatever might be the sources of conflict (religious, political, social, or other).

I began to look at the literature on sects by orientalists as a result of a research project (1965–1967) on the possibility of Sarvastivadin presence or influence in Burma. While I was unable to develop this project as far as I had wished, I concluded that there was no essential conflict between the views I have developed for this book and those put forward by the orientalists. The reader may consult Lamotte (1958), [5] Bareau (1955, chap. 4), and Frauwallner (1956). Dutt (1962) is also interesting but curiously reticent about schisms in Buddhism. I regret that the most impressive scholarship by Bechert (1966–1973) had not been completed nor made available to me during the period of my research. However, the conclusions I reached through my review of oriental scholarship did suggest that a task well worth performing would be to document more carefully the linguistic usage of such key Pali terms as *gana* and *nikaya,* which seem to be taken for granted rather than taken to pieces in this literature.

Had I proceeded to write this book with the approaches of both the orientalists and the anthropologists in mind, I might have succeeded in

5. Especially interesting are the excellent summary and bibliography in chapter 4, section 1, pp. 571–578.

making clearer the way in which a monkish faction arises without the implication, initially at least, that sectarian developments would follow. It may well be that there are levels of factionalism on which monks can be described—either by themselves or laymen—without the assignation of the term *sect*. An example is discussed later in the book where laymen in the Shan States identify a "Vipassana *gaing*" among the sophisticated monks of the city. By this they mean to refer to the fashion among certain monks connected with the government's Buddhist Revival program to be greatly interested in meditation. Although I have thought of this in terms of sect, I might have been wiser to speak of faction. The world of factions would be the world of little groups which I describe at the end of Chapter 5 in which Burmese strive for individual autonomy more than they strive for each other's defeat, with the result that innumerable groups survive long after their visible social functions have disappeared, perhaps to wait in the wings for a new role another day.

If such groups could be called factions, then the term *sect* might be freed for closer scrutiny of the mechanisms of actual sectarian formation by monks themselves, on one hand, and by lay power, on the other. Since splitting the Sangha is a heinous crime, any sectarian divisions must be justified in some way consonant with religious ideals such as "purification," and thus one might profitably investigate carefully the Buddhist etymology of the terms involved. Such research would have taken me beyond the province of my expertise. Accordingly, I tended to concentrate on the Burmese situation itself as I could discover it from chronicles, monastic literature, and laymen's publications.

It became clear that monks do declare themselves to be sects (*nikaya*) in their own literature and that kings also play a role in the recognition of this process of monastic definition. Some might argue that only kings could give ultimate sanction to sect existence, while others might feel that monks have been perfectly capable of handling this by themselves. The matter certainly requires further clarification, but it is certain that the rhetoric of purification is used by both kings and monks to justify such potentially divisive activity.

My editor and I now feel, at a late stage in the composition of the book, that, had an approach combining factionalism and sectarianism been followed from the beginning, certain unruly facts we have noted might have been more easily accommodated. For instance, when Burmese informants speak of a lack of importance of sects in Burma, they are thinking (or would like to be thinking) of a number of factions which never get as far as becoming sects proper. Such an approach might explain why those monks whom I have identified as a Pakokku sect tended, in answering questionnaires, to refer to themselves not as Pakokku but as Thudhamma. If, as seems clear, the pressure was coming in that case from the political lay authority over the monks, rather than vice versa, it would be perfectly understandable for the monks to disclaim secthood. On the other hand, it appears in the case of Shwegyin, Dwaya, and other groups that the monks themselves initiated divisive activities, in which case one would expect to find and does find all the paraphernalia of sectarian self-definition, such as self-reference in terms of a *nikaya,* organizational reports of structure and sect history, sectarian identification papers to be carried by members, and so forth.

We trust that the reader will realize the difficulty of definitively settling the matter of sectarianism in Buddhism and will approach what follows as an exploration of approaches to the problem rather than a final statement. We have tried to open up the issues involved, and in doing so we have been led to ignore what usually goes into the making of a book on Buddhism. We have had to take it for granted that the reader knows something of basic Buddhist philosophy, ethics, and metaphysics. I am not too concerned in this work with the supreme task of the monk, his reason for being a monk, or related matters; and we have had to exclude a large amount of sociological material about the layman's role in the monk-layman relationship. Other information that a reader might believe to be indispensable to a work such as this has been omitted. This book, for instance, contains virtually no description of the Sangayana itself (the Sixth Buddhist Council), the vast event toward which all the religious programs of Nu's government tended for several years after his becoming prime minister. The Sangayana is so treated because, on the one hand, it was widely reported in the world press, and, on the other hand, more importantly, because I believe that the Sangayana was a mask for other activities, the understanding of which is more crucial to a knowledge of the nature of Sangha-state relations than a detailed re-hashing of the surface events of the Sangayana could ever prove to be.

By this, I do *not* mean to call into question the good faith of the Nu government or to deny the strong religious forces at work during the Sangayana. It called forth much good energy, it was a great event for

Burma, and it sparked off a number of important consequences for the life of the average religious Burmese Buddhist, but these are not the sides I wish to stress at present.

In previous publications, I have tried to show that Burmese Buddhism is a complex creation, composed at the very least of three strands: (1) Theravada Buddhism proper; (2) a complex of belief and ritual I have called "messianic Buddhism"; and (3) the world of the *nat*s, known to observers as "animism," or the spirit-cult world. My conclusions have often been debated by other scholars, without always being correctly understood. This book does not represent more than a fraction of what I have to say on the matter of Sangha and laity relations in Theravada Buddhism in Burma, but it *does* constantly take account of these other layers. Whatever I may say that might cause the reader to feel that I might lack respect for Burmese Buddhism, the principle feature of the complexity studied is the degree to which the highest level (Theravada) informs and draws into itself all the other levels. If I say that Burmese Buddhist life as manifested both by Sangha and state constantly strives *toward* the highest ideals of Theravada without always achieving them, it should be remembered that such striving may be the best that mankind can expect and that, today, the striving is no longer even true of the largest area our species inhabits on this earth.

1. Early Sangha History

En fait cependant, les traditions historiques de
la Birmanie doivent, des qu'elles sont quelquepeu
anciennes, commander un scepticisme total.[1]

The anthropological field work to be discussed later in the book cannot be understood properly apart from the complex historical forces that developed in the almost two-thousand-year relationship of Sangha and state in Burma. A vital awareness of the past in Burmese society obliges those from an alien culture who seek understanding to consider carefully the Burmese view of their own history, a view deeply imbued with Buddhism because the accounts of the past were preserved in the monasteries by scholarly monks and passed on through centuries until a vernacular literature developed and court laymen began secular chronicles in the eighteenth century. The "history" thus preserved is strongly tinged with monastic views of events and is therefore of great use in trying to comprehend the nature of the Sangha over time.

Early Strains upon Sangha Unity

When Buddhism actually came to Burma is not known, but chronicle tradition includes a trip to Lower Burma by the Buddha himself by air, with "many hundred monks," in 536, followed in 309 B.C. by the arrival of the missionary monks Sona and Uttara with five others from the kingdom of Emperor Asoka in India.[2] Chronicle traditions for Upper Burma tell of missionizing in 523 B.C. and of a holy sage, or *arahat,* who lived atop a mountain where he received the teachings of the Buddha in person. Upper Burma also claims to have received in 309 B.C. a full mission from Asoka, thus asserting its position as the religious

1. Dupont 1959:14.
2. Pannasami 1861:42. The five monks represent the minimum number required in order to perform ordinations of new monks. A Burmese Sangha could thus be started with these five.

equal of the Lower Burmese.[3] In these legendary accounts are preserved a rivalry between Upper and Lower Burma that is of great importance in understanding the history of the Sangha.

Only for brief periods in history, under particularly strong kings, did a unified "Burma" exist in the form we know it geographically today. Not only were the hill tribes difficult to incorporate into the valley kingdoms, but also ethnic groupings such as the Shans were seldom made truly subordinate to central authority. The most dramatic and divisive rivalry, however, existed between those peoples we might speak of today as ethnic Burmese and those known as the Mons, or Talaings, in Lower Burma. Both inhabited what today is considered Burma, but historically the two peoples have preserved a sense of cultural separation and identity even up to modern times. The Mons eventually lost the bitter struggle to the Upper Burmese in over a thousand years of destructive intermittent warfare between the two Theravada Buddhist kingdoms, and inevitably the monkhood itself became involved in the contention. The rivalry can still be traced in the chronicle histories of premedieval days, where each side strives to promote its claim to a visit from the living Buddha and to the establishment of chapters of monks ordained by Asoka missionaries. The Mons of Lower Burma also claim the famous Theravada monk Buddhaghosa and see him as carrying key texts to and from Ceylon in the fifth century A.D., thus strengthening the Mon assertions of greater Theravada orthodoxy.[4]

The state of archaeological research in Burma is such that, despite the heroic efforts of Gordon Luce in making the early Chinese sources and the inscriptions of Burma available to scholars, the premedieval history of Upper and Lower Burma is still shrouded in mystery and controversy. Enough data are available, however, to determine with considerable certainty that Theravada Buddhism was established in Burma by the time the Pyu kingdoms of Upper and Lower Burma flourished in the middle of the first millennium A.D. Fragments of both Pali scriptures and Sanskrit epigraphs discovered at Pyu sites, in addition to statues of the Buddha going back to the third century, strongly suggest both northern and southern Indian Theravada Buddhist influences.[5] It can be fairly safely assumed that a Sangha, or order of monks, naturally accompanied

---

3. Pannasami 1861:61–62.
4. Ray 1946:24–33.
5. Ray 1946:33–73. See also U Mya 1961.

these symbols, and we know that by the time Chinese sources report on the Pyu, whose kingdom extended from the area of Prome in the south quite far into Upper Burma, the monastery played a vital role in the lives of the residents of Burma. Part of the Chinese T'ang dynasty (618–905) chronicle reads as follows: "They are Buddhists and have a hundred monasteries, with bricks of glass ware embellished with gold and silver vermillion, gay colours and red kino. The floor is painted and is covered with ornamented carpets. The king's residence is in like style. At seven years of age, the people cut their hair and enter a monastery; if at the age of twenty they have not grasped the doctrine, they return to lay estate."[6] The influence of the Sangha is seen, therefore, to have been then as pervasive as it is today—an important corrective to the generally held view that it was not until the eleventh century that "pure" Theravada Buddhism came to upper Burma. The parallelism of monastery and royal palace also suggests an early close symbolic relationship between king and monk that is a central theme of this book. This relationship was an important premedieval pattern in both Upper and Lower Burma.

Despite the above evidence of a form of Buddhism suggesting a Theravada presence in the first millennium, much data for both the Pyu and Mons in premedieval Lower Burma also indicate the existence of Hindu, Mahayanist, and, later, Tantric influences as well. I have argued elsewhere that Buddhism today as it incorporates spirit, or *nat,* worship and Brahmanistic elements such as astrology on one end of the scale is best approached as a continuum of religious practices with the Pali Theravada forms on the other end, the totality of the people's devotion to all parts of the continuum constituting Burmese religion.[7] It is helpful to consider historical Buddhism in the same light, and thus claims for a "pure" Theravada faith in any place or time should be approached with skepticism. "Animist," Hindu, Mahayanist, or Tantric elements were probably not wholly absent from Ceylon, India, Upper, or Lower Burma in the days before the great empire of Pagan in Upper Burma began to gather momentum under the leadership of the famous King Aniruddha in the eleventh century. I therefore suggest that the unity of the premedieval Sangha was strained by a multitude of religious forces from the continuum of these religious practices, just as it was strained by the

6. As quoted in Harvey 1925:12–13.
7. See Mendelson 1961a:230–231.

Mon-Burmese rivalry. The Sangha as a social body has always been under pressures from both internal factors involving monastic movements toward various positions in the religious continuum and external factors relating to political forces in which the relationship between king and monk introduces political considerations having profound effects upon the monkhood.

Monastic Factions in Early Pagan

With the decline of Pyu power in Burma during the last centuries of the first millennium, the way was opened for the rise of the Upper Burmese center of Pagan and the Lower Burmese or Mon kingdom at the city of Thaton. The Pyu were either extinguished or transmuted into what we know ethnically and culturally today as "Burmans," but the significance to Pagan of the Pyu civilization is attested to by one of the greatest Pagan kings, Kyanzittha, who in the eleventh century traced his traditions back to their capital city.[8] After the disappearance of the Pyu, however, the main Burmese culture centers became Pagan and Thaton. Most Burmans readily accept the famous chronicle account of King Aniruddha's conquest of the Mons at Thaton in 1057 as the starting point of pure Burmese Theravada culture, and they will also argue that Aniruddha captured not only king and city but also the Mon Sangha itself and brought hundreds of monks and the Pali scriptures north to Pagan in the train of the captured King Manuha.[9] Even more importantly, many Burmese will assert that the Buddhism introduced was "pure" and that it has remained the same ever since. These or similar popular assumptions have strongly influenced many scholarly works.[10] Similarly, many Burmese tend to conceive of a unified body of monks in one ecclesiastical organization or Sangha that has come down

8. Kyanzittha claimed to have been Vishnu in an earlier birth and to have been present as that god at the founding of the Pyu capital, Sirikhetta. See Durioselle 1960:114. J. F.

9. *Glass Palace Chronicle* 1829:77–80.

10. See, for example, Bode 1909:10–15; Htin Aung 1967:32–33; Harvey 1925: 25–31; Donnison 1970:216; Smith 1965:12–13; Sarkisyanz 1965:6–7. Ray (1946:80–83, and 97–104), while giving the chronicle details of the introduction of "pure" Buddhism, does note that the absence of contemporary inscriptions confirming the events is curious. Htin Aung (1970:16–31) discusses the complexity of the Buddhism of the day and notes Mahayanist elements at Thaton and Pagan, while seemingly accepting the historicity of the chronicle accounts of events and of the Theravada faith of Aniruddha.

virtually intact since the "pure" Mon Buddhism came to Pagan in the eleventh century under the leadership of the famous monk Shin Arahan, who is said to have converted King Aniruddha to the orthodox Theravada faith and to have purged the Sangha of heretical beliefs and members. No matter how one evaluates the Aniruddha reign in terms of fact and legend, the available evidence does not support the concepts of "pure" Buddhism or a unified, unchanging Sangha, as I shall attempt to show.

In the first place, it is doubtful that any "pure" form of Theravada Buddhism existed in 1057 at Thaton or even in Ceylon, for a Sinhalese king had to send to Pagan in c. 1070 for a chapter of Burmese monks to revive his own weakened Sangha.[11] As noted by Dupont (1959:11–15), it is equally difficult to accept the concept of a purely Theravada Thaton, since the available data suggest strong Hindu and Mahayanist presences at the time it reportedly "civilized" the Upper Burmese conquerors. Furthermore, some writers, like Luce (1953:11; 1959a:75–82) and Ray (1946:82–83), tend to see Pagan as founded by relatively uncivilized tribes who migrated from the north and were then civilized by the culturally superior Pyu and Mons; this view may reflect the strong influence of Mon notions of history, rather than a fair and accurate interpretation of Burma at that time.[12] The data available are not yet adequate to make a final judgment, but in any case it is quite possible that both Pagan and Thaton had a continuum of well-established Buddhist and non-Buddhist religious practices idealized in retrospect as "pure" Theravada. At Pagan the Sangha itself was probably spread out on that continuum in terms of monastic orthodoxy.

The nineteenth-century Pannasami, himself a monk and author of the *Sasanavamsa*, notes that older chronicle accounts of the key figure in the Pagan Sangha at the time, Shin Arahan, do not all agree, and he gives three versions from the ancient sources, concluding as follows: "Thus although there appear various views of various teachers, yet the fact that the Elder Arahanta [Shin Arahan] came to Arimaddana [Pagan] and established the religion there is alone sufficient here. It should not be undervalued" (1861:67). The importance of Shin Arahan is not denied by any of the older chronicle versions; what the various texts

11. Ray 1946:99.
12. See also Than Tun 1960a:47.

disagree about is the monk's monastic background, and throughout this book it will be evident that in the Sangha one of the most significant ways of promoting sectarianism is to assign to famous monks of ancient times a monastic career or teacher-pupil lineage that emphasizes certain elements on the religious continuum which the chronicle writer himself wishes to promote. Thus the Thaton Mon chronicle traces Shin Arahan to the Sona and Uttara missionaries of Asoka. Another chronicle claims he came from Ceylon to Sirikhetta, now Prome, in the old Pyu area. The third version sees him as coming from Lower Burma (where religion was said to be weakening) to the forest life of Upper Burma.[13] These three versions represent respectively Mon, Ceylonese, and Upper Burmese factions, the major factions in the Sangha throughout its history in Burma, the importance of which will be noted throughout this chapter.

Most versions of Shin Arahan's career stress the point that he converted King Aniruddha to Theravada Buddhism, after which event they joined to purge the Sangha in Burma of its wayward monks and false beliefs. The purge of the "sham ascetics" clearly illustrates the classic king-monk relationship that is the heart of the perennial attempts of the state to unify the monkhood. Some Burmese sources, such as the *Glass Palace Chronicle* (1829:59, 70–75), identify the purged monks as the Ari, infamous for serpent (Naga) worship, spirit idolizing, use of alcohol, falsification of texts, chants to evade guilt, and even the practice of *droit de seigneur*. While there is no doubt that some of the chronicle criticism of the Ari is forced and highly biased, a number of factors connect the Ari with Hinduism, Mahayana, and non-Theravada Hinayana. I have tried to review in detail elsewhere (1961b:576–577) some of the complexities of the nature of the Ari and the extent of their influence. Perhaps the most important point to note here is that some scholars identify the wayward Ari with forest monks,[14] those members of the Sangha who forsake the village or city life for the asceticism of the forest, usually with the implication of a more self-denying regimen and a concentration upon solitary meditation. It is not likely that the "Ari" are simply forest monks; rather, they probably represent factions within the total Sangha whose practices were not considered orthodox by Shin Arahan's standards. There is even evidence that two other orders of

13. Pannasami 1861:64–67.
14. Than Tun 1959c.

monks existed besides the one to which Shin Arahan belonged: "And thou [King Aniruddha] hast asked—Is there any monk of the Order, save myself [Shin Arahan], a disciple of the Lord [Buddha]? Yea, verily; besides myself there are the *paramattha* Order and the *samuti* Order."[15]

Significantly, both Sangha divisions mentioned by Shin Arahan bear names also used in reference to nineteenth-century Sangha factions. Since the *Glass Palace Chronicle* was written in 1829, the terms may represent the familiar pattern in the chronicles of projecting issues contemporary with the writers back into the past. The term *paramattha,* sometimes *paramat* (English transliteration), can mean truth in the ultimate sense, but it is also used derogatorily to describe those whose pursuit of ultimates lures them into nonorthodox extremes. The term *samuti* (perhaps from the Pali *sammuti*) appears to relate to general consent; that is, it was perhaps a division in the Sangha that by common consent was not under the direct control of the king and those monks who supported him. Both terms will be discussed in more detail in the next chapter, but here it suffices to point out that not only the Ari but also these two other Sangha factions existed in addition to Shin Arahan's own. Such factions, we suggest, were inherent in the Burmese Sangha from the start.

The whole matter of Shin Arahan and the chronicle accounts of his purification of the monkhood is further complicated by the fact that most Pagan inscriptions up to 1173 were written in the Mon language[16] yet contain no mention of the above events. The earliest mention is in the Kalyani Inscription of 1476, which, interestingly, was written at the orders of the Mon king Dhammaceti. Ray notes that there have been many examples in history of deliberate Upper Burmese neglect of Mon contributions and that failure to mention the story of Shin Arahan may have been due not so much to its untruth but to bitter racial hostility between Mons and Upper Burmese.[17] Luce (1959a:65) has suggested that perhaps it was King Kyanzittha (1084–1113) who, culturally very much a Mon, received Shin Arahan and introduced the competing forces of Sinhalese Theravada Buddhism to Pagan. Luce, in his latest work (1969:61), sees Kyanzittha as one who "led Burma out of the East

15. *Glass Palace Chronicle* 1829:74.
16. Luce 1953:18; 1959b.
17. Ray 1946:154–158. See also Bode 1897:32–33, for Mon-Upper Burma Sangha rivalry.

Bengal Tantric Mahayanism of Aniruddha's youth and lodged it finally in the Theravada fold." Htin Aung (1970:16–31), in contrast, following the chronicles, sees Aniruddha as *the* Theravada reformer and stresses Thaton's influence—not Ceylon's—upon Burmese Buddhism at Pagan. Scholarly differences aside, it is clear that wherever the Theravada Buddhism came from, it spurred a remarkable efflorescence at Pagan that created one of the most spectacular of all Asian religious sites. The surge in faith was most likely fed from many sources, including Mon, Tantric, Mahayanist, North and South Indian Buddhism, but certainly a major flow of religious influence came to Pagan from Ceylon.

Sinhalese Sectarian Pressures

We have already noted that the famous monk Buddhaghosa is said to have had Burma-Ceylon contacts in the fifth century and that Aniruddha sent monks to Ceylon to help revive the Sangha there in 1070. From this latter contact Sinhalese Pali scriptures are said to have reached Pagan and to have been compared with the Pali scriptures captured earlier from the Mons at Thaton, with the versions being found to be alike (suggesting Mon-Ceylon equality).[18] Of course, this account, like the version of Shin Arahan's life that gives his place of origin as Ceylon, was probably influenced by the fact that Pannasami, the nineteenth-century monk-author of the chronicle, traced his own distinguished monastic lineage to Ceylon. The Sinhalese scholar Godakumbura (1966:148–149) has actually proposed that the monks who went to Ceylon in the eleventh century to revive the Sangha there were Ceylon monks who had previously fled the wartime chaos in Ceylon and taken sanctuary in Burma, and were not Mons or Upper Burmese. In any case, there was apparently monastic contact of some sort in the eleventh century, although the next century was to witness much more important events.

Most of the writers in our field have touched upon the story of the mission of the Burmese monks Uttarajiva and Chapata in the twelfth century to Ceylon and the establishment of the Sihala Sangha, those groups of Burmese monks who traced the purity of their tradition to Sinhalese (Sihala) Theravada Buddhism.[19] Previous to this mission,

18. Pannasami 1861:71.
19. Chronicle accounts: Pannasami 1861:72–74; *Glass Palace Chronicle* 1829: 146. Histories: Harvey 1925:55–56; Ray 1946:110–118; Bode 1897:20, 1909: 19–20, 23–24; Than Tun 1959d:67. Epigraphy: Dhammaceti 1476:50–66.

chronicles tell of the residence in Ceylon of the monk Panthagu ("successor" to Shin Arahan), who left Burma for voluntary exile after King Narathu went back on his promise to avoid royal fratricide. He returned to Burma in 1173 after the death of Narathu, possibly establishing the contacts that promoted the visit of his "successor," Uttarajiva.[20] In 1180 the Mon monk Uttarajiva went from Thaton to Ceylon with a novice, Chapata, and they both visited the Mahavihara Sangha center, which represented a strong monastic tradition royally supported. Uttarajiva saw Chapata ordained in the Ceylon tradition, and then both returned to Burma at different times to found reformist programs that deeply affected the Sangha in Lower and Upper Burma. Two points, belonging more to the realm of projection rather than to fact, may be concentrated upon here.

The first point involves the attitude of the Burmese Sangha toward the reform movements initiated by the returning Uttarajiva and Chapata. Ray sees the success of the reformers in Burma in starting the Sihala Sangha traditions as "the first frank admission of the superiority of the Sinhalese over the Burmese Order."[21] Granted that the visit to Ceylon implied respect for the Ceylon Sangha, is this an entirely correct view? The fifteenth-century Kalyani Inscription can be read to show the Ceylon monks welcoming the Burma monks as equals:

"We [the Ceylon monks] are the spiritual successors of Mahamahinda-thera,[22] who established the Religion in Lankadipa [Ceylon], while you [Uttarajiva] and the other priests in your company are the spiritual successors of the two *Mahatheras* [great monk teachers], called Sona and Uttara, who established the Religion in Suvannabhumi [Burma].[23] Let us all, therefore, perform together the ceremonies incumbent upon the Order." Having spoken thus, they performed the *upasampada* [monk's] ordination on Chapata, the twenty-year-old *samanera* [novice].[24]

20. See *Glass Palace Chronicle* 1829:132–133; Ray 1946: 109–111; Harvey 1925:55; Godakumbura 1966:149. These monks were most likely not heads of the entire Burmese Order as the term "successor" might imply. More will be said on this subject later.

21. Ray 1946:112, 130–131; Harvey 1925:50–56.

22. *Maha* (P): great; Mahinda: the missionary monk from King Asoka to Ceylon in the fourth century B.C.; *thera* (P): elder.

23. Suvannabhumi: golden land. Some scholars believe the name in early records probably refers to Sumatra, but the Burmese chronicles claim it refers to Burma. See Harvey 1925:310–311; Law's notes in Pannasami 1861:xvi; and Coedès 1964:40.

24. Dhammaceti 1476:8.

Furthermore, we find that Uttarajiva was not reordained in Ceylon but only the novice Chapata was. It was thus Chapata who founded the main divisions in the Sihala Sangha. The Kalyani Inscription describes the break that separated the Sihala from the established Pagan Sangha:

"As the *Mahathera*s of Lankadipa [Ceylon] associated with our teacher, the Venerable Uttarajivamahathera, in the performance of ecclesiastical cere-monies, it is proper that we should now perform such functions after associating ourselves with the priests of Pugama [Pagan], who are the spiritual successors of Sonathera and Uttarathera [Sona and Uttara, Asoka missionaries].

"However, our teacher, Uttarajivamahathera, who was a native of Ramannadesa [country of the Mons], was formerly the sole head of the Church; but now, the priests of Marammadesa [Upper Burma] have become Lords of the Church; and we are not disposed to associate with them in the performance of ecclesiastical ceremonies." Thus, through pride, Chapata-mahathera declined to associate with the priests of Pugama in the per-formance of ecclesiastical ceremonies, and he performed such functions separately.[25]

Is this not a case of a feeling of superiority on the part of the Mon monk Chapata, fresh from Ceylon, in regard to the Upper Burmese—and all the more interesting for being recorded in a Mon inscription? And does this also suggest the view that the Mon monk Uttarajiva, at any rate, did not get reordained because he considered that the Mon Order was just as good? The possibility thus exists that the basic division in the Sangha in Burma at this time was between a Mon-Ceylon faction and an Upper Burma faction centered at Pagan, to which Chapata brought his reformist ideas. It should also be noted that the refusal of Chapata to join with the Pagan monks in "ecclesiastical ceremonies" would prevent him from participating in ordinations with the Pagan Sangha. If monks are ordained by separate "ceremonies," then perhaps one has to say that sects have developed. Furthermore, if one is to think of sects as groups of monks differentiated by such rituals, then a behavioral basis might be sought for the definition of the term *sect*. But is it the differing notions of sacred Pali texts that triggers factionalism in the Sangha, or is it differing judgments of behavior that invites varying interpretations of texts to support or condemn variations in monastic comportment?

In this book the position will be taken that the primary cause of division in the Sangha is a difference in the behavior of monks, though it

25. Dhammaceti 1476:10.

is fully realized that variations in behavior are often supported in monastic debate by reference to sacred texts. When a group of monks acts in such a fashion that they cannot join with others in ordination or eating rituals, then a "sect" will be said to have been formed. Quite often reference is made to Pali scriptures or the wording of Pali rituals to justify the departure from the norm, but the emphasis in this book will be upon not the textual arguments in all their complexity but upon the formation of a group under a leading monk whose position inspires others to follow the patterns he sets for them. The matter is most complicated in terms of sect identification, for to split the Sangha is the heinous crime for which the archetypal Devadatta was undone at the time of the Buddha;[26] thus, leaders of new monastic groups are reluctant to identify themselves as sects, although outsiders might so label them. Further difficulty is caused by the role of the state in perhaps favoring and encouraging sect formation in order to promote political ends or to purify the Sangha. Many differences of opinion, therefore, arise among both Burmese laymen and monks regarding sectarianism, and the outside observer finds a complex situation at every turn.

To return to Chapata's introduction of the Sihala Sangha at Pagan, we can see this new faction as sectarian in nature, but it did not remain a unified sect for very long. The four monks ordained in Ceylon whom Chapata brought back to found his new sect differed among themselves. One, Rahula, fell in love and left the order. The others, Ananda, Sivali, and Tamalinda, established their own factions.[27] Whether they were sects with separate ordinations is not clear, but, as Bode points out, their differences were based on disagreements over the application of rules in the Vinaya.[28] From this time on, we find definite groupings within the Burmese Sangha that trace their tradition to Ceylon orthodoxy and its ordinations and are thus known as the Sihala Sangha. In general the Sihala Sangha seems to have considered itself distinct from those monks who traced their tradition back to Shin Arahan and were known as the Arahanta, or Maramma[29] Sangha. The Sihala Sangha is also

26. Devadatta: the cousin of the Buddha who not only created a schism in the Sangha but tried twice to kill Buddha. See Davids 1890:163, 228; Cowell 1895, 3:289.

27. Pannasami 1861:72–74.

28. Bode 1897:21. See also Ray 1946:116.

29. I.e., Burma proper, Upper Burma as distinguished from the Mon kingdoms. Also spelled Mramma or Myanma. See Bode 1897:3.

known as the Latter Order and the Maramma Sangha as the Former Order.[30] The distinction was retained over the years, even into the nineteenth century.

Monastic Lineages and Historical Rivalries

Any exploration of the early Sangha factions and sects involves an evaluation of Burmese chronicles, many virtually unanalyzed in Western literature, and since we will refer to them often in this chapter a few words of introduction are necessary. On the one hand, there are secular chronicle writings, such as the *Glass Palace Chronicle,* which has been mentioned above. On the other hand, there are ecclesiastical chronicles, the best of which has already been referred to as the *Sasanavamsa,* written in Pali in 1861 by U Pannasami. The latter text, unlike the seventeenth-century chronicle of the same sort, the *Gandhavamsa,* has been translated into English. Much less accessible to date have been Burmese-language chronicles of the same kind. We shall use one particularly, the *Thathana Linkara Sadan* by Maha Dhamma Thinkyan,[31] which the *Sasanavamsa* follows very closely (but with significant differences in evaluations of the monks described); it also gives extra data on monks which are not contained in Pannasami's work. More important still, the Burmese work gives us the Burmese names of the monks, and in a number of cases, the *sayadaw* names. The title *sayadaw* is now a term of respect for any monk who has spent usually ten or more years in the Sangha and often is the "abbot" of a monastery, but more loosely it is also a term of respect for all monks.[32] The *sayadaw* name is usually the name of the monastery of which the monk is the head or the name of the place with which he is associated. Frequently, there is no connection between the Pali names of monks and the Burmese *sayadaw* names, so

30. Harvey 1925:56; Ray 1946:117.

31. Also known as *Sasanalankara.* Written in 1831 by Maha Dhamma Thinkyan (Thingyan), the 1st Maungdaung Sayadaw (see n. 32). See Tet Hoot 1961:58. J. F.

32. Htin Aung (1966:18–19) notes that the word formerly meant only the royal teacher but was extended to all highly respected monks during the late nineteenth century. In a sense, any monk was potentially available as adviser to the king. Certain *sayadaw* titles were handed down from monk to monk, and the individuals in the succession are differentiated by the terms "1st, 2d, 3d, 4th," etc., before the title, as in 1st Maungdaung Sayadaw, 2d Maungdaung Sayadaw, and so forth. This system seems to have started during the early nineteenth century. J. F.

that the information contained in the *Sasanavamsa* cannot be linked up with other information found in other Burmese texts or collected in the field in Burma. Working from the *Thathana Linkara Sadan*, however, I found this linkage a little easier to accomplish. The greatest gap, here, however, is in the field of pagoda and monastery *thamaing*s, local histories which contain important matter but can be handled only by one fully competent in Burmese. It must be hoped that these will be researched in due course. Ray (1946:97), who has used most of the sources referred to here—though apparently not the *Thathana Linkara Sadan*—mentions the *thamaing*s as being of little use to him. I would hazard to guess that they become more useful as the nineteenth century is approached. Finally, use is made of the Payapyu Sayadaw's *Thathana Bahu Thuttapakathani*, written in 1928, which follows the other chronicles closely but has extra information on a number of points and extends the account of the Sangha down to British times.

Study of these religious chronicles reveals that a history of the Burmese Sangha involves elaborate tracing of teacher-pupil relationships which are closely linked with, if not central to, sectarian divisions within the Sangha. Thus a monk writing in the twentieth century documents his tradition back through a succession of famous *sayadaw*s (teachers) until he reaches the missionaries of Asoka, who of course represent orthodoxy traceable to the Buddha himself. Bode (1897:56) calls this monastic record a "spiritual pedigree,"[33] but perhaps it is better to think of it as a monastic lineage, with the usual geneological manipulations of data so familiar to anthropologists, such as the telescoping of two or three people into one, the tendency of several lineages to identify with illustrious and famous ancestors through rather arbitrary linkages, and the removal from the lineage of monastic "ancestors" whose orthodoxy is deemed inadequate. These lineages or "lines" in Burma usually involve such monks as Shin Arahan (Arahanta), Chapata, or his pupils Ananda, Sivali, and Tamalinda, with fairly regular graftings to such branches by still later monks who traveled to and from Ceylon. It is difficult to determine if the Ceylon connections are so highly valued because of a reputed superiority in Pali scholarship and textual holdings or because the Burmese (as indeed the Sinhalese in return) looked to a distant Theravada land as almost mythically preserving the ideals they

33. The Pali term for monastic lineage is *theraparampara*. *Thera*: elder or respected monk; *parampara*: tradition or lineage.

so often could not actualize in terms of Vinaya orthodoxy. In any case, the lineages in the chronicles, with all their intricate detail, can be usefully approached to discover the historical dimensions of Sangha sectarianism.

In addition to the lineages traced to almost legendary figures such as the monks Arahan and Chapata, the chronicles also trace more recent lines or traditions. The general organizing principle of transmission of Theravada tradition from monk to monk is known as the *parampara*,[34] or the succession and handing down of orthodox teachings from the earliest days to the present. Quite often the writers of chronicles will exclude from their version of *parampara* all monks whose behavior is unacceptable to the writer and leave only one lineage such as the Parakkama,[35] which Pannasami in the *Sasanavamsa* traces in great detail to its origins in Ceylon (see Appendix C). The general concept of lineage is thus reified into particular lines, such as Parakkama, and monks considered *parampara* by one writer will sometimes be rejected by another. By consulting a number of chronicles, I have found other lines, such as the Pakhangyi, the Myauknan-Nyaunggan, and the Manle, and I note that monks who are versed in the Vedas (that is, Indian lay lore contained in Brahmanical works) are also of use to kings as royal advisers but are often excluded from *parampara* lists. The importance of the "orthodox" traditions to the monks involved cannot be stressed enough and, in order to imagine a proper Sangha history of Burma, one would have to include all these lines of tradition in such a survey. The problems involved, however, would daunt any but a Burmese, as is clear from an examination of the Parakkama line alone.

It is thus of critical importance that the main chronicle source for this chapter, the *Sasanavamsa,* was written by a monk who claimed descent from a Ceylon-oriented lineage (Parakkama), and it could be

34. Succession, series; see n. 33 above for *theraparampara.* Also known as *acariyaparampara* (line of teachers).
35. The origin of the word *Parakkama* is difficult to determine. It could be a person or place. Pannasami (1861:88) refers to a Mahaparakkama monk who settled a drink controversy in Pegu. [*Parakkama* might also refer to the tradition in Ceylon under King Sirisamghabodhi-Parakkamabahu of the twelfth century. It was this tradition to which the Burmese monk Uttarajiva turned and from which the Chapata sects traced their lineage. See Pannasami 1861:44. See also Bechert 1970:765–766, for a discussion of the forest and village monk division at the time of King Parakkamabahu II of the thirteenth century in Ceylon. J. F.]

argued that he wrote the whole of Burmese religious history in the light of the Sihala Sangha's development. The author's slighting of the early Pagan period and his subsequent concentration upon the introduction of Ceylon Buddhism could be cited to support Ray's view that the chronicles are biased toward Ceylon, but it must be made clear that lines other than those of the Sihala Sangha are included in the *Sasanavamsa,* such as those coming from Shin Arahan.[36] Variations between chronicles are also evident in tracing lineages.[37] Similar variation can be found in assigning a lineage to a famous monk: Ariyavamsa (see Appendix C) is said in the *Sasanavamsa* to be of Chapata lineage, but is identified in the *Thathana Linkara Sadan* as of the Arahanta line.[38] Such differences suggest loyalties of the authors more than ecclesiastical fact. It is also noteworthy that monks of whom the authors disapprove, such as Silavamsa and Ratthassara, both poets, are included.[39] One can say, therefore, that the chronicles, if handled with care, can tell us much of the inner dynamics of the Sangha over time, particularly if different works are carefully cross-checked.

The duration of these different lineages varies and they often mix in confusing fashion. The Sivali and Tamalinda lines, after being established in Lower Burma from Pagan, did not last long beyond the Pagan period, while the Ananda line remained intact a little longer. The Arahanta line changed its name to the Kamboja Sangha in parts of the country. There were also two more Sihala groups descending from monks who had gone to Ceylon independently of Chapata. In essence, however, the main division in Pagan times was between the Arahanta

36. Pannasami (1861) identifies the following as being of Arahanta (Shin Arahan) lineage: Silabuddhi (p. 78); the monk who persuaded Razadarit to turn back (p. 100); Tisasanadhaja (p. 108); the Le-Dat Sayadaw, head of the Sangha for Anaukpetlun (p. 115); and the Pakhangyi line of *sayadaws* (p. 121). The Saga monasteries held men of both Arahanta and Ananda lineage, thus indicating less than sectarian differences. Saddhammakitti (p. 104), Tipitakalamkara (p. 111), and Nandamala (p. 134, leader of the two-shoulder party in King Singu's time) were of Chapata's line, which is not exactly the same line as the author's.

37. For example, Pannasami (1861:72–74) identifies five lines after the time of Chapata: Chapata, Ananda, Sivali, Tamalinda, and Arahanta. Maha Dhamma Thinkyan (1831) lists five: Arahanta; Uttarajiva and Chapata; Chapata and Sivali; Ananda; and Tamalinda.

38. Pannasami 1861:104; Maha Dhamma Thinkyan 1831:142, 146.

39. Pannasami 1861:104–105; with more detail, Maha Dhamma Thinkyan 1831:146–150.

(Upper Burman) line and the Chapata (Mon-Ceylon) factions, although monks could cross these demarcations on occasion, as when the monk Tisasanadhaja "studied a book with the Elder Saddhammakitti" and traveled with him; the former is Arahanta, the latter Chapata.[40] The complicated process of recording discipleship and tradition over several hundreds of years cannot inspire too much confidence in the accuracy of these lineages, but they do suggest forces at work that have produced divisions if not sects within the Sangha as a whole throughout Burmese history. Of course, other criteria for factionalism sometimes drew supporters from otherwise separated lineages. One of the most long-lasting of these revolved around forest monks.

The Forest Monks as Reformists

The origin of the forest monk phenomenon is traceable to the early history of asceticism in India, and the ideal home of the Buddhist holy man has always been the solitary retreat in the Himalayas, as countless Jataka tales reiterate almost like a refrain as they tell stories of the Buddha's previous lives. An association between the forest life and orthodox sanctity has been commonly made, as though only in solitary, world-renouncing withdrawal could the search for Buddhist release and enlightenment take place. Yet there are contrapuntal voices that recall Buddha's rejection of extreme asceticism and his adoption of the middle way symbolized in the monastery, which is, as Tambiah says, "as much apart from the village as it is a part of the village" (1968:48). This ancient argument in Buddhism has involved the distinction between gamavasi monks and aranyavasi or vanavasi, monks—the former residing in towns and villages, the latter in jungle or forest areas. The forest monks, much like hermits, did not necessarily cease to belong to a mother community which might well be of the village kind. Later in time, forest monks began to appear in forest communities, devoting themselves no longer to meditation alone but indulging also in cultural and educational activities, as did town and village monks; in short, they seem to have been treated in some places as separate sects. This process has also been recorded for Ceylon.[41] We must, however, be very careful to keep in mind at all times the distinction between a solitary forest-

40. Pannasami 1861:104–108.
41. Rahula 1956:196–197; Ames 1963:52; Yalman 1962.

dwelling monk (one, for instance, who might retire to the forest late in life to live and die meditating) of any particular sect, and *groups* of forest-dwelling monks living in monastic communities to which a sectarian color might come to be attached.[42]

Following Luce, Than Tun has put forward a theory about a group of Burmese forest monks in monastic communities that arose in the thirteenth century. These monks were rivals of the Ceylon components in the Sangha, and they acquired great power and royal patronage, largely through the process of acquiring and developing land in relatively unpopulated areas, which helped the kingdom itself to expand its domains. Their leader was one Mahakassapa, and he is shown to have been, in all probability, the rival of certain monks who were sent to Ceylon in 1237 and 1248 "with perhaps the chief object of soliciting Sinhalese help to stop the growth of this sect of 'forest dwellers.' "[43]

Than Tun further suggests that these forest monks were neither more nor less than the famous Ari monks whom Shin Arahan is said to have purged. As noted above, I do not find this part of Than Tun's position convincing, although I am prepared to accept the possibility that the Ceylon factions were in competition with the forest monks in the thirteenth century. Certainly, however, the Arahanta (Upper Burma) traditions cannot reasonably be reduced to the level of unorthodoxy encompassed by chronicle accounts of the lax Ari, nor to that of the landed, liquor-drinking denizens of the forest described in Than Tun's articles. In contrast, the forest monks apparently represented to Pannasami, the author of the *Sasanavamsa,* a tendency toward orthodoxy in behavior, and his portrayals of them are usually quite sympathetic and supportive.

Other aspects of the forest monk movement are revealed in the thirteenth-century dispute over lands dedicated to seven monasteries built by King Uzana II. The argument involved the rules for looking after the fields associated with the monasteries, and three monks left for the "forest" (i.e., a mountain meditation monastery and a mountain cave): "Those Elders [who left] were called those who walked alone. But the remaining monks were called village-dwellers who walked with many. From that time onwards there were separate groups (of monks):

---

42. For details on modern forest monks, see Spiro 1970:54, 224, 313, 365.
43. Luce 1959a:61–68, 1959b:86; Than Tun 1959a, 1959c, 1959d:58, 67–68; Luce and Pe Maung Tin 1939:273.

forest-dwellers and village-dwellers. There was also a class of the Order known as monks who were recipients of the taxes on the fields and lands dedicated to a monastery."[44] Pannasami clearly favors those monks who departed from the place where such laxness in the rules was allowed,[45] and he notes that what he calls the Sangha "Parakkama" tradition was still in the nineteenth century associated with the forest place where the dissenting monks retreated. As we shall see later, Pannasami identifies himself with this Upper Burmese tradition, even though he is a Ceylon-oriented monk. Pannasami also clearly recognizes that monks who were "modest and of good behavior" (1861:91) could be village monks as well, but he is not tolerant of abuses of monastic land, of those "recipients of the taxes" in his third category above.

We obtain a further insight into this same forest–village monk division by studying the *Thathana Linkara Sadan,* which gives us the Burmese names and more details. The chronicle says that some monks contested land arrangements at the Campaka Monastery, and the monks Thathanadara and Parakkama left, one to live at the foot of the Tuywin Hill, the other to live at Taungbilu near Sagaing.[46] The brothers came to be known as "lone forest dwellers."[47] Later, the chronicle refers to a "Parakkama Saya" (respected teacher) of the East and one of the West going to Taungbilu. When Ava was being built, they crossed over the Irrawaddy River to Sagaing and stayed to the west of the Andawmu Pagoda. They set up two abbeys, the West Parakkama and East Parakkama. We thus have, in this chronicle, corroboration of the *Sasanavamsa*'s assignment of the Parakkama tradition to the protesting monks. Furthermore the monks who departed are clearly identified as the Arahanta line, and the orthodox monks who remained are noted as of the Ananda (Ceylon) line.[48] The *Thathana Linkara Sadan* thus re-

---

44. Pannasami 1861:92. See also Maha Dhamma Thinkyan 1831:125–126.

45. See also Maha Dhamma Thinkyan 1831:177.

46. Taungbilu: Tiriya Mountain, later the abode of the Tiriyapabbata Sayadaw. See below.

47. Maha Dhamma Thinkyan 1831:127–128.

48. The following summarizes Pannasami's (1861:91) and Maha Dhamma Thinkyan's (1831:125) data on the monks and monasteries involved in the forest–village split. The first name given is Pannasami's Pali designation; the second (in parentheses) is the Maha Dhamma Thinkyan's Burmese designation. Asterisks designate the Arahanta line or forest group; the rest are of the Ananda line.

veals a pattern we will meet again in the nineteenth century: the internal reformers of the nineteenth-century Sangha see themselves as "lone forest dwellers" fortified usually by an infusion of Sinhalese "orthodoxy" into the Arahanta tradition but traced not through Chapata lines but through later (and therefore less subject to unorthodox decay) "pilgrims" fresh from reordination in Ceylon. Even more fascinating in terms of the longevity of Burmese cultural patterns is the vital role played by the Sagaing site in the thirteenth-century drama, for it was also to Sagaing that the "lone forest dwellers" of the nineteenth century retreated to create the major sectarian movements under King Mindon, sects that exist in Burma today.

The foregoing example of thirteenth-century division in the Sangha raises serious questions about Than Tun's view of the forest party as the Maramma (Upper Burma) Sangha and the village monks as the Sihala (Ceylon) Sangha. An alternative view is suggested: that the Sihala Sangha traced in its lineages and lauded in its chronicles those monks in either forest or village whom it considered orthodox in behavior, and that it criticized unorthodox behavior wherever it was found, including the "forest." Forest monks whom Pannasami, for example, admires are those who do not found landed estates but who meditate or live strictly by the Vinaya rules of the monkhood wherever they may reside.

It should also be made clear that land was quite frequently donated to the Sangha by both kings and laymen. There is plentiful material in the epigraphy studied by Luce and Than Tun regarding such gifts and others. Land, as well as the agricultural produce thereof, often including slaves to look after and till the lands, was given to monasteries, to pagodas, to ordination sites, and to Buddha images. Donations often included enough to keep an institution going after it had been started.[49]

Sayadaws	Monasteries
*1. Suddhamahasami (Thuddhammamahathami)	Campaka (Sampaka)
2. (Nyanadaza)	(Weluwun)
3. Gunarama (Gunabirama)	Jetavana (Zetawun)
4. Adiccaramsi (Adeissawunthi)	Kulavihara (Kula Kyaung)
5. Suddhamalamkara (Thudhammalingara)	Golden Monastery (Shwekyaung)
*6. Varapatta (Warapatta)	Nicageha (Ein-nein)
*7. Siripunnavasi (Thiripunnawathi)	Dakkhinakoti (Taungzun)

49. Than Tun 1959a:120, 122, 124, 1959d:59, 61–63, 65–66; Tin Hla Thaw 1959:137.

Land ownership by monks frequently led to disputes and lawsuits, some between monks and kings, some between monks and laity, and others among monks. Occasionally the kings would try to reclaim lands their predecessors had given in piety, but in three such thirteenth-century cases the kings were proved wrong by the monks and the land was given back to them.[50] Some kings disliked seeing an increase in religious land from which no revenue was obtained, and "the tendency during Pagan times was to confiscate religious lands where the evidence was weak."[51] It may be, although Than Tun does not say so specifically, that one of the reasons for the landed "forest" monks' decline after the fifteenth century was that more and more land had come to be populated and was thus unavailable for donation by royalty. Another possible reason is that the progressive Sinhalization of the Sangha worked against the abuses of a landed monkhood. It is perhaps also important that, the more the king was in control of his land and wealth, the more he could prevent laymen from helping the Sangha to political power through land and wealth donations. Too much materialism in the Sangha triggers both internal monastic reformers and lay purification movements, and the forest monks Pannasami favors are more likely to be the reformers than the reformed. Occasionally in early Burmese history a king acquires the power and motivation himself to carry out massive disciplining of the entire Sangha. Such a king was the fifteenth-century Dhammaceti.

Royal Purification for a Unified Sangha

King Dhammaceti of the Mons had been a career monk himself for many years before a queen resigned the kingdom to him.[52] He thus knew personally the situation in the Sangha at the time, and his royal reforms have a sharpness of focus that reflect that firsthand knowledge. Above all, he had a desire to hold the monkhood up to the demanding standards of the Vinaya.

As noted in the Introduction, the Vinaya, or Book of Discipline, is one of the three fundamental texts in Theravada Buddhism, and its importance in the history of the Sangha cannot be overemphasized. It contains a central core of 227 rules to be followed by monks, as well as

50. Than Tun 1959d:62.
51. Than Tun 1959c:109–114.
52. Harvey 1925:117–120.

commentary upon each rule, based upon the tradition that the Buddha made each rule as it became necessary to correct unseemly monastic behavior which might not produce the esteem in which he wished his Sangha to be held. The rules deal with such obvious matters as sexual behavior and taking life, but they also define more subtle norms such as good taste in eating, walking, or even avoiding certain topics of secular conversation. It would be safe to assert that the Vinaya has been the core of Sangha concern throughout history, and royal traditions, as well as internal reformist tendencies within the Order, have kept the Vinaya's dominion supreme.

The Vinaya pervades Dhammaceti's fifteenth-century program for the Sangha. A reading of his Kalyani Inscription itself is necessary in order to appreciate the relentless thoroughness with which the king thought out and organized his purification. He studied the Vinaya and all its commentaries thoroughly before he arrived at any decision, and his remarks on the subject came to be a charter for subsequent ordination procedure in Burma. The key to his effort was insistence upon reordination in the Mahavihara tradition in Ceylon, the concept being that the Theravada tradition of the Mons had been broken by war and backsliding and that a new infusion of orthodoxy from Ceylon was needed to unify the Sangha and mold all the sects into one, with one ordination rite. Sixteen Burmese monks were ordained by the strictest standards at the Kalyani River in Ceylon, near the ancient Mahavihara monastery, where the Buddha himself is said to have visited. Once back in Burma, these monks organized ordinations at a ritually purified river site near Pegu renamed Kalyani. The king notified all the monks of the realm that they had to be reordained or leave the Sangha. They were warned also that they were losing all their previous seniority in the monkhood, since they had to start at the beginning, according to Mahavihara custom, by becoming laymen, novices, and then reordained monks.[53]

The inscription claims that these ordinations were carried out for 800 leading priests, to whom the king gave gifts and titles, as well as 14,265 young priests. There were also 601 new monks, raising the total to 15,666.[54] Seniority, the main criterion for leadership in the Sangha, was thereby in the hands of those sixteen monks reordained in Ceylon. This was an effective means of establishing new leadership and at the

53. Dhammaceti 1476:74.
54. Dhammaceti 1476:83.

same time removing the barriers between the sects caused by different ordination rites existent before the king's unification of the Sangha.

The excesses in the monkhood that Dhammaceti's reforms sought to eliminate are enumerated in the inscription in great detail. He seeks to remove those "sinful priests" from the Sangha who practice medicine, "the art of numbers," carpentry, crafts, astrology, painting, turnery, or cotton and grain trading, as well as the more obvious "gamesters, roues, drunkards," robbers, or men in the service of the king. We can also note the royal concern with the matter of monastic materialism of all sorts. He asks monks possessed of "gold, silver, and such other treasure, corn, elephants, horses, oxen, buffaloes, male and female slaves" to give them up.[55] Those guilty of such offenses as described above were by royal command defrocked and forced to become laymen. The inscription sums up the royal purification as follows: "It was in this manner that Ramadhipatiraja [Dhammaceti] purged the Religion of its impurities throughout the whole of Ramannadesa [Lower Burma], and created a single sect of the whole body of the Priesthood."[56] Ray (1946:192) has argued that this reform was decisive and set the pattern in Burma once and for all. Does this mean that the whole Sangha of Burma was re-ordained? In the absence of complete statistics, it is very difficult to say.

It is helpful, however, to consider Dhammaceti's program as a very important moment in the Sinhalization process for the Burmese Sangha. It is unlikely that any reform was decisive or that unity in the Order, if actually achieved, was ever more than momentary, but Dhammaceti's Vinaya emphasis, his stress upon ordination proprieties, and his admiration for the orthodoxy of the Ceylon Mahavihara traditions are all enduring Burmese patterns of emphasis. The point to stress is that Sinhalization is a process in Burma that had no real end: the Sangha was perpetually questioning itself and its values, and the degree of Sinhalization prevalent at any given time can only be defined relative to the degree of non-Sinhalization which it was, at any given time, opposing. Available evidence shows that there long remained refractory elements. It does, however, appear that as a result of Dhammaceti's reforms, the majority of the Sangha become more and more orthodox, or Sinhalized. Such problems as the forest–village conflict continued, despite the efforts

55. Dhammaceti 1476:79–80, 82–83.
56. Dhammaceti 1476:83. It is worth stressing that ordination may well have been one of the modes of sectarian definition, as it might well be today. J. F.

of Dhammaceti and other kings. These royal efforts to hold the Sangha to its ideals of unity introduce the question of how the kings actually worked with the monks of the Order.

Monastic Leadership and Royal Power

We have already recorded that kings like Aniruddha are said to have influenced and controlled the Sangha through such particularly prestigious monks as Shin Arahan. The difficult questions, however, are whether or not there was in early times a leader of the Sangha and whether the monkhood has been an organization with a hierarchical structure requiring such a head, or *thathanabaing*. In the first place it is reasonably clear that the "kings" we are dealing with, say, in Harvey's chaotic Shan Dominion period (1287–1531), are not the same kind of rulers as those we find in the Toungoo Dynasty period (1531–1752) and subsequently, up to the British period. The former are mere princes in a very troubled land, with constantly shifting frontiers to their "states;" the latter reigned over the whole of Burma, however much frontiers may have changed with the hazard of conquest. This certainly implies that the monks favored by the rulers must also have differed. Very roughly speaking, our chronicle texts tend to report royal preceptors (who taught the king as a prince) rather than "heads of the Order" up to the time of King Bodawpaya (nineteenth century), after which the latter title seems appropriate. There is a broad correlation between this conclusion and Than Tun's comment that, for the former period, one finds reference to preceptors but not to *thathanabaings*, or heads of the Order. His picture of a number of powerful *sangharajas*, or rulers of the Sangha, with what look like strong local affiliations,[57] corresponds broadly to the political picture we have from sources such as Harvey. The role of the *thathanabaing* is best seen, therefore, not so much in terms of the headship of the Order as in terms of a bridge between the royal power and the Order, or, perhaps more accurately, certain sections of the Order. The true situation would then depend to a great extent on the balance of power. The stronger the king, the more likely he would be to impose his choice; the stronger the Sangha, the more likely they would be to

---

57. Than Tun 1959d:66–67. Than Tun 1959c:114 also refers to many *sangharaja*s (lit. king of the Sangha, or leader, chief, head of a particular Sangha) among the forest dwellers, according to localities, led by one who was also a royal preceptor.

impose theirs on the king. In the former case, seniority in the Sangha, which is so important to the monks, would not matter overmuch because the determining factor would be that the monk chosen had been the king's teacher. In the case of a weak king, the monks would be most likely to promote and follow that monk who had the greatest seniority in the Order, and there would also be a tendency for such senior monks, in the time of weaker kings, to overlap reigns.

There exist, however, Burmese traditions that trace the office of the *thathanabaing* back to the time of King Minkyiswasawke in the fourteenth century.[58] Some British writers even refer to "primates" before this. Harvey (1925:55–56, 60), as noted earlier, sees the monks Panthagu and Uttarajiva as "successors" to Shin Arahan, followed by the monk Sihama Upali.[59] These early medieval monks are not officially designated in the chronicles as *thathanabaing*s, and thus it seems more accurate to start with the fourteenth-century material produced by combining chronicles and epigraphy; it is complex and often conflicting, but the data are summarized in Appendix A. The details regarding the first two reigns are most confusing,[60] but Than Tun's information (1959c:114–115) on the fifteenth century is very interesting, suggesting that during that period there were many *sangharaja*s (one a woman!) heading groups of monks and that these leaders must not be confused with other monks in the position of *thathanabaing*. As the chronicles treat the histories of the various monks, they do not always agree on the lineages represented by various *thathanabaing*s. For example, the monk Saddhammatthiti under King Narapati in the fifteenth century is said by Pannasami (1861:104, 161) to be of the Chapata line (see Appendix C) but said by Maha Dhamma Thinkyan (1831:142, 146) to be of the Arahanta tradition—a difference that reveals more about the Ceylon-Upper Burma rivalry in these

58. A list of *thathanabaing*s was made by the Khemathiwun Sayadaw (a famous survivor of the last *thanthanabaing*'s council) in response to a request from the Ministry of Religious Affairs in 1958 or 1959. A list of leaders of the Order is also found in the "Simla Document," written by a Burman in Simla, India, during World War II, also known as "The Problem of the Pongyi" by Tin Tut (1943). See Bibliography. [Thanks to Robert Taylor for this reference which is now (1973) declassified. J. F.].

59. See also *Glass Palace Chronicle* 1829:119, and Chan Htoon 1903:25. Stewart (1949) avoids discussing the issue until the time of Bodawpaya.

60. See Than Tun 1959c:100–102, 107, 114; Bode 1897:29; Maha Dhamma Thinkyan 1831:136–140, 176; Pannasami 1861:100.

two writers' nineteenth-century attitudes than it reveals about the fifteenth-century monks themselves. Actually, individual chroniclers vary in their willingness to include a particular *thathanabaing* in the Parakkama lineage or in the broader *parampara* tradition.[61]

For example, at the turn of the seventeenth century the Le-Dat Sayadaw is said to have been the *thathanabaing,* but he is not accepted as a member of the Parakkama line.[62] The chronicle focuses instead upon the Taungpila Sayadaw, who is said to have been the king's teacher and may have succeeded the Le-Dat Sayadaw (see Appendix A). The *Sasanavamsa* contains a very significant passage dealing with this period:

And these two Elders were of the same standing. The great Elder who was residing in the Tiriyapabbata monastery [the Taungpila Sayadaw] having talked with him, went away afterwards. The Elder Jambudhaja [the Shwe-O-Min Sayadaw of the Pakhangyi line][63] followed him to show him the path. Then the great Elder who was a resident of the Tiriyapabbata monastery said to the Elder Jambudhaja: "Reverend Sir, I am the king's favourite, the teacher of the king; it is you who should go before me." Then the Elder Jambudhaja said to the Elder who was a resident of the Tiriyapabbata monastery: "Reverend sir, you are the king's favourite, the teacher of the king. In the world, the teacher of the king indeed dwells in the state of striving, therefore, it is you who should go ahead of me." And in this connection it should be understood that both the great Elders spoke thus in regard to the common custom out of respect for each other.[64]

The *Thathana Linkara Sadan* text explains this rather cryptic episode more fully. The monks are presented as having taken a fancy to each other; they are of the worthy line of the Elders and have enjoyed visiting. "The same standing" means that their seniority in the Order is equal. The Taungpila's view, which is presented as being in accordance with Dhamma, or the orthodox teachings or Law of Buddha, and which is contrasted with the "inferior" worldly view of his friend, is that people will naturally think that the first man in line will be the king's teacher and that he wishes to proceed second in order to prevent them from

61. *Parampara* (Pali): succession, series, one after the other. The tracing of the orthodoxy eventually back to the Buddha himself. See nn. 33 and 34 above.

62. He is of the Pakhangyi line, a lineage descending from Arahan. The line appears to go back to King Thadominbaya, founder of Ava. See n. 36 above. The head monastery in Pakokku township was the Shwe-O-Min.

63. It is another monastic lineage mentioned briefly in the chronicles. See n. 62, above.

64. Pannasami 1861:121.

thinking this. The Shwe-O-Min, on the other hand, is afraid of being accused of disrespect by walking in front of the king's teacher.[65]

This episode suggests some very important aspects of Sangha leadership. The king could invite certain respected monks to the capital to join an executive council that had general responsibility for the welfare of the Sangha, including such matters as monastic discipline, property disputes involving monks, and communication between the state and the Order. Available material documenting the early existence of these councils is inadequate, but some of the data we shall examine later in the context of the eighteenth- and nineteenth-century Thudhamma Councils suggests that, in these matters, the *thathanabaing* was never more than primus inter pares; thus, any act would be promulgated by the *thathanabaing*-in-council, not by him as the sole ruler of an ecclesiastical organization called the Sangha. We know enough about Vinaya egalitarianism to realize that a truly orthodox monk will decline to stand out as leader of the Order or will pretend to decline and will thus opt, officially or not, for a primus inter pares position. In the Taungpila–Shwe-O-Min episode above, the monks' behavior illustrates the two possibilities open to a Sangha head, and the Taungpila's self-effacing behavior is clearly considered to be superior to that of his friend. As we shall see, monks continually refused the position of *thathanabaing* right into King Mindon's time in the nineteenth century, and this refusal, whether in the case of forest monks or not, has usually been taken as a sign of rigid orthodoxy. Possibly there was a strong motivational conflict in the case of a powerful monk called to the leadership of the Order: his own charisma would impel him to act as leader, while his feeling for Vinaya might lead him to pay, or seem to pay, great attention to the opinions of his council. This is yet another difficult and unexplored topic in the history of politicoreligious relations. It may be that such difficulties always stood in the way of any policy aiming at the unification of the Sangha in Burma.

The Taungpila's Parakkama orthodoxy is further illuminated by his retreat at the age of sixty to the forest life at Tiriya Mountain near Sagaing, after which time he was known as the Tiriyapabbata Sayadaw.[66] From the *Thathana Linkara Sadan* account we learn that Taungpila is

---

65. Maha Dhamma Thinkyan 1831:177–178. The significance of Sagaing was explained above.

66. Pannasami 1861:111, 121, 162.

synonymous with Tiriyapabbata.[67] It is from this monastery, however, that a divisive one- and two-shoulder robe controversy arose in the eighteenth century (discussed below); thus, its monks eventually departed from the strict orthodoxy claimed by Pannasami's line. The monastic lineages, we thereby realize, cut across other factional divisions in the Sangha, just as the holders of the office of *thathanabaing* represented different points of view either promoted by the royalty or supported by the monkhood at large. Monasteries also do not necessarily remain constant over time in terms of the issues dividing the Sangha. The position of *thathanabaing*, consequently, is perhaps best seen as a link between the king and the Sangha, but this link is very sensitive to royal wishes, and thus the state has an opportunity to exert its influence one way or the other through the *thathanabaing* and thus to affect issues important not only to the monks but also to the political realm as well.

Autonomous Monasteries and Political Intervention

In summation, we may assume that, from early times, there had to be communication between the king and the Sangha and that this had to be mediated by some sort of organization on the latter's part, however, rudimentary. The simplest form of this seems to have been a royally appointed senior monk—very frequently the king's own preceptor— acting as the interpreter of the court's desires to the Order and appointing a number of other monks in different parts of the realm to look after local issues.

Since, however, a Burmese state with fixed frontiers did not appear until recent times, there have been only royal centers achieving greater or lesser degrees of impermanent control over the surrounding countryside. These centers of power rose and waned rapidly; in this sense there is no better illustration of the Buddhist Law of Impermanence. Thus, as in everything else to do with political or religious authority, a permanent Sangha organization could hardly be set up in a situation where such fluctuations brought with them the rule that each new king appointed his own officials and discarded his predecessor's. However, patterns of allegiance within the Sangha were probably more permanent than those set up by the court; a *sayadaw* of age and standing in any given local community automatically became the center of the monks in

67. Maha Dhamma Thinkyan 1831:178.

the area around his monastery and probably enjoyed their allegiance for the duration of his life quite independently of the flux of events at the capital.

In a sense, therefore, I would agree with Cady that the Sangha is "an aggregation of individual ascetics rather than an organized church community."[68] Basically speaking, the monastery (*kyaung*) is the perfect ecclesiastical unit. At certain times and in certain conditions, however, the single ecclesiastical unit has grown into a much larger institution, consisting, in many cases, of a "mother" monastery with "daughter" or branch monasteries in various parts of the country. These larger complexes, known as *taik*s (sometimes called *kyaungtaik*s), may offer a variety of advantages, such as advanced education, a division of labor, or just sheer companionship, and many become the monastic equivalent of a university. It is important that, among the larger ecclesiastical units, the university types of *taik*s are in the majority.

Since the small monastery is virtually impregnable to political designs, because of the number of such monads scattered over the land, central authority turns to the larger *taik*s when it seeks to influence the Order. But since these central *taik*s often are the centers of sectarian power, they are likely to have vested interests that can be amenable or made tractable to the polity's designs. Further, if political power is going to obtain a foothold in the Sangha, it will do so by working upon the vested interests of certain sects against those of others. The fact that factions and sects exist, indeed, means that the political power *can* work upon the Sangha. We will turn next to a bitter factional argument in the Sangha which was resolved only by royal intervention and power—the famous dispute over the wearing of monks' robes.

The Robe Controversy and Royal Favor

The one- and two-shoulder robe argument which so divided the Parakkama line of Pannasami seems to have begun in the time of King Sane, at the beginning of the eighteenth century. Briefly, the party the chronicles favor, the *parupana,* held that the robe should cover both shoulders when monks went out to the villages for their daily food. The *ekamsika* party held to the view that one shoulder only should be covered. The quarrel dragged on, fed by the fact that successive kings

68. Cady 1958:58. Cf. Harvey 1925:326.

had preceptors or *thathanabaings* of different parties who reversed their predecessors' decisions. King Bodawpaya put an end to it a hundred years later by an "inquiry" which clearly reveals the iron hand in the velvet glove, and orthodoxy (*parupana*) was finally established in the whole land.[69]

As noted earlier, the Parakkama line contained one-shoulder advocates, and these may have been disciples of the great Tiriyapabbata Sayadaw, whose forest retirement we have already discussed. Thus there may be a link between the forest monkhood and the one-shoulder party, but it is tenuous. The forest–village rivalry, however, must have had some relationship to the robe controversy, for the *Sasanavamsa* tells of a village monk leader who incited his followers to attack and burn the books of forest dwellers, only to be stopped by royal intervention.[70] The one-shoulder party also made an unsuccessful attempt to legitimize their claims through Ceylon connections.[71] Adding to the confusion of rival claims is the fact that kings apparently had no criteria beyond personal preference in the selection of their preceptors, and it seems that, when one party in the conflict was in the ascendancy owing to royal privilege, the other party lay low, with some striking exceptions, such as the courageous eighteenth-century monk Munindhaghosa, who faced up to King Alaungpaya and his one-shoulder *thathanabaing* Atula.[72]

In the long history of the one- and two-shoulder controversy, Atula stands out in particular. The *Thathana Linkara Sadan* (1831:187, 233) tells us that he was the disciple of the Taungbilu Sayadaw, a Parakkama monk. At this point the Parakkama line seems to become too trying for U Pannasami, a two-shoulder advocate. He shifts his attention henceforth to rather obscure persons whom we seem to find mentioned nowhere else in the chronicles, and his lineage emerges from obscurity only just before Bodawpaya's time (see Appendix C). Atula (Maha Atula Yasa Dhamma Raja Guru), Pannasami's object of disdain, was stoutly

69. Pannasami 1861:123–135; Maha Dhamma Thinkyan 1831:103ff. See also Ray 1946, ch. 5. It is probably significant that in the *Thathana Bahu Thuttapakathani* (Payapyu Sayadaw 1928:103) the *parupana* party is identified with the Thudhamma sect, the major segment of the Sangha in Burma today.

70. Pannasami 1861:125; Maha Dhama Thinkyan 1831:182. The former source says that the forest monks were to be attacked because they did not wear headgear. The latter source says the contrary!

71. Ray 1946:24–33.

72. Pannasami 1861:128–131.

opposed by a long series of monks, beginning with Sujata, then Munindaghosa (the monk who unfrocked himself before appearing in front of King Alaungpaya rather than let the king take the risk of killing a monk), and two monks of Maungdaung village who may have been connected with the subsequently famous Maungdaung line of *sayadaw*s from which Pannasami came. Atula must have been a very strong person, and, indeed, some Burmese authorities regard him as *thathanabaing* over the five reigns from Alaungpaya to Bodawpaya.[73] The chronicles at least agree that he was the king's teacher during the reign of King Alaungpaya (1752–1760), founder of the terminal Burmese dynasty. We can safely assume that there was much more to the case of the one-shoulder party than appears from the biased accounts of the authors of the chronicles. On the one hand the question is one which goes beyond the boundaries of Burma. The Siam sect of Ceylon was a one-shoulder party, and I believe that, until King Mongkut's reform, inspired by a Mon sect, most Thai monks dressed this way also.[74] On the other hand, some monks the Burmese authors would like to claim for their party (monks of the Taungpila line) became involved, embarrassingly enough, with the one-shoulder group. It is also highly unlikely that Atula was as foolish as the texts make him out to be or else he would scarcely have been able to renew his attacks over so long a period. But clearly no satisfactory conclusions on this issue will be reached until the sectarian behavior of the Sangha throughout Southeast Asia has been studied.

Atula's successor is Nyana, the Taungdwingyi Sayadaw, and he is referred to as King Naungdawgyi's (1760–1763) teacher (see Appendix A). He was a two-shoulder leader and well-known writer who came from Taungdwingyi, a famous origin-place for Burmese literary men.[75] Some twentieth-century sources state that Nyana continued as *thathanabaing* through the reign of King Hsinbyushin (1763–1766), but the

73. Taw Sein Ko 1893:8.

74. For Mongkut's reform, see Lingat 1958 and Griswold 1961. Fascinating iconographical problems of a kind which might have led to clothing controversies are discussed in Dupont 1959:290–291.

75. Stewart 1949:12, n. 1. The Payapyu Sayadaw (1928:104) tells us that Nyana's earlier name was Maung Hpyaw so that he became known as the Hkingyihpyaw Sayadaw or Taungdwingyi Hkingyihpyaw Sayadaw. An alias is Makaralopa Sayadaw.

chronicles name the monk Candovara as this king's teacher.[76] He appears to have been a one-shoulder man, though the sources are not clear here. The same uncertainty surrounds the case of the next *thathanabaing,* Mayavattaka, who is also known as the Manle Sayadaw. The situation here is a curious one. The *Sasanavamsa,* at any rate, does not indicate that the Manle Sayadaw became head of the Order, king's preceptor, or anything else. Instead Pannasami (1861:133–134) stresses another monk, Nandamala, who was manifestly of the two-shoulder party, and Bode (1909:73) goes as far as to declare him head of the Order. Does this mean that the Manle Sayadaw was a one-shoulder man? His discipleship to the two-shoulder Taungdwingyi Sayadaw makes this a little unlikely. Another interesting feature is that the Manle Sayadaw became a member of King Bodawpaya's council of monks but not *thathanabaing.*[77] All this indicates that the shoulder-covering dispute was blurring lineages and loyalties considerably by the end of the eighteenth century and the situation was not as clear-cut as the orthodox writers of our texts have made it out to be. Factionalism and sectarianism in the robe controversy seem to have overwhelmed all other distinctions, such as Sinhalese and forest traditions, and thus the stage was set for strong royal action to impose the unity in the monkhood which had been so elusive for both monks and kings since the early eighteenth century.

Bias in Ecclesiastical Sources

We are now on the eve of King Bodawpaya's momentous reign, and it is time to reflect upon some of the basic patterns of the Sangha's history, bearing in mind that what passes in the sources for the history of the Sangha may indeed be overly weighted in favor of Pannasami's Parakkama lineage with its Sinhalese emphasis. The material we have reviewed on groupings and subgroupings in the early Burmese Sangha can be classified into two main areas of acculturation. The first regards the extent to which there was a Mon-Burmese rivalry in the Sangha, a rivalry which has accounted for certain biases in the stories told by our sources, mainly the chronicles. The second aspect of acculturation

---

76. The modern sources used are basically the lists of *thathanabaing*s given in Tin Tut 1943 and the Khemathiwun Sayadaw's paper for the Ministry of Religious Affairs in 1958 or 1959. See n. 58 above for more details.
77. Payapyu Sayadaw 1928:105, 197.

regards relations between Ceylon and Burma and the fact that the *Sasanavamsa,* especially, was written by a monk who claimed descent from a Ceylon sect. There are also some major sectarian activities running like threads through the history in our sources. The quarrel between forest monks and village or town monks, as well as the shoulder-covering controversy, are examples of such sectarian activity. It is still uncertain how far the sectarian disputes are related to the acculturation problems involving the Mon and Ceylon influences, though certain hypotheses have been advanced.

It should also be remembered that the Parakkama line is not the only lineage about which we have data. We noted above the allegiance of the Shwe-O-Min Sayadaw of the Pakhangyi line, who exchanged ideas on precedence with the Taungpila Sayadaw. Some information exists also on the *sayadaw*s of the Myauknan line, one of whom appears to have been Aggadhammalamkara, a famous seventeenth-century contemporary of the Taungpila Sayadaw, with whom he exchanged courtesies as to his scholarship.[78] The importance of lineage and discipleship in these discussions should be clear by now: both the *Thathana Linkara Sadan* and the *Sasanavamsa* constantly refer to visits and periods of study by one monk to and with another, the flavor of which can only be obtained by a perusal of the originals. We should also note that there is no doubt that great affection and friendship often united monastic peers of certain periods, despite the obvious rivalries. The period of Tipitakalamkara, the famous young monk of Prome, who vied with Ariyalamkara, the famous young monk of Ava, both in scholarship and for monasteries is most suggestive in this respect.[79] The texts also make clear the extent to which friendship counted when monks of this standing, who were close to the king, were considered for promotion. A young monk coming up to Ava or Sagaing from the surrounding countryside differed little from a young writer coming up from the provinces to a Paris or London.

The Vinaya and Sectarian Differentiation

In reference to sects and traditions, we should also note that the monks of Burma cared greatly for grammar and textual lore, right from the early stages of contact with Ceylon, as Bode and Ray have stressed.

78. Pannasami 1861:122; Maha Dhamma Thinkyan 1831:173, 179–180.
79. Pannasami 1861:110–112; Maha Dhamma Thinkyan 1831:164–166.

This interest, if we are to believe the chronicles, was shared by the laity so that good housewives of Pagan would pause to pass the time of day with their gossips and discuss the finer points of Pali grammar. Many stories told in the *Sasanavamsa* illustrate this emphasis: the monk who attained textual knowledge in the teeth of what was considered to be old age is still a hero in Burma and was depicted on posters during my stay in Burma.[80] Another story tells of the monk who made noises of disapproval about a text read aloud by the great monk Ariyavamsa: the latter had made two small errors of grammar, but the Master gave the critical monk his own robe as a token of the highest honor.[81] The criterion here is the same as that governing the *parampara* (lineage): the greatest exactitude in transmission of knowledge is required: the texts must not be veered away from by so much as one jot. We, of course, have stressed the importance of the behavioral basis of the Vinaya in sectarian and lineage differences, but we are aware that other textual issues were sometimes involved.

This same strictness we find in connection with texts seems closely related to the process of "purification" and "reform" of the Sangha itself. One recalls King Dhammaceti's intense reflections on the Vinaya texts; such emphasis can be seen at the heart of his reforms. The passion for exactitude in ordination halls (*simas*) is part of the whole pattern: if the ordination is incorrect, the monks are not monks and the religion is not the religion. The fact is that the various themes—the lineage of monks, the ordination, the purity of texts, the orthodoxy of one's "theology"—are all linked together in a complex of beliefs and rituals which determined the very nature of the Buddhist Order everywhere, but especially the traditions of Burma. Orthodoxy, however, is relative, and the early history of the Sangha must be evaluated very carefully in terms of the writer's particular sectarian affiliation or lineage. The tendency of chronicle writers to refashion monastic history to favor their own side, of course, makes scholarly evaluation difficult for us, but, on the other hand, such factionalism is dramatic tribute to the critical importance of sectarian issues in the Burmese Sangha.

In this chapter the behavioral aspects of cleaving to the Vinaya have been stressed. In the larger monasteries, however, the emphasis frequently turns to scholastic pursuits, and the *taik*s become higher insti-

80. Pannasami 1861:85–87.
81. Pannasami 1861:103–104.

tutes of learning, with great emphasis upon the sacred Pali texts. While this book does not examine these scriptures at any length, their importance to the Burman, monk or layman, is considerable, and to a great degree the Burmese have tried to live in accordance with them. The scriptures could be said to form the basic preoccupation of the Sangha, that its whole life revolves around them and that the interpretation of the scriptures, both in theory and in practice (*pariyatti* and *patipatti*), remains the one overwhelming task and responsibility of the monkhood. Differences in interpretation of the scriptures and in educational systems are very slight; but he who has a certain view of the texts or any part thereof will wish to teach them in a way corresponding to those slight variations. Thus differences of textual interpretation at one monastery may lead to larger and larger complexes of *taik*s and eventually to sect formation, even though the structure of the Sangha is such that a dissenting monk, if the source of the conflict be minor, can always retire into a small monastery or into another monastery and there live up to his own idea of Buddhism in undisturbed peace.

In ideological terms as well as—to a surprising degree perhaps—in practical terms, the function of the Sangha, from its own point of view as well as in many respects from that of the laity, is to provide a context wherein a way of life propounded in the Theravada scriptures can be led to the best advantage and under the best possible conditions. The Vinaya above all other scriptures is seen by laity and monks alike as the key to preserving that way of life for the Sangha.

During the period reviewed in this chapter, sects cleaving to Vinaya have been looked upon favorably by political authority, which did not want the Sangha to acquire land and power and thereby to interfere in politics. Thus we can notice royal favor bestowed since Pagan times upon reformist factions and sects within the Sangha, whether they were Mon monks from Lower Burma, Sinhalese sects claiming an ultra-orthodoxy, forest monks renouncing materialism of all sorts, large *taik*s that represented high standards of academic discipline, or lineages that claimed to follow the pure path of the Elders. Yet the ever-present factionalism, as dramatically evident in the robe controversy, continually threatened monastic unity and traditional allegiances, presenting both severe problems of disciplinary control for the kings and their monastic leaders and, of course, opportunities for royal power to enter into the religious realm for its own ends. Faced with these dangerous situations, the monks of Burma always turned to the Vinaya as a secure port in such storms. Strict observance of the Vinaya's ancient rules became the ultimate position of safety for the Sangha.

It is worth noting here, however, that, after King Mindon in the late nineteenth century and especially after Independence in 1948, the laxer sects were the ones favored by the political authority, and in this century the stricter Vinaya sects became the enemies of a religious Revival program which entailed participation in politics. The process of reformation discussed in this chapter can be interpreted as evolving, in a sense, beyond itself, so that it became in modern times self-defense on the Sangha's part against an active polity rather than self-defense on the polity's part against an active Sangha.

2. The Sangha during Royalty's Last Century

This chapter will concentrate upon the critically important years between the ascent of King Bodawpaya to the throne in 1781 and the overthrow of the last Burmese monarch, King Thibaw, at the hands of the British in 1885. This final century of royal rule witnessed momentous changes in Burmese national life. The country was forcefully introduced to the reality of colonialism as, starting in 1824, piece by piece its territory fell under the control of English troops. Quite understandably these changes involved the fate of the Sangha and of Buddhism itself.

A Strong King and Enforced Sangha Unity

The period begins with the aggressive and powerful King Bodawpaya's rule of a politically unified Burma; this king naturally sought to create a unified Sangha as well, but his enigmatic personality with its strange fluctuations of opinion on religious matters did not quite provide the necessary stability of leadership. Available evidence on his reign contains records of continuing factionalism in the monkhood that traces back most certainly to the patterns discussed in the previous chapter. The one- and two-shoulder argument, for example, was still very much a problem, and King Bodawpaya forcefully brought the matter to a close, although his vacillation makes it difficult to establish the order of events. The texts tell us that the king, realizing that monks would not discuss the robe controversy freely in his presence, sent out commissioners among the monasteries. They found that the one-shoulder party could claim no textual authority for their views, and the king accordingly decreed in favor of the two-shoulder party. Ray, commenting on this, finds it strange that the one-shoulder party should have given in so soon and, in view of Bodawpaya's authoritarianism, suggests that the king had already decided in favor of two-shoulder orthodoxy and coerced the opposing monks into acceptance. The king would have been supported in this by his teacher, who came from Maungdaung, the village, as Ray rightly points out (1946:231–233), which furnished objectors to Atula of one-shoulder fame in the time of the previous king Alaungpaya. The *Sasanavamsa,* on the other hand, describes this teacher as arriving after the decision. The monk in question was Nyana, who was known as the 1st Maungdaung Sayadaw.[1] In any case, in 1784 Atula came back to the attack for the one-shoulder monks, armed this time with a textual authority, but he suffered the epic defeat described at length in the chronicles.

Ray has suggested that the one-shoulder party drew strength by having some of its group on the new Council of Elders that Bodawpaya appointed (see Appendix B), and indeed this interpretation would be fortified if we could show that the Manle Sayadaw, a council member, and perhaps others, had been one-shoulder men. Unfortunately little more than speculation is possible here. The Payapyu Sayadaw's history tells us that Atula was expelled from Upper Burma and that at this time the two-shoulder party became known as Thudhamma (presumably from the name of Bodawpaya's Council of Elders, the Thudhamma Council) while the one-shoulder heresy was known as Sulagandi, from the contrived text used by Atula, the *Culaganthipada.*[2] The term Thudhamma, it should be noted, is the first of the sectarian names which were to be used in Mindon's reign and which still exist in contemporary times. Furthermore, insofar as the Sangha is said to have been made "one" again by Bodawpaya's action after Atula's defeat, we have some support for the argument made later in this chapter that, in Mindon's time, the Thudhamma was the Order itself, i.e., the body from which subsequent sects split off, rather than one major sect among minor ones.

At the time of the defeat of the one-shoulder monks, Bodawpaya seized the opportunity of reorganizing the Sangha, and, after building the new capital at Amarapura, he named a number of leading monks to important monasteries there. Finally, in 1788, he placed his teacher

1. Pannasami 1861:135. The Payapyu Sayadaw (1928:114) gives the 1st Maungdaung Sayadaw's name as U Myat Nei. [Tet Hoot (1961:58), as noted above in Chapter 1, n. 31, identifies the Maungdaung Sayadaw as the Maha Dhamma Thinkyan and the author of the *Sasanalankara.* J. F.]

2. Payapyu Sayadaw 1928:111–3. Here Atula's name is given as U Pan Htwei. Maha Dhamma Thinkyan (1831:233) refers to a book written by the Hsounda Sayadaw in which Atula's lineage is traced from the Taungpila Sayadaw, but the remainder of the lineage is composed of monks I was unable to identify.

Nyana, the 1st Maungdaung Sayadaw, at the head of the Order, with a new title. Later in his reign, Bodawpaya appears to have had trouble with his Sangha, and at one time the *thathanabaing,* Nyana, was obliged to disrobe.[3] But there are records in Western sources of interviews, before this crisis occurred, with Bodawpaya's head of the Order, who is most likely Nyana.

Toward a Portrait of Sangha Leaders

Descriptions of Sangha leaders provide precious insight to the nature of the *thathanabaing*'s position. One of the first outside observers of a Sangha head was the Italian missionary Father Sangermano, at the end of the eighteenth century, who wrote as follows about Bodawpaya's *thathanabaing:*

All the Talapoins [monks] who live in the different Baos [monasteries] of a province are under the jurisdiction of a superior, who corresponds to the provincial of our religious orders; and those of the whole Empire are subordinate to the Zarado (Sayadaw), or grand master of the Emperor, who resides in the capital, and may therefore be called their General. The Baos are . . . completely cased with fine gold both within and without, particularly those which the Emperor and his sons built for their Zarado. [1833:90]

Sangermano's contemporary, the Englishman Symes, devotes several pages to the monasteries and their sculptural glories; in the midst of some rapturous prose, a description comparable to Sangermano's is found:

We beheld the Seredaw [*sayadaw,* i.e., the *thathanabaing*] sitting on a satin carpet. He was encompassed by a circle of Rhahaans [monks], from whom he could be no other ways distinguished, than by his preserving an erect position; whilst the others bent their bodies in an attitude of respect, with their hands joined in a supplicating manner. . . . He received us with much politeness, and in his looks and demeanour affected more liveliness and complaisance, than any of the fraternity I had hitherto seen. His appearance denoted him to be about forty years of age; not meagre and austere as they usually are, but fat and jocular. I presented to him my offering. . . . I noticed the magnificence of the kioum [*kyaung,* monastery]: he replied, that such sublunary matters did not attract his attention; he was on earth but as a hermit. I desired his prayers; he said they were daily

3. Stewart 1949:5–6; the Payapyu Sayadaw 1928:114; Sangermano 1833:61. See also Mendelson 1961b:575.

offered up for the happiness of all mankind, but that he would recommend us, to the particular protection of Gaudma. He made some observations on our appearance, which I did not understand, and he even smiled; a relaxation very unusual in a Rhahaan.   [1800:388–389]

Earlier in his book, Symes appears to have encountered a provincial head of the Order, and this man's magnificence may give us a clue both to Symes's surprise at meeting a pleasant *thathanabaing* and to the degree of independence probably enjoyed then as now by the heads of the Rangoon Order (although one should not take too seriously judgments depending on the temper of author and interviewee on a single day of each other's lives). Symes continues:

I had heard much of the veneration paid to the Seredaw, or head of the Rhahaans at Rangoon, and by chance . . . I met him returning from the pagoda. . . . His years and abstracted appearance induced me to ask who he was; on being told, I turned and joined company with him, for he would not have stopped or gone out of his way had a monarch accosted him. He entered freely into conversation, but kept his eyes fixed invariably on the ground before him; he was a little old man of seventy-five, and still walked with firm step on even ground, but when he ascended the stairs of his dwelling he required support. He goes every day at the same hour, to the temple, to offer his devotions, and performs the journey, which, going and returning, cannot be less than four miles, on foot. . . . I was, however, disappointed in the expectations I had formed; he betrayed a worldly pride inconsistent with his years and sacred function; he announced with much pomp, that he was the head of the Church of Rangoon, and ostentatiously displayed his sacerdotal titles, engraven on iron plates, that had been conferred on him by the present and the late king. He seemed to possess little of the humility which distinguished the aged prelate of Pegue,[4] and I left him impressed with much less reverence than I had entertained for his character before our interview.   [1800:212–213]

These writers were not afraid to comment upon their personal reactions to individuals, which we may take for what they are worth, remembering what the authors were likely to be sticklers for national as well as religious pride. While it is still possible for a foreigner to gather an impression of overweening pride from certain leading *sayadaws*— I once served as ad hoc chauffeur to two of them and have never felt so small in my life—it must be remembered that in many cases "proud" behavior means different things in different societies and that much of it

4. Symes had previously visited a highly respected monk at Pegu and had been very much impressed. J. F.

in monks stands simply for the detachment their lay followers expect from them. Returning to the facts, and assuming that in all cases the writers were actually meeting the dignitaries they described, what do we have?

Most accounts agree that the *thathanabaing* at a certain period, say during the eighteenth century, had great power over the monks in the whole kingdom, although beyond general disciplinary policing it is not easy to gather the exact nature of that power. While the *thathanabaing* was, in dress and many aspects of behavior, not very different from an ordinary monk, the quarters in which he lived and the ceremony he found himself the center of—whether he cared for such or not— marked him as a person apart. Of most interest, perhaps, are the details concerning the personal qualifications of the *thathanabaing,* the rules of succession to that dignity, and the matter of delegation of power. Unfortunately Symes does not note the exact nature of the "iron" (probably copper) plates held by the Rangoon monk so we cannot know whether these were titles of office or titles of distinction such as educational ones, but we do gather from other sources that such provincial designations of status were known, though these older writers do not describe the details of the subordinate offices. One frequently mentioned point is that the *thathanabaing* was not necessarily a very senior member of the Order; Symes's was about forty. His main qualifications had to do with his influence over the ruling king.[5] Since each ruler tended to discard his predecessor's officials, this absence of seniority is not surprising and fits well with my general thesis. But, to be fair, was this the whole question? Obviously, an old man is not necessarily an energetic one, and some kings may have desired an energetic *thathanabaing;* other kings might prefer an older, less vigorous monk for obvious political reasons. When the modern period is considered later in this book, the ages of the monks connected with the Burmese "Revival" will suggest similar political factors.

The question raised regarding the qualifications of leadership, in view of the absence of an adequate ecclesiastical history of Burma, may be an academic one, yet it is worth asking such questions for the sake of other scholars in the future. Today the same monks tend to hold offices over the years even when provision exists, in "democratic" constitutions of the

5. Nisbet 1901, 2:124.

sects, schools, or societies concerned, for their being changed. In this pattern they are not very different from laymen, but there is another aspect to the question. Not only monks but also certain monasteries sometimes tend to assume succession to important posts. For example, if the presiding *sayadaw* of a certain monastery serves on some monkish council or board and dies, the next presiding *sayadaw* of that same monastery takes his place. We thus doubt that the discontinuity in royal Burma was as great as it is sometimes claimed to have been.

Leadership Through Councils and Officials

Our understanding of the office of the *thathanabaing* during the reign of Bodawpaya is further complicated by the king's creation of the Council of Elders. Although hundreds of years earlier, as noted in Chapter 1, according to Than Tun's data, a number of local *sangharajas* (literally Sangha rulers) under a *mahasangharaja* may well have met in a council, no evidence whatever exists about either the responsibilities of a head of the Order or of a royal preceptor, or about any devolution or sharing of power on his part, until Bodawpaya's resign. The *Sasanavamsa* tells us that the king dedicated monasteries to four great elders (the Min-O, Manle[6] Hsounda, and Min-ywa Sayadaws), then to five more (the Nyaunggan, Shwedaung, Hsinte, Meidhi, and Lawkahmankin Sayadaws).[7] Bodawpaya's nomination of nine monks to monasteries, following a prophecy and certain astrological directions, suggests a strong magical motivation connected with both the monasteries and the founding of the new capital of which they were a part.[8] He then created eight posts to help the first four great elders, who, "on account of old age and weakness, will not be able to purify the religion according to their wish."[9] These eight posts went to the following *sayadaws* in order: the Shwedaung, Bagaya, Kato, Meidhi, Mountaw, Salin, Hsinte, and Maungdaung. Thus, among the monks who received monasteries, Nyaunggan and Lawkahmankin were appar-

6. The monk Silacara, a disciple of the Manle Sayadaw, was later famous as a forest monk (see Pannasami 1861:144). This could mean that Bodawpaya had elected a forest monk; it could also imply, however, that passage from village to forest monkhood could be accomplished with some ease, or that at any rate monks from different camps could be teachers and disciples of one another—a pattern we observed in Chapter 1.
7. Pannasami 1861:135–136.
8. For confirmation of this idea, see Than Tun 1960b. J. F.
9. Pannasami 1861:136.

ently not on the council. Finally, he made the Maungdaung Sayadaw "Lord of the Religion": an example, perhaps, of the primus inter pares argument.[10] There is no evidence that all these monks were entitled *thathanabaing*. More details on these Council of Elders members is given in Appendix B.

I could find no reference to provincial dignitaries at this time and thus conclude that Stewart (1949) has combined material belonging to Bodawpaya's and later reigns in writing about such district Sangha officials as *gaing-gyok*s, and so on, though this does not necessarily mean, either, that such dignitaries did not exist earlier than King Mindon. The Khemathiwun Sayadaw writes that at the time of the 2d Maungdaung Sayadaw *thathanabaing* (1839–1846 and 1852–1865) a liberal assistant to a minister of the Hluttdaw[11] introduced a system whereby single control by the *thathanabaing* was transformed into collective control by the council.[12] Was it not until the reign of King Mindon, therefore, that the primus inter pares principle appeared in the regulations? This seems unlikely, though it is not impossible; at any rate the spirit of the arrangement was, as we have seen, present before Mindon's time.

Connected undoubtedly with some of Bodawpaya's attitudes toward Sangha organization is the troublesome question of religious lands which was touched on in the previous chapter, where we saw that kings preferred to limit, as far as possible, the amount of land owned by the monks, because such land could not be taxed. Stewart, discussing the matter, disregards the earliest evidence we have reviewed and, with a glance at King Thalun, passes straight on to latter data:

The Nyaungyan Dynasty (1605–1752), which moved the capital from Pegu to Ava, took some steps towards delimitation of religious lands. Apart from King Thalun's inquest of 1638, one of the objects of which was to ascertain the lands held by monasteries or dedicated to pagodas, the appoint-

10. Ray 1946:234, 274 and subsequent authors have misread texts and refer to eight members of the council, where I find twelve. Stewart (1949:4) confuses Bodawpaya and Mindon data.

11. This official was also governor of the city of Yaw; he wrote a text called the *Yaza Dhamma Thingaha*, a guide for royalty in ruling the country (*yaza*: king; *dhamma*: law; *thingaha*: friend; i.e., a law that is a friend of the king).

12. Four-page mimeograph emanating from the Khemathiwun Taik, West Sector, Mandalay, not dated. Ms. in Mendelson papers. The Khemathiwun Sayadaw was one of the Thudhamma Council members in the 1930s.

ment of a civil official, called the *Mahadanwun*, with jurisdiction in such matters, is believed to have been first made under this dynasty. The order appointing him gave him power to decide whether land belonged to a pagoda or monastery, or to the State, and, in consultation with the clerks of the monasteries, to prepare lists of persons cultivating religious lands. Such persons were not to be allowed to escape from their servile status by getting their names entered in the lists of any category of state servants. [1949:4]

Bodawpaya's attitudes varied considerably, and it seems that he decided at one time that the Order had too much land and thus launched an investigation of religious titles in 1784. In the course of his collection of all dedicatory inscriptions throughout the realm (some one thousand of them now to be found at the Mandalay Arakan Pagoda and the Amarapura Patodawgyi Pagoda), he appears to have confiscated some lands and attempted to reduce the glory of the monkhood.[13] It was no doubt all these activities that led to the creation of the office of *wutmyewun* (ecclesiastical lands official) with powers similar to those of the *mahadanwun* of King Thalun's reign, the latter official being now concerned with the enforcement of monastic discipline.[14] We have here in embryo much that is relevant to the question of ecclesiastical discipline in modern Burma.

Another Reformist Sectarian Movement

The mercurial temperament of King Bodawpaya in religious matters is revealed in another important area that illustrates how sectarian tendencies continued despite this strong king's solution of the robe controversy and his efforts to unify the Sangha. I refer to the so-called Paramats,[15] a group of most unorthodox believers. It is necessary to go into the matter in some detail.

13. Ray 1946:239–40.

14. *Wutmyewun* (B): *wut mye:* ecclesiastical land; *wun:* official; an official appointed by the king to supervise and keep records of Sangha lands. The *mahadanwun* was appointed by the king to supervise discipline in the Sangha (see Glossary for word derivation). See Stewart 1949:5; Scott and Hardiman 1900, 1, pt. 2:6; and Payapyu Sayadaw 1928:128.

15. *Paramattha* (P): the highest good, ideal: truth in the ultimate sense, philosophical truth; more generally speaking, those Buddhists at the end of the Theravada religious continuum who insist that in reality nothing really exists. The term has, in Burma, connotations of taking religious matters to extremes and is somewhat derogatory.

We first meet this kind of group as the "Zodi" or Zawti (see Glossary) as described by Father Sangermano:

The Zodi . . . began by making a great stir throughout the whole kingdom, and thereby excited the zeal of the Emperor [Bodawpaya], against them. It is believed that great numbers of them still exist in divers parts of the empire, but they are obliged to keep themselves concealed. They are of Burmese origin, but their religion is totally different from that of Godama [Buddha]. They reject metempsychosis, and believe that each one will receive the reward or punishment of his actions immediately after death, and that this state of punishment and reward will last for eternity. Instead of attributing everything to fate, as the Burmese do, they acknowledge an omnipotent, and omniscient Nat, the creator of the world; they despise the Pagodas, the Baos [monasteries], or convents of Talapoins [monks], and the statues of Godama. The present Emperor, a most zealous defender of his religion, resolved with one blow to annihilate this sect, and accordingly gave orders for their being searched for in every place, and compelled to adore Godama. Fourteen of them were put to a cruel death; but many submitted, or feigned to submit, to the orders of the Emperor, till at length he was persuaded that they had all obeyed. From that time they had remained concealed, for which reason I have never been able to meet with one of them, to enquire if any form of worship had been adopted by them. All that I could learn was that the sect was still in existence, and that its members still held communications with each other. They are for the most part merchants by profession. [1833:89]

Here we note the extremism of the sect, their worship of a transcendent deity (the Nat), and their dislike of monks, images, and other appurtenances of the Sangha.

Yule also writes about what appears to be the same phenomenon:

During the reign of Mentaragyi [King Bodawpaya], in the end of the last and the beginning of the present century, a latitudinarian or heretical doctrine had considerable diffusion in Burma, among the intelligent of both sexes. It is repeatedly mentioned by Judson[16] in his Journals and letters. He calls its followers sometimes semi-deists, sometimes semi-atheists, but it is difficult, from the slight notices alluded to, to get any accurate idea of their doctrine; indeed, it appears to have varied with the individuals. One held the fundamental doctrine that Divine wisdom, not concentrated in any existing spirit or embodied in any form, but diffused throughout the universe, and partaken in different degrees by various intelligences, and in a very high degree by the Buddhas, is the true and only God. This seems very nearly Mr.

---

16. Adoniram Judson, an American Christian missionary and scholar.

Hodgson's *Prajnika*[17] doctrine, and not inconsistent with Buddhist tenets. In other cases the sectarian tenets took the shape of a mere universal scepticism; and in others of a nearer approach to deism, with entire rejection of Gautama. This sect of Judson's is probably the same with that of the *Zodi,* of whom Padre Sangermano says (undoubtedly giving too exact a definition of their creed): [Yule then cites Sangermano[18] as above]. . . . I have been told that this deistical sect is still numerous, but I have not been able to obtain any information regarding them.   [1858:241–242]

The most complete information to date is given by Scott:

The only sect which has at any time started any doctrinal heresy is that of the Paramats. They reject the worship before pagodas and images, and pray only to the Nyan-daw, the godlike wisdom, which abides like a mountain of fire in the heavens, invisible to mortal eyes, and taking no interest and exercising no influence over mundane things. These dissenters pay reverence to the ordinary brethren of the yellow robe, keep the Ten Precepts, repeat the Bawana[19] . . . and the Ittipi-thaw,[20] but they never go near the shrines, and recite their prayers and invocations in the jungle or in open fields . . . A cardinal fault in them is that they give no alms. . . . The sect was founded at the beginning of this century by a pongyi [monk], called by his followers Shin Tabaung. He lived at Sinbyugyun, "White Elephant Island," a place half way between Mandalay and the British frontier, and the dissent would probably never have spread beyond that district, or outlived the life of its originator, had it not been for King Bodaw Paya. When the Thenga [Sangha] refused to recognize his claim to be the fifth Buddha of this world cycle, he espoused the cause of the Paramats, imposed penalties on all monks who would not accept their tenets, and went so far as to force a Thathanabaing, one of the heads of the Order, to marry, marriage being permissible under the doctrines of the dissenters. This gave the schism a prominence which it could not otherwise have attained, and enabled it to last down to the present time, though its numbers never very great, have steadily dwindled away. There are perhaps more Paramats in Prome than in any other town in Burma, Lower or

17. *Prajna* (Sk): *Panna* (P): "transcendental wisdom" in Mahayana Buddhism. J. F.

18. At Sangermano's mention of the religious zeal of the emperor, Yule adds a note: "This was in the early and pagoda-building days of Mentaragyi."

19. *Bhavana* (P): subjects for meditation, concentrating on something. Scott mistakenly thought the word referred to a chant of praise to the Triple Gem (the Buddha, the Law, and the Sangha). J. F.

20. Possibly *itti patti go* (B): literally, come and examine. Perhaps a reference to Anussati, the prayer of worship to the Triple Gem. See Pe Maung Tin 1964:6. J. F.

Upper. Their most prominent doctrine is that the Shwe-Nyan-daw existed before the world began, and will exist for all eternity. Ideas may arise from the influence of external objects, but when they have been freed from their connection with bodily creations, they have an independent existence, and when once they have come into being continue to live. This is explained by the assertion that the quasi-deity of the Buddha is founded only on his supreme wisdom. Buddha means, etymologically, "the wise," and Shin Gautama was simply an incarnation of the pure Wisdom. Men believed they actually saw him when he was already really a deity—nothing else than the inspiring Nyan-daw, which made the five Khandas[21] appear to have an actual earthly existence. Occasionally an energetic Sadaw [*sayadaw*] excommunicates all the Paramats under his jurisdiction, and forbids all the laity to sell to them, or have any communication whatsoever with them, but as a rule they are let alone. The movement is too feeble to threaten any real danger to religion, and has never gained many adherents among the laity. [1909:147–149]

One or two points must be made here. As usual, the changing behavior of Bodawpaya causes trouble: in other sources he appears to have persecuted Paramats. Perhaps we are to follow Yule and claim that he persecuted them early in his reign but joined with them later, although Stewart does not refer to Paramats at all (only to *pwe-gyaung*[22]) in his account of Bodawpaya's disrobing of a *thathanabaing*. The matter is far from clear. What is it exactly that this sect was and was not allowed to do? Marriage for monks seems wholly inadmissible as part of their doctrine. In another work, Scott confuses the matter further. Giving an account of Paramats similar to that in his earlier book, he writes, "The *Paramats* of the early years of last century called themselves *Tongaing* and *Yongaing*"; but Scott states a little later that Bodawpaya "sided with the *Yongaing*" in the matter of his claims to be Metteya.[23] He thus, according to Scott, sided with Paramats against Paramats. Not satisfied with this, Scott goes on to split up Paramats into different

21. *Khandhas* (P): the five "bundles" or conditioned elements of human existence; the five bundles of phenomena that create the illusion of self; more generally in this case, the earthly being. J. F.

22. Nineteenth-century, nontraditional, rather secularized schools in monasteries.

23. Metteya (Maitreya) is the Buddha who is to come at the end of the present era. For more detail on Metteya in relationship to messianic Buddhism, see Mendelson 1961b:574–579. [The references by Scott to the Tongaing and Yongaing involve the one- and two-shoulder controversy. Tongaing: *toun gaing* (B): one-shoulder sect; *youn gaing* (B): two-shoulder sect (Judson, 1966:485, 846). Scott conjoins the *paramat* and robe issue. J. F.]

groups: "These *Paramats* are, perhaps, represented most nearly in the present day by the *Sawti* sect, which is fairly strong in some parts of the Shan States, and has its headquarters at Nam-kham, near the Chinese border. The *Sawtis* neither support nor reverence the mendicants nor their monasteries, and their leaders seem to correspond most nearly to what we should call lay brethren" (1911:378).

Considering the variety of usage for the word *paramat,* we might best accept it as a relative, category term attached to a variety of extremist sects by outsiders knowing little and caring less about historical details. Paramat belief and practice are important during the reign of the king who solved the one- and two-shoulder controversy and who is often credited with unifying the Sangha because they are evidence of sectarian activity, and, even more important, they suggest considerable royal involvement in Paramat sectarian affairs, if we can believe Scott's description of Bodawpaya's bid for divinity.

Thus, during Bodawpaya's reign, we see the end of the one- and two-shoulder controversy, the appointment of a *thathanabaing* in the person of the 1st Maungdaung Sayadaw, the royal donation of five monasteries at the capital, the appointment of a Sangha Council of Elders (with some regional representatives), the support of land and disciplinary officers for the Order, and, in general, evidence of firm control over and interest in the orthodox Sangha. But we can also find suggestions of a remaining forest monk controversy, the defrocking of the *thathanabaing,* royal confiscation of monastic land and wealth, the possible appointment to the council of monks of dubious orthodoxy, and, finally, some dabbling with sectarian religious affairs of the Paramats in an attempt to control the Sangha as a whole. For these reasons, Bodawpaya's role is unclear, but existing evidence does not support a view of a totally unified Sangha at this time.

Early Nineteenth-Century Monastic Leaders

As we leave the Bodawpaya era, we enter the period covered by the reigns of Bagyidaw, Tharrawaddy, and Pagan (1819–1850). In terms of the *thathanabaing* history for this period (see Appendix A), King Bagyidaw (1819–1838) took as his teacher and head of the Order one Pyinnyasiha, who, interestingly enough, was established in the same monastery as the 1st Maungdaung Sayadaw (the Ratanabhumikitti Monastery of the Asokarama Taik); he was also known as the Salin

Sayadaw after his origin-place.[24] This king also honored the monk Silacara, a disciple of the Manle Sayadaw, whom he "placed as foremost among the monks who were forest-dwellers" and provided with a monastery in the country of Rajagara.[25] It seems as if forest monks frequently are those who refuse to become royal preceptors because this would entail an urban residence; nevertheless, their place in the prestige system is not impaired even though they might refuse official and administrative honors.[26] During this period King Bagyidaw made a significant investigation of Sangha lands that may be related to forest monks. The *Sasanavamsa* tell us, however, that the monks were properly in possession through an extraordinary charter myth going back to the Bodhisattva![27] Thus we see that the familiar causes of Sangha factionalism continue.

With the assumption of power by King Tharrawaddy (1837–1846), the The-in Sayadaw was appointed *thathanabaing*. This monk, also known as Suriyavamsa, was a disciple of the 1st Bagaya Sayadaw, a member of Bodawpaya's council, who, together with the 1st Maungdaung Sayadaw, had been a disciple of the Min-O Sayadaw, another member of the same council and one of its most senior monks (see Appendix B). Appendix C shows how Pannasami's Parakkama lineage includes the The-in Sayadaw, the 1st Maungdaung Sayadaw, and the 1st and 2d Bagaya Sayadaws. The The-in Sayadaw was appointed *thathanabaing* at an advanced age and died two years later. He was followed in 1839 by his disciple U Nyeyya, the 2d Maungdaung Sayadaw, who became *thathanabaing* at the age of forty-one.[28] It is this monk who was Pannasami's teacher (see Appendix C), and he was therefore apparently in the Parakkama line.

When King Pagan (1846–1853) came to the throne, he seems to

24. The Salin Sayadaw, however, is not included in the Parakkama line by Pannasami (1861:161–162). J. F.

25. Perhaps it is significant that this forest monk was the pupil of a monk (the Manle Sayadaw) who *is* considered to be in Pannasami's *Parakkama line* (1861: 161–162). [There would seem to be a claim by Pannasami of a link between the forest and reputed "orthodoxy" when a member of the Pannasami line is not appointed as *thathanabaing* by the king. J. F.]

26. Pannasami 1861:144.

27. Pannasami 1861:145–146. See also Maha Dhamma Thinkyan 1831:221–227 for further discussion of land matters. [Aung Than (1965:5) says that Bagidaw restored many lands confiscated by Bodawpaya. J. F.]

28. Pannasami 1861:147.

have appointed the 2d Bagaya Sayadaw, not the 2d Maungdaung Sayadaw, to be *thathanabaing*. A certain amount of confusion about this period in Sangha history is perhaps traceable to the conflict of two principles, the royal choice of head of the Order on the one hand and the continuity of seniority on the other, a conflict we have already noticed to some extent in the case of Atula and the Manle Sayadaw. Here, however, no sectarian issues clouded the problem: all the monks involved were orthodox. Stewart (1949:6) writes that Mindon, the next king, "left U Nyeya [the 2d Maungdaung Sayadaw], who had been *thathanabaing* since 1839, in office." On the other hand, the Khemathiwun Sayadaw's list[29] names the "2d Maungdaung Bagaya Sayadaw" as the *thathanabaing* under King Pagan, omitting to record the death of The-in Sayadaw and the latter's succession by the 2d Maungdaung Sayadaw (see Appendix A). Apparently, on the Kemathiwun Sayadaw's list the 2d Maungdaung and 2d Bagaya Sayadaws have been telescoped together, since the former monk was *thathanabaing* when Pagan became king, but the king replaced him with the 2d Bagaya Sayadaw. At least one record of King Pagan's reign, however, continues to call the 2d Maungdaung the *thathanabaing sayadaw*, perhaps because a variation of the primus inter pares principle was at work.[30] An interesting aspect of the 2d Bagaya's stay in office is that he was given the title and seal of *thathanabaing* four times.[31] It is not at all clear why these reconfirmations took place all within one reign. But the importance of this monk can be appreciated later as we note that a Bagaya Sayadaw is named as a master of the originators of the modern Dwaya sect in the Khemathiwun Sayadaw's account (see Appendix D). This Bagaya title is one of the most important in the records of the modern Sangha. The 2d Bagaya Sayadaw (see Appendixes C and D) was the master of the 2d Min-O Sayadaw as well as the famous Bhamo and Thingaza Sayadaws of King Mindon's times. Both the The-in and the 1st Maungdaung Sayadaws were, in turn, masters of the 2d Maungdaung (U Nyeyya), who was reappointed *thathanabaing* in Mindon's time. Thus we can see the lineages crossing, and we can establish a picture of a kind of oligarchy of ruling monks.

A Western perspective on the Sangha at this complex period in Burma

29. See chapter 1, n. 58.
30. Payapyu Sayadaw 1928:124.
31. Payapyu Sayadaw 1928:124. He is listed here as the disciple of the The-in Sayadaw. [See also Pannasami 1831:149. J. F.]

is found in the observations of Bishop Bigandet, a missionary whose writings are perhaps the most thorough of the foreign sources from the mid-nineteenth century. He serves as a transitional author between the travelers and diplomats of the 1800s and the first observers with genuine scientific detachment, in the late nineteenth and early twentieth centuries. On the *thathanabaing* he says:

In the kingdom of Ava,[32] the keystone of the Talapoinic [monkish] fabric is the *superlatively* great master residing in the capital or its suburbs. His jurisdiction extends over all the fraternity within the realm of his Burmese Majesty. His position near the seat of Government and his capacity of king's master, or teacher, must have at all times conferred upon him a very great degree of influence over all his subordinates. He is honoured with the eminent title of *Thathanadau-paing,* meaning that he has power and control over all that appertains to religion. It does not appear that peculiarly shining qualifications or high attainments are required in him who is honoured with such dignity. The mere accidental circumstance of having been the king's instructor when he was as yet a youth, is a sufficient, nay, the only recommendation for the promotion to such high position. Hence, it generally happens that each king, on his accession to the throne, confers the highest dignity of the order, to his favorite Phongie [monk]. In that case, the actual incumbent has to leave the place to his more influential brother, and becomes an ordinary member of the fraternity, unless he prefers leaving the society altogether, and reentering into the lay condition.   [1858:251]

After describing the great respect accorded the *thathanabaing* when he preaches at the palace and sits in the king's place or goes about in a gilt litter attended by a large retinue, of his rich monasteries, and of the silence surrounding him, Bishop Bigandet goes on to describe a meeting with the *thathanabaing* and comments on the more recent history of his office.

When the writer visited that dignitary, he was much amused on his approach to the place, to meet with those mute guardians who by all sorts of signs and gestures were endeavoring to make him understand that he must walk slowly, noiselessly and beware to speak aloud. When admitted to the presence of the Tsaia-dau [Sayadaw], he was not a little surprised to find a man exceedingly self-conceited, who thought that to him alone belonged the right of speaking; his language was that of a master to whom no one is to presume to offer the least contradiction. He appeared quite offended, when

32. Ava: capital of Upper Burma at times. Even after Mindon moved the capital to Mandalay, Western writers continued to refer to the "Court of Ava." J. F.

his visitor was compelled to dissent from him on certain points brought forward during the conversation. The writer left him with an impression very different from that which a worthy English Envoy,[33] in the end of the last century, entertained of a similar personage, whose mild, benign and pious exterior captivated him to such an extent as to elicit from him, a request to be remembered in his prayers.

In our days, the power of the Thathana-paing is merely nominal; the effects of his jurisdiction are scarcely felt beyond his own neighbourhood. Such, however, was not the case in former times. Spiritual commissioners were sent yearly by him to examine into, and report on, the state of the communities throughout the provinces. They had to enquire particularly whether the rules were observed or not, whether the professed members were qualified for their holy calling or not. They were empowered to repress abuses, and whenever some unworthy brothers, or *black sheep,* was [sic] found within the enclosure of a monastery, he was forthwith degraded, stripped of the yellow garb, and compelled to resume a secular course of life. Unfortunately for the welfare of the Order, these salutory visits no more take place; the wholesome check is done away with. Left without a superior control, the Order has fallen in a low degree of abjectness and degradation.   [1858:252][34]

Such is the extent of the evidence on monastic leadership during the period between the death of King Bodawpaya and the accession of King Mindon in 1853. The available sources do not provide enough information to explain the full significance of the shifts in Sangha leadership. One only senses that old factions and rivalries continued through all three reigns. Bigandet's assertion, however, that the power of the *thathanabaing* was weaker than before is certainly based on fact. By 1852 the second war with England had been lost, and Lower Burma was in foreign hands. Whatever formal powers the *thathanabaing* actually had were restricted of necessity after 1852 to Upper Burma alone.

Royal Control and Sangha Independence

Under such conditions King Mindon (1853–1878) assumed the throne, and he faced not only a diminished kingdom but also a series of serious problems involving the role of the Sangha in Upper Burma and

33. I.e., Symes. See interview earlier in the chapter. Symes was perhaps more understanding and respectful than was the "Bishop." J. F.

34. See also Malcolm 1839, 1:264 and Yule 1858:241. [The Bigandet passage is typical of the Christian missionaries' fascination with the "abjectness and degradation" of the Sangha, surely as much a fond hope as a piece of reliable reportage. J. F.]

in British Lower Burma as well. His reign, as we can see in retrospect, was of critical importance in terms of his effect upon the Sangha, for it under his rule that most of what we know as the modern Burmese sects had their origin. The matter is complex and will require considerable explication. The question of Sangha leadership will be considered first.

The status of the *thathanabaing* during Mindon's reign presents a number of problems. No doubt following such authors as Bigandet, Nisbet states that "the archbishop [i.e., *thathanabaing*] formerly exerted much greater power than he was allowed to possess after the accession" of King Mindon in 1853:

Under this monarch, who was not inclined to brook any interference with his political power,—and the priesthood or "Assembly" had undoubtedly considerable influence among the people,—the authority of the *Thathanabaing* was much more nominal than real. Formerly his jurisdiction extended to all the territories under the sway of the King of Burma, and he sent emissaries to examine and report on the state of discipline, to enforce rigid obedience regarding the instructions to priests, and to expel from the Assembly those who were found to be unduly lax in the performance of their vows. During the latter days of the court of Ava, however, the archbishop was shorn of much of his former power, though otherwise treated with the most illustrious and respectful attention.   [1901, 2:124]

Stewart furthermore points out that Mindon was a different kind of king:

Naturally pious and holding what we may call the orthodox view that the business of the Order should be religion, he [Mindon] was at great pains to maintain amicable relations with it and so was able to effect the reform in discipline which he considered necessary with the general approval of the monks themselves. . . . He made liberal monthly offerings to the monks in the capital (one of whom rather gracelessly criticized them as being made from State revenues and not from privy purse). He commenced his revision of the Scriptures from 1860. . . . He cancelled his own orders resuming lands in several districts on representation by the monks. When he introduced *thathameda* [household income tax] in 1861, cultivators of religious lands were excluded from assessment. Sayadaws all over the country were invited to address the King direct on civil matters and were given official papers for the purpose; royal orders are on record explicitly stating that village headmen and other officials of similar standing were appointed on the recommendation of the local sayadaws. Extraordinary care was taken to consult the clerical authorities on any question having a bearing on the Religion. . . .[35]

35. Scott and Hardiman (1900 1, pt. 2:6) seem to differ with Stewart regarding

Someone has said of King Mindon that he was his own Prime Minister. For the greater part of his reign he was his own Thathanabaing. [1949:6, 7]

There are clues in the two passages above to both the past and the future, but these authors have not worked out their full implications. To begin with, King Mindon himself appears to have been something of a bridge between the old royal order and the new world of the Europeans, and there is evidence that he was amply conscious of this. In some ways he faced toward the past; one of the sentences omitted in the above quotation runs, "He crucified U Po who had maintained that genuine *rahan*s [monks] were almost impossible to find."[36] In other ways he faced resolutely toward the future, and his religious program clearly foreshadowed the policy of the U Nu government a century later, as will be noted at a later stage.

Stewart's provocative analysis of the Mindon era also contains the following observation:

The result of this policy [the King's support of the Sangha] was a change in the attitude of the Order. Hitherto it had preached and taught generally indifferent to dynastic changes and inculcating [sic] at most a passive loyalty. It now became more actively loyal. It was prepared to believe that the welfare of Buddhism and of Burma were bound up together and to give the civil power its cordial co-operation, even at some sacrifice of its independence. [1949:7]

Granted that there was a new element under Mindon, the assumptions made by Nisbet and Stewart seem to rely on insufficient evidence. Is it certain that before Mindon the archbishop, as is implied in the passages above, always exerted great power, or that monks had been generally indifferent to dynastic changes and preached "at most a passive loyalty"? My reading of history suggests rather that relations between Sangha and king were determined by the strength of the king at any given time. It is easy to imagine that in centrifugal periods the loyalty of monks could easily evaporate, just as, in centripetal periods, under such strong kings as Bayinnaung or an Alaungpaya, monks, being Burmans, after all, followed the fortunes of their leaders and were as loyal to them as any other citizen. In short, the writings of Nisbet and Stewart and perhaps

---

the assessment of cultivators of religious lands. Perhaps "cultivators of religious lands" are to be distinguished from the so-called "pagoda slaves."

36. Stewart 1949:6. U Po seems involved with the Paramat issue, which will be discussed again later in this chapter.

others imply a "before" and "after" Mindon attitude which I cannot share.

Because of the uncertainties and inconsistencies in documentation for this period, it is difficult to see exactly when and why the *thathanabaing* stood out above what has become known as his Thudhamma Council[37] or, on the other hand, merged with it as primus inter pares. Beyond the personal power of any particular *thathanabaing* or lack of it, was his position in this respect a function of the relative power of the lay ruler? Perhaps the *thathanabaing* faded into his council under the "strong" king Mindon. Thus under a "weak" king, such as Thibaw (1878–1885), Mindon's successor, stronger monastic leadership was possible, as Stewart's observation (1949:7) implies: "Obstruction to civil authorities was perhaps treated as rebellion, for we find the Thathanabaing threatening to have his *Gaing Gyok*s [district officials], etc., along the lower course of the Irrawaddy tried by the Thudhamma Council for alleged resistance to collection of taxes." But Scott and Hardiman (1900, 1, pt. 2:4) note the fact that these very *gaing-gyok*s, were the officials the government normally used to persuade the people to pay these same taxes. Apparently on certain occasions the Sangha hierarchy, which existed between the Sangha at large and the king, favored one side, while on other occasions it favored the other; and the balance depended a good deal on the general distribution of royal power at any given time. Just as the *thathanabaing* served as a bridge between Sangha and king, so the provincial officials could serve as bridges between the *thathanabaing* and local monks and laymen. Mindon's genius may well have been the realization that more prestige and recognition for the monks meant increased loyalty and obligation on their part to the throne, while at the same time the throne's transformation of the neutral bridge into an instrument of royal power could effectively enable the king to control the Sangha he pretended to set free. Unfortunately, as we shall see, the realities of a divided country[38] and the traditional antagonism of the Sangha to centralization frustrated his plans.

The Origins of the Mindon Sects

Mindon's purposes in his strategy with the Sangha leadership are discussed by Stewart:

37. See discussion in the first chapter.
38. The British were in control of Lower Burma as of 1852, and thus Mindon could not effectively control the Sangha there.

Possibly he found it easier to work the system of co-operation without a titular head of the church. *But he was in rather a weak position* in regard to any doctrinal question. One such question he does seem to have shelved, and it is from his reign that we must date a cleavage in the Order which still persists. On the death of the Thathanabaing U Nyeya [Nyeyya] in 1865 King Mindon *wished to appoint* one of a Puritan sect known as the Shwegyin Gaing [i.e., sect], but the Chief Queen wished the appointment to be given to one of the Thudhamma[39] Sayadaws. . . . His successor [King Thibaw] appointed two Thathanabaings, the Taungdaw and Shwegyin Sayadaws. The Taungdaw Sayadaw had no qualifications or claim to the office apart from his having been King Thibaw's teacher when he was an obscure prince, and the Shwegyin Sayadaw (1822–1893) did not choose to act with him, but confined himself to the control of his own following. There has been no rapprochement, and the Order in Upper Burma is to-day divided into two sects—Thudhamma and Shwegyin.   [1949:7; my italics]

In the above account, Stewart does not appear to have made up his mind regarding Mindon's role in this matter. On the one hand he speaks of a "weak" position of the king; on the other he refers to a royal "wish to appoint" a Shwegyin Sayadaw as *thathanabaing*. The accounts of the beginning of the Shwegyin sect are still a subject of some dispute in Burma today, and in considering the history of this important sect two factors should be kept in mind. First, Mindon's religious policy of recognizing the Shwegyin sect possibly had some political purpose. Did he divide the Sangha in order to rule? Second, accounts of the Shwegyin history differ according to whether they emanate from Shwegyin or Thudhamma sources. Such factors are of great importance for an understanding of both the phenomenon of sectarianism in general and the U Nu program in particular.

The Sangha under Mindon, instead of having the orthodox or Sinhalized unity the chronicles imply, reveals the sectarian process continuing. We see the hiving off of such sects as the Shwegyin and the Dwaya, whose major concern, as so often, was with yet closer attachment to pure Vinaya behavior, and yet it is most interesting that Pannasami (1861:149–161), the author of the *Sasanavamsa,* though he records Vinaya discussions under Mindon in which he took a leading part, does not mention the Shwegyin or Dwaya sects specifically. Apparently the times had at last caught up with him and he found himself in effect challenged by a further wave of Sinhalization after thinking as he

---

39. As used here by Stewart, Thudhamma refers to the largest or main sect in the Sangha from which reformist sects split off.

wrote his book that he and his line were at the very apex of orthodoxy. Such evidence suggests that reformation movements or concern with Vinaya purity is a process without end in the Burmese Sangha.

The development of the Mindon sects can best be seen as a series of splits from a main body. If the Thudhamma is considered the norm, a spectrum can be established which begins with a set of disciplinary, "puritanical" sects differing from Thudhamma only in the degree of severity of adherence to certain Vinaya rules, and which ends where differences in doctrine appear to place certain small sects completely outside the pale of accepted Buddhism.[40] We shall find in the sources and among informants that the term *paramat* is frequently applied to such latter sects. Should one meet Paramats, however, and one may still do so in monks of the Hngetwin sect (see below), one may well discover that these monks consider themselves very much within the pale, defining themselves as the Sangha closest to the Buddha's original wishes and showing the other sects as more or less removed from this ideal. The notion of "orthodoxy" in Buddhism is awkward because of the absence of a "church." Thus Sangha groups defined as *paramat* constitute, by stressing the "ultimate or highest sense" of doctrinal points, a kind of superorthodoxy recognized as such by other monks. At the same time, the average monk and layman see *paramat* views as dangerous to the sociological basis of normal lay-Sangha relations. This passage by Scott describing the Mans suggests a reason:

In Burma proper the nearest body to the *Sawti* [Zawti, as discussed above] are the *Mans,* who also are anti-clericals. They sprang into existence half a century ago, but now seem to be dying out, though there are still some communities of them in the Pegu and Tenasserim Divisions [in Lower

---

40. "Sect" is being used here as an approximate, if slightly unsatisfactory, substitute for the word *gaing* (B). Spiro (1970:315–320) suggests "branch" as a gloss for the term *gaing*. A *gaing,* from the Pali term *gana* (a chapter of monks), is, sociologically speaking, a group of *taik*s who recognize the somewhat charismatic leadership of a *sayadaw* who is considered the leader. It may at first have practices or beliefs (such as ordination rites, unique textual interpretations) no different from other established sects, but it may develop such differentiating characteristics and become both a self-defined and lay-defined sect, or what is known in Pali as a *nikaya*. Lay definition by a wealthy lay supporter (*taga*) usually precedes self-definition. The difficulty is that the Burmese word *gaing* (collection, assemblage) is used by informants to cover both the Pali *gana* and *nikaya*. The problems involved with these terms are discussed in the Introduction. A further difficulty is that *gaing* can also have messianic overtones (Mendelson 1961a, b, 1963b, c). J. F.

Burma]. The Founder was a man named Maung Po,[41] who was a doctor to King Mindon, and propounded his theories, or heresies, about the time Mandalay was being founded. All orthodox Buddhists reverence *Paya,* the Buddha, *Taya,* the Law, and *Thinga,* the Assembly of the Religious, the "Three Gems." Maung Po rejected the third, which he maintained to be a mere afterthought, or growth, and not doctrinal, and taught that there was no obligation on the part of the laity to minister to the wants of the monks, either in the way of food, shelter, garments, or medicines, which the regular Buddhist considers the four necessaries. Beyond this the chief point of his teaching was that every man could and should work out his own salvation. . . . King Mindon put an abrupt end to Maung Po by having him impaled, but his chief disciples and followers fled to Lower Burma, and still maintain a party there.   [1911:378–379][42]

Such sects appear to have endangered the Sangha as a whole, and a definitely anticlerical trend is found in the mid-nineteenth century when movements in the Sangha to form stricter sects were initiated, many with the help of Lower Burma.

In modern times, such sects probably mask some of their more extreme differences in order to placate any lay forces that might desire some form of excommunication. The point is important because some of the Paramats, as well as some of the more extreme sects reported under other names in the historical literature, may join forces with non-Sangha groups and soteriological movements I have considered elsewhere under the term "messianic Buddhism" (1961a, b; 1963b, c). It is therefore important when studying the historical documentation to discriminate between the peripheral Paramat groups and the Thudhamma, Shwegyin, and Dwaya sects (the three major bodies that developed from the Mahagandi and the Sulagandi sects).

Available sources on this nineteenth-century period present a plethora of names of sects, and at first sight the data seem hopelessly confusing. Nisbet (1901, 2:117), writing of the Bodawpaya period, divides the Sangha into "two rival schools of *Tongaing* and *Yongaing,* roughly corresponding to High Church and Low Church." He sees the king as siding with the Yongaing party and unfrocking the rest. As we have seen above, the king decided in favor of the two-shoulder party, and thus we can identify the Yongaing with them and the Tongaing with the defeated one-shoulder followers of Atula. Scott, who associates the Yongaing

41. U Po, whom Mindon is said to have "crucified." See Stewart 1949:6.
42. See also Foucar 1946:50.

with Paramats, claims that Bodawpaya chose this sect because the others refused to recognize his claim to be the future Metteya Buddha.[43] Writing of post-Bodawpaya events involving the Tongaing and Yongaing sects, Nisbet concludes, "These two parties have various names in different parts of the country, but they are best known respectively as the *Sulagandi,* or *Dwaya* (lit. 'a hole or aperture'), and the *Mahagandi,* or Kan (lit. 'a deed, an action')" (1901, 2:117). The names Sulagandi, Dwaya, and Mahagandi lead us to much more familiar territory which will now be reviewed.

Sectarian Purification Movements and Issues

The Mahagandis were in the late nineteenth century the majority group, the Sulagandis the reformist minority. In the matter of discipline, the Sulagandis (the Tongaing) objected to the increasingly popular practice in the Sangha of wearing silk robes or robes not strictly compounded of torn strips of cloth sewn together. They criticized the habit of the more lax monks in not eating directly from the begging bowls as they came back from their morning rounds but either selecting pieces from the bowls or throwing the contents of the bowls to dogs and birds and eating specially cooked meals. The Mahagandis (the Yongaing) countered that more food could be given to the poor and the animals in this way and that cooked meals also originated from alms and donations. Other denunciations by the Sulagandis included the wearing of monks' sandals and shading their heads with umbrellas on most occasions, handling money, attending *pwes,*[44] and holding noisy functions in monasteries at certain times such as the end of lent.[45] The doctrinal difference is best summarized by Scott: "The Puritans [Sulangandi] believe that man is endowed with Free Will. The Broad Churchmen [Mahagandi] deny the existence of Free Will, and assert that a man's whole life is controlled entirely by *Kan,* the influence of past good or evil deeds on future existences. The Sulagandi attribute all the importance to the intention; the Mahagandi think that the action is sufficient, and the intention immaterial or taken for granted" (1911:380). This

---

43. Scott 1909:148; 1911:378. See also Stewart 1949:5, and Mendelson 1961b.

44. Public entertainment often involving theater, music, and dance.

45. Nisbet 1901, 2:117; Scott 1909:149–151; 1911:379. During "Lent," i.e., the *wa,* or rainy season, monks and laymen traditionally observe more self-denying rules.

doctrinal difference reflects the main preoccupation of the Sulagandi with discipline and intent. A review of Htin Aung's discussion (1966: 22–23) of the events of 1855 also helps us to identify the Dwaya sect[46] with the Sulangandi position described above. Scott (1909:151–152) tells us that the head of the "Sulgandi" was U Okgansa of Okpo Monastery in the Tharrawaddy District, who was at one time invited to Mandalay to take charge of a monastery there but declined the king's offers and stayed to see the "victory" of his sect in the south. This monk is identified by Htin Aung (1966:23) as the Okpo Sayadaw and is said to have founded the Dwaya sect in Lower Burma.

The British sources for this period were written predominantly from a Lower Burma point of view, which seems to have led to some misleading emphases on their part. Scott is explicit about this:

The quarrel [between the Mahagandi and the Sulagandi] is at present limited to Lower Burma, where the greater wealth of the country and the introduction of foreign luxuries among the laity have led to corresponding indulgences in many of the monasteries, against which the Sulagandis protest and preach with feverish energy. The austere party is strongest in Maulmein [Moulmein], Henzada, and Pegu, and faction feeling runs so high that street fights between the scholars of the two sects are very common, and often so embittered that the English authorities have to interfere to restore peace in the town, for the laity take sides with equally bitter animosity. [1909:149]

Writing later, Stewart restores the balance by showing that the quarrel also existed in the same form in Upper Burma; he mentions the important Shwegyin sect, which is scarcely mentioned by earlier writers, and he refers to Mindon's desire to nominate a Shwegyin *thathanabaing* on the death of U Nyeyya in 1865—a wish that was crossed by the chief queen's desire for a Thudhamma *thathanabaing,* as noted earlier in this chapter. Stewart then continues:

A friend and fellow-pupil of the Shwegyin Sayadaw's, the Okpo Sayadaw, U Okgantha [Okgansa], started a similar Puritan movement in British Burma. His following became known as the Dwaya Gaing [sect], from its interpretation of *kayena, vacaya, manasa*[47] in the prayer used at the commencement of an act of worship as ("I adore the three Gems) through the

---

46. "Dwarya" in Htin Aung.
47. Possibly from *kayadvara* (P): the outlet of the senses; *vaca* (P): word, speech; and *mana* (P): mind, consciousness. J. F.

medium (*dvara*) [door] of my body, my speech, and my thought," instead of the traditional interpretation "by the deeds (*kan*) of my body etc." The movement spread to Arakan, so that in Lower Burma and Arakan the Order is divided into Kan and Dwaya Gaings. Other names, which seem to be equivalent to these, are Mahagandi and Sulagandi (the Great and the Little Sect), which were very familiar a generation ago but are perhaps not so well known at the present day. [1949:7]

And in a footnote he adds: "The Thudhamma and Shwegyin sects are also represented in Lower Burma." Here are two possibilities. Insofar as the name "Kan Gaing" is virtually unknown in Burma today, though one informant said it had existed for a brief time, it seems likely that there was never any real difference between Kan and Thudhamma. Thus an all-Burma Thudhamma Mahagandi can be contrasted with a predominantly Upper Burma Shwegyin Sulagandi and a predominantly Lower Burma Dwaya Sulagandi. Or perhaps the disorganization of the Sangha in Burma consequent upon partition in early British times was such that the Lower Burma majority of monks thought of themselves as a Kan sect and later remerged with Thudhamma when Burma became entirely British. The issue needs further investigation. But certain data strongly suggest that the words Mahagandi and Sulagandi have often been used in situations where people wished to define majorities and minorities without being quite sure of the sects involved.[48] In this context, another question may be raised. Nisbet claims that at the Fifth Buddhist Council, held by Mindon in Mandalay, the king favored the Kan sect while the queen favored the Dwaya.[49] It is curious that this should have been so

48. F. K. Lehman has suggested (personal communication, 1973) that the term *Sulagandi* may also refer to a text which was deeply involved in the one- and two-shoulder robe dispute, which Pannasami (1861:138–144) discusses at length as the *Culaganthipada*. Sulagandi: *cula* (P): small, minor; *ganthipada* (P): a glossary or commentary. [The one-shoulder monks under Atula based their case on this text which they said was written by Moggallana, a disciple of the Buddha. According to Pannasami, it was instead written by a Moggallana who lived in the twelfth century during the reign of King Parakkamabahu (the exact time of the Parakkama monastic lineage's origin) as part of a text known as the *Vinayaganthipada*, the author of which Bode (1909:75) lists as a Ceylon monk named Joti. The correspondence between the monk's name, Joti, and the use of that word by Paramat sects (Zawti, Zodi, from the Pali *joti* may signify a link between the Paramats and the Sulagandi. If this interpretation is correct, then Mahagandi would perhaps be a complementary term, signifying that the two-shoulder monks had the greater (*maha*) text (*ganthipada*). J. F.]

49. Nisbet 1901, 2:118. [It seems likely that Nisbet is wrong in this case. J. F.]

if Mindon, following Stewart, liked Shwegyin better than Thudhamma—unless the Mahagandi-Sulagandi controversy really was only a Lower Burma matter, Shwegyin and Thudhamma in the north being considered as one main body. Insofar as some informants in Burma told me that Mindon had chosen Shwegyin, while others swore he had done nothing of the sort, this seems to be a matter on which partisans of different sects differ. Nisbet may well have derived his information from a Thudhamma supporter.

For convenience' sake, the names Thudhamma, Shwegyin, and Dwaya will be retained and the terms Mahagandi and Sulagandi will be considered less precise designations which are used, if at all today, by laymen who do not need too great a degree of precision in their discussions of ecclesiastical affairs. Whatever the terms, it is possible to find the widest range of interpretation of them. A Mandalay informant who had been, when much younger, a *thathanabaing*'s secretary told me that Kan and Thudhamma were one, as Shwegyin and Dwaya were one. Thus the Shwegyin were said to use the word *dwaya* (means of perception) rather than *kan* (deeds) in the morning prayer. However, the head of the Hngetwin sect,[50] who rejected the positions of the Thudhamma-Mahagandi, Shwegyin-Sulagandi, and Dwaya groups, claimed that the Shwegyin and Thudhamma sects both used the *kan* formula, while the Dwaya sect used the *dwaya* wording, of course. His own Hngetwin sect used still another wording, the *panama* formula.[51] The question as to whether Shwegyin used the *kan* or *dwaya* formula, or, indeed, some other, remains obscure.[52] Htin Aung's view that Shwegyin represents a

50. This modern sect will be discussed later.
51. Meaning salutation, obeisance (P). Part of the wording of the Buddhist Common Prayer, referring to permission to be forgiven for offenses committed by deed or mouth. See Pe Maung Tin 1964:31. J.F.
52. F. K. Lehman (personal communication, 1973) suggests that the matter is more complex than Stewart realized, and he believes that two so-called Buddhist Common Prayers (see Pe Maung Tin 1964:31 for one of them) are involved here. Both begin with the same triple invocation, *Awakatha* (B) or *Okasa* (P), but one asks pardon for offenses, and the second stresses acts of worship to achieve merit as a means of forgiveness. Furthermore, the first prayer involves the concept of offenses done by unintentional acts, and the second involves positive acts of worship or begging of pardon which Lehman interprets as the *dvara* or "means" whereby positive intention is stressed. The Dwaya sect, he suggests, may put into the first prayer the "intention" wording of the second to stress the positive intentions of the worshiper rather than his acts. This interpretation provides a doctrinal basis to the sectarian differences rather than an "artificial formalist controversy."

compromise between Thudhamma and Dwaya adds to the possibility that the Shwegyin used *kan* and thus, in a sense, could be included in the Kan sect. One Dwaya source even claims that leading Thudhamma and Shwegyin monks in Mindon's time used the Dwaya formulas. This is presumably an attempt to give the Dwaya interpretation a wide acceptance it did not seem to have. A Rangoon civil servant even opined that Hngetwin was probably the same as Sulagandi but did not like to be called so. A similar informant claimed that Sulagandi really meant "minor arts" and that members of this group were hermits, alchemists, medicine men—in short, the people I have studied elsewhere as *weikzas*.[53] It should be clear by now that, even to educated laymen, the terms have had no precisely determined and collectively sanctioned meanings. They have been used even by monks as part of the armory of rhetoric differentiating one human group from another whose differences are based on more serious dissent, the causes of which must still be determined.

Before discussing the Burmese sources concerning the origins of each of the Mindon sects, I shall briefly summarize the complex material just presented. It appears that the two-shoulder party, traced so carefully by Pannasami and presented by him as the apex of orthodoxy, became by Mindon's time the majority group in the Sangha, known variously as Yon, Ayon, Mahagandi, Kan, or Thudhamma. But the process of "reform" caught up with the majority. The one-shoulder monks, sometimes called the Atin sect, with their *Culaganthipada* text,[54] became known as the Sulagandi and then the Dwaya sect of the Okpo Sayadaw;[55] these later groups claimed the orthodoxy they denied to the successors of Pannasami's two-shoulder, Sinhalese line.

In other words, the evidence is clear to the extent that King Mindon

---

Lehman also sees the *panama* wording of the Hngetwin sect as part of the second version of the Buddhist Common Prayer.

53. See Glossary. Mendelson 1960, 1961a, b, 1963b, c.

54. Pannasami 1861:141. See n. 48 above.

55. For an identification of the Ayon gaing (two-shoulder) monks with the Thudhamma monks and the Atin gaing (one-shoulder) monks with the Sulagandi gaing, see the Payapyu Sayadaw 1928:113. If, on the other hand, Htin Aung (1966:30) is correct in speaking of a later Sulagandi in Lower Burma, arising out of the Okpo Sayadaw's views, then the name Mahagandi may have been identified with the majority party, i.e., mostly Thudhamma, in that controversy. The difficulty is that Htin Aung does not in any way document his assertions.

faced a host of factional movements within the Sangha that also involved strong emotions among the laity. The orthodoxy represented by his *thathanabaing,* the 2d Maungdaung Sayadaw, as well as by Pannasami, was challenged seriously by a number of reformist groups in Upper and Lower Burma. Mindon himself seemed to have mixed feelings on the matter of the reformist factions, and certainly the records available indicate that he made overtures to both sides. A close analysis of the histories of the sects engendered by his reign may help to elucidate the entire matter of sectarian formation and development in Burmese Buddhism.

The Dwaya Sect's Early Development

Perhaps the oldest of the "Mindon sects," that is, those that trace their origins to the *sayadaw*s of Mindon's time, is the Dwaya sect, generally agreed to have been founded by U Okgansa, the Okpo Sayadaw. The Mindon sects were founded for the most part by monastic schoolmates, if not by friends. Stewart (1949:7) refers to the founder of Dwaya as a friend and fellow pupil of the Shwegyin Sayadaw and tells us that the Okpo Sayadaw "started a similar [to Shwegyin] Puritan movement in British Burma." A rather vague but interesting reference to the beginnings of Dwaya is contained in a Report to the Ministry of Religious Affairs, Upper Burma Office, by a Mandalay Dwaya representative, U Khameinda:

In the reign of King Taninganwe . . . who ascended the throne in 1714, first mention was made of the *Atin* and *Ayon*[56] parties, with U Okkamsamala speaking for the *Ayon* side. Since then, the following monks have demonstrated the correctness of worshiping through the three Dwaya[57]: U Varasabodhi in the fourth year of the reign of Mahadhammayazadipati (1733); *Thathanabaing* U Nyeyya [2d Maungdaung Sayadaw]; the [2d] Bagaya *Thathanabaing*[58]; and his disciple the Dakkhinarama *Taik Sayadaw* Jagarabhivamsatipitikadhara MDRDRG.[59]   [1959:10]

    56. *Atin: ahtin* (B): visible (the robe put on casually, over one shoulder); *Ayon: ayoun* (B): to put on, as a priest's garment (to cover properly, as a Buddhist statue). J. F.
    57. "To worship through the medium (*dvara*) of my body, my speech and my thought," instead of by the deeds (*kan*) of my body, etc. as quoted above from Stewart 1949:7.
    58. King Pagan's *thathanabaing.* See Appendixes A and C.
    59. I have not yet been able to identify this last monk. For an explanation of MDRDRG, see Appendix A.

Clearly the Dwaya sect is here attempting to go back to the two-shoulder orthodoxy of the eighteenth century in order to prove its case and perhaps reject Sulagandi status: the matter is probably one of sectarian rhetoric rather than factual truth.[60]

The facts that we do have indicate that the Okpo Sayadaw was born in 1817, founded his Dwaya sect in 1855 in Okpo, Henzada District, and died in 1905. Htin Aung (1966:22–28) presents Dwaya as a Lower Burma challenge to the Thudhamma Council. The Okpo Sayadaw claimed that Vinaya was sufficient: no support or patronage was needed from lay power. He insisted that the intention of a donor was more important than his action: the sincere small gift of a poor man of greater merit than the huge, casual gift of a rich man. This chanced to have certain important effects for Burmese jurisprudence. The Okpo Sayadaw also challenged the ordination method of the Thudhamma Council, a severe criticism in view of the importance of control of ordination procedures in ensuring orthodoxy, as was noted in the last chapter during the period of King Dhammaceti's fifteenth-century Sangha reforms. The founder of Dwaya does seem to have been something of a troublemaker. He is said (perhaps as a way of commenting on his "intention rather than action" theory) to have gone up to a Prome pagoda with his shoes on in violation of the age-old prohibition of footwear in sacred places. In Pegu he did the same, at the Shwedagon also. Eventually there was much censure. The community approached two of his disciples, who asked the Okpo to explain matters in a book. Some four authors then replied to him. After a while (the informant compared this to the days of Pope and Dryden!), the Okpo replied, insulting his critics. The famous Ledi Sayadaw entered the melée, and many books were exchanged.

There is some difficulty in ascertaining the lineage of the founders of the Dwaya sect (see Appendix D). The Shweman Sayadaw claims that Dwaya was started by the Myatheindan Sayadaw, master of the Okpo Sayadaw and pupil of the 2d Bagaya Sayadaw. The biography of the Shweman Sayadaw further recounts the episode of how the Thingaza, Bhamo, and the (2d?) Min-O Sayadaws all studied under the 2d

---

60. It will be recalled that the two-shoulder orthodoxy was associated with Mahagandi. This raises difficulties about Htin Aung's (1966:30) interpretation of Sulagandi. The linkage between the monks of the early and mid-eighteenth century and those of Mindon's time is very difficult to establish clearly.

Bagaya Sayadaw and decided to live not far from each other in the neighborhood of Shwekyetdaung village near Sagaing between the years 1855 and 1859, with King Mindon instructing his officers to build monasteries for each.[61]

Apparently three "generations" of important monks are involved (see Appendix D): (1) that of the 2d Bagaya Sayadaw and 2d Maungdaung Sayadaw as *thathanabaing*s; (2) their pupils and friends, including such monks as the Thingaza, Thilon, Myatheindan, Bhamo, and 2d Min-O Sayadaws; and (3) pupils of the second generation and their friends (later to be rivals)—the Shwegyin, Okpo, Weluwun, the Shweman Sayadaws—who became the new leaders of the various sects that were to be the dominant groups in the late 1950s. Much can be learned from studying this pattern. As so frequently in Burma, a relatively small group of leaders start as fellow pupils and end as rivals: a process not unknown in politics, as the recent history of the AFPFL shows very well.[62] The "Mindon sects" can also be viewed in the light of this friend-rival situation. The general lack of acrimony in today's Sangha relations may well be due to these historical factors, as well as to an amiability on the part of monks generally.

Some evidence in Burmese sources suggests that the Dwaya sect arose out of the Shwegyin, though a parallel development is more likely. Tin Tut (1943) writes, "The most important of the sub-sects is the Dwara sub-sect of the Shwegyin sect. Its origin lay in a difference of opinion with the majority of the members of Shwegyin sect on the text of the Burmese Buddhist Common Prayer." The Report to the Ministry of Religious Affairs of the Union of Burma refers to such an argument, but the only source to date it is the booklet *The Present Religious Events,* which refers to a split over recitation methods around 1897–1898.[63] If it is true that Dwaya was founded in 1855, a roughly parallel evolution may have developed with commensality and other contacts allowed up to the late 1880s, when a definite split occurred. *The Present Religious Events* refers, without dates, to a split within Dwaya after the death of the Okpo Sayadaw into Henzada and Ingapu branches, with U

61. Sandawara, n.d.:59.

62. Anti-Fascist People's Freedom League: the wartime and postwar political party of Aung San, Nu, Than Tun, Mya, and others that split into various factions in later years.

63. Pyinnyaramikamaha Sayadaw 1958:69.

Mala of a Rangoon monastery as head of the former and U Wiseitta as head of Ingapu Dwaya. Other documents mention a reconciliation in 1944, some thirty years after the split, as will be discussed in a subsequent chapter.

Although there have been doctrinal differences, based apparently on the interpretation of a point in the *Anguttara Nikaya*,[64] the rules of the Dwaya sect and its basic organization do not differ greatly from those of the Shwegyin sect, the stress being laid on increased behavioral strictness rather than inherent difference in textual matters. Dwaya monks are not allowed to associate with monks other than those listed by the *maha nayaka,* or the leader of the sect.[65] They must not harbor enemies of the state and they are to have nothing to do with courts of law. The rules concerning food, drink, and abstention from shows are as usual. Though machine transport is allowed if there is a lay steward (*kappiya*) to buy the ticket, pony and bullock carts, trishaws, palanquins, and other traditional means of transport must be avoided. Umbrellas are not to be used outside the monastery, except for sickness, rain, or the presence of a tiger or leopard. The emphasis is thus basically upon what I have called before cleaving to the Vinaya; it is the fundamental criterion for sectarian differentiation. On the basis of this Vinaya emphasis, the Okpo Sayadaw would not participate in King Mindon's Fifth Council,[66] and he was never consulted by the king.[67] Instead, his sect represented a challenge to both the king and the other monks led by the 2d Maungdaung Sayadaw and U Pannasami, that is, the Thudhamma Sangha.

The Shwegyin Sect's Early Development

Burmese sources provide helpful information on the Shwegyin sect, the origin of which, as pointed out, is still somewhat obscure, though it is certain that the sect proper began in the reign of King Mindon. The crucial point in the origin stories revolves around the question of

64. One of the five Nikayas, or Sutta Tipitaka (the dialogues or discourses of the Buddha). The Sutta are one of three basic divisions of the Buddhist Pali Canon (the Tipitaka). I was not able to identify these "doctrinal differences."

65. *Maha:* great; *nayaka:* leader master. It has been reported by H. D. Evers (personal communication, June 1967) that the terms *maha nayaka* and *anu nayaka* [township] are used at the Malwatte Vihara, Kandy, Ceylon.

66. The Fifth Buddhist Council, held to purify and confirm Theravada Buddhism; the main emphasis was on proper editing of the Tipitaka.

67. Htin Aung 1966:26.

whether the Shwegyin Sayadaw refused to call upon and submit himself to the Thudhamma *thathanabaing* or whether the latter was so impolite to the Shwegyin Sayadaw that this monk was unable to call upon the head of the Sangha. The first version is preferred by Thudhamma accounts, the latter by members of Shwegyin. A further point of confusion arises out of a statement often made to the effect that King Mindon was frustrated in his desire to appoint the Shwegyin Sayadaw as *thathanabaing*.[68] Some informants say that his chief queen backed a Thudhamma man and that the question was resolved only when King Thibaw nominated two *thathanabaing*s, one from each sect. Since the story gives us some insight into the origin of sects and the part royal support could play therein, it is worth examining the rather tangled evidence in support of the differing theories.

Replying to a Ministry of Religious Affairs questionnaire, the Shweman Sayadaw, a Thudhamma senior monk and patron of the Yahan Byo Ahpwe,[69] writes:

At that time—around 1859—though the Shwegyin Sayadaw was summoned and invited over several times by the *thathanabaing* U Nyeyya, the Shwegyin Sayadaw remained without hearkening. The reason was that he had King Mindon as his strength and thus just ignored the Thudhamma. When the matter was reported to the King by Thudhamma, Mindon said "Please treat it as a *gana wimokha* my Lords." The Shwegyin Sayadaw having received this *gana wimokha* took courage and formed the Shwegyin *gaing*. [1959:1][70]

The *Sasanavamsa* does not specifically mention the Mindon sects, but the troubles Pannasami refers to in obtaining the cooperation of the Sangha in swearing an oath before the Buddha occurred in 1858, just one year before the reputed break between the Shwegyin Sayadaw and the *thathanabaing*.[71] The need for such an oath probably is related to incipient sectarianism.

Answering a Ministry of Religious Affairs inquiry similar to the one

68. Pyinnyaramikamaha Sayadaw 1958:90; Panditta 1955:186–88.
69. Young Monks Association, a political organization discussed in detail in Chapter 6.
70. *Gana* (P): sect: *wimokha* (B-P): *vimokkha* (P): release, deliverance, emancipation; in other words, release from Thudhamma control.
71. It is also possible that Pannasami, as the pupil of that *thathanabaing* and as loyal supporter of Mindon, was trying to keep the Shwegyin Sayadaw within the fold and thus played down in the *Sasanavamsa* his opposition's role. J. F.

mentioned above, the Pattamya Sayadaw, AMP,[72] a Shwegyin senior, writes:

Although the Shwegyin Sayadaw had to go thrice to the *thathanabaing* who was of the Thudhamma Order and who was twenty three years his senior in age to pay his respect, the *thathanabaing* remained silent and cold. As he had to go back without saying a word, it dawned on the Sayadaw that there was no longer any need for him to repeat his visit. However, when he was again summoned with a tone of authority, he went to the King and submitted that he no longer desired to stay in the royal city and would return into the forest to carry on the work of the great Sasana.[73] When asked why he told his story, he said that he thought his presence in the royal city did not give peace of mind to the *thathanabaing* and that he had better leave. The king answered "My Lord, there is no need for you to leave on account of this. From today onwards none may summon you or require your presence. Please abide here in peace and comfort" [The King informed the *thathanabaing* to that effect] . . . and thus, commencing with the King himself, the Shwegyin Sayadaw and the monks of his Order were held in separate esteem and worshipped as an Order on their own.   [1959:2–3]

At the Shwegyin headquarters in 1959, I was told that the Shwegyin Sayadaw had called on the *thathanabaing* but was ill received. He was then summoned twice but refused to go. My source averred that no quarrel between king and queen ever took place. In view of the data presented here, it is difficult to understand Htin Aung's contention (1966:25) that "the ecclesiastical [Thudhamma] council did not consider the Shwegyin Sayadaw to be a rebel against their authority."

In his account of the sects quoted above, the Thudhamma Shweman Sayadaw gives the lineage of the Shwegyin Sayadaw's teachers as consisting of the following: (1) the Namaw Sayadaw from Dipeyin; (2) the Thilon Sayadaw; and (3) U Nanda, the Shangalekyun Sayadaw.[74] If the Shangalekyun Sayadaw had been the immediate master of the Shwegyin Sayadaw, it is easy to see how he could have been confused in some minds with founding the Shwegyin sect, though he was of course technically still Thudhamma because the Shwegyin sect had not yet been formed.

There is also some further evidence, though not definitive, that the

72. I.e., *Agga Maha Pandita Maha Thera* (see Glossary). A title and award instituted by the British to honor learned and respected *sayadaws*.

73. *Sasana* (P): teaching, doctrine; the religion taught by the Buddha: i.e., Buddhism.

74. Sandawara, n.d.:66.

Shangalekyun Sayadaw was as much of a rebel as his distinguished pupil must have been. The pamphlet *The Present Religious Events* tells, incidentally, how U Nanda, the Shangalekyun Sayadaw, was summoned on one occasion to Mindon's palace and told to prepare Vinaya instruction for other monks.[75] He prepared a text called *Alizzi Dhamma Winissaya,* which he had distributed around the countryside, and he invited many monks to the palace. Soon after, in 1855, an insulting letter apparently written by one "Maung Shan" was thrown into the compound of the minister of the interior. A young monk was told to throw an equally insulting reply into the compound of the Shangalekyun Sayadaw. The story then switches to a Bhamo Sayadaw, who was accused of being the author of the letters. The *thathanabaing* interrogated the Bhamo Sayadaw, who replied elusively, was brought before the king, and then was exiled to Bhamo, annoying his escorts by claiming that a royal prerogative granted him allowed him to take a detour through Pagan. The chief queen interceded for him after some time, and the king allowed him to return to Mandalay, though the Bhamo Sayadaw insisted on staying in Sagaing.[76] There he penned various insulting epigrams which brought him national fame because of the wit and sharp satire he directed against those in high places, both in the Sangha and in the government.

Htin Aung (1966:19) gives an account of the Bhamo Sayadaw in which the queen's liking for this monk is clear. According to this source, the Bhamo Sayadaw was a Thudhamma Council man but highly critical of Mindon's censorship devices. His struggle with King Mindon thus seems related to the king's attempts at Sangha purification. It may be significant that in the *Shwehintha Tawya Thamaing*[77] the Bhamo's name is given as U Panditta, which is also the name of Pannasami's opponent in the passage in the *Sasanavamsa* (1861:156) which may refer to the birth of the "Mindon sects." Since Pannasami was a Mindon supporter and Thudhamma monk, he was possibly trying to defend his position against both the liberal Bhamo Sayadaw and the pupils of the 2d Bagaya

75. Pyinnyaramikamaha Sayadaw 1958:64–68.
76. Htin Aung (1966:19–20) reports on monkish "migrations to the Sagaing Hills." Many of the 2d Bagaya Sayadaw's pupils were there, as was the Hngetwin Sayadaw. It seems to have been the seedbed of the "Mindon sects." For more information on these lineages, see Panditta 1955:45, 54–59.
77. Panditta 1955:67.

Sayadaw. Despite the rapport which apparently existed between Pannasami and Mindon, the king turned to the Shwegyin Sayadaw to effect his plans. The motivation of the king may be illuminated somewhat by a review of the character of the monk he chose to be the leader of the new reformist sect.

The most complete account that I could find of the Shwegyin Sayadaw's life and his contacts with King Mindon is found in a 1959 account by the Pattamya Sayadaw, a Shwegyin monk from the Pattamya Monastery in the West Sector of Mandalay. According to this source, the Shwegyin Sayadaw, U Zagara, was born in 1822 in Shwegyin, a village to the south of Shwebo. As a schoolboy, he worked under the village *sayadaw,* and he later worked as a novice under the country-famous Thilon Sayadaw,[78] returning only for a brief spell to his village to become ordained as a monk. He also took lessons in deportment from the *sayadaw*s of Mangyitanywa and Muweywataung and spent some time as a scholar at the The-in Monastery in Amarapura. While there, the future Shwegyin gave a verdict in favor of an accused in a case from another village. The complainants desired that the monk's judgment should be checked with Vinaya tradition. The case was taken to the heir apparent, Mindon, who was asleep in his chambers.[79] On being awakened and told the facts, Mindon appears to have been highly impressed by the monk's judgment and decided that he was a very extraordinary person.

Prince Mindon met the *sayadaw* again when he and the Kanaung prince left for Shwebo and encountered the Shwegyin monk in a rest house near the village of Hlatawgyi. On this occasion, after hearing a sermon by the monk, Mindon decided that he would invite him to the city when he became king and ordered his secretary to write down the names of the monk and his parents as well as the place of his birth. In 1861, after Mindon had taken Amarapura, had reigned there for a time, and had finally ascended the throne in his new capital at Mandalay, he made inquiries about the *sayadaw*. Mindon found that he was residing at a rural monastery near the village of Sheinmaja and sent his ministers to invite him to the city. After the monk refused, his parents

---

78. The Thilon Sayadaw played a key role in the formation of the Mindon sects (see Appendix D). Some idea of his lineage would be very helpful but it has not yet been discovered. J. F.

79. Mindon at this time was probably a monk himself. J. F.

were approached, and in his eighteenth year as a monk the *sayadaw* went to Mandalay.

Asked to point out a desirable residence, the Shwegyin Sayadaw indicated a site north of Mandalay Hill, and soon afterward a monastery of 262 pillars and a variety of lesser buildings were erected at a cost of 553,222 *kyats*. A total of five main constructions were given over to the Shwegyin Sayadaw as his place of residence. It was after this that the episode with the 2d Maungdaung Sayadaw as *thathanabaing* took place and the Shwegyin sect came into being.

This story is told very much as an "origin myth" of a lineage might be told, with stress on the omens and signs that usually mark out great events. One of the important omens in stories of kings and their favorite monks or teachers is the pattern of the two parties meeting in early life and then again later, when the consecration of one by the other occurs after full power is achieved. In the Shwegyin Sayadaw's story above, the "first occasion" is the Shwegyin's judgment at Amarapura, the "second occasion" the meeting at Hlatawgyi. This Shwegyin history also reveals the importance of lineage. Since there are few other social relations knitting the individuals of the Sangha together, it might be expected that the "line" of teachers and disciples should receive special attention, and indeed this relation has been sanctified in Buddhist texts from very early times. In Burma, the stress on these lineages in the texts appears to be one of the few ways available of reconstituting some degree of ecclesiastical history—although, as an anthropologist might suspect, the upper reaches of any lineage tend to become blurred, and certain personages at the top are lumped together or otherwise confused.

The Shwegyin sect thus clearly traces its origin to Mindon's actions and plans, and we might well ask what that king's policies really were. While much research remains to be done on this matter, a number of signs point to an overcompensation on Mindon's part as a result of the British menace to Upper Burma due to their military occupation of Lower Burma, with a corresponding reaction on the part of the Sangha that was to have far-reaching consequences. On the one hand, there was a centralization of Sangha powers vested in Mindon's Thudhamma Council,[80] which was favored by the king's religiosity and his champion-

---

80. According to the Khemathiwun Sayadaw, Mindon in 1862 appointed eight Pitakama *sayadaw*s, holders of awards known as the *sakyi tazeit,* and on a later, unspecified, occasion added another two. The first eight *sayadaw* names were:

ship of Buddhism. But his concern for the Lower Burma situation meant that his "favors" involved a certain degree of politicization of the council: these were state monks, to a great extent. On the other hand, there was the perennial refusal of many Sangha leaders to submit to anything smacking of lay discipline. For example, the king appears to have tried to curb growing luxuriousness among monks by putting stronger disciplinary powers in the hands of ecclesiastical censors, yet, while some of the council monks agreed strongly with the austere measures, they violently protested the interference of laymen in Sangha affairs. The careers of some of the great monks of the time illustrate the tensions involved. Such *sayadaw*s as the Thingaza, Bhamo, and Hngetwin were patronized by the king, queens, or princes, but they spent only short terms on the council or left in a huff. Thus the cliffs of Sagaing became a great center for monks who sought solitude and escape from political control, thereby decentralizing the Sangha by deserting the council and the capital monasteries for the *tawya,* or "forest."

The story of Mindon's championship of the Shwegyin Sayadaw also suggests that his policy may well have been to play off various monks on his council against each other and to use the *thathanabaing*'s position to create antagonism among the great monks of the time, who, as noted above, were part of a small oligarchy of masters, disciples, and friends. A number of factors produced a sectarian "peeling off," with the great monks stressing the Vinaya purity of their case, partly as a way of going along with the king and with the tradition of not causing divisions in the Sangha, and partly as a way of revolting against the royal politicization of the leadership of the Sangha, which only a cleaving to the Vinaya would seem to ward off. A further combination of factors seems to have clinched the matter. Monks involved with incipient sectarian formation found a haven in Lower Burma. For conditions existed there that could only hasten the formation of sects: monks were no longer dealing with one view of Buddhism versus another but with Buddhism versus non-Buddhism, or even anti-Buddhism.

Siputtara Sayadaw	2d Maungdaung Sayadaw
Minde Sayadaw	Meiktila Sayadaw
(2d?) Salin Sayadaw	Ok-kyaung Sayadaw
Pakhangyi Sayadaw	Sitaw-myinwun Sayadaw

Htin Aung (1966:32) says the Thingazar (alias Thingaza) Sayadaw was on the council in 1860 but left after a few years to promote Thudhamma reforms.

The Founding and Growth of the Weluwun Sect

The Dwaya sect, of course, fits the pattern for the Lower Burma situation just introduced, and the Weluwun sect also has a strong Lower Burma posture. Before visiting an extremely well-kept monastery in Taunggyi in the Shan States in April 1959, where I went in search of a school for tribal people, I had only heard of the name Weluwun in connection with two large monasteries in the Bahan and Kemmendine quarters of Rangoon, though I had been puzzled by the frequency with which this name occurred in connection with monkish establishments. On inquiring, as I always did, as to the sect of the *sayadaw* in Taunggyi, I was told that he belonged to a Weluwun sect which had begun not long ago in Rangoon, the present Patama Sayadaw (aged 94), the third in the Patama line, residing then in Kemmendine. I also learned that the first *sayadaw* had belonged to a Gu-ko-lon, or Nine-Caves, sect. The monks present were very keen to inform me that sects grew up only for disciplinary purposes and without any aim of splitting the Sangha, but they were unable to tell me more about their organization. Before leaving, however, I was able to secure a booklet which turned out to contain a history of the sect written at the time of the installation of the third president around 1954.[81]

The lineage of the founder is traced to four outstanding monks whose names we have come across in connection with other sects: (1) Thilon Sayadaw, (2) Shwegyin Sayadaw, (3) Okpo Sayadaw, and (4) Thingaza Sayadaw.[82] There is a strong suggestion throughout the text—which I have unfortunately been unable to confirm entirely—that the Weluwun sect originated out of the Dwaya sect, both being Lower Burma sects of the Henzada region.

The chronological presentation of the Mindon sects will be interrupted long enough to discuss briefly here the highlights in the Weluwun sect's development, as the factors in its history are basic to an understanding of the growth of any sect. In 1863, a pupil of the Thingaza Sayadaw, the Nine-Caves Sayadaw (U Nandiya), built nine impressive meditational caves in Myanaung, Henzada District, where for forty years he

81. The cover of this booklet was ripped off; therefore no bibliographical details can be given.

82. See Appendix D for lineages of these monks and the relative position of the Nine-Caves Sayadaw.

taught his monks *pariyatti* disciplines, that is, the scholarship and theory of Buddhism. One of his disciples was U Puntawuntha, who entered the monkhood in 1884 and was to become the Weluwun Sayadaw. In 1895, U Puntawuntha began to teach at the Htupayan Monastery in Thonze, Tharrawaddy District, where he came to the notice of U Hpyu, a trader of that town. In 1897 the trader invited the *sayadaw* to Rangoon and established him in a temporary residence taken over from a nunnery in a bamboo grove of Bahan quarter. Here, though already famous, the *sayadaw* carried out further studies under a famous Mandalay teacher, the *"Pitaka taya saya paramatta widu."*[83] It is here that, from a habit of his disciples of muttering *"weluwun, weluwun"* (bamboo grove), the monk is supposed to have become known as the Weluwun Sayadaw. We note the existence of a very important pattern here: recognition by a rich *taga,* or donor, followed by an intensive building program of "daughter" monasteries. The *sayadaw* began to set up Weluwun monasteries at Inya Road in Rangoon (1906), Bassein (1909), Myanaung (1919), and Kemmendine in Rangoon (1916). He resided and taught in the Kemmendine monastery, and it became the headquarters of the new group, which at this stage is best thought of as a *gaing,* that is, an organization that has incipient sectarian leanings as it grows.

By 1919 the Weluwun Sayadaw appears to have had a following of about five hundred monks. At a meeting in that year he named as head of the *gaing* the Kyaikhto Sayadaw, who had been a fellow student when he studied with the 1st Pwinhla Theingon Sayadaw at Prome. The Kyaikhto Sayadaw died in 1940, and the Weluwun Sayadaw himself was installed as *maha nayaka* (leader). In the same year, he brought together the Pwinhla Theingon *gaing* of Prome and the Anaukchaung Dwaya *gaing* of Bassein under his authority. Note here that there is a further suggestion of amalgamation with some part of the Dwaya sect. At this stage the *gaing* had become sufficiently large and well organized to be seen by others as possibly bidding for sectarian status.

The Weluwun Sayadaw died in 1943, but the uncertainties of the war years prevented another installation until 1953. Another Weluwun Sayadaw of Myanaung, the "heir apparent," had died before his installation, and the 89-year-old Sandayon Sayadaw from Thaton was elected

---

83. Pitaka (P): the Pali Canon; *taya* (P): three; *saya: hsaya* (B): teacher, expert; *paramatta: paramattha* (P): highest truth; *widu* (B-P): *vidu* (P): wise man. One who knows the Pitaka at the highest level.

head of what we now can define as a sect, with four assistants who were to become leaders serially. We note a pattern in the full development of some sects by the time the third or fourth leader has taken over. These assistant heads provide a good illustration of the strict seniority principle: (1) Weluwun Sayadaw of Myanaung, the new incumbent (age 83, monk age 64); (2) Weluwun Sayadaw of Kemmendine (age 83, monk age 58); (3) Weluwun Sayadaw of Kyonpyaw (age 74, monk age 53); Pwinhla Theingon Sayadaw of Prome (age 72, monk age 52). Insofar as three hundred presiding *sayadaw*s of the districts are said to have taken part, we may note another pattern that will acquire importance by and by: the importance of the monastery of origin—a consideration which is not surprising if we reflect that it is in the important abbeys that candidates sophisticated enough for leadership will have acquired the habits and the craft to become ruling *sayadaw*s of the Sangha.[84]

The Hngetwin Sect's Origin and Claims to Orthodoxy

It is customary to de-emphasize the doctrinal originality of new sects and to emphasize the Vinaya concern of such groups as the Shwegyin, Dwaya, and Weluwun, but perhaps my lack of philosophical sophistication and textual familiarity precludes me from noticing subtleties in interpretation of the scriptures which often form the basis of sectarian debate on doctrine. This lacuna on my part may be graver still in the case of the Hngetwin sect to be discussed now, for this group, rightly or wrongly, is often referred to as *paramat*. Among reasonably educated laymen I found the view that the monks of the Hngetwin, or Satubumika, sect are extremists. Their opinions resemble the exposition in the Reverend Nyanatiloka's *Buddhist Dictionary* under *"Paramattha"* (1950: 116):

"Truth (Phenomenon, expression, exposition) which is true in the Highest Sense" as contrasted with the mere "Conventional Truth." The Buddha, in

84. The close-knit nature of this sect comes out very clearly in the list of student travels of the Sandayon Sayadaw (see Appendix D). Born in 1865 in Myanaung, Henzada, he studied under U Eindathara, then under the Payagon Sayadaw and Nine-Caves Sayadaw (two of his ordinators) at the Payagyi Taik, Mandalay, returned to the Nine-Caves, after a brief spell with the Mota *thathanabaing* and the Mainkaing Sayadaw of Sheweyesaung Taik in Mandalay, and finally studied with Mahadhammikarama Sayadaw of Thaton, who made him *sayadaw* of the Sandayon Taik in 1902. We also see that Weluwun monks could study with Thudhamma worthies without trouble.

explaining his doctrine, sometimes made use of the so-called conventional language, sometimes he used the philosophical mode of expression corresponding to reality in the highest sense. In the ultimate sense, existence is a mere process of continually changing physical and psychical phenomena, within which, or beyond which, no real Ego-entity or personality can ever be found. Thus wherever in the texts mention is made of a person, a self, or rebirth of a being etc., . . . this should not be understood as said in the ultimate or "highest sense" (*paramattha*) but as a mere conventional mode of speech (*voharavacana*). The only actual realities are those physical and psychical phenomena, though only of momentary duration arising and passing away every moment. Cf. *anatta.*

Thus the *paramat* interpretation of the Buddha's doctrine is the most highly sophisticated available and can be interpreted in a favorable light. Informants recognized, however, that in Burma the term was usually an abusive one. One stated, "Yes, the Hngetwin work in the *paramat* sense where nothing really exists, but this is an extreme opinion and it can become a mad one." Another, voicing the usual view of Hngetwin, told me that "they believe there is no merit in feeding the crows by presenting food on altars and pagodas at *pwes* and festivals, and they feel that candles are merely lighting the way for the mice to find the food. When you think of it, it is silly to throw away food so that even the poor cannot have it. The Hngetwin people would have men eat the food which is placed at pagodas, not just throw it away." A third told me that "the mind should be concentrated on the virtues of the Buddha, not wavering while making offerings." And a leading Hngetwin monk at Mandalay said that alms food was not presented to images because "the Buddha should be kept in one's heart so that if the monks are fed the Buddha is fed too. And in any case people should be fed, not images. If you lead a good life, there should be no need for you to make offerings." Thus *paramat* doctrine can be viewed favorably as being of a highly sophisticated order or unfavorably as undermining the ordinary practices felt by the large majority of Burmese Buddhists to be part and parcel of their religion, and it is the latter, rather fearful view that seems to prevail.

Whether this sect actually is the Paramat sect referred to in earlier sources, or whether it has been confused with some other sect or sects, possibly the Zawti, is difficult to determine. The Paramats studied earlier in this chapter as part of the Bodawpaya period also seem to have assumed the "no food for the crows and mice" view referred to above; but, in addition, they had a "semi-atheistic" heresy (Judson's words) revolving around their reverence for the concept of the Nyan-daw, or heavenly wisdom as a pillar of fire (see Chapter 1 above). I have as yet no evidence that the Hngetwin sect shares an interest in this older concept—as opposed to the Zawti whom I interviewed in the Shan States and will discuss later—and thus the Hngetwin may have been maligned and confused with such a sect as the Zawti, or perhaps it has changed its colors and abandoned some of its more heretical opinions in favor of greater orthodoxy.[85]

Htin Aung (1966:20–25) considers the Hngetwin (Ngettwin) Saya-daw to have been "the first challenge to Mindon," and he lists the following doctrinal objections with which the Hngetwin Sayadaw challenged Mindon's Thudhamma Council: (1) pagoda offerings dirtied shrines and encouraged rats; (2) taking the five precepts before a monk[86] is unnecessary because, if a layman does not follow these precepts automatically in daily living, he is not even a Buddhist no matter what he recites; (3) monks should not be ordained unless they have been trained in meditation; (4) no gifts should be made to the Sangha unless they are given, not to be property of individual monks, but to the Sangha as a whole; and (5) no monk should reside anywhere any longer than one or two years. These were serious challenges to the Thudhamma Council. Even though the Hngetwin Sayadaw had been the tutor of Mindon's chief queen and had been a prominent leader of the forest monks at Sagaing, he had to leave Upper Burma on account of his difficulties there with the king and the council. But he found that British rule in Lower Burma gave greater freedom of expression. In 1885, at the age of about fifty-six, he settled at the Lepaw Monastery in Kungyangon, Hanthawaddy District. This can be counted as the foundation year of the sect.[87] In 1886, at its second anniversary, the Paramisan Monastery was built within a ten-acre plot near the Lepaw, donated by one Daw Gyi. In the course of 1887–1888, the *gaing* received the name Hngetwin from a stream near Mingun in the Sagaing Hill Range, where the

---

85. For more on this view see Purser and Saunders 1914:22, 56.

86. To "take the precepts" is to ask a monk to recite the basic five rules of Buddhism which the laity tacitly agrees to follow as they are recited.

87. Htin Aung (1966:25) holds that the Hngetwin Sayadaw would not permit the formation of a separate sect until 1887.

founder originally meditated and studied.[88] The name appears to have helped the *gaing* to spread better than its original Satubumika name, though this growth was effected under ceaseless criticism, reference being made by critics to a Hngetwin *gaing* law (*taya*), or separate Hngetwin teachings (Dhamma), as if the sect were outside of orthodox Buddhism. It is in such passing remarks as these that one senses the possibility of an original heresy as discussed above.

By 1893 the founder had written several works which were distributed in Rangoon, Maubin, Dedaye, Pegu, and as far north as Shwebo, and by 1909, at the age of eighty, he had built twenty monasteries in Upper and Lower Burma. In the same year he died at Thaton, leaving the Hngetwin *gaing* in the hands of four leaders and about five hundred monks. The early leaders were all Lower Burma men, and Hngetwin in modern times still seems to have more establishments in the south than in the north. By this time the *gaing* apparently takes on sectarian dimensions in terms of a self-defined sense of individuation in relationship to other monks.

I was fortunate, after many inquiries, to be able to interview the presiding *sayadaw* of a Hngetwin *yeiktha*,[89] the Thassathindanpya Sayadaw, Nan-yaw U Zagara. The name Nan-yaw came from his village of origin in Thongwa District, Lower Burma. He had been in Mandalay for eight years and reckoned his following among the laity at around two thousand. This *sayadaw* was most impressive and fierce looking and sounding, though humorous and very kind. He prided himself on his system of teaching. This was based on a bag of small round nuts which he disposed in patterns on a floor or a table to explain the abstruse points of doctrine or sect organization to a foreigner who had hitherto consorted with only the most lax of Buddhists.

The Shweman Sayadaw has written that "the Hngetwin people contend that leaning between the action (*kan*) and the doors (*dwaya*) one pays obeisance by the door of the mind, the door of the word, the door of the body. The reason for the Hngetwin Sayadaw's forming the sect was

---

88. Htin Aung (1966:20) identifies Hngetwin as meaning a "cave of birds" at Sagaing, where the *sayadaw* meditated. It is reasonably clear that this sect prefers the name Satubumika [B-P?]: possibly from *sādhu* (P): good, virtuous; *bhumi* (P): ground], not Hngetwin, as the latter apparently is perceived as derogatory. J. F.

89. Literally, a shady place; a term used to signify a pleasant place donated to the Sangha; a retreat.

that the monks in his entourage should not lean either toward the Dwaya or the Kan *gaing*s, when these two so momentously split."[90] In other words, the Hngetwin people, by their variation on the famous formula, set themselves midway between the two conflicting sects. This was a Thudhamma view of the matter. However, my informant, U Zagara, delighted me by doing everything in his power to show that, strictest among the strict, the Hngetwin were the best and most highly evolved of Buddhists and he did this by grading the other sects on a scale, with the Hngetwin in the purest position. His exposition shows once again how the relative positions of the different sects on a continuum differ according to the sectarian affiliations of the speaker, a point of great importance in both our historical and theoretical intrepretation of the growth of these Sangha sects.

The bulk of U Zagara's explanation to me, with the aid of the little diagrams made out of nuts, was concerned with the special position of Hngetwin. He told me that there are four basic kinds of Buddhists. First and lowest come those who keep no precepts (*sila*)[91] but take the Three Refuges.[92] They believe a good deal in *weikzas*[93] and *nats*[94] and are forever holding *pwe*s and making offerings. Then come those who keep five precepts, turn to the Three Refuges, and make donations to monks with a good deal of *pwe*. In this class he seemed disposed to lump Thudhamma, Shwegyin, and Dwaya, though elsewhere he gave the latter two some preference in his scheme. A third category keeps eight precepts, turns to the Three Reguges, and makes donations with some *pwe*s. I am not quite clear on this point but believe that here he placed

90. Sandawara, n.d.
91. *Sila* is the Pali word for the Precepts, or the basic behavioral observances kept by Buddhists. See below. The Five Precepts include refraining from (1) taking life, (2) stealing, (3) lying, (4) illicit sexuality, and (5) taking intoxicants. The full Eight Precepts include also (6) eating after the noon hour, (7) watching or participating in *pwe*s, (8) sleeping in a high or ornate bed. The full Ten Precepts would include (9) wearing perfume, jewelry, or other luxurious adornment of face or body (sometimes one of the Eight), and (10) handling money. [See Spiro 1970:45–46. J. F.]
92. The statement that one makes in turning as a Buddhist to the Buddha, the teachings, and the Sangha for refuge.
93. Persons supremely adept in messianic Buddhism. In some respects, a wizard who has mastered magic powers or arts, such as "astrology, alchemy, cabbalistic signs, *mantra*s . . . and medicine." See Mendelson 1961a:230–231.
94. Spirits or gods.

Hngetwin lay followers. The fourth and highest category definitely includes Hngetwin, and such Buddhists keep twelve precepts, the Three Refuges, and the three *shikos*[95] of the Buddha, Dhamma, Sangha; they also make donations without music and *pwes*.

In U Zagara's scheme, the twelve precepts of Hngetwin are divided into three groups of four, relating to the body (*kaya-kamma*), the mouth (*vaci-kamma*), and the mind (*cetana-kamma*).[96] Group one (body) includes abstention from (1) killing; (2) stealing; (3) adultery (even with the consent of one's own wife); and (4) drink, smoking, drugs. Group two (mouth) covers abstention from (1) lying; (2) insults and disturbances; (3) abuse; and (4) shows and *pwes* of all sorts, which must not even be discussed. Group three (mind) includes abstention from (1) jealousy; (2) revenge; (3) the manifestations of the five passions; and (4) a living earned by any of these. These suggest that U Zagara's scheme is little more—in purely sociological terms—than an elaboration of the original five precepts without any great advance in thought, an elaboration that is of far greater importance to the monastic world than to the outside observer. To the latter it is barely thinkable that sects can arise solely on the basis of such rhetoric; the main causes must be elsewhere. It remains to be said that the Hngetwin use orthodox ordination procedures like all other sects; that their ordination ritual is the same as Thudhamma's and the others; that they consider themselves as outside the *nikaya* system;[97] and that they have not sought government recognition and wish to have nothing to do with courts, as they settle their disputes among themselves.

The pattern is by now familiar, and we note that such small, easily managed sects as the Hngetwin arose at a certain time and place, mostly the time of Mindon in Lower Burma. They represent the results of a number of historical and sociological factors bearing upon Sangha organization at that time and place. Was this the only way for the Sangha to remain independent from and uncontaminated by political control? Was the fear of contamination expressed by an ever stronger

95. Three *shiko* (B): here a reference to the formulaic use of the term *panama* (P): salutation, bending, adoration, bowing down.
96. *Kaya* (P): the body; *kamma* (P): deeds; *vaci* (P): speech, word; *cefana* (P): intention.
97. I.e., the governmental recognition of the existence of sects such as the Shwegyin that are given proportionate representation on government-created boards, councils, and the like.

stress on Vinaya discipline? Are the differences more rhetorical than real, in that the very creation of a sect must be rationalized by some differences from the main body, though the important need is the creation of a small group rather than the following of any particularly original way? These are the kinds of questions to keep in mind when similar developments are reviewed in the post-Mindon period.

Educational Excellence and the Pakokku Sect

There is only one sect remaining of the groups that can be said to constitute the "Mindon sects," and this group's origin is far from clear, although the "Pakokku" name itself signifies a highly respected tradition in the Burmese Sangha. Mandalay, Rangoon, and Moulmein apart, Pakokku District, together with Pegu and Myaungmya in Lower Burma, shares one of the highest monk populations in Burma. Pakokku, an isolated town on the west bank of the Irrawaddy and the gateway to the Yaw and Chin countries to the west, has long been famous as a center of proud and independent monastic learning in Burma; as the saying goes in one Pakokku monastery rule book, "You are illiterate until you have been to Pakokku." In this context of independence the development of the sect named after this town took place, and it reveals the Old Burma in its most conservative northern form.

I do not know when the Pakokku sect started, though I was told in Pakokku that the first *sayadaw* of the Mahawithudarama, or Central, Monastery—one of the "big three" that dominate the town—was U Ganda, the Yegyo Sayadaw. This monk is almost certainly U Gandhasara, the Yesagyo Sayadaw, who is said to have left Mandalay after disagreeing with Mindon's Thudhamma Council when, at the death of the 2d Maungdaung Sayadaw (U Nyeyya) in 1865, the *thathanabaing*'s monastery was given to the Parakkama Sayadaw.[98] He had four disciples, among whom the leadership of the Pakokku sect was rotated. It should be clearly stressed that Pakokku never considered itself a sect but saw itself rather as an association oriented to, and concerned mainly with, religious education. The Pakokku sect played a key role in the educational plans of the U Nu period, and its history will be discussed later. The important point to stress here is that once again a sect's origins, such as we can discover them, are rooted in the Mindon era and involve

98. Payapyu Sayadaw 1928:129, 179.

the rivalry not only between the sect founder and the council but also between the queen's and the king's predilections in 1865.

The Mindon Sects and Royal Efforts at Control

At this point the "Mindon sects" can be reviewed. Characteristically the sects try to present themselves as being ever stricter than their neighbors, and this is in fact rhetorical self-appraisal rather than a judgment based on an absolute criterion of differentiation. Sectarian distinctions involve esoteric doctrinal points best left to the textual scholar and comparative religionist. I have stressed, instead, the discipline in the sects (sanctioned, it is true, by age-old Burmese custom) as a reflection of the crumbling social order in these difficult times. It is obvious that, to stay within the pale of acceptance, a sect must not be open to the accusation of splitting the Sangha. Thus, each sect is virtually obliged to differentiate itself according to "good" criteria such as disciplinary fervor. Indeed, the very move to Lower Burma in the case of some sect founders (or the attempt at alliances in Lower Burma on the part of others) brought with it new problems; for the move to Lower Burma, apart from freeing a sect from the orthodoxy of the north, brought with it the still greater problem of the dissipation in social life that could erode Buddhist behavior—the "greater wealth of the country and the introduction of foreign luxuries" which Scott has commented on in his description of the Sulagandi.

There is considerable evidence that the new sects, far from attempting to meet new situations by creative thinking and new modes of organization, were in fact reacting in highly conservative fashion by attempting to recreate within themselves the pure Sangha of eternal Burma. Because of their size and manageability, they inevitably took upon themselves— and with greater success—the very functions the *thathanabaing* was supposed to have had in the olden days. They sanctified the sect by the use of "lineage myths," relating themselves to famous monks and monasteries of the past and to such events in early Buddhism as the Great Councils, when the texts of the Vinaya were purified—a point of great interest in view of Mindon's Fifth Buddhist Council and the AFPFL's Sixth Council. This emphasis, together with the writing of new "sect" texts on old subjects and new "sect" commentaries, must be seen as part of the rhetoric of differentiation used as a cover for quite other ends. In some cases texts were written to launch a sect; in others, texts were obviously written because a sect already launched needed strengthening. An old tendency is confirmed in the situation of leadership centers in those localities where the majority of the sect monks had congregated and where famous abbeys had been established, which grew to be sect headquarters and training grounds for new leaders, so that frequently the principle of monastery seniority overruled individual seniority in the monkhood as a basis for leadership. As will be demonstrated in detail later for modern times, sect documents for this period stress constantly the themes of unity, discipline, and control. Organization is remarkably similar throughout the different sects: a tight oligarchy at the top, usually for life, despite pretences of re-elections; local administrations responsible to it through lists of monks sent to the center during each rainy season (Lent); the importance of the prestigious monasteries (usually teaching institutions or *taik*s); a tight registration system with individual record cards; the encouragement of an ample literature about the sect, such as rule books, lives of the founder, commentaries on the Tipitaka from the sect's point of view, and so forth; and, of course, much lip service paid to democracy and equality. These, of course, were the functions and duties of the *thathanabaing* ideally as the bringer of unity, discipline, and control to the Sangha in royal times.

But in the Mindon period, times were different. The sects that developed equipped the Sangha, so to speak, with an answer to the disintegrative forces in the colonial acculturation process, and they also developed an organization that the total Sangha had seldom achieved in earlier royal times. Since they did for themselves what the *thathanabaing* was supposed to do, they were naturally unresponsive to efforts of the political center to discipline them. This attitude of the sects toward both King Mindon's and U Nu's political efforts helps to explain why Mindon's Fifth Council failed to unify the Sangha[99] and why, as we shall see, U Nu's Sixth Council had similar difficulties.

There is strong reason to believe that Mindon wished to hold as many of the reins of power as possible in his own hands, and that in the process he deliberately or by omission allowed the power of the thathanabaingship in his own time to be weakened. His aim was apparently to

99. Payapyu Sayadaw 1928:137–139. The major supervisors were mostly monks of the Thudhamma Council, such as the Minde, 2d Maungdaung, Pakhangyi, and Salin Sayadaws. Also mentioned were the Sibontara, Mekkhara, Thitseingyi, Ingan, and Bangyi Sayadaws.

divert the loyalty of the Sangha to himself by taking it away from the *thathanabaing*. In the process he appears to have directly and personally encouraged the splitting away from the main Thudhamma body of at least one sect, the Shwegyin, which he may have wanted to make the instrument of his own religious policy. But his plans were not successful. Faced with the weakening of the Order as a whole as well as with the potential liberty allowed by a Lower Burma out of the king's control, the Sangha seems to have begun to realize that it should reconstitute itself into small, easily governable groups in order to preserve both its self respect and its power to act for itself outside the sphere of political control. This process most likely was at work in the evolution of the Mindon sects. The British noncommittal attitude to Burmese religion further provoked and favored this outcome and, by the time the Burmese regained control of their affairs and wished to reinstate a united leadership of the Sangha, it was too late, for they found well-organized bodies sure of their ground and very vocal in defense of such an active Sangha as there could be said to be. A consideration of post-Mindon sects will show that the sects that may have begun as instruments of political policy were, by the time of national independence, a power themselves which political authority could only come to terms with as best it could.

Continuing Sectarianism under Burma's Last King

With the death of King Mindon in 1878, time was running out for the old system. When King Thibaw took over, he appointed two *thathanabaing*s, one his own teacher, the Taungdaw Sayadaw, and the other the Shwegyin Sayadaw, thus giving recognition to both Thudhamma and Shwegyin factions. Apparently, Mindon had let the office of the *thathanabaing* remain vacant after the death of the 2d Maungdaung Sayadaw in 1865. As noted above, there was controversy when the 2d Maungdaung's monastery was assigned to a Thudhamma monk, the Parakkama Sayadaw.[100] The Taungdaw Sayadaw is generally recognized to have had few qualifications beyond having been the royal preceptor

---

100. Presumably this monk is in the Parakkama lineage traced in Appendix C; he would be the natural successor to the 2d Maungdaung Sayadaw, Pannasami having died a few years after he wrote the *Sasanavamsa* in 1861. In Scott and Hardiman (1900, 1, pt. 1:48) it is said that the San Monastery of the deceased king's teacher was handed over to the "Pyi *sadaw*," who had been a queen's teacher also. J. F.

when Thibaw was but an obscure prince, and the Shwegyin Sayadaw took no part in the Thudhamma Council's affairs. Interestingly, the Pahkan Sayadaw,[101] to whom the 2d Maungdaung Sayadaw had handed over affairs, became known as a *samuti thathanabaing*[102] insofar as the monks agreed to call him *thathanabaing* and to bow to his will. He continued as a recognized leader after the death of the Taungdaw (in 1895) until his own death in 1900.[103]

The data on Thibaw's council of monks is difficult to follow. According to the Khemathiwun Sayadaw, the king is supposed to have added two monks to Mindon's roster, but the list of twelve then given does not correspond well at all to what we know of the composition of the Mindon council.[104] There may have been two lists of Mindon council monks, or perhaps reconfirmation customs brought about changes in titles, even though the same monks were involved.[105] What is clear, however, is that the sectarian issues of the Mindon reign continued unabated into the reign of Thibaw.

Nisbet, in describing the sectarian issues of those days, writes:

When a layman of the High Church party has built and endowed a monastery (*Kyaung*) and the priest living there has died, the founder (*Kyaungtaga*) very naturally objects if a monk (*Pongyi*) of the Low Church party enters and takes possession of it. Sometimes such things cause heartburnings and bickerings in the villages, but on the whole the differences are far more nominal than real. In proof of this the statement may be made that it is not easy to find anyone in a jungle village who can explain what differences really exist between the doctrines of the two parties. The village monks always belong to one or the other rival schools, and the villagers accordingly consider themselves adherents of the same sect. Beyond the fact that *Sulagandi* are stricter in performance of religious duties and in the

101. The Pahkan Sayadaw may be the "Pahkangyi" Sayadaw of Mindon's council, who is listed in Thibaw's council as the Pahkan Sayadaw. There is also Taw Sein Ko's "Pakan" Sayadaw (1913:217), whom the British would not recognize as a proper *thathanabaing* candidate. J. F.

102. *Samuti: sammuti* (P): consensus, generally accepted choice. In other words, *thathanabaing* by general consent of the Sangha, not by appointment of the state.

103. Payapyu Sayadaw 1928:146, 189. Also see Stewart 1949:7.

104. The *sayadaws*' names are as follows: (1) Mahawithudarama, (2) Mandalarama, (3) Mingala, (4) Sangyaung, (5) Mahakhemikarama, (6) Taungdaw, (7) Thetpun, (8) Hladwe, (9) Pakhan, (10) Wiseittarama, (11) Mahawiseittarama, (12) Mahadhammazawtikarama.

105. Spelling idiosyncrasies in the various transcriptions into English from Burmese also confound the matter. J. F.

observance of ritual and rubric than the *Mahagandi,* the people in general really know little and care less.   [1901, 2:118]

Scott (1909:144) has made the same point more concisely: "Heresies, therefore, never originate with the people; any there are come from the monasteries, but even these relate more to matters of discipline and internal regulation than to real points of faith."

Here Scott is a little more helpful than Nisbet, describing how, in the period of writing, the vernacular presses of Rangoon flooded the country with controversial tracts from both parties, causing the laity to enter the discussion and to adopt sides until the battle became so fierce that highly respected monks such as the Thingaza Sayadaw, a Thudhamma monk from Mandalay, went as early as 1873 to Lower Burma to help to settle the sectarian strife in Rangoon, Prome, Henzada, Pegu, and Moulmein.[106] In 1880 he was received at Danubyu by a large crowd of women who spread their own hair over his path to the monastery. He made numerous inquiries and finally halted at Henzada to give his decision. But when he heard that monks had been betting freely on his decision, he was enraged and refused to favor either side, although he remained preaching in Lower Burma for a considerable time, urging the Sangha to stop airing its disputes in public. Htin Aung's information on the Thingaza Sayadaw is precious because it shows how this Thudhamma monk attempted to regain the allegiance of Lower Burma for Mandalay, and the delightful tales forming the body of Htin Aung's book allow us to understand the nature and the appeal of Thudhamma orthodoxy against the claims of the smaller rivals. Despite the countrywide honor given to this monk in 1884, an attempt was made on his life in Henzada: some denounced the followers of the Okpo Sayadaw, and Htin Aung (1966:33) reports, "The Okpo *Sayadaw* himself denounced the action and came to worship the Thingaza *Sayadaw* in person." Such was the intensity of the rivalries and the strains upon the Sangha as a whole during the final days of the era of the kings.

106. See also Htin Aung 1966:31–33. Tales 23, 48–56, and 58 in this book illustrate some of Thingaza's methods in opposition to the Sulagandi which is now fairly clearly identified with Dwaya, although Htin Aung is still vague on this point at page 30, saying merely that "their [Sulagandi] ideas were not new, as they borrowed freely from the new rules of conduct advocated by the Okpo *Sayadaw.*" See Appendix D.

The Elusive Sangha Majority

At this moment in history, as Thibaw was about to be deported in 1885 to India and the whole of Burma was about to become a British colony, the Sangha can be seen as a large, virtually autonomous Order, elusive insofar as it lacked a high degree of organization and leadership and elusive also in that it had such a great turnover of personnel, being composed both of career monks and of temporary members in the act of initiating themselves into manhood by a brief stay in the monastery— an Order seemingly composed of individuals or small groups of ascetics, living off their peasant patrons in their thousands, apparently holding the balance between rulers and ruled by their mercy and charity, otherwise aloof and detached from society and its works. This overwhelming majority of the Sangha might be called "passive," in sociological terms, but it provides an important avenue of social mobility for talented youths who could use the informal ties within the Sangha to benefit from the disciple–master relationships, the local patterns of allegiance, and the sectarian and educational offerings at the monastic "universities." There thus can be said to be a certain coherence to this passive, non-political part of the Order. On the other hand, an "active" part of the Order can be identified, made up of certain sect groups within the Sangha as a whole as well as great monasteries and their dependencies which are often tied to educational facilities. My hypothesis is that, beyond the occasional great scholar or hermit tucked away in a small monastery or hermitage who, for some personal reason or another, would receive and accept a political charge, the men who formed the bridge between Sangha and the throne were the leaders of the great establishments, and it is they who were concerned with such matters of government as concerned the Sangha and the throne. A glance at the list of great monasteries and at the titles of the *thathanabaing*s and council *sayadaw*s we have discussed in this chapter supports such a hypothesis, and similar patterns in modern times confirm it. In its very nature, the Sangha is a body which simply does not need self-government, or government of any kind. In an ideal society, with peace prevailing, it is the most perfectly anarchic and individualistic of bodies.[107] Its simple strength, residing in the patron-monk relationship, still enables a

107. "Anarchic" in the sense that it would theoretically, under such ideal conditions, need no secular, outside laws. J.F.

great number of monks to survive today in the way in which it appears the Buddha once wished them to survive. Their peaceful Buddhist life has been constantly threatened by political rebellions against secular power, which never managed to strike dynastic and administrative roots for any length of time. Such troubles, as the first twelve years of national independence in modern Burma have proven, are not a thing only of the royal past. But there has also been an element of change from the early days of the kings, which is the intrusion of the outside world, of alien cultures, into the small closed world of royal Burma. The traditional patron-monk relationship has been endangered by a host of new factors, and the advantages which may have been gained in the colonial period by the semblance of a more ordered governmental system have perhaps been lost just as quickly by the disorder and conflict in the minds and hearts of the faithful. The nature of the Sangha and of its relations with the laity thus being such that a very low level of organization is necessary, efforts to impose an organization from above can have only one purpose: strengthening the political authority of the imposers. The implications of this are many, and they shall be explored in subsequent chapters.

3. The Nature of the Modern Sangha

Before the political involvement of the Sangha in the colonial period that followed the overthrow of King Thibaw in 1885 can be meaningfully discussed, some basic aspects of the Order, such as its demography, its sociological parameters, its educational role, and its basic organization, must be examined. The material spans a broad period of Burmese history, including both the colonial and modern eras. Basically, we shall be attempting to understand the sociological nature of the Sangha and its place in Burmese society.

The Monastic Population

In researching this book, I made great efforts to determine the number of monks in the Burmese Sangha over the years, but the situation in regard to statistics is little short of disastrous. The earliest estimate is Malcolm's, made in 1839:

The company of priests is very great, but I found few places where the exact number was known. From the data I was able to obtain I think their proportion to the people is about as one to thirty. In some places it is greater, in others less. Ava, with a population of two hundred thousand, has twenty thousand priests. The province of Amherst, with thirty-six thousand souls, has one thousand and ten. Tavoy, with a population of nine thousand, has four hundred and fifty. [1939, 1:99]

Writers after 1891 tend to quote the census of that year and each other. Scott and Hardiman (1900, 1, pt. 2:3) quote a figure given by Taw Sein Ko (1913:216) to the effect that under Burmese rule *pongyi*s (monks) comprised 3 percent of the population of Upper Burma, including the Cis-Salween Shan States, while in Mandalay "members of the order" numbered 13,227, about 8 percent of the population. In a later account, Scott (1911:372) reviews the 1891 census, like Nisbet (1901, 2:127), and adds that the 1901 census figures are not comparable. Brown (1925:106), probably working from the 1921 census, reports that the "country contains about seventy thousand monks, and less than eight thousand nuns." Christian (1945:197), Andrus (1948:26), and others, working from the 1931 census, conclude that there were about 120,000 monks in all of Burma, the former recording "nearly twenty thousand" for Mandalay. Tinker has a remarkably high figure:

> Altogether there are said to be 800,000 monks in Burma, equivalent to one adult male in 10. [He adds, in a note:] This figure was quoted in a government statement in Parliament (*Nation*, 5/3/54). It is far higher than prewar estimates, among which the figure of 120,000 is given by Christian. The Social Planning Commission has produced an estimate (1953) of 100,000 (Dept. Information, *Burma, the Sixth Anniversary*, p. 53). This is probably a distinct underestimate. [1957:168]

Later than this, one has to revert to local estimates by such researchers as Pfanner and Ingersoll (1962:346), who suggest that approximately 2.5 percent of the total Burmese population is in the Sangha "throughout a block of forty-seven villages in the Pegu District," well over half of these being temporary novices (*koyin*).

Faced with such statistics, the researcher then turns to census figures for British India which begin to be useful for Burma in 1881 (Burma 1883:353, 429), but immediately one is overwhelmed by the confusion of terms used in each census to define different categories of religious practitioners. In the 1891 census (Burma 1892:268–269) "*pongyis*" (monks) are defined as heads of monasteries, "*upazins*" (probationary monks) being distinguished from them, but this distinction "is not a lasting" category. *Pothudaws* (actually lay males in attendance) and "*methila*" (lay females, now known as nuns) are classed as "religious mendicants" but may or may not be included in later categories. By the 1901 census (Burma 1902:144), *koyins* (novices) are included in the category "religious mendicants" along with monks, thereby clouding the data. In the 1911 census (Burma 1912:327), non-Burmese, such as missionaries, are included with the monk figures, and lay supporters at the monasteries also seem to be counted in with them. By 1921, however, *koyins, methila, pothudaw,* and *yathe* (hermits) have been excluded from the total figure of religious practitioners (Burma 1923:241). In the last colonial census, that of 1931 (Burma 1933:170–171), the figure includes "other indigenous races" such as Christians. A Ministry of Religious Affairs source, c. 1958, provides further figures which are included in Table 1.

Table 1. Estimated monastic population since 1891

Year	Monks only	Monks and koyins	Total population
1891	46,000	78,000—	7,606,000
1901	55,000—	64,000	9,253,000
1911	53,000	62,000	10,610,000
1921	58,000	67,000	11,715,000
1931	60,000	69,000+	13,102,000
1958	76,000	108,000+	18,000,000

Source: Official census reports and Ministry of Religious Affairs interview, c. 1958.

Notes: All figures are rounded off to the nearest thousand. A minus sign indicates that the actual figure is probably smaller than that reported in the source; a plus sign indicates that it is probably larger. Figures are for Burma proper, excluding the Shan States, the Kachin State, the Chin Hills, and other hill areas.

The figures in Table 1 are, at best, my educated guesses arrived at by estimating the numbers involved in the nonrelevant areas and subtracting them from the census totals. Unfortunately, there is no way of subtracting *koyins* (novices), or Christians and others from the monk figures when they are combined in the census. For example, *"koyins"* in the 1891 census seems to be a category that also includes *maungyin,* or monastic schoolboys! The difficulty here as elsewhere is to distinguish between a real *koyin,* real in the sense that he is likely to become a monk, and a *koyin* merely undergoing a temporary initiation or *shinbyu:* a distinction which may have operated only in later decades when *koyin*s and "scholars" were separated. The "real" *koyin* would tend to be an older boy.[1] A further difficulty consists in estimating the effects of shifts in the frontiers of districts over the years. Therefore, only extreme changes in the monk population are likely to be significant. However, there are a number of such significant changes, and they tend to square with predictions based on other materials.

Using the same census and government figures for 1891 to 1958, I also looked for regional variations in ecclesiastical populations, and,

1. *Koyin*s (B) may also remain novices permanently for a variety of reasons, never planning to become fully ordained as monks.

while the same problem with terms exists, the following patterns were apparent: a steady rise in the monk population in Rangoon; a drop in the Mandalay numbers after 1901 to a low point in 1911, followed by a gradual rise to 1958; a gradual increase in the number of monks in Lower Burma so that by 1958 there were more in Lower than in Upper Burma; and a general correlation between population density figures and the concentration of monks.

What conclusions can be drawn from the foregoing? In view of the limitations of the data available and my lack of sophistication in dealing with them, it would be rash to ascribe much independent value to any conclusions based on them. Rather, any hypotheses should be compared with those drawn from material set out elsewhere in this book. With these qualifications, the following points are proposed.

First, the number of monks in Burma, during the British period at any rate, appears not to have been as high as the estimates of most previous writers, even if the Shan States—a relatively unknown quantity —are taken into consideration. There is ample evidence of the difficulty of differentiating between "real" or professional monks and novices in the available figures, but previous guesses seem high even for monks and novices taken together. This point obviously has some bearing on the extent of monastic influence on Burmese life in general and politics in particular.

Second, the figures, such as they are, do not seem to bear out a theory of a catastrophic decline of the Sangha during the British regime as a whole, though there apparently was a decline at its outset. The complaint, often heard from monks during my stay, that the number of novices had declined through the years does seem to be true, however. This ties in with what we know of the drain of educational facilities from monastic to lay schools and undoubtedly has had a long-term effect on recruitment into the Sangha, an effect that may well have grown serious by the 1950s. When a monk in the political arena argues that the Sangha has declined numerically, he is probably talking largely about recruitment.

Third, during the British period, the center of gravity of the Sangha appears to have shifted slowly southward toward the Delta and the neighborhood of Rangoon—a shift entirely understandable in terms of population movements in Burma after the opening up of the Delta. Mandalay city, however, has retained its strength, partly it appears by drawing on the ecclesiastical population of Upper Burma. Marginal districts in Upper Burma, such as Katha, Yamethin, Magwe, Minbu, and Lower and Upper Chindwin, have declined rather sharply since 1911–1921, whereas those of Lower Burma, excepting perhaps Akyab and Bassein, appear to have held their own. In Lower Burma, Moulmein, after a heavy fall between 1891 and 1901, possibly to the profit of Upper Burma, has remained an important Lower Burma Sangha center, second to Rangoon. The traveler going south from Mandalay and Sagaing—even though he passes through Prome, Pegu, and Rangoon—does not again obtain the same impression of northern ecclesiastical richness until he reaches the heart of the old Mon empire.

Finally, by and large the pattern of concentration of the ecclesiastical population seems to parallel that of the general population—that is, the monk lives where his lay supporters live. This confirms expectations based on a relatively simple donor-recipient relationship. With proper statistics, much more research could be made into the relationships among population densities, richness of the land, and Sangha population. Such economic problems are tantalizingly suggested by the crop figures for 1931, for instance, where such important ecclesiastical areas as Sagaing and Pakokku are found to have very low percentages of rice cultivation.[2] The lay associations in other districts which exist to collect and send rice to the monks of such areas thereby acquire a more immediate economic motivation than research has so far afforded them. Generally speaking, however, traditional centers of learning such as Mandalay, Sagaing, Pakokku, and Moulmein are no exceptions to the monk–lay supporter proximity rule in that they are situated in reasonably dense and rich areas.

Such are the basic facts and conclusions in terms of the Sangha's numerical presence in Burma. Quite obviously the sheer numbers alone reveal the importance of the monkhood's existence in past and present Burmese society. I also tried to comprehend the degree to which there might be a property base for the Sangha's influence in Burma.

Sangha Property and Buddhist Law

Throughout the first two chapters we have seen the importance of the Vinaya in terms of sectarian validation and definition, and in the matter

2. Burma 1933:35.

of monastic property it plays a key role as well. Over the years a considerable body of ecclesiastical and secular law on Buddhist matters has also evolved in close harmony with the Vinaya, and it also must be studied if one desires to understand the Burmese view of how property is to be donated by the laity and then handled by the monks. I conducted no original field research on the legal aspects of this matter, so only the briefest possible summary of the relevant legal source material will be given here. The main references used are the most recent ones: May Oung (1914), Mootham (1939), and Lahiri (1951).[3]

In current Burmese usage, religious property is normally divided into three classes. The first consists of property vested in the public at large and is made up of pagodas, rest houses, ordination halls, and religious edifices not defined by the other classes, together with their structures and lands. Such properties, unless they come under the jurisdiction of archaeological or museum authorities, are usually administered by lay trustees. The most famous instance in Burma is of course the powerful body of Shwedagon Pagoda trustees.[4]

The second class of religious property is known as *sanghika*.[5] This is normally divided into (1) *catudisa*[6] *sanghika*, property belonging to the Sangha of the "four quarters," .ie., the Order in general; (2) *aramika*[7] *sanghika*, property belonging to the Sangha of a particular locality; and (3) *ganika*[8] *sanghika*, property belonging to a particular sect of the Sangha. Any attempt to be more precise leads to difficulties of definition. May Oung, for instance, seems to confuse *aramika* and *ganika*, while Lahiri's attempts to clarify procedure for the inheritance of these different properties begs several questions: it is not at all clear what is meant by "the presiding monk of a locality," "the Sangha in general,"

---

3. The major source for specialists is of course Gaung (1902–1909), but its greater complexity dictates its omission from consideration here; likewise there seems no reason to go into the details of Lingat's classic "Vinaya et droit laïque" (1937) at this stage. Case references which can be found in the above authors will also be avoided. Detailed cases can be found in Dunkley (1928, 1941), but the layman should be warned that some cases are arguable and some have been reversed.

4. May Oung 1914:192–193; Lahiri 1951:348–349. Mootham (1939:132–133) has some extra detail.

5. *Sanghika* (P): belonging to the Sangha, the Order.

6. *Catuddisa* (P): the four quarters of the globe.

7. *Aramamika* (P): belonging to a monastery.

8. From *gana* (P): sect.

and other such expressions. *Sanghika* properties are apparently best administered by one form or another of trusteeship.[9]

Sanghika property is further divided into *garubhan,* or "heavy property," and *lahubhan,* or "light property."[10] *Garubhan* in turn is classified under five headings, the main ones being garden trees and garden lands surrounding the monastery, and the monastery itself plus the land on which it stands;[11] *lahubhan* includes everything not defined as *garubhan,* such as robes, begging bowls, and the other small requisites of the monk. *Garubhan* property is impartible (that is, indivisible in inheritance) under any circumstances whatsoever while *lahubhan* is partible. The sources have many discussions of the rules for handing down small *lahubhan* objects to disciples and helpers.[12]

The limits of authority of presiding monks over *sanghika* property belonging to the order as a whole are most fully discussed by Lahiri, but there are still many questions. My own hypothesis would run something as follows. Property known or suspected to be *sanghika* can, if completely vacant and manifestly unused, be occupied peacefully by individual monks in the exercise of their duties, with the possibility that challenges to such occupation may have to be decided by some authority (such as an ecclesiastical court) at a later date. Long-established *sanghika* properties are handed down to the next eldest monk in some cases, in others to members of a trustee board which coopts new members as old ones die out.[13] Agreement as to which monk or monks are abbots at any given time is not in normal circumstances hard to attain. There are, however, more limits on the authority of a *sanghika* abbot in

9. May Oung 1914:193–194; Lahiri 1951:346–347; Mootham 1939:133. Lahiri's remarks on trusteeship and authority, however, seem to be the soundest and most concise.

10. *Garu* (P): heavy; *lahu* (P): light; *bhanda* (P): goods.

11. The other categories consist of four kinds of sleeping requisites; nine varieties of brass and iron utensils; and eight kinds of building materials and utensils of wood and clay. Exhaustive lists of all properties are in Gaung 1902–1909, 1:396–398.

12. May Oung 1914:194; Lahiri 1951:348; Mootham 1939:133.

13. F. K. Lehman (personal communication, 1973) notes that there is a further subdivision of *sanghika* property into that which is controlled by the Order and that which is in the hands of lay trustees, in whom the power of appointing the head monk is vested. The latter type of arrangement, he points out, enables the lay trustees to consider the appointed monk as a field of merit for them—a privilege denied if all control is in the hands of the monks.

getting rid of a monk who has become undesirable than on a similarly placed abbot in an individually owned monastery (see below), though definition of these issues requires a detailed reference to Vinaya and much more research into what happens in practice. Any reader familiar with behavior regarding religious property realizes that, where goodwill and common sense prevail, matters are easy enough to handle, but there are incredible loopholes for those with bad will and disputatious spirit. In the latter case, even though the majority of the Burmese Sangha are law abiding, land and property squabbles can become one of the greatest causes of dissension in the Sangha.

The third type of monastic property is *poggalika:*[14] property vested in individual monks. *Sanghika* is the norm, *poggalika* being at best an unhappy compromise with human nature. Traditional Buddhism has always considered *sanghika* a more "meritorious" type of gift than *poggalika.* As May Oung (1914:194–195) points out, an early judgment, relying mainly on Vinaya, strongly doubted that a monastery could be given at all in *poggalika* fashion to an individual monk. Later judgments, however, recognized that most property which a monk is entitled to hold would take in *poggalika* form in actual practice.

It has always been felt in Burma that *poggalika* ownership of property is limited. To begin with, it is Sangha-tied, so that, if a monk leaves the Sangha, he loses the right to dispose of the property. A *poggalika* gift of monastic property may be made to another monk while the giver is alive as easily as a gift of, say, paddy land to a layman, but gifts intended to take effect after a monk's death are invalid. If a monk dies or leaves the Sangha without correctly disposing of the property, it becomes *sanghika,* and a monk must be elected to ownership of the property by a valid Sangha election.[15] A number of questions have remained obscure or are still contested, such as whether a donor can take back or be granted the right to elect a successor to a *poggalika* property. May Oung cites a case in which even *sanghika* property was given back to the poor descendants of donors by a kind *thathanabaing,* and later sources seem to stress the *poggalika* owner who surrenders to the donor the right to elect successors.[16]

14. *Puggalika* (P): personal, individual.
15. May Oung 1914:195–196; Lahiri 1951:341–343; Mootham 1939:135.
16. May Oung (1914:192); Lahiri (1951:343).

Poggalika gifts can be made to two, three, and four monks jointly, the survivor(s) becoming sole owners, but the process can be perpetuated by cooption of further members. Lahiri (1951:352) states that such gifts are "very common nowadays to prevent *poggalika* property from becoming a *sanghika* property."

But *sanghika* is today the more usual kind of property, and my informants claimed that the government preferred it to *poggalika*. Most likely the vast majority of village monasteries are *sanghika,* though surprises may await the research worker in villages with more than one monastery.[17] The great traditional centers, such as the "university" monasteries at Pakokku and the most venerable institutions in towns and cities, are likewise, as far as can be determined from the land records, *sanghika.*

A number of informants stated that, although they could not provide figures, they believed there has been a definite increase in *poggalika* property in modern times. The reasons they offered were revealing, and all had to do with the alleged decline of the Sangha and a consequent change in lay attitude toward monks. Specifically, a land records officer said that "bad" monks taking refuge in the Sangha after some misdeed bought or arranged to have bought for them property they then held as *poggalika*. Perhaps more importantly, other informants noted that people needed more and more to pick out a good monk and to endow him with goods of his own that no bad monk could take from him. Another informant, discussing the "decline of the Sangha" said simply, "People do not know right from wrong any more. Monasteries are no longer run on proper Vinaya lines and the lay officers [*kappiya*][18] attached to them do not know what to do."

While the role of the original donor, once a monk dies, is not clearly delineated in available legal sources, and while most informants held that donors could not interfere once the gift was made (an "ideal" picture like many others, perhaps), I interviewed one highly respected lay steward (*kappiya*) in Kemmendine, Rangoon, who held that donors

17. An estimate obtained from the Settlement Office, Mandalay, in August 1959 suggested that Mandalay, Sagaing, Kyaukse, and Meiktila districts had at least one monastery in every village, and that 50–60 percent of the villages had two.

18. *Kappiya karaka* (P): lay attendant of a monk, one who traditionally acts as steward and transacts monastic business for the monks to prevent them from Vinaya violations.

could, if still alive and if there were no clear successor, ask a monk from the outside to take over. A case might arise, for instance, in which a famous teaching monk, in a monastery with a floating population of students, might not have around him a suitable successor. If there were no successor forthcoming at all, my informant suggested, the donor could sell the land. The more *sanghika*-like this land had been, however, the more difficult it would be to sell it to Buddhists, though, of course, Muslims or other non-Buddhists might buy it. The apparent unorthodoxy of this—*sanghika* land, officially, can never be alienated—coming from such a pious and informed man suggests the extent to which the real picture, in towns especially, might differ from the ideal.

Little information is available on the extent to which monasteries in Burma today possess agricultural land worked for them by villagers, either collectively or in restricted groups of families or trustees. As noted previously, in royal Burma, the large monasteries often had such land, but the more the Sangha follows Vinaya, the less likely it is to have land, and vice-versa. The relation of monastery size to settlement size and proximity to a settlement probably are additional factors. Obviously, the average small village monastery, containing one or a few monks directly dependent on the village, will not need such lands, whereas a large "forest" monastery may require them in one form or another. Certainly, some monasteries are known to possess such real estate. One Rangoon informant, discussing his monastic education in an untypically large (population five hundred) village in Singu township, Mandalay District, where there were nine monasteries in all, told us that his monastery had two hundred acres of land growing tobacco, rice, and vegetables, worked by villagers under a lay steward appointed by the *sayadaw,* who looked after the sale of surplus goods for the monastery's profit. The informant added that when the great wooden gong was struck all able bodied men and women had to repair to the monastery and do whatever work was to be done, in teams. A forest-dwelling *sayadaw* had criticized the *sayadaw*s in the informant's village for being princes rather than monks but, despite their respect for the critical *sayadaw,* the village monks had not changed their ways. I was repeatedly told of such occurrences in the Shan States, and the size of some of the monasteries in Pindaya, for example, suggests that they may have owned agricultural lands. Apparently Buddhist law still holds that nothing prevents a monk from receiving paddy lands, though this is somewhat dubious from the Vinaya point of view and tends to occur as *poggalika* rather than *sanghika*.[19]

In August 1959 the Settlement Office, Mandalay, reported that some rich men evaded the Land Nationalization Act by making gifts to monks, leading to a slight increase in monastic lands. In these cases, monks were said to have hired laborers to produce a crop for the upkeep of the monastery, but was felt that the usual tithes were not likely to be paid to the donor in such cases. A lay informant who had been a pagoda trustee in Rangoon stated categorically that large monasteries in the city did not own land outside it, nor indeed did most of the monasteries he dealt with. On the other hand, several pagodas outside Rangoon did have land lying fallow in the mid-1930s; this land was not cultivated then or at any later date he knew of, but the possibility of acquiring such land through the good offices of a local monk could not be excluded. He also stated that the decline of faith and the growth of poverty could be held responsible for the failure of present-day communities to look after pagoda land. In Pagan, I was told that only the Ananda temple had land in quantity: much of it, looked after by trustees, was used to provide big spreads for the pagoda festival. The large Pagan pagodas (the Ananda, Shwegugyi, Gawdawpalin, and Shwezigon) are cared for by trustees at Pagan and thus can be said to be still "alive," not just monuments to past devotion.

Another factor leading to monastic involvement with land lies in the special nature of the university or teaching monasteries (*taik*s). Examination candidates at such institutions are often spared by the head monk the duty of doing daily rounds for food in their villages or towns. Thus the lay supporters (*taga*s) of the university monasteries may well be tempted to invest in land in order to provide food for those candidates. The history of the Shwehintha Monastery is informative here. An undated reference in its written history refers to the purchase by its lay association of "thirteen acres of paddy land on behalf of the *sayadaw*s. The villagers of Lepanchaung, out of a pure desire to do charity and obtain merit, had the whole plot ploughed and sown in a day, the crop reaped and winnowed in another, and the harvest stowed in a barn on a third."[20] The history also reports that admissions to the monastery were

19. May Oung 1914:195–196; Lahiri 1951:339; Dunkley 1928:164; and 1941:106.

20. Panditta 1955:18. The monastery itself stood on 22.75 acres and "from a distance looks like woodland, drawing toward it the hearts of men."

very severely controlled, partly because of the pride it took in its achievements and standards, but partly also because food had to be found for its Pali students.[21] The constitution of the lay association for the upkeep of the monastery mentions two kinds of gifts to the monastery: (1) gifts made for a set purpose, and (2) gifts made to earn interest: in this latter case money obtained from loans could be used to invest in land and immovables on behalf of the monks, and mortgages could be arranged.[22] All of this, notably, is in lay hands, although in such situations there can be a tug of war between monkish qualms regarding Vinaya restrictions on property and the laymen's desire to support the monastery generously.

This brief review of the property customs and laws involving the Sangha should make clear the care with which the Burmese have tried to preserve the ideals of the Vinaya and yet deal directly with the realities of human nature. The whole subject of the tension between monastic donations by the faithful laity and Vinaya restrictions on same is an interesting sociological aspect of the Sangha's presence in the country that needs much more study.

The Lay Steward as Insulator

Law, of course, is not the only means that the Burmese have used to keep the Vinaya alive. Historically, another mediating force between the monks and the lay supporters (*taga*s) has always been the monastery's lay steward, or *kappiya,* but in recent times these men have had to face the trying conditions that confront the *sayadaw* of any urban monastic compound: the difficulty of keeping up large establishments in modern conditions, the shortage of land in towns, the temptation to let relatives live in the monastery compound so that they may provide services in an otherwise indifferent city environment, and so forth. The highly respected lay steward from Kemmendine mentioned above emphasized the great care necessary to run a monastery at all "in these days." In terms of property, though a new builder must still get permission from an original donor to add to an existing establishment, the care of buildings by generation after generation of one family has by and large broken down. The patron, or *dayaka,* should go on looking after the buildings, but in the bustle of modern life many are content to give to

21. Panditta 1955:101.
22. Panditta 1955:200–206; 20.

the monk and forget. Thus the lay steward inherits the patron's worries, and stewards today are difficult to get. Monks are consequently tempted to do their business themselves and may tumble to the advantages of owning *poggalika* land. Paradoxically, even a very pious layman might not help, for once a gift has been made to the Sangha, the merit is won, and if a bad monk mismanages the gift, that is no concern of the giver.

The financial records of the Kemmendine monastery in which the lay steward worked illustrate the complexities involved. The cost of building, maintaining, and running a monastery in urban conditions and in an environment which is not homogeneously devoted to that one institution can be considerable. This small monastery had been a cooperative venture. The plot of about one acre had been garden land belonging to a layman who paid some seven rupees a year to the Rangoon Development Trust. The lay steward had had to approach the Ministry of Religious Affairs in order to get the land declared religious land, when the Development Trust had failed to act. The land is *sanghika* but is recorded in the presiding monk's name. The ordination site, or *sima,* is in his name also. The land was donated around 1946. The lay steward himself gave the first building, a dining hall, in 1950, at the cost of 5,000 *kyat*s.[23] The second building (4,000 *kyat*s), in which the monk lived, and and another building, the fifth (2,500 *kyat*s), were given by the monk's niece. The third building (15,000 *kyat*s) had been given by a famous politician, and the fourth (25,000 *kyat*s) by a lawyer. A rich merchant had built a small building for a particular monk (600 *kyat*s); a number of cubicles had been erected by various persons at 1,000 *kyat*s each. The wall, at 150 *kyat*s a section, represented many small donations, but virtually the whole back part had been paid for by the monk's brother. The informant estimated that in British times the monastery would have cost, in toto, around 20,000 *kyat*s; it had actually cost 80,000; by 1960, the cost would probably be more than double that.

The monastery cost some 70–80 *kyat*s a month to run, including 20 *kyat*s for a cook, employed by the lay steward, who acted as substeward. In addition 10 *kyat*s a month was paid for electricity. Coolies were occasionally engaged to keep the garden tidy. An average of 100 *kyat*s a year went into repairs. Total costs ran thus to something like 1,200

23. A Burmese *kyat* is worth about 20 cents in United States currency (as of 1975).

kyats per annum. The lay steward sent his boys[24] to about one hundred persons scattered all over Rangoon who called the monk "their" *sayadaw* and who occasionally kept the sabbath together at the monastery. Collections took place once a month, with receipts and accounting. Owing to Vinaya prohibitions about storing food, the lay steward had to see that stores in his house were very carefully kept, since certain products might become scarce now and then. The role of the cook as sub-steward simplified this a little in that food could be stored by him provided that the monk had not touched it with his hands.[25] The monks usually had boys with them in the morning carrying biscuit tins or other storage containers in which anything other than curry and rice could be kept for a little while.

The lay steward stressed that relatively few monasteries are run like this today. In the old days stewards had been *luthudaws*, that is, men wearing white robes and living with the monks, acting without pay or reward. Today ideas have changed, he said: people think it is a disgrace to retire to a monastery in their old age, and stewards, like the cook at the monastery, virtually have to be paid servants. As for boys, they are very hard to find since so few go to monastic schools nowadays. Monks often have to pick them from among relatives and almost bribe them with an education, clothes, pocket money, and so on. Or they can try to get an orphan or a pauper. The many squatters found in city monasteries since the war and insurrection may have been a godsend to some monks.[26]

Nothing seems to prevent a very orthodox monk from looking after accounts. A monk-scholar I met supervised building and well-digging,

24. They are young boys who live at the monastery with free room and board, in return for which they perform tasks of many sorts for the monks, including manual labor, shopping, cooking, and so forth. Most go to school at the monastery or nearby. J. F.

25. The *kappiya* was being even stricter than Vinaya required in this respect.

26. One boy at the monastery discussed here was born of a Buddhist father and a Muslim mother. To save him from the latter's family, he was sent to live with nuns in a monastery. The monk from this monastery taught him and did not wish him to go to a lay school. It is obviously a very difficult situation, since the layman may have doubts as to whether a monk is asking for him for his salvation's sake or because he needs a layman in order to remain a monk. A rather dubious Shan monk in Rangoon had rich Chinese lay supporters and never had to go out for food. A cook took care of whole meals brought in cooked, or large bags of rice, each big enough for a month. Money had to be presented formally to the monk, but "it was not given to servants, for fear of stealing: the *sayadaw* chanted over it when he used some to clear the debt."

looked through bills, and checked cheating—no doubt in his scholarly role as much as in his religious role. He is also said to have owned *poggalika* property in other parts of town. But his attention to the lay steward's procedures was scrupulous. Many other monks, however, were seen receiving money and other gifts. Some have accepted the notion that "modern" living does not allow them to do otherwise.

Monks and Kinship Networks

Another related matter which requires very thorough investigation in Southeast Asian social contexts, mostly above the village level, is relations between monks and their kin, for, despite the ruling that monk and family are dead to each other in matters of ownership, property, and the like, many monks still appear to maintain good relations with their families, much as a parish priest might among ourselves. Here there are two principal questions: to what extent does family allegiance to particular monasteries encourage children to go on following the same *sayadaw,* and to what extent do monks lean on their kinsmen for sponsorship and general support? We will consider the latter question here.

The village situation is virtually unknown since, although parents are as likely as not to look after their children during a novice's passage through a monastery and to look after their ordination as monks should they wish to have a career in the Sangha, most monks apparently do not "practice" in their village of origin. Kinship may nonetheless play a role in calling them to a particular village; there is evidence that in particular local districts, in Upper Burma for instance, around Mandalay, Kyaukse, and Sagaing, it may play a greater role than is commonly suspected.

In my wanderings around the monasteries I saw many cases of kinship influences. At the monk-scholar's establishment discussed above, two of five main buildings were built by the monk's elder brother and his niece. Another not untypical case involved a monk whose grandmother had built a monastery for him, within the larger compound or *taik,* after he had been in the Order for five years. He had since done thirty-five more years and was fed every day by a niece living nearby. One monk with whom I visited a great deal in Rangoon had an extended kinship network in the city and enjoyed visiting his relatives. He was fed regularly by one lay donor who lived near his monastery; however, he had breakfast twice a week with a niece of his, married to a member of Parliament and living with three children in a suburb near the Kaba Aye Pagoda.

Relations were informal, but the whole family formally bowed (made a *shiko*) to the monk on his arrival and departure. He also visited a sister's husband who had been a member of the upper house in British time; a younger brother at Monkey Point Road, with three sons and daughters, whose father-in-law had become a monk in 1948 at the age of seventy; some cousins living in a three-generation household near the Shwedagon Pagoda, as well as some lifelong friends whom the monk had first taken on a pilgrimage in India some years before.

The same monk gave us some information on a rather dramatic case of family cooperation. A certain monastery founded in 1922 in Rangoon had had as its *sayadaw* an Upper Burman from Sagaing District, born around 1880. The monastery was now run by a body of seven monks, all sons of the *sayadaw*'s brothers and sisters: "grandnephews who were poor in Upper Burma and on whom the *sayadaw* took pity so that he gave them the monastery." Our monk, who found it awkward to comment on this, claimed that the place was *sanghika* and thus "democratic," but ultimately he admitted that the seven grandnephews, aged 25 through 39, had the last word. The monastery had at the time 68 monks and 16 novices. I found no other case as marked as this, but extensive research into these questions is obviously needed.

The question of "squatters" on monastery lands which exercised the Ministry of Religious Affairs in 1958 and 1959 may be partly linked to the question of kinship. I found at least one monastery in which "impoverished" relatives of the first *sayadaw* resided on the premises. A number of monks spoke of laymen living on the lands they had donated, and some of these seemed to be kin. One reason why the question was hard to discuss is that such people found it easy to evade taxation. While I was in Burma the Ministry of Religious Affairs was instructing deputy commissioners to clear such squatters in the districts. The problem was undoubtedly related to war refugees and was aggravated by the monks' need for lay stewards and supporters. This was commented on when controversy broke out at the large Thayettaw Monastery (*taik*) in Rangoon, where two thousand families were supposed to have set up living quarters. One party of monks apparently called in the officials; another party later asked them to rescind their orders.[27] The intentions

27. *The Nation,* Jan. 10, 15, 1959.

of the ministry, announced in July 1959, are part of the general registration problem which will be discussed in Chapter 6. The monasteries and shrines were to provide lists of names of present donors and benefactors, as well as descriptions of the nature of funds obtained for upkeep (private or public), with names of fund raisers and of "all members of the religious communities under their charge." Much of this data collection was rationalized by the claim that the ministry could not otherwise reply to foreigners who inquired about noteworthy shrines in Burma.[28] Such governmental concerns can be seen as part of a continuing process in Burma in which both the private laity and the government engage in a constant dialogue over the real sociological dimensions of the ideal Sangha.

Food and Modern Lay Donors

The heart of the laity's support of the Sangha is undoubtedly the donation of food (*hsoon*) within the framework of the Vinaya's ancient patterns. Here we can realize the essence of the lay supporter's (*taga* and *tagama*) role. In this usually daily interchange, both laymen and monks test, in a sense, the operation of the Vinaya in this critical area of Sangha support.[29] The complexity of the Vinaya is such that a complete knowledge of it in addition to a reasonably lengthy period in the monkhood itself, or at least in residence at a monastery, would be necessary in order to assess how carefully the Vinaya is observed in Burma. By and large, since expert knowledge of the whole Vinaya is a specialty among monks themselves, a reasonable knowledge of the 227 rules of behavior set out in the *Sutta Vibhanga* section of the Vinaya, or more conveniently in the *Patimokkha,* is the most we can expect. In regard to a number of these rules, even though no detailed study of the matter was intended or carried out, I observed some laxity.

One rule frequently broken was the injunction forbidding monks to eat or partake of "solid food or soft food that was stored."[30] Similarly, I found variations in the rules discouraging monks from selecting certain households on alms tours or picking and choosing among foods,[31] thus

28. Ibid., July 24, 1959.
29. The great bulk of the food eaten by monks should be obtained on food-collecting rounds from neighborhood households.
30. For the Vinaya rules, see Horner 1938–1952, 2:339.
31. For the Vinaya rules, see Horner 1938–1952, 2:317, 3:129.

depriving some of the laity of their merit-making potential.[32] In a like manner, rules are infringed every day regarding the unmonkly behavior of indicating to lay donors the kind of goods and services that are required instead of letting gifts come unsolicited.

The importance of food in the monk's life has been commented on pithily by the English translator of the Vinaya: "The rules on eating are important for monks, for taking nothing but food given in alms involved a threefold maintenance of correct attitude: towards the laity, towards members of other sects, and towards fellow-monks. . . . It might indeed be said that monk's attitude towards eating and robes epitomizes his whole attitude towards the society of the day."[33] A rather untypical young monk with scholarly leanings, an interest in medicine, and various personal problems related to his fitness for his vocation gave me one of the best pictures of a monk's point of view, a valuable testimony insofar as we rarely have anything but the orthodox textual statement of what a monk should feel about walking for alms food:

It can become very burdensome in a town because of the long distances and the transport difficulties. People are always inviting me to sit down and while away the time with them. They tell you all their stories and all their problems—I'm sorry I don't know more about your work because I could probably help you. They don't like it if you miss them for a day so that it is better not to start unless you want to be a regular. Look, so and so has just come in with a full bowl and is going out again. . . .

Yes, it does happen that people refuse. You just stand in front of the door with your eyes down and go away after a moment if nothing happens. . . .

I usually visit about twenty houses of a morning, but as often as possible I get food from a *taga* because I do not really like going out. They help me in this monastery as I am studying. For instance I read until very late at night, so I could get up at 8 a.m. instead of 5 if I wanted to. They also allow me to eat with a spoon, but of course if I'm out, I have to eat with my hands. I have had trouble in the past with indiscriminate eating of curries—too much acid—but this is getting better. [Transcription from field notes.]

I examined the alms food collected by two monks and a novice one morning; it consisted of three large bowls full of rice and forty-two

32. For a full discussion of the importance of merit in Burmese Buddhism, see Spiro 1970:92–113.
33. Horner 1938, 2:xxx.

smaller silver containers with a large variety of dishes. The novice, my informant, sorted and apportioned the latter on two separate tables: one for the head monk and the other monk, and one for himself. The monk, washing up the silver after the meal, commented, "The waste involved in this food business is deplorable. The surplus is usually given to poor people, but this is a poor part of town anyway!" A confidential and therefore anonymous American report by a sociologist—unusually reliable considering that it was based on only two months' study—states, "The food, once back at the monastery, all mixed up together in the black pottery bowl that is so vital a part of monkish equipment, is simply thrown aside or fed to the dogs; the monks themselves do not eat it." This kind of statement was heard on other occasions, and I can only state that it is completely contradicted by most of my information: the monks *do* eat the food!

A monk may well equate the amount of food (or other gifts) he receives with the amount of power he has over his donor, as is clear from a remark made by one of my most valuable informants, a great legal expert and retired civil servant. Commenting on the fact that monks of the Dwaya sect still refused to eat with other sects, though less consistently than they had done in the past, and that Shwegyin sect had now virtually given up endogastronomy, this gentleman pointed out that the Nyaungyan Sayadaw, head of the Thudhamma monks and president of the Sixth Council, had once offered a 160-dish meal to a Dwaya monk at the height of a controversy which kept Dwaya monks from participating in the Sangayana.[34] The informant added, "It was to show his power." On another occasion I attended a ritual feeding of monks (*hsoon*) given by a person who had lost his father. The friendly presiding monk's first remarks upon noticing my presence included a joking question to the host as to when *I* would be feeding them.

How much the Burmese spend on food for religious purposes is difficult to determine because of the great variety of occasions on which it is given, the variations in household wealth, and differences between village and urban patterns. The most common donation of food, of course, is to monks making their daily alms rounds. An analysis of a 1958 unpublished survey[35] of five hundred different Rangoon households

34. Sangayana: The Sixth Buddhist Council so much promoted by U Nu. It will be discussed in detail in Chapter 5. The meal has a potlatch aspect.
35. Mimeographed, Central Statistical and Economics Department of the Min-

indicates that the feeding of rice and or curry to monks on their rounds and the giving of tins of rice to nuns accounted for only 1.2 percent of the total household food budget. Probably not included in such figures are such events as family death ceremonies or housewarmings, when a number of monks are invited to the home and fed with special honor. Monks are also fed at *shinbyu* rituals, when novices are taken into the Sangha and often concurrently girls' ears are bored. The same is true on other religious occasions such as *katthein,* or robe donation rituals. At such events many lay guests are usually also fed by the family, as a kind of residual merit-acquisition value is associated with feeding any-one. Also food presented at the Buddha altar (*hsoondawgyi*) at such times may later be eaten by the poor or distributed to animals. There are thus many ways in which a household gives food for religious purposes.

Obviously the more wealthy the family, the more it can give, as Nash (1965:33–43) pointed out for village life.[36] I would also agree with Pfanner and Ingersoll (1962) that the major burden of supporting the monks is borne by the wealthier households. Furthermore, sharing food with friends and relatives, which can also be socially prestigious, is often found to cost more than gifts to monks. For example, I attended a monthly meeting of a Government Pensioners' Buddhist Association at Rangoon for which 320 *kyat*s had been collected by its members by subscription, but only 20 *kyat*s went to the monk who preached (at considerable length); 25 *kyat*s went for two other smaller meetings and 275 *kyat*s went for breakfasting the one hundred or so members, paying the cook, and so on. The ideal picture of support of the religion is phrased by Kell (1959:137–138): "The general opinion is that one should use one-third of one's income." Even if one were to meet such a goal, however, it is still uncertain how much support would actually reach the monks themselves.

Variations in the methods of support can also be seen in urban pat-terns. Food, as noted by Kell (1959:138), can be handled in the cities by any of the following procedures: calling at houses by arrangement between *sayadaw* and householder; forming street associations with rotation systems; collecting at food markets in towns and surrounding restaurants; taking potluck in streets where the monk is unknown; or

---

istry of National Planning, Rangoon, 1958. The report, but not the figures, ap-peared in *The Nation,* Jan. 10, 1958.

36. Cf. Spiro 1970:453–468.

sending food to the monastery for old or honored monks.[37] While attending a pagoda festival at Paungde, I found that the people had an unusual feeding arrangement during Lent. On each of the 120 days of Lent, one household was found to feed all the three hundred-odd monks. of the town for one day. Tiffin carriers for curry were sent the night before; and then between 4:30 and 6:00 the next morning the monks arrived to collect rice. The cost was supposed to vary between 350 and 600 *kyats*. Such inventiveness is often at the mercy of circumstances, however. The army regime's clean-up of Rangoon streets in the late fifties did away with many little *zayats* (rest houses) in which laymen had fed monks their first meal of the day. Commenting on this, a layman said that the monks had adapted to getting a first, very early meal in this way, thus reserving the discomfort of house-to-house collection for the second and last meal. He predicted that monasteries without resident cooks would in future hire them for the first meal. A university professor commented that lazy Rangoonites preferred to serve the second meal at 10:00 A.M. rather than stay up all night cooking! Of course, major factors in much urban religious support of the Sangha are the earnest efforts of lay Buddhist associations, a topic discussed in more detail later in relation to the "Revival" period of the late fifties. There are thus a number of ways in which the donor-recipient pattern so basic to food distribution can be modified and expanded beyond the archetypal village pattern anticipated in the Vinaya.

The "Decline of the Sangha" Issue

In addition to stresses caused by property, recruitment, and food, a number of other tensions result when the modern monk faces social change with his classical Vinaya viewpoints—an issue of grave concern to the Sangha, the laity, and foreign observers alike in terms of the "decline of the Sangha" issue.[38] During my stay in Burma in 1958–1959,

37. F. K. Lehman (personal communication, 1973) writes as follows: "There is yet another system in Upper Burmese and Shan villages, whereby various households in no especial order bring food offerings to the kyaung each morning. This works better during the season when many village youths are temporarily in orders, which is also usually the slack season in agriculture. It also works more generally only where the *kyaung* normally has very few permanent monks or novices. It is also better served on duty days. In many such villages no monk ever walks his rounds."

38. Beginning with the nineteenth-century rebellions led by monks and

I made careful notation of news regarding monks in both the English-
and Burmese-language press reports; significantly, there were very few
cases of monk misbehavior noted in the Burmese press but quite a few
examples in English sources such as *The Nation*. Undoubtedly some
Burmese feel that the English-language press, much of it controlled by
non-Buddhists, is eager to pick up the unsavory detail, true or false.
Since it is extremely difficult to tell real from false monks in an organization like the Sangha, and since many of the crimes and misdeeds recorded could be ascribed to false monks, one can not use them to prove
any thesis regarding the alleged decline in Sangha discipline. Cases of
intra- and intermonastery fighting are, of course, of a more serious
nature; it should perhaps be remembered, however, that warrior-monks
have frequently appeared in Buddhism, as in Japan and Tibet, without a
decline necessarily being hypothesized. Factionalism among monks
can be vicious anywhere. Burmese monks are not men in the abstract—
though they are often written about as if they were—but Burmese men,
members of a culture which historically has always included a strong
component of violence. It would be strange indeed if all the violence
were to be found on the side of the laity and none on that of the monks,
even though psychologists argue that the monk's role may well be one
to which those Burmese most anxious to escape violence naturally turn
for salvation.[39]

I witnessed no monkly violence myself, so that the reports of others
must be invoked exclusively here. A fairly wide variety of trespass cases
have been reported, but the following two examples will suffice as
illustrative of one type of problem.[40]

In July 1958, a monastery in Bahan, Rangoon, split into two parties.
Each tried to oust the other, and the police had to guard the monastery

---

ex-monks, many observers of Burma, including many Burmese themselves, saw the
Sangha seriously declining as an ideal, with a secularization and corruption of its
way of life producing the degree of political involvement and laxness in behavior
that was seen as characteristic of the Sangha in the post-independence period. J. F.

39. Spiro (1967, 1970) has dealt with this range of problems.

40. Other examples include the full battle between the pro-Sangha Parliament
monks of the Mingalarama Taik and their opponents at the Pyinnyaramikamaha
Taik in Rangoon, when police had to use tear gas to restore order (*The Nation*,
Mar. 1, 19, 20, 1959; *New Times of Burma*, Mar. 19, 1959, Apr. 27, 1959);
and the 1954 killings at the Thadu Taik (see Smith 1965:206–207; *The Guardian*,
June 14, 1958; *The Nation*, Jan. 17, 1959).

until calm was reinstated. One paper reports that the abbot had asked the civil authorities to oust the rival; another paper states that the rival had asked the same.[41] The second incident occurred earlier in the same month. Two monks residing in a Rangoon monastery, having built up followings among the laity in their different monasteries, came into open conflict. The abbot tried to get an eviction order from a civil court, and his rival was told to leave, with twenty followers. On appeal, the later was given a while to shift. During that time the abbot felled a tree on his rival's side of the compound. Enraged, the rival wished to fight. One of his supporters rushed to the headquarters of a political party opposite the monastery and phoned the police. The abbot assured the police that no fighting would take place and the police retired.[42]

I also kept watch on reports of monks involved in individual crimes of various sorts, such as stealing or confidence tricks, problems with women, and violence to self or others. Two cases were reported of monks arrested for traffic in opium,[43] two involving theft and refuge in the Sangha after misappropriation of large sums,[44] one kidnapping,[45] a case of two monks in a pilgrimage racket designed to smuggle goods and foreign exchange to India,[46] a report of a monk accused of carrying medical supplies to insurgents,[47] and one example of a monk confidence man who tricked a school mistress out of a valuable ring on the pretext of chanting mantras over it to increase her holdings and wealth.[48]

There were accounts of three monks involved in clandestine affairs with women, one resulting in a paternity charge, another culminating in a mortal assault on a boy and his companion who had gossiped about an older monk's affair with a young girl, and a third involving a trishawman's wife and a monk.[49] For "embracing and kissing in a railway carriage" a monk and a girl were imprisoned for three months, an

---

41. *The Nation,* July 24, 1958, and *Bama Khit,* July 27, 1958, respectively. It is not impossible that political factionalism may be at work both in the quarrel and in the reporting.

42. *The Nation,* July 9, 1958.

43. *The Burman,* Jan. 28, 1958, Sept. 28, 1959.

44. Ibid., Nov. 28, 1958, and *The Nation,* Sept. 21, 1959.

45. *The Nation,* Jan. 9, 1959.

46. *The Guardian,* Jan. 27, 1959.

47. *New Times of Burma,* Jan. 11, 1959.

48. Ibid., June 28, 1959.

49. *The Nation,* July 17, 1959, Oct. 28, 1959, and Oct. 14, 1958, respectively.

appeal being denied on the grounds that obscene acts in public places were too frequent and that an example had to be made.[50] Finally, I read of a monk who wounded his own abbot because the abbot had threatened him in order to gain the monk's sister in marriage.[51]

Violence between monks was also reported on occasion. Three cases were noted of monks or novices attacking others in the monastery, often with apparently minor provocation: one from school ragging, one from a quarrel over possession of a book, and another from a derogatory note found during a Pali exam.[52] An equal number of incidents of violence led to the death of someone in the monastery; in one incident, a novice, lightly reprimanded by the presiding monk, killed him with a dagger; in another, a monk was discovered dying in a pool of blood, and a missing colleague was sought; in a third, an abbot who had spent twenty-eight years in the Sangha turned himself in to a village headman after running amok in his monastery and killing one monk and badly wounding a companion, both of whom he had invited to his monastery to spend the rainy season.[53] In addition, two cases of suicide were reported, one due to mental torment and conflict, another concerning a seventy-six-year-old *sayadaw* who thought it was time for him to leave the world, and an account was given of a monk hospitalized with acute stomach pains seemingly related to his agonies over his five children, whom he had left to join the Order.[54] These data of course require much more careful analysis in terms of individual psychology, and particularly in terms of the violence component, which some observers have seen as typical of the Burmese.[55]

As noted above, it is questionable whether these difficulties relate to the alleged "decline of the Sangha" or instead represent merely the human weakenesses and failures that are part of any ideal scheme. All are clear violations of Vinaya in the eyes of most observers, but all issues involving the Sangha are not so. A particularly interesting case in terms of its modernization dimensions is that of the bus disputes.

50. Ibid., June 30, 1959.
51. *The Burman*, June 8, 1958, and *The Nation*, June 11, 1958.
52. *The Nation*, Oct. 23, 1958, Sept. 24, 1958, and Apr. 5, 1959, respectively.
53. *The Burman*, Nov. 9, 1958; *The Nation*. Oct. 14, 1958; and *The Nation*, July 26, 1959.
54. *The Nation*, Aug. 13, 1958, Sept. 14, 1959; and Sept. 18, 1959, respectively.
55. See, for instance, Hitson and Funkenstein 1959 and Sein Tu 1964.

On August 6, 1958, a monk hit a girl conductor with his slipper for having asked him for a fare and beat her again when she asked him a second time. The incident was widely reported and prompted a number of editorials.[56] One paper took the line that such behavior was unmonkly in a socialist society and in a modern context where gentlemen did not slipper ladies.[57] Another paper, however, pointed out that monks were not supposed to carry money and that, since most bus owners were devout Buddhists, they should view free passage as a form of alms to the Sangha, especially as city life virtually required that monks travel on buses to collect their food.[58]

A young urban monk's comments on the money issue from my field notes may be instructive: "Yes I do get money of my own. You cannot get on in a town without it. You cannot even get into a bus without it. But then some bus conductors don't take money from monks and sometimes people in a bus might spontaneously offer to pay for me." The basic quarrel apparently arose because of differences among bus companies, some being permissive, others not. Some were prepared to seat two monks in front but not more, and some companies were happy to give free passage for food collectors but demanded payment by monks on personal travels. It was found, during discussions with an activist monastic group known as the Sangha Party, that some drivers would pull up ahead of bus stops or beyond them in order to keep monks from boarding the bus.[59] The points involved here are (1) the difficulty of adapting traditional relations between monk and lay donors to an urban situation involving unusual distance and the need for transport; (2) the reluctance of Buddhist laymen to modify a system of offerings in a way which would oblige them to lose fares on buses from paying passengers; (3) the uncertainty involved in the lack of any courageous, clear-cut decision, to the detriment of monk-laity relations. Such was the need for clarity that the Sangha Party, perhaps only temporarily, advised all monks to pay fares. As usual, the key problem is the nature of the monk's relationship with the laity in a period of rapid modernization.

56. See *The Nation, The Guardian,* and *The Burman,* all on Sept. 7, 1958.

57. *The Nation,* Sept. 8, 1958. The conventional paean to the "holy" ideal monk of olden times is then repeated.

58. *The Burman,* Sept. 8, 1958.

59. Ibid., Aug. 8 and Sept. 18, 1958. See also a letter from the "Student-Sangha" in *New Light of Burma* (in Burmese), Sept. 26, 1958.

Charismatic Monks and Their Followers

The constant need for lay support persuades some monks to enter into activities that involve non-Vinaya behavior with popular appeal, such as making special charms. It is difficult to estimate how many monks acquire lay supporters through curative and even magic powers: that these procedures exist we know, but the matter is extremely complex and involves the study of messianic Buddhism, which I have dealt with elsewhere.[60] A civil surgeon with whom I discussed the matter on a medical basis told me he was impressed with the small number of monks who cure nowadays, but that when they do cure it is certainly to acquire prestige and supporters. Injections, thought to be cure-alls since the first antiplague shots around 1900, were the greatest danger. He knew at least one monk who consulted him if the case seemed difficult. Certain curing monks, such as the Sewungaba Sayadaw, were much talked of in Burma and were constantly touring the country selling their wares and building monasteries with the proceeds. This kind of activity is probably tied, however, to what I have termed *gaing*s, that is, group-ings of laymen and some monks centering around charismatic figures who are reputed to possess great powers in such areas as alchemy, meditation, medicine, astrology, and other esoteric arts and skills. These *gaing*s are often incipient sects in that they acquire a strong Buddhist ideology as they develop, no matter how unorthodox their origins and beginnings may have been. One alchemist monk recognized that alchemy attracted rich people and that alchemist monks might therefore be well off. He added that alchemy was a return to the lay supporter of his kindness and that monks had a duty to protect and lengthen the lives of benefactors.[61] Among famous *gaing sayadaw*s who were widely respected in Burma while I was there, the following may be mentioned: the Yok Gan Sayadaw, a teacher of the director of the Institute of Advanced Buddhistic Studies; the Webu Sayadaw, thought by many to be a *arahant* (one who will not have to be reborn) and said to walk above the ground; the Yakyaw Sayadaw, master of many army officers and of politicans as important as U Kyaw Nyein; the Man Aung Kyaung

60. Mendelson 1961a, b; 1963b, c. See Spiro 1970:186–187 for a view of messianic *gaing*s which differs from mine.

61. At the same time, a *monk* alchemist would be careful to say that no profit must be made out of alchemy: any profits should be used to buy more materials.

Sayadaw U Nandiya of Mandalay; U Nyanika and the Patheitawa Sayadaw of Shwebo; U Wilatha of Setkya Monastery on Sagaing Hill, patronized by some Ministry of Religious Affairs officers in Mandalay; the
Ngwejantha Sayadaw of Moulmein, a famous *se-weikza* or medicine
master whose body disappeared at his death, though his robe "remained
propped up as if by two knees"; U Ohn Gain and U Eindacarya,
alchemy masters; and the famous and controversial meditation-master
the Sunlun Sayadaw, held by some to have become an *arahant* on
visiting the Webu Sayadaw. Many monks familiar to us from the political
records are claimed by some to have been *gaing* adepts: the Shwepyigyi
Sayadaw, U Kalyana, who is said to have worked out a charm for U Ba
Maw to bring him back into power after his exile by U Saw; the great
Bagaya Sayadaw, a famous wrestler in his youth who had attained
invulnerability; and the Mohnyin Sayadaw, whose astounding pagoda
and meditation center outside Monywa (with its multitude of messianic
features) may have cost him the favor of the Buddha Sasana Council
(see Chapter 5), are among them. Many monks were and are against
these *gaing* involvements and are extremely reluctant to discuss them;
some even asked that they not be written about at all. On the other
hand, the famous preacher, the Ledi Sayadaw, appears to have wished to
conciliate all parties and to show, using various lesser-known Pali texts,
that *weikza* powers were no different from those one could obtain
within strict Theravada.[62] Finally, we should note that a number of
*gaing*s are said to have been founded by monks.

Most monks, however, do not obtain supporters in this manner. More
important in the usual situation is the personal factor. The impression a
particular monk makes on a layman met more or less by chance is
generally acknowledged to be of great importance in Burma, and, as can
be noted in the evolution of sects, a rich layman's encounter with the
monk in question almost always marks the turning point when a personal *gaing* following becomes organized into a sect. The layman estab-
lishes the monk in a monastery, just as the king used to "make" monks
in this manner by calling them to the capital and establishing them

---

62. Ledi Sayadaw (1955). These very complex matters must be left for study
elsewhere, but basically a "purification" system is at work here where by *gaing*
*weikza*s are fitted into a scheme below the *ariya-weikza* of Theravada (that is,
powers acquired by meditation as a monk). It should be stressed that, from within
a *gaing* perspective, many monks are claimed to belong to the system who would
not necessarily make such claims themselves.

there. In royal times we noted conflicts of conscience balancing off court and prestige against forest and the stricter religious life. A layman has to be very sophisticated indeed to establish monks "in the forest" since this causes him inconvenience in providing the necessary support. Nevertheless a number of my informants, especially those laymen interested in meditation, "followed" *sayadaws* in distant and sometimes inaccessible centers they had helped to set up.

It is even harder for a nun, or *methila,* to inspire a layman to become a lay supporter, but such cases occasionally arise. The following one illustrates another selection principle: kinship and friendship. The speaker is a retired Mandalay official who traveled with me to Monywa:

Most nuns become so out of disappointment in love or poverty but that is not always the case. This person who has just helped us here in Monywa is the daughter of a rich merchant of Homalin. He was Chinese, her mother Burmese. Her father opposed her entry; she had to escape from home. She joined at twenty-eight and has now been in six years. She is above *dhammacariya*[63] rank and gets 800 *kyat*s from the government and rice from scholarship associations. Students live with her.

My wife does not take to nuns usually but there is something special about this one and she wants me to build her a *kyaung* [monastery] on a plot of land we have in Sagaing. This is now under dispute.[64] For the moment she does not want to come where there are such bad monks. An old blind woman has offered to retire from her house and leave her that. And yet again some rich rice millers we met are ready to build her a *kyaung* for forty persons any time she wants it. We met her because she was a pupil of my cousin, who is a nun in the Mohnyin Sayadaw's pagoda's nunnery.

Of course, there can be extremes on either side of the monk-laity relationship. While some *taga*s have great power over the monks they support, we noted cases where the monks clearly tyrannized their supporters by making it altogether too clear just what kinds of food and necessities they desired, such as walking sticks or robes. Also, however,

---

63. Dhammacariya: teacher; a Pali exam on the Tipitaka which monks and nuns may seek to pass. Success brings prestige, a title denoting a lectureship level in teaching Buddhism, and often some material support from government or lay associations.

64. It was not known how the judgment would be made: civil court or ecclesiastical court. Probably five monks would be named on each side to arbitrate. (Incidentally, the old monk, who was holding our informant's land illegally, was eighty-two and "likely to die soon.")

some monks were like the Kyaungdawya Sayadaw, who was so admired and revered that when he went alone for alms food, he so inspired the laity that what he obtained was sufficient for one hundred monk students and had to be carried by two lay stewards with staves and slings.[65]

Two Exemplary Monasteries

I have been dealing with extremes or departures from the norm of Vinaya purity. Perhaps now a brief portrait will be welcome of two institutions in which the utmost attention is given to scrupulous observance of the Vinaya code. Informants were virtually unanimous, all over Burma and at all times, that the personality of the leading monks in a monastery was of cardinal importance in giving the monastery its tone. The authority of an abbot in full possession of his powers is an awesome thing to study.

The history of the Shwehintha Monastery at Nyaungdon, already referred to, gives a persuasively detailed picture of strong Vinaya observance.[66] The repeated comment, running like a litany through the history of this monastery (taik), acquires value and poignancy by contrast with the data we have reviewed: "It is because of this that the taik stands firm." Many of the leading themes of this chapter are exemplified in its history. One of the main reasons for the smooth operation of the monastery, apart from that of the personalities of the monks concerned, is that here there is no such thing as "my donor" and "your donor," or "my pupil" and "your pupil." The abbot has quietly insisted that all gifts should be made to the monastery as a whole, not to individual monastery units or to specific monks. He also has demanded that monks, although placed in an individual monastery, should pay allegiance to the entire monastery compound (taik) as a unit alone and to its officers: the abbot, the taik-ok, and the taik-kyat.[67] The educational process of the laity must help the supporters pass from veneration for one monk or monastery to veneration for any monk of the unified taik. Poggalika or privately owned gifts are not allowed: they are encouraged to be sanghika. The officer-monks alone decide who shall be the head of such and such a monastery, and these heads are shifted every three years or

65. Panditta 1955:20.
66. Panditta 1955.
67. The taik-ok is an ecclesiastical official below the district leader who serves as warden, chief administrator, and discipline officer. The taik-kyat is his assistant.

so, in order that no allegiance may develop to one monastery rather than to the whole *taik*. Any monk can plant trees for shade and comfort, but all flowers and fruit belong to the *taik:* there are thus no *poggalika* trees. All head monks have to visit the officers at least twice a month. This is a large *taik* with something over thirty member monasteries held together.[68]

The constant theme of the *taik*'s history is that the temperament of leaders is made gradually manifest: when a monk is made an officer, it is because the laity and the other monks have been calling him by the title for some time. The leader is not necessarily the most obvious man for the job: a modest disciple will not push himself forward. The implication is that the laity should leave the choice to the wisdom of the *sayadaw*s. The simple discipline of the leaders, their refusal to stand out and claim special privilege, is also stressed. The founder U Thila always traveled on foot; he gave all offerings received to local monks and never mentioned property or offerings, though he did erect forest or *tawya,* monasteries. The kindness and consideration of another early *taik* leader, the Sankyaung Sayadaw, are brought out in a number of telling details. With his friends, the leaders in the positions of *taik-ok* and *taik-kyat,* he would personally tend to the sick, however unpleasant, and he had even been known to clean the *taik* toilet sticks. In a world where certain masters were so stern that monks would not dare approach them until they had left the monastery for four or five years, or so punctilious that they would even dictate the type of paper to be used in addressing them, the Sankyaung Sayadaw would often recall and negate set punishments and he never minded how he was addressed. His regard for the sacredness of the ordination area (*sima*), was great, and he would allow his feet to to roast on hot roads rather than wear sandals. Monks of his *taik* would not attend the festivals at monk's funerals or accept gifts from these (because some of the money might be from criminal sources); they would even refrain from using water that had come from wells erected because a monk had asked for them or from bowing at shrines and images obtained in the same way. Such refinements of Vinaya are now very rare. It is no wonder, however, that when the author of the *taik*'s history visited the *taik* after the death of one of the early leaders, he had a vision among the trees that the old master had planted, and it seemed

68. Panditta 1955:38–44.

that the trees were bowing and saying to the departed and revered *sayadaws* of old that, since they were no more, the trees were sad. Only the trees alone were left to bear witness to the works of the honored leaders.

Our second example of scrupulous attention to the Vinaya is a monastery run by one of the most famous "Vinaya *sayadaws*" in Burma during the fifties. He was U Zanakabiwuntha, the Mahagandayon Sayadaw, whose monastery was on the outskirts of Amarapura. The contrast between the extraordinary establishment—by no means used a showplace, as it could well have been by politicians and others—and the average Burmese monastery today is great. It was first built around 1908 as a meditation monastery for "forest monks" by a Thudhamma monk; the second *sayadaw* had been Shwegyin, and the third was the monk named above. The place was entirely *sanghika* and housed eighty-one monks and novices. About twenty others were visiting, preparing both for *patamabyan* and *dhammacariya* Pali examinations. Among examples of the way in which the Mahagandayon Sayadaw kept rules that had been "overlooked, forgotten, or even ignored by almost every other monk in Burma" are the following: separate buildings were maintained for each function, such as eating, sleeping, learning, and so on; refectory tables were set up on platforms; monks prepared and dyed their own robes, ate only out of bowls, received children as *thudaws* (lay disciples) before receiving them as novices, and so on. The neatness and spotlessness of the place were remarkable and were ensured by the work of daily cleaning and sweeping disciplines reminiscent of those in certain monasteries of Japan. I was told, indeed, that monks there did not sit for Vinaya examinations because each day the whole *Patimokkha*[69] is recited in turn by the monks in addition to the fortnightly recitals required by discipline.

The daily routine was extremely strict:

4:00   Monks rise and meditate until dawn.
5:00   Bell rings. Breakfast in dining hall. Sometimes cooked in the monastery out of the *sayadaw*'s "writings' fund"; sometimes brought by lay supporters.
5:45   Wooden log is struck. Assembly in Lecture Hall. *Sayadaw* gives instructions for the day. "This lasts until letters are visible in the

69. *Patimokkha* (P): the basic 227 rules in the Vinaya covering monastic behavior.

books." Punishments are meted out on the spot. Novices are dismissed and lectures begin. After first set of lectures, all monks go out with bowls while *sayadaw* writes, for about an hour. Bowls left in dining hall. Monks bathe. Assistant *sayadaws* (*dhammacariya*s) lecture in two shifts.

11:30   Midday meal. Baths and naps allowable after this; activities must be very quiet.

13:00   Sayadaw's lecture, followed by assistants'.

16:00   Cleaning and sweeping of halls, rooms, yards, paths, etc. Tasks allotted individually. Followed by ginger juice plus jaggery made by lay servants or visitors and shared out by monks.

18:00   *Paya-shiko* (honor to the Buddha).

18:30   Recitation of the day's lectures; in the case of examination candidates as late as 24:00. Some monks attend lectures in the dark with no lights and no books. Recitation in normal voice; no shouting aloud.

20:30   Log is struck. Meditation.

21:00   Sleep permitted for those not otherwise engaged.

Such is the outline of a day for the most orthodox of the orthodox. Such exemplars, we must always remember, continue to exist as a means whereby all who observe the Sangha may avoid the overconcentration upon its falterings and reputed decline.

Traditional Monastic Education

No portrait of the modern Sangha would be complete without a description of the vital educational role played by the monks. The present situation cannot be properly understood apart from the past, and thus we will review some of the history of this important facet of the monkhood's presence in Burma.

The prevailing image of the monk which lingers in my mind is that of a long, lean brown finger following in the wake of a line of rotund Burmese script, occasionally harpooning a word with a swift jab, yet always infinitely patient, infinitely ready to explain and interpret. While the noise of boys' voices shouting their lessons aloud is no longer a hallmark of life in the village monastery as it used to be, it is prevalent enough to give us a picture of traditional education in Burma. Writer after writer, whatever his opinion of monastic education, has repeated the opinion that to it, and to it alone, has been due the preservation of Burmese culture until very recent times, and that it has made that culture, within its limitations, one of the most impressively literate on earth. Little detailed information on the old curriculum and its history is available, but some printed sources and informants' accounts can be combined to present a picture of this education as it was at the time of the arrival of the British.

Stewart (1949:6), in an excellent short pamphlet based on his study of such Burmese classics as the *Myanma Okchokpon Sadan,* the *Thathana Linkara Sadan,* and the *Thathana Bahu Thuttapakathani,* can say little about the ratio of secular to religious education in monastic schools until the period of Bodawpaya, when he notes "a great increase of secular knowledge." Bodawpaya was an ardent collecter of Sanskrit works from India, some of which were translated, and many artists and craftsmen were invited to court from distant parts. The Order appears to have become interested in this knowledge, and monasteries in which it was taught were called *pwe gyaungs.* Here astronomy, astrology, medicine, massage, divination, horsemanship, swordsmanship, archery, arts and crafts, boxing, wrestling, music, and dancing were taught. Some time after 1812, in which year a boxing match took place at court between novices and lay boys, Bodawpaya apparently became fearful that rebellion might be planned in these monasteries and he thus suppressed them. Stewart surmises that royalty may have feared a process whereby commoners were acquiring an education in subjects previously open only to princes and officials and that there may well have been at this time a popular movement for better and more general education, as witness the Kinwun Mingyi's swordsmanship, learned in a *pwe gyaung,* and his desire that this skill remain unknown.

Secular subjects, largely of an Indian nature, were taught in Burma from at least the Pagan period onward and probably earlier. There is much evidence that, from early times, hermits and wizards of various sorts, either as individuals or as groups, studied, practiced, and taught such secular subjects. The evidence also suggests that these hermits and wizards often found new recruits after a wave of orthodoxy in the Order of monks proper had driven the unorthodox from the fold. At different periods, the Order was perhaps more or less tolerant of the practice and teaching of secular subjects by monks. Stewart (1949:6), at any rate, claims that the *pwe gyaung*s "survived into Pagan Min's reign (1846–1853) at least, and some of their studies were still pursued unobtrusively in King Mindon's reign."

The culture thus transmitted was only a small part of the Buddhist culture available to the monks themselves: school taught a set of basic ritual texts, basic ethical texts, and a number of works that could be argued to afford growing boys some notion of how to grapple with the world around them. A bare list of such texts would make poor reading and inform little. Instead I offer a substantial description by a sophisticated informant of about fifty years of age, representing the state of monastic education in Upper Burma around the middle of the second decade of the twentieth century. This account is, I believe, more descriptive than those at present available:

I am speaking of my village in Singu Township, some fifty miles north of Mandalay. I believe the pattern of monastic education there held good for the whole of Upper Burma and I do not think it has undergone marked changes to date. The village is a very large one—500 houses—and it was and is more prosperous than most of the other fifty-odd village tracts in the area. The Japanese occupation brought soaring prices, but, on the debit side we have had the insurgents. . . . Would you believe it, the village had no tea shop until 1948, in spite of Indian and Chinese traders. So you see, prosperous, but not very sophisticated . . .

There were nine monasteries in all around our village, built "far from the madding crowd." I cannot remember any nuns, but the monks catered for girls up to ten years, after which they had to leave, so we did have coeducation after a fashion. There were a presiding monk and his assistant teachers, all unpaid, of course. I suppose there were from twenty-five to forty pupils in each of the monasteries.

I was sent to school at the age of six. It was a great day in my life. My mother and father had requested permission from the *sayadaw,* and he had chosen Thursday as the day of learning in my case. I had a special bath, my hair was knotted, I wore my best clothes. My father carried tidbits and plain tea, my mother, rice on a tray, covered. Aunts and uncles also came to shower blessings—who would not on such an occasion? We had to arrive before 9:30 a.m. so that the food could be eaten in our presence. My parents said, "Bring him up to be worthy; barring eye injuries and broken bones, you can injure him to bring him up learned and worthy."

The educational process began with elementary ritual formulas and with the vowels, consonants, and combinations thereof contained in the *Thinbongyi:*[70]

And, believe me, the monks practiced that: "Spare the rod and spoil the child," is that not so? I was put under an assistant and taught my first lesson that very afternoon. The monk recited the twelve vowels and I repeated them after him. First came a prayer, *Namaw Buddhaya Theikdan*—"I

---

70. Burmese alphabet book.

worship Lord Buddha, may he help me complete my education," etc. Then *A, Aa, I, Ii,* and so on. I had to memorize this before I went home. Next day I traced circles, the *wa* character—it is a popular belief that learning must start on a Thursday and writing on a Friday. I wrote on a long black slate with sandstone and steatite pencils. A wooden slate of *letpan* or *salut* wood was smoothed and smeared with thick boiled rice water and rubbed with charcoal, then dried in the sun: we loved this daily process, but above all we loved rainy or sunless days! We had to pay attention to the clockwise direction of our strokes (this is now being lost and after 1920 there were no slates . . .). I traced circles and recited vowels the whole day. It took me a week to master circles; I practiced on kitchen walls and the bedroom walls and, if I went wrong, I was beaten with split bamboo. The *wa* came first because from it arise all the consonants.[71]

I interrupt this informant's account to insert a relevant section on the learning process for the monastic schoolboy as described by Scott (1909:16–17):

A little explanation starts him off, and for the next few days he [the new boy] is engaged in shouting out their sounds at the top of his voice. Nobody minds him, for all the other scholars are similarly engaged in hallooing, and the monks derive a sense of comfort and a virtuous consciousness of doing good from the noise. . . . If a boy stops shouting, it is a sign that he has stopped working—and if he is not meditating mischief, it is probable that he is about to go to sleep, and he is corrected accordingly. The method is an admirable one for keeping the boys occupied—much more so than civilized Western methods—though I fear a council of English head-masters would scout the idea. . . . Doubtless it is a primitive method. . . . Nevertheless everybody learns in the end, and then they are set to read in the same way, and gradually advance in the immemorial regulation subjects.

But let us return to my informant's account:

Then came the stage of mastering all the consonants and learning to remember all the letters by sight. So, in the first year, one learns the *Thinbongyi* and the principles of the Burmese language, though some say Pali is the main thing and Burmese comes accidentally; in the next we copied the *Jataka*[72] passages from palm leaves or books, though boys were rarely trusted with books. Bright boys took two months, but there were some who took two years! Punishments were beating, drawing water, sweeping, cutting grass. The worst was standing instead of playing.

We learned prayers and recited them, one or two a day. Just from joining

71. The *wa* is supremely important in messianic Buddhist symbolism as a character from which everything arises and to which everything returns.
72. Stories of lives of the Buddha.

in with old people, you know—there was no special lesson. The first prayer would be before the monks' meal (other monasteries had this one early in the morning). All monasteries had the second in the evening just before going home. This one ended with a verse saying we were going home to waiting parents saddened by a long day's separation. . . .

All the time the writing and the learning went together. It took me two to three years to learn writing. At the end of the second year I learned the thirty-eight blessings of the *Mingala-thok* (*Maha Mangala Sutta*)—the five precepts were automatically incorporated in prayers, by the way; there was no special course on them. One important thing, I think, is that the meaning of the Pali was never explained. Children just like repeating, and the monks exploited this delight. We learned the meaning from here and there, not from the teachers. We were often asked by parents and friends about our progress at school and they used these opportunities to explain things. The *Mingala-thok* is, in fact, a moral code and everybody in the village was interested in driving it home.

Reciting is a daily routine. Explanation comes only when a child can recite any piece at any time without notice, without forethought, almost in his sleep. It took me six months to get the *Mingala-thok*, frontward, back to front, in every way. The monks never pushed, they just waited and waited. The memory of such things remains very late in life.

After the *Mingala-thok* came the *Loka-Niti*, a sort of guide to the world of men. I think it was compiled by a royal minister some six hundred years ago. It took me about two years to learn this; again all the Pali before any meaning.

Along with the Pali passages, there were verses in Burmese written by learned monks. These form part of Burmese literature, as one discovers to his great surprise on arriving at a university. Books, incidentally, were very rare and treasured. I had to pay homage to a book before taking it out. I remember proverbs like "one letter is worth a pagoda" or "one letter means one Buddha." About twenty years ago even newspapers were treated with respect. Well, after four or five years we were allowed to read full *Jataka* tales in prose, which were considered to be very sanctified things. A special privilege was to read the ten last great *Jataka*s. These were about young boys, sometimes, to inspire young boys. It was a splendid thing for young brains: all that courage and determination and good citizenship.

At about the age of ten I was initiated as a novice. It is the greatest occasion in the life of a young boy. From the day a boy is born, his parents think of their first duty to him as the novitiate. Of course this is a different topic. I forgot to tell you that if a mother notices a punishment bruise on her son, that is, from a monk, she hits him again in the same place. You can see that we are heavily and thoroughly indoctrinated. . . .

I have quoted at length from this material partly because it is a fine and lively description, partly because it shows very well how, from the very beginning, a pattern is set—one very different from that known to a European schoolchild, yet just as formative and perhaps more lovingly remembered. Burmese observers often stress that this is not merely an educational system but the beginning of a way of life which will never cease to influence the Burman, however high he may climb in his life. And indeed, upon retirement from work, the Burman very often seeks to reconstitute this world of his childhood as much as to lay up a store of merit now that he is free of social responsibility. Burmans very often equate social responsibility with irreligiousness—especially in middle-aged men—and life is conceived as a circle, the old retired person returning to the religious purity of the very young.

There is probably no better way of ensuring undeviating allegiance to a number of ritual and moral precepts than the method described above. The lessons are unforgettable, and they ensure that all those subjected to them respond to social situations in roughly the same way and find themselves members of one same universe of discourse. This "layman's Buddhism," as Stewart has called it, still forms a common background of experience for all but a very small minority of Burmans.

Respect for tradition and for the written word are assimilated from the beginning. The form of teaching, the sanctity of books and writing or printing in general, and the authority ascribed to classical writers all contribute to this unquestioning allegiance. At the same time, while there is little choice of subject, the individual is left free to develop in his own time and at his own rhythm. There is no separation into classes and streams; there appear to be few if any rewards for learning faster than the next man; the infinite patience of the teachers waits for all to catch up in time.

The texts and precepts pertaining strictly to Buddhism and the order in which they are taught seem fairly standard: the praises to the Buddha, Dhamma (law), and Sangha; the *Mingala-thok;* the *Yatana Shwe Gyaing* (prayers for the conquest of external and internal moral enemies); the *Namakara* (formulas of homage); the *Payeik Gyi* (*Maha Paritta,* or "formulas of the Great Protection"); the *Loka-Niti* and the *Jatakas*. In addition other subjects taught or picked up by the way form part of the Burmese religious tradition but do not pertain strictly to "orthodox" or "pure" Buddhism.[73] These include an understanding of lucky and unlucky days, the position of *nats* (gods and

73. Stewart 1949:10.

spirits) and planets on certain days, and other astrological knowledge. Scott tells how the monks taught the details of Burmese cosmology (this would not contradict the spirit of the Buddhist texts) and how often traveling *saya*s (teacher-experts) dealing in astrology, medicine, necromancy, plays, and poetry would stay at the monastery and impart some of their knowledge to the more adventurous boys. A whole world view was taught—one very different from and infinitely richer than today's traveler might guess. As for lay subjects, there were very few: the pupils were taught addition, subtraction, and the multiplication table up to nine times nine.

There appear to have been few punishments, except in the case of moral shortcomings, such as disobedience and dishonesty which, according to Mi Mi Khaing (1945:4), were treated very severely. Various lenient correctives, such as lazy boys running around the courtyard with others on their shoulders, are described by the same author, but my informant made it clear that, in many, perhaps most cases, punishments were designed to involve the pupils in looking after many aspects of monastery life: Mi Mi Khaing writes:

He [my father] and all the other scholars performed the domestic tasks of the monastery, swept and rubbed the good hard wooden floors, the monastery grounds and pagoda steps, because in these precincts all comers went barefoot; they drew water for drinking, and for the bath of the older monks; they followed the monks on their rounds, two of them bearing a pole on which was slung a covered tray, to take any food donated in excess of what would go into the monk's bowl; they waited on the monks at meals. . . . In the evenings they went home to eat the meal which the monks abstained from, but came back at sunset to recite the lessons of the day and many past days all over again, to join in the assembled night prayers, to sleep in the monastery and rise again before the dawn. [1945:3]

Thus the boys, and especially the boarders, familiarized themselves with monastic life against the day when they too would for a time join the Order. Perhaps as day pupils they also learned some respect for the ways of the monastic exemplars of the community, but above all they participated in the running of the monastery. As we shall see later no small part of the desire of many present-day monks for a resumption of monastic schooling comes from the realization that if there are no pupils there are not only no future monks but there is also little help in running the affairs of a monastery. Schooling is thus intimately associated with recruitment of both monks and the essential servants.

Monastic schooling is very clearly a community venture in our informant's account of his childhood in Singu township. We know that monastic and parental authority reinforced each other: the five things a child is immediately taught to respect are the Buddha, the Law, the Order, parents, and teachers. A more graphic example of reinforcement is the informant's tale of a mother's adding to a bruise inflicted by a monk. More generally, the monks set down in broad terms what must eventually be interpreted in particular terms by the parents, relatives, and friends of the child in explanations given to them after their lessons. In this way, two disparate and contradictory aims are achieved: on the one hand, the monks do not sully themselves with interference in everyday affairs, teaching only lofty principles in the most general and timeworn terms; on the other, these principles are related to the daily life of the community by being interpreted by the child's kin and friends. Thus, many of the aims which in our culture need specific groups (parent-teacher associations for the most part) for success were achieved in an informal fashion, and the broad ties uniting the village and the monastery were made from the start in the lives of the village's members.[74]

This general picture should illuminate the realm of traditional learning in Burma and the potential opposition to any "progressive" ideas that might threaten Burmese monastic education. In the colonial period, this cherished monastic system declined under the pressures of governmentally and privately supported lay and mission schools and a general secularizing trend in the curriculum. The first colonial architect of such massive educational change was Sir Arthur Phayre.

The Colonial Legacy in Education

Phayre's policy, first enunciated in correspondence with the government of India in 1864 and subsequently embodied in his report of 1865, was based on the evidence that monastic schools were the only available local schools in the countryside. He suggested that any attempt on the

---

74. The following dialogue between myself and the informant previously cited is instructive. E.M.M.: "Was the question of obedience to precepts ever discussed?" Inf.: "No." E.M.M.: "What did you do in case of doubt?" Inf.: "Teachers are too much revered. Parents were asked." This willingness to accept runs right through: Even Abhidhamma (the philosophical book of the scriptures) is taught before questions are asked. I knew of one great Abhidhamma teacher who had great difficulty with Europeans because they persisted in asking questions as they went along instead of waiting until the end of the course.

part of government to set up additional schools in villages would meet with failure and that the only sensible policy would be to expand the monks' teaching of reading and writing by means of some six or seven books to cover basic subjects: geography, surveying, arithmetic, anatomy, ancient history, geometry, and astronomy. By the time these manuals came into use, new and competing Anglo-vernacular schools built in provincial towns with colonial or mission financial backing had made their mark; high schools and colleges came later. In this way Phayre thought mass primary education would be effected at little cost and the prevailing educational system would suffer little disturbance.

This, by and large, was the government policy from 1865 to 1917, when the Education Department ceased to be the sole authority concerned with vernacular education. While practical methods varied, the basic aim was clearly to secularize the curriculum and methods of the monastic school. However, difficulties were encountered from the very beginning. In 1867–1868 only 41 monastic schools were using the new textbooks, and only 91 pupils were nominally studying them. In 1868–1869—I quote the few available figures—170 books were distributed, and 82 pupils were studying them. By 1870 the efforts of the first director of public instruction, appointed in 1866, and his four circuit teachers were of little avail, and steps had to be taken to assist lay teachers and schools. A training school for masters and mistresses was opened, the circuit teachers were paid off, and four deputy inspectors were appointed. The causes for the failure were identified as the success of the newly created private mission and lay schools, the need for lay schools for girls who were not admitted to monastic schools, and, above all perhaps, the difficulty of dealing with jealous and independent monks.[75] The fact that monks had their own means of subsistence and were thus outside the sphere of governmental control was also noted. Nevertheless, the government persisted in its efforts, and every kind of makeshift was tried to persuade the monks: the use of itinerant teachers, rewards to pupils and teachers, grants to schools based on results, special concessions in regard to the curriculum, but in 1912 the director of public instruction noted that the itinerant teacher system had been found wanting and had thus been abolished, and that a classification of monastic schools as "B" schools with a restricted curriculum had offended the monks. In

75. Burma, 1936.

addition, monks recognized no responsibility for teaching secular subjects; stricter members of the monkhood even considered geography and arithmetic irreligious pursuits. Many monks disliked the appointment of lay teachers to their monastic schools, and the lay teachers working at the monastery, in turn, disliked the authority of untrained monks and preferred to open their own schools outside the monastery or assist other lay school managers. Furthermore, most monks objected deeply to the indignity of being interviewed by government inspectors and of having to keep up attendance and progress registers. At the same time, too many such inspectors revered the yellow robe too much to exact full standards of efficiency from the monks. The inefficiency was enormous: more than 80 percent of children left monastic schools after one or two years' attendance.[76]

During the colonial period, the change in the Burmese educational system was dramatic. For example, in 1891 there were 2,434 monastic schools and only 757 recognized lay schools, but by 1938 there were only 976 monastic schools, while lay schools numbered 5,255.[77] By the time of the Vernacular Education Committee's 1924 report, it had been concluded that the Phayre concept of recognizing and incorporating monastic schools into the government's realm was a failure. The committee held that the cardinal error had been to suppose that the Sangha would ever look at education as anything but a secondary occupation; in the traditional system, the monk obtained his comforts through the slight effort of teaching a few subjects known to him by heart, but the "modern" world called for less conservatism and a far more varied and competent education. The committee suggested, therefore, a "progressive" policy: monastic and lay schools should henceforth be put on an equal footing. There was to be no more favoritism in the case of the former; only efficiency could determine the issue. Both types of school should conform to the same curriculum and take the same examinations. The only exception would be for parallel lay girls' schools to be set up in villages where the monastic school did not admit female pupils: duplication would probably not be on a large scale since, out of 74,161 pupils in monastic schools, 12,272 were said to be girls. Here, then, and in spite of courtly bows in the direction of the monks, there appeared to

76. Taw Sein Ko (1913:263–268) shows this well and discusses the conservative attitude of the *thathanabaing* toward the problem.

77. Burma 1948:8.

be a recognition of a plan that would become an instrument of their further decline.

This "progressive" viewpoint, however, began to change by the late twenties and thirties. A report in Burmese by a 1928 Committee on Buddhist Religious Instruction for Buddhist Pupils in Vernacular Lay Schools under Buddhist Management, made public in 1932, recognized that Buddhism was not being taught well in the Burmese lay schools. Furthermore, the problem in Anglo-vernacular schools was even greater than in Burmese schools since pupils in the former stayed longer and were meant to attain high posts in the community. Most such Anglo-vernacular schools were under Christian missionaries, who were excellent educators but had difficulty teaching moral and ethical subjects since their system was shared neither by their pupils nor by the latters' parents. This committee of 1928 suggested a number of ways of increasing the attention paid by headmen, township officers, inspectors, teachers, and students to Buddhism through such initiatives as instruction in Buddhism in normal and primary teacher training schools and the preparation of more Buddhist textbooks for all grades of students.

This same emphasis is found in the 1936 Vernacular Education Committee's report, which reviewed all the problems noted by earlier studies, but unfortunately the 1936 committee had nothing original whatsoever to offer toward the solution of a problem it knew had been insoluble for well on seventy years. The 1928 and 1936 documents, however, taken together with the aggressively "progressive" 1924 report, reveal the nature of the dilemma. At first the British government had been unwilling to tamper with a system so uniform and so widespread that it constituted a permanent temptation to those who could see money better spent than in an expensive duplication of schools all over the country. In terms of educational plans, however, the monkhood had, on the whole, been quiescent, so much so indeed that by 1924 its incapacity to participate in an education fit for a modern world had finally been accepted. Now, however, other political and nationalistic forces were at work, and the monkhood had begun to assume a vanguard role in a land which wished to be rid of its masters, as will be seen in Chapter 4. Allusive and imprecise as the remarks of the 1936 committee, are, their caution suggests a realization that the problem of a Burmese Buddhist education, and hence the whole problem of the role of the monastic schools, was acquiring new, revivalistic overtones. The irony of a situation in which traditionalism might change from a negative into a positive value was beginning to be felt and it was a problem independent Burma would itself inherit.

The loss of the educational role, formerly the exclusive realm of the monk, has had profound effects upon the Sangha's place in modern Burmese society. The movement to place education into secular hands was a legacy of colonialism that left a vacuum in Burmese life, for the specifically Buddhist nature of the traditional learning process was lost in the transfer to lay schools. Lay associations, formed in the realization of such a loss, attempted to promote Buddhism to make up the difference, and we shall see how the twentieth-century nationalist politicians also assumed the task, not always to the liking of the Sangha.

Some Evidence of Monastic Hierarchy

In the final section of this chapter a portrait will be attempted of the general structure of the Sangha and the monastery as it has existed in the past and has survived into the present. Information on the nature of hierarchy in the Burmese Sangha is extremely difficult to obtain, basically because many monks themselves often have no clear notion of the system such as it exists. Fortunately, after months of searching, I was able to obtain one document of a kind that has by and large disappeared from Burma, although it was said to be common in royal times, and the army regimes of the late fifties and early sixties wished to reintroduce it. This is the Shwegyin sect's *Wazo Thangadawmya Sayingyok* for 1956, a list of monasteries and monks in Rangoon, Hanthawaddy, and Insein which contains precious details about the social organization of nearly nine hundred monks and novices.[78] That it is a Shwegyin document should not be surprising, because such sects have created, as I argued in the last chapter, organizational substitutes for the duties formerly performed by the king's *thathanabaing*. While the Shwegyin system cannot be assumed to be the organization model for the entire Sangha, it does correspond quite well with my impressions about the Order as a whole gained through field work.

First of all, this Shwegyin document indicates that there is a sense of geographical organization to the sect's affairs. It can be summarized as follows:

78. Shwegyin Taik 1956(?).

htana   = an area of jurisdiction over *taik*s
taik   = a cluster of monasteries (often with a central abbey)
kyaung   = a monastery as individual unit
kyaungthit= a new or offshoot monastery

The local jurisdiction units (the *htana*s) do not exactly reproduce lay district boundaries, since one *hatana* may claim a monastery or two from another secular district, but the overlap is minimal. The basic unit within the *htana* is the *taik,* which we may generally consider for the entire Sangha as a cluster or group of monasteries. *Taik*s are determined roughly by size (though not entirely—in Twante there is one monastery that has more novices and monks than any of the *taik*s there). Apart from the sect headquarters *taik* in Rangoon—which contains twenty monasteries—all *taik*s are listed as being coterminous with a single monastery: although we do not know the sizes of these buildings, this usage is strange since the term *taik* usually seems to imply an assembly of monasteries within a compound. Thus, the Shwegyin monks generally seem to conceive *taik* in the sense of an "abbey," which is probably "served" by monasteries not within its immediate boundaries. It is interesting that 74 percent of these monasteries have only one to five monks living in them, with 83 percent having five or fewer novices. Even in cities, therefore, Shwegyin monasteries are usually very small units of the *taik*. We also find the term *kyaungthit,* which seems to mean "new monastery" or is used with the meaning of "daughter monastery." In Yedashe Road, Rangoon, for example, there are an "old" monastery and a "new" one. One *taik* in Rangoon contains only a single monastery, called a "new" monastery. *Taik*s can be mainly administrative, such as the Rangoon headquarters *taik,* or teaching institutions, such as the largest establishment described in the document, the Medini Taik in Kanbe, with sixty monks, twenty novices, and, incidentally, the local Vinaya expert.

Accompanying the geographical concepts of *htana* and *taik* are a host of Shwegyin titles that reveal the existence of a hierarchy that is rather complex and not at all clear from the data available to me. The sect is headed by a president (*nikaya maha nayaka*), below whom is a Mandalay-based Supreme Council of other great leaders (*maha nayaka*), but below that level I can only list the terms used in an approximation of their relative status to each other:

htana hsaingya wunhsaung	officer of an ecclesiastical area or center
ahpwe agyo tawhsaung	protector of interests
agyo tawhsaung	assistant protector of interests
gaing-gyok	district officer
gaing-ok	subdistrict officer
gaing-dauk	assistant to subdistrict officer
Winido gaing-dauk	Vinaya expert
Patimokkha kyaunghsaung	
gaing-dauk	Patimokkha leader
taik-ok	*taik* leader (warden)
taik-kyat	assistant *taik* leader (deputy warden)
sayadaw	head of *taik* or monastery, often with over 50 years in Sangha
pontawgyi	head of monastery, with an average of over 35 years in the Sangha
pongyi or	over 10 years in Sangha, usually senior
kyaunghtaing pongyi[79]	or presiding monk in the monastery
kyaung-pongyi	possibly an assistant to either of the two levels above
upazin	monk with fewer than 10 years in the Sangha

Apparently *gaing* positions rank above those at the *taik* level, but I was not able to pinpoint any geographical area specifically related to them. Not all districts in the Shwegyin statement contained such officials. It is clear, however, that the Shwegyin sect ascribes a restricted meaning to the terms *sayadaw, pontawgyi,* and *pongyi.* Shwegyin *sayadaw*s seem to be monks with considerable seniority, and they are usually in charge of *taik*s rather than monasteries. *Pontawgyi*s generally have seniority in their monasteries and are head monks as well. *Pongyi*s have at least ten years in the Sangha (nineteenth-century usage), whereas in common modern parlance the term *pongyi* is used for any monk. However, titles in the present-day Sangha are simply not to be trusted. Indeed a monk once told me that men within the Sangha could recognize the sect of most monks by the way they used key hierarchical terms. These slight variations are usually lost on the layman.

Unfortunately I was unable to discover information about the specific functions or duties of any of the offices represented by the titles. It

79. *Kyaung* (B): monastery; *htaing* (B): to sit; head of the monastery. The Rangoon equivalent is *kyaunghsaung* (B): *hsaung* (B): to bear responsibility; thus to have responsibility for the monastery.

might be useful, however, to introduce here for comparison with the Shwegyin material Nash's observations on the organization of the Sangha as he observed it. He reports that, at the village level, each monastery is "virtually an independent entity" and each of the presiding monks "is a self-sufficient authority." There is, however, "a vague notion of *taik,* a group of monasteries tied together by the authority of an especially venerable monk." In the "outer circle" this was a *sayadaw* in Legyi village with authority over some twenty villages. He settled internal Sangha questions such as disciplining and even expulsion, for which a quorum of monks is necessary; Nash writes, "But, in all the time Nondwin villagers can remember, no one has ever been expelled from a monastery in the region, and the *taik* has never formally convened. The only organizational reality it has is that when the 21 or so monks from the region are assembled, they sit in rank order descending from this venerable *sayadaw*" (1965:144).

Above the *taik* level, Nash (p. 144) feels that there is an "even vaguer level of organization called the *gaing.*" To village monks this refers to the doctrinal divisions in the Sangha, that is, to sects. The other sense in which this word is used among village monks is for "the group of followers of a given *sayadaw,*" whether laymen or monks. Nash's observations thus parallel mine.

Field Questionnaire: Facts and Fancy

In an attempt to learn more about monastic organization and monks themselves, I developed a modest questionnaire. The authorities with whom I discussed the possibility of administering it to monks were uniformly discouraging, especially since my stay in Burma coincided with government attempts at monastic registration which the monks regarded, as we shall see later, with deep suspicion. Nevertheless my simple questionnaire in Burmese produced some responses in a number of places. Packages of them were deposited either by myself or by agents with trusted *sayadaw*s and were later collected and analyzed. Unfortunately it was not possible to follow these up with interviews. A number of questions dealing with newspapers and other printed matter read by monks, meditational practices, Buddhist associations, and Sangha political groups produced unsatisfactory results which could not be used, either because standard answers were given or because the questions were not answered at all. In the case of a question relating to desire to stay in the Order for a lifetime, the overwhelming majority said that they hoped to do so, again a standardized formula. Other disappointments included the fact that certain answers were apparently dictated—written in by one person in the case of a Shwegyin monastery—while in another case a misreading of the questionnaire deprived me of a whole series of important data.

A first questionnaire (type A) was administered to 42 novices and 58 monks in a highly respected monastery of the Shwegyin sect in Amarapura and to another 20 monks among my students at the Sangha University at Rangoon, the latter residing in various monasteries, including the university's own. A similar but lightly enlarged questionnaire (type B) was administered to 13 novices and 102 monks in various places. These included a 46-monk monastery of the Hngetwin sect in Mandalay; a 7-novice, 27-monk monastery of the Shwegyin sect in Mandalay; the Shweman Sayadaw's monastery (Thudhamma) of 6 novices and 7 monks, also in Mandalay; and 22 monks from one of the vast teaching monasteries at Pakokku. The total of respondents was thus 235, including 55 novices and 180 monks. Although the sample is very small, this is perhaps the first survey of its kind. The data acquired on origin and occupations are summarized in Table 2.[80] The results of ordination age questions are given in Table 3.

A review of the ordination data in Table 3 will show that 60 percent of the novices were ordained between the ages of ten and fifteen. This figure might have been higher if I had better figures from the Amarapura Shwegyin monastery and if the rather untypical Hngetwin establishment were excluded. The monk ordination figures in Table 3 reveal that 62 percent of the monks were ordained between ages 18 and 20. In orthodox procedure, novice ordination should always precede monk ordination, as may be seen from Sinhalese classical sources. When a man is of age to become a monk, his monk ordination follows more or less immediately upon his novice ordination. The age for monk ordination is said to be 20, and if the nine months spent in the womb may be counted toward this age, then the ordinations at 19 make sense, but the age of 18 is hard to account for unless I have had trouble with Burmese dates.

80. See Spiro 1970:331–350 for a discussion of motivational aspects of monastic recruitment.

Table 2.   Questionnaire results: Origin place and occupation

Area of origin (N = 214)	
Village born	86%
Town born	14%
Upper Burma	79%
Lower Burma	21%

District of origin (N = 210)	
Upper Burma	
Pakokku	41
Mandalay	28
Shwebo	22
Magwe	16
Sagaing	15
Myingyan	10
Monywa	10
Misc. from Upper Burma, Shan and Kachin States	24
Lower Burma	
Pegu	7
Pyapon	7
Misc.	30

Occupations of members of family
Father (N = 211)

Farmer	65%
Merchant	20%
Craftsman	3%
Medical practitioner	3%
Headman	1%
Official	1%
Misc. (army, mechanic, etc.)	7%

Older brothers (N = 122)

Farmer	47%
Merchant	21%
Teacher	12%
Craftsman	4%
Official	4%
Monk	3%

Table 2. Continued

Army personnel	2%
Student	2%
Medical practitioner	2%
Misc.	3%

Younger brothers (N = 101)

Farmer	36%
Schoolboy	33%
Other	31%

Table 3. Questionnaire results: Ordination ages of novices and monks

Age of Ordination		Number	Percentage
Novices (n = 171)	6 – 9 yrs.	15	9
	10 – 12 yrs.	53	31
	13 – 15 yrs.	50	29
	16 – 20 yrs.	27	16
	21 and over	26	15
Monks (N = 119)			
	18 yrs.	11	9
	19 yrs.	26	22
	20 yrs.	37	31
	21 – 30 yrs.	24	20
	31 – 40 yrs.	6	5
	over 41 yrs.	15	13

Possible ordination location responses were birthplace, nearby village or town, township or district center, and further afield. Out of 213 respondents, 71 percent were ordained as novices in their birthplaces, and of the 155 monk respondents 48 percent were ordained as monks in their birthplaces. For the rest, numbers were about equally divided between near and distant ordinations. Of the relevant total, 37 percent were ordained both as novices and as monks in their birthplaces. The proportion of fathers still resident in the respondent's birthplace (type B questionnaire) was 88 percent; of older brothers 60 percent, and of younger brothers 62 percent.

Educational standards were not too high. Of 157 persons, 42 had passed the *Patamange* Pali exam, 26 the *Patamalat*, 26 the *Patamagyi*, and 29 the *dhammacariya* (see Appendix G). Responses to questions on food collection from rice donors were as follows ($N = 200$):

12 visited no households at all
56 visited 1–19 households
77 visited 20–39 households
36 visited 40–59 households
 6 visited 60–79 households
13 visited 80 or more households

The discussion of food-collecting habits earlier in this chapter has prepared us for variations due to such factors as town and village patterns, the scholars' more sedentary habits, and various types of communal feeding by lay groups.

There were 163 answers to a question about personal lay supporters, but in 45 cases the responses were the same as those for food collection; many respondents apparently did not distinguish between the two categories. As for those who did make a distinction, their personal lay supporters often live in the monk's original home place or ordination place, while food donors are obviously resident in the monastery area. A more subtle distinction between ordination sponsors and other types should obviously have been made in the questionnaire. The figures are as follows:

 9 persons had no personal lay supporter
99 had 1– 9 lay supporters
32 had 10–19
13 had 20–39
 6 had 40–59
 4 had 60–79

Thus 61 percent of the total had only 1–9 lay supporters. There was a slight tendency for a high number of food-collecting donors to go with a low number of personal lay supporters. This fact may indicate that the categories should not be radically separated and that, for instance, a monk visiting many households might well find his nonfood needs satisfied by one or more of these.

Another question concerned the frequency with which monks from the same area clustered in the same residences when away from home. This is related to a number of interesting problems such as the extent to which an abbot might draw on his home village for recruits, the tendency

of relatives to enter the same establishment, and so forth.[81] Out of the
13 persons living in the Shweman Sayadaw's monastery in Mandalay, 3
novices and 2 monks came from the same village in the Madaya area,
not many miles from the monastery, while a novice and a monk came
from the same village in the Thaton area of Lower Burma. There was
no special indication that these monks and novices might be closely
related by kinship. Of the 35 persons from the Shwegyin monastery in
Mandalay as many as 13 came from 8 villages in the Gangaw area
(Pakokku) and 3 others came from a single village in the Pyapon area
of Lower Burma. This is an important area for further research,
separately and in relation to the question of *poggalika/sanghika* property factors.

I also tried to assess awareness of sectarian distinctions among the
respondents. Apart from the Mandalay Shwegyin monastery, which contained a Thudhamma sect man, the monasteries were one-sect establishments (that is, excluding specifically "teaching" monasteries in which it
is accepted that different sects may reside together). The curious
exception—curious in view of the abbots' fervor for his rather unusual
sect—was the Hngetwin monastery. Of the 46 monks here, 24 called
themselves Satubumika (Hngetwin), 19 Thudhamma, 1 Shwegyin, and
1 "Buddha *gaing*," while another did not answer at all. One of the
Hngetwin monks claimed to have started as Thudhamma, become
Shwegyin, and lastly joined Hngetwin. Twelve of the Hngetwin men had
been ordained at this monastery, ten of these being middle-aged or older
at that time. Most of the Thudhamma men recognized the authority of
gaing officials in their own ordination places so that, while the abbot did
not say so, it appears that he accepted nonsect members who wished to
learn his meditation system. The monks in this monastery came from
more varied places and professional backgrounds, and, being mostly
older, it was natural that they were exceptions because they had former
professions: 17 out of 24 had been farmers. Educational achievement
was very low: I suspect, though this requires further research, that educational and meditational achievement may tend to be mutually
exclusive, in practice. Another interesting feature of this monastery is
that food-collecting habits were strongly influenced by the wealth of the

---

81. Lehman (personal communication, 1973) points out also the phenomenon
of mass ordinations, which are often sponsored by a major village *taga*. Monks
who join the Sangha as a group may stay together for a while.

monastery patron, a cigar manufacturer whose religious donations included the *nat* establishments on Mount Popa as well as this most orthodox of monasteries! Her name cropped up twice among the food-collecting responses and she was listed as personal supporter four times, while the abbot himself was cited once for unknown reasons.

One of the most important questions concerned the extent of monks' knowledge about the organization of their sects, since this might indicate how strictly the sects are in practice organized. Questionnaire A did not include a question on this, so I have no results from the Amarapura Shwegyin monastery; but the Mandalay Shwegyin monastery received B questionnaires, and it was there that the correct answers were apparently dictated or even filled in by the same person. In view of earlier material about the Shwegyin reviewed above, there can be little doubt that this sect knows itself to be well organized, but the reason for the Mandalay Shwegyin response to the questionnaire is puzzling.

Hierarchy-awareness tests were carried out in two situations, the Pakokku and the Hngetwin monasteries. Of the 22 participants in Pakokku, all claimed to be Thudhamma, except for one Dwaya, who gave the correct answers for his sect. Eight persons abstained from answering the hierarchy questions. Among the 13 Thudhamma monks who answered 5 claimed there was a *thathanabaing,* while 2 stated there was no such office at the time. Of the five, two only wrote in the word "thathanabaing." Two others claimed that two successive reigning *rattagurus*[82] were *thathanabaings* (one of these was wrongly identified). One claimed that the rattaguru of the Pakokku sect, nominated in 1956, was *thathanabaing.* He was correct if the Pakokku group is actually taken to be a sect: the situation is curious for in the very heart of Pakokku territory no one else claimed it to be a sect. The two others who claimed no *thathanabaing* gave the name of the abbot of their own monastery: the Mahawithudarama Sayadaw.

Ten men recognized a *gaing-gyok,* nine of them (including the two monks who claimed there was no *thathanabaing*) naming the Mahawithudarama Sayadaw. The other respondent, who had named the Pakokku *rattaguru* as *thathanabaing,* also claimed him as a *gaing-gyok.* At the *gaing-ok* and *gaing-dauk* levels there was confusion in conceptual-

---

82. *Rattaguru* is a title of honor given by the government to highly respected *sayadaws,* based partly upon seniority in their particular sect. See Chapter 6.

ization of hierarchical structure, though one monk who claimed the Mahawithudarama Sayadaw as *gaing-gyok* and three other *taik sayadaw*s as *gaing-ok*s seems nearest to the truth.[83]

In comparison, the Hngetwin meditation monastery figures are interesting. Among the 46 monks there, 18 failed to answer the relevant questions at all. Of those 12 who did identify themselves with the monastery as a *gaing*, three recognized a standard *thathanabaing-gyok-ok-dauk* system. The *gyok* in this hierarchy was named as *thathanabaing* by two others, who mentioned no other officials; another monk identified the one the others thought of as *"thathanabaing"* and made him an *ok*. Of the remaining six, one cited "Satubumika" as *thathanabaing* (!), four placed their ordaining monks in various positions, and the last showed a similar confusion. This is an extraordinary result for a sect which contrasts itself so sharply with the others.

Of the 16 non-Hngetwin respondents from other monasteries, mostly Thudhamma, two gave "Satubumika" as *thathanabaing;* another had a named but unidentified (as to location) monk in that position, while a fourth had a Pakokku Mahawithudarama Taik monk there. Twelve recognized various patterns involving two or three officials: of the 26 monks named, as many as 17 belong to monasteries where the respondent was ordained or ones neighboring those, and some of these may be correct answers. In two cases, recognition of office was coupled with ignorance of the name of the monks involved.

The Shweman Sayadaw's monks all named the Shweman as their *gaing-ok,* giving no other names. The Mandalay Shwegyin monastery monks referred to the Shwegyin *rattaguru* as *thathanabaing* and said that there were *gyok* and *ok* monks but did not give the latters' names. As we have seen, the Shwegyin answers were apparently standardized, and we cannot know what the monks would have replied if left to themselves.

If this data is compared with the description of the hierarchy contained in the Shwegyin *Wazo* lists considered earlier, the conclusion as far as hierarchy recognition is concerned is that, while some pattern is known to most monks, there is no standardized reaction to the questions. While the Shwegyin and Dwaya monks seem to recognize a definite strucure, the Hngetwin and Pakokku respondents are definitely confused.

---

83. The usual descending order of these titles is: *gaing-gyok, gaing-ok,* and *gaing-dauk* (see Glossary).

More Thudhamma answers would perhaps have given us a still vaguer picture. The confusion prevalent regarding the lower ranks of the hierarchy is particularly notable, for one would expect monks to know their immediate superiors best of all if there were a working hierarchy. Instead the Sangha seems to be an army knowing its generals and colonels (without a clear understanding of the meaning of those ranks) but not its captains and lieutenants.

Though not conclusive, this interpretation gains some force when it is put beside Nash's formal statements, referred to above, about the "vagueness" of the *taik* and *gaing* levels of organization in villages. If hierarchical awareness among fairly sophisticated members of city monasteries is vague and confused, the situation in villages—and therefore among the great majority of the Burmese Sangha—cannot help but be more so. Here Nash is helpful again:

> But the persistent theme always returns: each monk is self-sufficient; each monastery is self-regulating; there is not a real enforceable hierarchy in Burmese Buddhism. It is as Mendelson (1961) reported. Even at the national and urban levels, a series of autonomous monks and monasteries without an organizational format exists. Whatever organization there is results from the charisma of a given monk, not from the structure of Buddhism. [Nash 1965:144][84]

The conclusion seems inescapable that there is no great degree of organization or formal structure in the Sangha today. I have attempted to describe the minimal structures which I could discover and to give some of the basic characteristics of the monkhood as it has existed and does exist in Burma. My conclusion is that the strength of the Sangha is quite obviously to be found not in its national ecclesiastical structure but in such fundamental areas as its adherence to the Vinaya, its *taga* and *tagama* relationships, its role as culture carrier in education, and, most importantly, its ability to discipline itself through the formation of small, governable monastic groups such as *taik*s or sects, which are the Sangha's best defense against the efforts of those who would use it for secular ends. In these small groups, the questionnaire data suggest, it is not the total ecclesiastical structure of the Sangha that the monks were familiar with but the more important network of discipleship of teacher and pupil, the very lineages so important in the history of the Sangha as presented in the first two chapters.

84. For more on monastic structure, see Spiro 1970:310–320.

4. Nationalism and the Sangha

After the fall of royal Burma in 1885, the country became a colony of the British Empire, with all the strains that such a status imposes. In a sense, no sooner had the British taken over than indigenous forces of resistance were created that we now describe as nationalistic. The Sangha was not uninvolved in this national process of self-definition and liberation. Decades of armed resistance to the British followed King Thibaw's final plea for Burmans to defend their country. Nationalism can therefore be said to have begun as colonialism entered the scene. The development of nationalism is now reasonably well documented in a number of works, and a review in detail is not necessary here, but the role of the Sangha in this period must be extracted from such available political accounts to discover those items that afford definite proof of monastic participation in lay affairs. British writers did not study the Sangha at all closely, so that generalities overwhelmingly prevail in their description of the monks' role in the development of nationalism. Such expressions as "the monks" or "a number of monks" or "a majority of monks" must do service for unavailable statistics and details. In Cady's *A History of Modern Burma* (1958), a work which depends heavily on British sources, the expression "political *pongyis*" becomes little more than a cliché. Apart from adding a little material from biographies in Burmese of a few leading *sayadaw*s, our task here is a rather negative one: measuring the extent of our ignorance so that future researchers may be aware of the problems that need tackling.

Early Rebels: Monks or Ex-monks

A genuine criterion does not exist for determining exactly who, among the monks, participated in lay nationalist movements. All politically active monks tend to be labeled by colonial authorities as "political agitators in the yellow robe." This label is very ambiguously used at times: when an author wishes to strengthen his contention that monks were involved in the matter in hand, he will stress the religious identity of the participants at the expense of their political role; when he wishes to defend the monkhood, he writes that no "real" monks participated, only agitators in the robe, as in the case of Saya San, the leader of the peasants' revolt in the thirties. The official report on Saya San's rebellion (Burma 1934) tells us that he put on the yellow robe more than once in the course of his activities. One rarely reads an account of his rebellion that does not bring in the fact that Saya San was an ex-monk.[1] What is meant by monk in this instance? Are not all Burmese men to some extent ex-monks? Most adult males traditionally joined the Sangha, no matter how briefly. Have authors, in other words, made the necessary distinction between temporary and lasting membership in the Order? Cady (1958:57) has made this point, stating that individuals who wished to enjoy the status implied by the yellow robe without full responsibility for keeping the rules remained as novices within the Order, though this does not prevent him elsewhere from forgetting this. The truth is that few pointers exist to indicate whether nationalist or "political" monks were temporary or not. On the other hand, evidence is clear that fully ordained, "career" monks did participate in politics. In short, the fact that the Burmese Sangha is an open institution and that people can go in and out of it as they please, makes the definition of a "political *pongyi*" extremely difficult, if not impossible. Consequently, discussion must be limited to the appearance of the yellow robe in lay affairs, whether meetings, the courtroom, or riots or disorders of one sort or another. Further research is needed before much more can be said.

Most authors agree that the period of monastic "leadership" of the nationalist movement (which preceded the development of lay political parties with primarily lay programs) was a backward-looking one. The shock of conquest, it is argued, caused the people to forget the unpleasant aspects of royal times and to gild the lily of ancient institutions. For some time, religion was the only unifying factor available, the only way Burmese nationalism could begin to express itself. Throughout the period we are studying, references to efforts at reviving the kingship constantly recur; and the major example, though only one of many, is the Saya San rebellion. I have dealt with the ideology behind such efforts

---

1. Saya San will be more fully discussed later in this chapter.

elsewhere (Mendelson 1960, 1961a, b) and cannot go into the matter extensively here. It must be said, however, that members of the Sangha were not necessarily the only Burmese to participate in this kind of revivalism: also involved were a large variety of *sayas*[2] whose various magical techniques were closely associated with the idea of a royal revival. I have no doubt, from very scattered evidence, some of it in the Saya San case itself, that some political *pongyi*s were in fact *saya*s themselves or worked in close cooperation with such *saya*s. A great deal has been made in the literature, especially that predating the origins of the present-day Burmese government, about the leftist inclinations of young nationalists. In the course of time, monks certainly arose to share these leftist inclinations and to work for programs that were predominantly lay ones. A much larger body of monks may have been influenced by nationalistic ideas which had nothing whatsoever to do with leftist views, though, in the course of time the messianic elements in both revivalism and socialism blended to some extent.[3]

Monks were definitely involved with the early outbreaks of resistance to the British colonization, but there is only the most meager evidence for Sangha participation in the repeated outbreaks of rebellion in Arakan and Tenasserim in the 1830s, which arose mostly, according to Cady, "from convictions that an indigenous ruler was required to foster the Buddhist faith" (1958:9). The same is true of the outbreaks in 1852, following the annexation of Pegu by the British.[4]

Royalist feeling asserted itself most strongly, of course, when the British took over the whole of Burma in 1886. Royal pretenders appeared from all corners of the land, many self-styled as "princes" with more noble ambition than regal blood in their veins. Others were vestiges of monarchs past who had placed offspring in charge of various towns. Whether real or pretending, these claimants raised what following they could and caused the British much trouble. Scott and Hardiman's *Gazetteer of Upper Burma and the Shan States* (1900) remains the classic source for information on the monks' role in these incidents, though they see the participating monks as "bad monks," ignoring the fact that many seem to have taken off their robes before attacking. We

2. Teacher or expert of sorts in often estoteric areas such as astrology, folk medicine, charms, and the like. Usually the term implies deference and respect.
3. Sarkisyanz (1965) has explored this blending in considerable detail. J. F.
4. See also Furnivall 1948:200.

will briefly review the cases they mention, noting in passing how many monks involved were from Upper Burma as well as the presence of the revivalist theme already noted.

The first case is that of the Myanchaung Sayadaw, a Shan from a village in Lower Burma. He went to Mandalay and obtained from the Taingda Mingyi (Prince) an order to create a diversion in Lower Burma in favor of the king. His attack was launched in 1885, with forces composed mainly of Shans, who looted the Burmese peasantry. His efforts affected Shwegyin District and portions of Amherst, the Salween, Toungoo, and Pegu, before he was captured by Christian Karens in 1886 and hung. He had claimed the power of conferring invulnerability. Of this incident Scott and Hardiman write:

This rising cannot be attributed to monkish discontent. It was arranged for before Mandalay was occupied, and there is good ground for believing that it was really what the leaders professed it to be, a political diversion in favour of the Burmese Government. In this respect it differed from the plots and risings which took place after the annexation, and it gives an excellent example of the use made of the sacred order by the Burmese Government. [1900, 1, pt. 2:9] [5]

The next case concerns one U Ottama,[6] who in 1886 unsuccessfully attacked Salin in the Minbu District with upwards of 3,000 men. The north of Minbu remained in his control until the end of 1888. U Ottama appears to have established a small principality of his own, taking the title of *mingyi,* with an *atwinwun* (palace administrator) and two chief lieutenants, one "like himself, a monk who had thrown aside the yellow robe." He indulged in systematic pillage and exploitation of his area. At his trial in 1886 he claimed he had gone to get a commission from the Myinzaing Prince to fight the British. He was hung in 1889. Scott and Hardiman (1900, 1, pt. 2:9–10) quoting a letter written by a Mandalay monk to a brother monk in Tavoy, show how a link was made by the monks between the decline of Buddhism and the rule of the "ignorant, wicked and animal-like" foreigner, though even this letter acknowledges that Ottama *left* his robe, that is, the Sangha, before starting his rebellion.

5. Cady (1958:139) has summarized the data on the Karen Christian role in suppressing this rising.

6. Not to be confused with the twentieth-century nationalist monk of the same name, discussed later in this chapter.

Another monk, U Parama of Hsenwi, came to Mandalay and obtained from the *thathanabaing* an appointment as *gaing-gyok* (district Sangha official) in the Hsipaw region.[7] He joined the Myinzaing Prince's confederacy; then, on the death of that prince, he joined the faction of the Limbin Prince, who made him *"thathanabaing"* of the Shan States.[8] When Limbin surrendered in 1887, U Parama tried to get Kengtung to rise and later joined another pretender in Shan China. Scott and Hardiman write: "U Parama affords an example of affection for the State rather than for the Church, for a letter was sent to him from the *thathanabaing* in Mandalay advising him to be reconciled with the the British Government" (1900, 1, pt. 2:9–10).

Among other supporters of the Myinzaing Prince were U Rewata of Megawadi Monastery, Mandalay, and one U Einda, who did not himself lead but incited uprisings, notably in Henzada and Tavoy. They were imprisoned. U Thumana of Yandoon, originally a Shwebo man, was also implicated, because he had called on U Rewata to tell him that he proposed to incite the people of Yandoon, Pantanaw, and Maubin. He was also detained when it was shown that his whole monastery had been implicated in uprisings.[9]

Also involved with rebellious princes was the Modi Sayadaw of Mandalay. In 1887 the younger of two princes was brought to Mandalay and entrusted to the Modi Sayadaw. A conspiracy to take over Mandalay was quashed in his monastery, and the *sayadaw* was deported. Magical apparatus was discovered which was associated with royal pretenders: the elder brother had a *galon*[10] seal; the monks reportedly set fire to the Modi Monastery on the day of the younger brother's arrival in order to demonstrate his supernatural powers; bullet-proof charms were distributed; and an oath was taken with water in which a Buddha image had been dipped.[11]

Partly at the instigation of U Rewata of Mandalay (originally from Shwebo), U Sandima of Tavoy, was implicated in the uprisings there

7. Hsenwi and Hsipaw are in the Shan States.

8. The use of the title *thathanabaing* here by Scott and Hardiman is, of course, inappropriate, because it is not within the power of a mere prince to appoint one. It is the prerogative of the rightfully constituted king. J. F.

9. Scott and Hardiman 1900, 1, pt. 2:11.

10. From *garuda* (Sk): *garula* (P): mythical bird, the symbol used by Saya San.

11. Scott and Hardiman 1900, 1, pt. 2:11–13. See also Woodman 1962:347.

in 1888. U Tha Dun, also of Tavoy, gave up the robe after the murder of a British township officer and constituted himself the *mingala bo,* or chief lieutenant, of the Sindo Prince. He fled to Siam in 1888 but was sent back and hung.[12] Another Upper Burman, U Thuriya, planned a general rising in the Paungde-Tharrawaddy area in 1888. He joined with dacoits and proclaimed the authority of the Myingun Prince, the restoration of Burmese monarchy, and the goal of throwing out all heretical foreigners. Then he threw off his robe and attacked the railway; the revolt failed, and U Thuriya disappeared.[13] The next uprising was started in 1889 by U Po Lu, an ex-monk of Sandoway, together with a blind monk who was an expert in invulnerability charms. They marched into Sandoway with a rabble of country folk. Two other Upper Burman monks concerned, the Theingon Sayadaw and the Minbya Sayadaw, both disappeared. Po Lu declared himself a *minlaung* (pretender), and claimed Arakan. Scott and Hardiman write: "The monks were at the bottom of it and were doubtless inspired by the disaffected in Mandalay through the agency of itinerant mendicants" (1900, 1, pt. 2:15). Finally, U Kelatha and eighteen followers made an attack on Fort Dufferin in 1887. This monk, significantly, claimed to be an incarnation of the *setkya* prince[14] and laid claim to the throne of Burma.[15]

The data indicate that these were all backward-looking rebellions, the first of a long series which persisted well after the evolution of lay Burmese nationalism. Clearly in many cases monks simply became laymen in a time of crisis to act as officers to princes or as princes themselves. The monks were acting not so much as monks but as Burmese, like many monks who, throughout history, have been called from the Sangha as educated men to take over important lay posts, as well as, in some cases, the throne itself. Understandably monks from the areas most recently "pacified" by the British conquerors (Upper Burma and the Shan States) took the lead; these areas are the traditional center of Burmese rule—especially Shwebo it might be added, where one finds

---

12. Scott and Hardiman 1900, 1, pt. 2:13–14.
13. Scott and Hardiman 1900, 1, pt. 2:13–14.
14. The prince who will wield the supernatural circular weapon (*setkya*) as the world emperor. See Mendelson 1961b:564.
15. Scott and Hardiman 1900, 1, pt. 2:15. See also Cady 1958:137.

the symbolic "earth of victory."[16] The evidence for a network of monastic intercommunication is reasonably impressive, though we must remember that monks had been used often on diplomatic missions in royal times and were, as students, great travelers. I have tried to show elsewhere (1961a, b) how the *setkyamin* or *cakravartin* theme originated, probably in the time of Bodawpaya and Bagyidaw. In the royal past, the notion of a world emperor, with certain messianic overtones of tidying up the world for the coming Buddha, had probably been harnessed to duly constituted central authority, and it legitimized the careers of Southeast Asian conquest on which such authority embarked. Gradually, with the fall of Burmese royalty, the social area in which royal pretensions could be found was naturally enlarged by uncertain circumstances, and we begin to find among quite humble sections of the population and their *saya*s the notion of the "true," mysterious religious prince who could restore Buddhism to Burma. The case of U Kelatha illustrates the beginnings of this process.[17] Finally we may note that there is no evidence that large numbers of monks were involved in the uprisings; rather, most of them had seemingly accepted the ruling of the deposed king's *thathanabaing*.[18] This illustrates the contention of many authors that the Primate (and thus many more of the Sangha) could have given the British serious trouble during the period of military pacification had he wished to do so.

Sangha Leadership and a Missing King

A vital problem for both the Sangha and the British during the entire colonial period was what to do about the office of the *thathanabaing,* an issue that relates very closely to an understanding of the nature of the Order itself. In Chapter 2 the details of the last royal efforts in this area were traced. King Thibaw had appointed both the Taungdaw (his teacher) and the Shwegyin Sayadaws as *thathanabaings,* but the Shwegyin

16. The earth at Shwebo is special because the first king of the final dynasty reigned there. J. F.

17. For a later example, see Cady 1958:260.

18. King Thibaw's *thathanabaing* still exerted some influence until his death in 1894. Smith (1965:55) has made the point that a belated British attempt was made to bolster the *thathanabaing*'s authority as a direct result of the threat of the political monks; he quotes a 1921 source (*Rangoon Gazette Weekly Bulletin,* Dec. 9, 1921) for an order from the primate.

went his own way and, in effect, left the Taungdaw alone in the post along with an advisory Thudhamma Council. There was no *thathanabaing* for British Lower Burma, and therefore when Upper Burma was taken over in 1885 and the king exiled there was immediately a question of what should be done about the authority of the Taungdaw Sayadaw.

As Harvey (1946:26) has pointed out, Sir Edward Sladen, resident at Mandalay for five years before the annexation, and an expert in Burmese political and legal matters, proposed a path of wisdom which was not followed by his compatriots. Writing to the chief commissioner of British Burma in 1884, Sladen stated that he had found the *thathanabaing* system efficient in Upper Burma and recommended that it should be applied in Lower Burma, presumably with a separate *thathanabaing*. Sladen argued that the people of Upper Burma would probably welcome the British

. . . if only we did not interfere with religion so seriously as we have done since we took possession of [Lower] Burma.

We have studiously refused to recognize the Buddhist ecclesiastical code. . . . The result . . . is that the power of the priesthood to regulate church affairs is almost nil, their influence for good has vastly deteriorated, and Buddhism . . . is broken up into numerous sects and schisms, without and beyond all ecclesiastical control. The worst of it is, that the members of all these sects divide themselves socially as well as religiously, and the domestic relations of life have in many cases been materially disconcerted. . . . [In Lower Burma we should] recognize the Buddhist ecclesiastical code so far at least as it does not clash with any of our own codes of law and procedure. The main effect of this change would be that an archbishop and bishops would be appointed with lawful authority to control the priesthood and to decide all cases arising amongst them of a purely civil and religious character. By this means the present dissent from orthodox Buddhism would be effectually checked, and social order, wherever it has suffered by religious disturbance, would be practically restored. Nor must it be over-looked that this concession to the priesthood of a right they exercised and still enjoy under Burmese rule, would not only propitiate all orthodox priests in British Burma, but remove from the minds of those in Upper Burma any objection they may now feel to become at any near or remote period, loyal subjects of the British Government.[19]

19. This letter is quoted from the Simla Document (Tin Tut 1943), which refers to the (London) *Times*, Jan. 1, 1886. See also Pyinnyaramikamaha Sayadaw 1958:25, which refers to a seventeen-point order passed by Sladen in 1885: the fifth point protects Buddhism.

Harvey points out two occasions on which the Burmese themselves asked for a primate. In December 1886, at Mandalay, the Taungdaw Sayadaw, who had been tentatively recognized as primate but not confirmed in any of his rights, and thirteen of his colleagues met with the commander-in-chief, Sir Frederick Roberts, and promised to preach submission to British rule in every village throughout the land. At the same interview they asked to be confirmed in their jurisdiction over the Sangha. In March 1886 citizens of Rangoon told the governor general, the marquis of Dufferin and Ava, on a visit to newly conquered Burma, that they wanted a primate. Harvey (1946:27) concludes that it would have been extremely easy to staff the ecclesiastical commission with "our own men" and deplores the mistake which was made in allowing the opportunity to pass.[20]

Documentation is scanty on British relations with the *thathanabaing* in the early days of the annexation of Upper Burma: cooperation of a sort must have existed, with the British delaying somewhat until they should gauge the direction of the wind and the Burmese hoping for backing for the *thathanabaing*. Cady refers to a visit by the *thathanabaing* to Lower Burma, where the high commissioner, Sir Charles Bernard, discovered the Primate had little authority. When Sir Charles Crosthwaite took over from Bernard in 1887, he rejected the hierarchy's assistance.[21] The Taungdaw Sayadaw, famous neither for learning nor for administrative ability but deriving some prestige from having been Thibaw's personal teacher, died in 1895. The Mandalay elite among the laity and the Sangha could not agree on his successor, and two factions arose, one headed by the Megawadi Sayadaw, the other by the Pahkan Sayadaw, neither of whom was recognized by the British.[22] Interestingly, the Pahkan Sayadaw and the Taungdaw Sayadaw had both refused the Education Department's request regarding assistant teachers as far back as 1887.[23] According to one source, the Taungdaw had never been accepted by the Sangha, who regarded the Pahkan Sayadaw as the

20. Woodman (1962:338, 426) and Geary (1886:118–119) provide similar data for other areas.
21. Cady 1958:169. Smith (1965:38–57) has reviewed this question and provides other sources.
22. Taw Sein Ko 1913:216–223.
23. Payapyu Sayadaw 1928: 146, 189, 179, 191.

"*samuti*"[24] *thathanabaing,* but the Pahkan is said to have had other rivals, such as the Mogaung Sayadaw, who may have been the monk banished in Thibaw's reign for disrespect to the Thudhamma Council. Another source, however, sees the Mogaung Sayadaw as backed by the council in opposition to the Pahkan.[25] Clearly there were Sangha factions competing for the Taungdaw's title but the colonial government backed none of them.

In 1901 the venerable Kinwun Mingyi led the citizens of Mandalay in agitating for a primate. In October of that year a very large meeting was held at the foot of Mandalay Hill to elect a *thathanabaing* and voting proceeded. The Mota Sayadaw won, followed by the Taunggwin. Lord Curzon, the governor general of India, met the primate-elect in the northern capital in the following November and discussed arrangements with him and with local officials. However, the Mota Sayadaw died of fever in March 1902. Further elections were fortunately unnecessary owing to a clause in the rules to the effect that the runner-up in the election would succeed in such a case. Thus ended an eight-year inter-regnum marked by considerable "indecision" on the part of the monks in the capital.[26]

In more than one place in his papers, Taw Sein Ko (1913:216, 219) refers to the "political expediency" of recognizing a *thathanabaing.* Information from another source sheds some light on the eight-year interregnum. The periodical *Buddhism,* edited by the English monk "Ananda Metteya," published its first volume in September 1903, and it contained an account of the preparations for the installation of the new primate. The following passage describes the reasons for the monks' "indecision" in choosing a *thathanabaing:*

This introduction of Parliamentary methods, however, proved more or less a failure. The majority of the reverend gentlemen being much too overawed by the Vice-Regal presence to explain the position of affiairs, all the talking was done by one erratic monk who claimed, not without provoking general laughter, that the great thing needed for the preservation of the Religion was that *he* should be appointed Thathanabaing. "What was the use," as

---

24. *Sammuti* (P): consent, permission, that which is generally accepted. That is, the monk who is generally accepted by the Sangha as its head, as contrasted to a *thathanabaing* appointed by a king or the state. J. F.

25. Smith 1965:49.

26. Taw Sein Ko 1913:216–217.

several of the chief Theras [monks] in Mandalay asked us afterwards, when we pointed out the magnificent opportunity they had lost by not agreeing. "What was the use of the Uparaja [vice-regent] asking *us* to decide who should be Thathanabaing? The pupils of each great Thera will always think it to be wrong to vote for anyone else than his own teacher, and all the Theras will never agree. If the Uparaja, like our Burmese kings, had said, 'So and so *is* the Thathanabaing' then we would accept his selection and everyone would be very pleased.[27]

Possibly the election of Mota and the confirmation of Taunggwin on Mota's death were somewhat arbitrarily pushed through. The position of the colonial administration is expounded in the journal *Buddhism:* "The thing needed is a properly constituted Thathanabaing; but it will be many years before the whole Buddhist priesthood in Burma will understand the advantages of union, or the real benefits of an election: so that if the matter had been postponed until the monks could come to a fairly unanimous decision, it would have been long before the troubles that a lack of central authority in the Sangha have given rise to, could be rectified."[28]

According to accounts in *Buddhism,* the Burmese were uncertain of the government's aims. The people could not understand why the government was so fearful of exercising one of the main prerogatives of former rulers: naming a primate. Knowing how little monks understood elections and how disunited they were in the very nature of things, some even "saw in this very election itself only an attempt to shift the responsibility for the absence of a Thathanabaing on to the shoulders of the Mandalay theras."[29] Clearly it was the king and no one else who should nominate the primate, and the monks were upset at having to decide on one among themselves. On its side, the government felt that it had no authority to appoint a new *thathanabaing,* though it would recognize one chosen by the Sangha. The government apparently waited to recognize the Mota, wanting guarantees of support and the certainty of having the "right man."[30] As we shall see, the government later made out that it had wanted a *thathanabaing* all the time: if there had not been one it was only because the British could not find a primate to recognize.

27. *Buddhism,* 1, no. 1 (Sept. 15, 1903):147.
28. Ibid.
29. Ibid., 1, no. 2 (Dec. 1903):180.
30. Ibid., p. 192.

Belated British Support of Sangha Leadership

In any case, in November 1903 the Taunggwin Sayadaw was formally recognized, and he was given a *sanad,* or government charter, delineating his powers. A speech made by the lieutenant governor, Sir Hugh Barnes, on that occasion contains the essence of the misunderstanding which sapped the primacy of its strength. The speech[31] began with a review of the history of the question. He pointed to the British support of the Taungdaw Sayadaw until his death in 1895 and to the reason for delaying recognition of a successor: "It was [. . . the government's] duty, and their policy, to abstain from all official intercourse with the ecclesiastical organization of the Buddhist religion." Nevertheless, it was not true that Lord Dufferin had refused to recognize a primate, Barnes continued. In 1891 the Taungdaw's jurisdiction over both Upper and Lower Burma had been "formally notified to all District Officers." In 1886, in Rangoon, Dufferin had promised Buddhists that the government would respect Buddhism, recognize its dignitaries, and do its utmost to please the Burmese. Thus the 1903 action was not an innovation: the British had simply been unable to find a *thathanabaing* to recognize.

Barnes then reviewed the reasons for the present *durbar,* or official ceremony, wishing the British point of view to be clearly understood. There was, he stated, a practically unanimous desire in Upper Burma for a primate. The 50,000-odd monks in Upper Burma needed a central authority; moreover there were many ecclesiastical dignitaries in Upper Burma whose appointment rested with the *thathanabaing* and whose positions were thus likely to be disputed if a central authority did not exist. The government of Burma needed order in the "church" since, as was well known, the "church" had in its hands the education of the young.

The civil courts could not be expected to deal on their merits with Vinaya cases, as Barnes saw matters, and had no option but to enforce the orders of the duly constituted central ecclesiastical authority. At the same time it was important that "the Buddhist community should clearly perceive and understand the limitations of the recognition that is now given": that authority was administrative but not independent of the

31. Ibid., p. 197.

courts of law, and that the primacy must support law and order on pain of being abolished. These limitations were to be clearly outlined in the *sanad*. In the following crucial passage, having recognized that Burmese monks were virtually unable to understand democracy, Barnes throws the responsibility for monastic organization in democratic terms back onto the monkhood. The passage brilliantly sums up the misunderstanding over the role of the *thathanabaing:*

We English, you must remember, have our own Religion, our Christian religion, in which we firmly and devoutly believe; and though, in accordance with the wise policy enjoined by the Great Queen Victoria in Her Majesty's famous Proclamation of 1858, we abstain from imposing our convictions upon others and molest no one in the observance of his Religious Faith; and though we extend to all religious communities alike the equal and impartial protection of the law, and refuse to favour one rather than the other; that is the whole extent of our obligation, and no Religion but our own can claim from us anything more. Therefore, you must clearly realize that we cannot interfere in the internal affairs of the Buddhist Hierarchy, and that it is not our business to interest ourselves in the selection of its chief. These are matters for the Buddhist community alone. You must understand that we do not appoint your *Thathanabaing*. We merely ratify the selection made by the monks themselves, and we grant our official recognition of it for purposes of administrative convenience only and because the recognition is a prerogative which the people expect the ruling power to exercise, and one which has come down to us from the Kings of Burma.[32]

Against this background the *sanad* given to the *thathanabaing* must be viewed. Because of its importance, it is quoted in full here:

1. Whereas by ancient custom, ecclesiastical affairs in Upper Burma are superintended by a *Thathanabaing;* and whereas the Taungdaw *Sayadaw,* who was *Thathanabaing* in the time of the Burmese Government and was recognized as *Thathanabaing* by the British Government, died in 1895; and whereas on the death of the Taungdaw *Sayadaw* the appointment of a *Thathanabaing* remained in abeyance because the Buddhists of Mandalay and other places in Upper Burma could not agree on the selection of a successor; and whereas the Taunggwin *Sayadaw* has now been selected as successor by an influential and venerable assembly of monks at Mandalay; and whereas there is a general wish in Upper Burma that the Taunggwin *Sayadaw* should assume the office of *Thathanabaing,* and should be recognized as *Thathanabaing* by the Lieutentant Governor of Burma.
2. I, Sir Hugh Barnes, Lieutentant Governor of Burma, hereby declare that I

32. Ibid., pp. 196–197. Smith (1965:51) cites some reactions.

recognize the Taunggwin *Sayadaw* as *Thathanabaing* of Upper Burma, and I grant him this *Sanad* in testimony of the fact that I and my successors recognize him and will recognize him as such.

3. This position does not render him independent of the Courts of Justice in matters which are within the jurisdiction of those Courts. Nor does it confer upon the *Thathanabaing* authority to do anything in the enforcement of monastic discipline or otherwise, which is contrary to the Civil or Criminal Law. Nor does it exempt the *Thathanabaing* or other ecclesiastical authorities from attendance before the Courts.

4. But, subject to these provisos, I recognize the *Thathanabaing* as supreme in all matters relating to the internal administration and control of the Buddhist hierarchy in Upper Burma, the discipline of the monastic order, and the repression of abuses therein.

5. The Civil Courts will, within the limits of their jurisdiction, give effect to the orders of the *Thathanabaing* and of the *Gainggyoks, Gaingoks, Gaingdauks* and other Ecclesiastical authorities duly appointed by him, in so far as those orders relate to matters which are within the competence of those authorities.

6. The Government expects the *Thathanabaing* and *Gainggyoks, Gaingoks,* and *Gaingdauks* under his authority to use their influence on the side of law and order and to assist in the work of education. In consideration of the assistance thus rendered, I hereby promise to maintain the privileges at present enjoyed by religious communities in Upper Burma in respect of—

i). the exemption from *thathameda* [income tax] of all ministers, priests and teachers of religion and schoolmasters;

ii). the exemption from land revenue of land which, on 13th July 1889, belongs to the site and curtilage [fenced yard] of any monastery, pagoda or other sacred building and which continues to be used for the purpose of such monastery, pagoda or building;

iii). the free grant of land for sites of religious edifices;

iv). the free grant of Timber from Government forests for the repairs of pagodas, monasteries and *zayats* [rest houses].

7. This *sanad* is granted upon the condition that the Taunggwin *Sayadaw,* as *Thathanabaing,* shall continue to give his assistance and support to the government, and shall not contravene or countenance the contravention of its laws. I reserve to myself and my successors the right to cancel this *Sanad* now granted to him and to withdraw my recognition of the Taunggwin *Sayadaw* as *Thathanabaing* should he fail to observe the above mentioned conditions.

8. In order to assist the *Thathanabaing* in his functions, I hereby grant to him an official seal, and I authorize him to issue subordinate ecclesiastical seals approved by the Government.[33]

33. *Buddhism,* 1, no. 2 (Dec. 1903):197–199. This is also reported in the Simla Document (Tin Tut 1943).

The monk who received this sanad, the Taunggwin Sayadaw, had studied under the 2d Maungdaung Sayadaw as well as under the Bongyaw and Sankyaung. He was honored by King Mindon, whose chief queen was his lay supporter. The Taunggwin Mingyi invited him to administer the Taunggwin Taik, where he developed his fame as a Vinaya master to the point where the *thathanabaing,* the Taungdaw Sayadaw, appointed him his deputy in charge of Vinaya matters, a post that led to his election in 1901. Taw Sein Ko (1913:221–223) describes an interview with the Taunggwin Sayadaw in which the monk spoke of his concerns just before his formal appointment.

The primate represented himself as a man who above all hated schisms and would do his best to conciliate opponents, although we learn elsewhere, in a communiqué of his on education, that he did not approve the rules framed by the Shwegyin sect.[34] He told Taw Sein Ko that he was thinking of appointing an Advisory Board of three aged *sayadaws.* headed by the eighty-two-year-old Hladwe Sayadaw. He also planned to appoint a new Thudhamma Council of eight *sayadaws.* "Draft rules had been framed regulating the admission of monks into the Order, and their conduct while in orders, and defining the policy of the Buddhist Church. These rules would be submitted to the Local Government for approval, and, when approved, would have the force of law."[35] He would also appoint *gaing-gyoks* (district Sangha officers) and, their subordinates and, "in doing so, he would consult the wishes of the local monks and elders." The *gaing-gyoks,* and so on, were probably already in existence, and the nature of the thathanabaing-ship was such that the primate could do little more than ratify the wishes of the local populations of monks.[36] The primate was also preoccupied, according to Taw Sein Ko, with the succession question, about which Taw Sein Ko gave him some advice, describing how papal elections were held.[37]

In contrast to the Taunggwin's concern over schisms, the British

34. Taw Sein Ko 1913:268.
35. Taw Sein Ko 1913:222.
36. The British jurists seem to have accepted this; see May Oung 1914:202.
37. Note that Taw Sein Ko (1913:221) seems very much interested in establishing law and order in the Sangha, most likely because of the monastic role in rebellions only a few years earlier, as described earlier in this chapter. He also clearly expects the Taunggwin, unlike the Pakan, to cooperate with the British plans for education. J. F.

apparently did not realize the importance of sects, and Sladen, as noted above, seems to have expected British recognition of a primate to end all dissension. After the death of Thibaw the Shwegyin Sayadaw was not officially recognized, even though he had once refused the position of being joint *thathanabaing*. Two informants, one the surviving lay secretary to the Taunggwin who was then a retired barrister living in Mandalay, and the other the Sankyaung Sayadaw, a member of the Thudhamma Council, both told me that the Taunggwin's reign was viewed by the Shwegyin as a period of discontent. They said that intra-sect disputes were settled within the sect as usual but that Shwegyin–Thudhamma quarrels were sometimes brought to the primate for reference. In one case requiring the intervention of a court, the British policy regarding sects was quoted by May Oung:

It is not the policy of Government to interfere in matters of religion, and it would be utterly contrary to every British tradition to lay down that there should be but one Buddhist sect in Burma, and that every Burman who wished to embrace a religious life should accept the dogmas laid down by the Thathanabaing. It is expressly stated in the Sanad that recognition of the Thathanabaing by the State does not extend to matters of dogma, but it seems obvious that if the Thathanabaing had power to direct a monk to leave a monastery, and to enforce his order through a Civil Court without the merits being gone into, the life of a schismatic might be made intolerable, the way would be laid open to persecution, and the effect would be the same as if the Government openly recognized the Thathanabaing's authority on matters of dogma.   [1914:204]

It so happened that the court ruled in favor of the primacy in this case, but the possibility had been raised of challenging the *thathanabaing's* power by taking disputes to a civil court, as in *sanghika* or *poggalika,* property ownership questions, particularly if sectarian issues were involved.

The Undermining of the Sangha Hierarchy by Civil Courts

Such a position by a civil court contrasts significantly with a much earlier judge's ruling in 1893, on an appeal concerning the primate's authority to settle a property dispute within a monastery (*U Teza v. U Pynnya*):

There is no doubt some difficulty in defining exactly the position of the Buddhist Church in Upper Burma under the present Government. Under the Burmese Government the State and the Church were in a sense one, under the same sovereign as head, much as the English Church is part of the State under the English Sovereign. With the annexation of course the former relations of Church and State came to an end, but I conceive that what the State has not taken away is still left to the Church, and that the presumption is in favour of the Church's retention of its privileges until the contrary is shown. Consequently, in the absence of any proof of a different state of things, it must be taken that the constitution and authority of the ecclesiastical hierarchy have been preserved along with the property of the Church.[38]

A letter from the *thathanabaing* himself to the court in this case points out that in Burmese times there was a hierarchy of appeals to *taik-ok*s, *gaing-dauk*s, and so on, up to the Thudhamma Council, whose decision was final and that the Hluttdaw, or royal council of laymen, never allowed any appeals from such decisions. The letter then expresses views with which some judges were sure to concur:

It is a task of great difficulty for laymen to master completely the subject of the canonical laws of the *Vinaya* prescribed for the guidance of the *Sangha*s; and if appeals are allowed to be entertained by the Courts of justice under the present constitution from the decisions of the said *Sayadaw*s [i.e., on the council] given by the ecclesiastical bench in accordance with the *Vinaya* . . . it will tend to lessen the authority of the *Sayadaw*s over the Buddhist priesthood in future, if this privilege is to be continued and vested in courts of Justice.[39]

His position is supported by a further quotation from the judge's opinion:

The measure of authority claimed for the *Thathanabaing* and the *Thuddhama* Council of *Sayadaw*s as the ruling body of the Buddhist Church is moderate, and there appears to be no good reason why it should not be recognized by the Civil Courts of the country. So long as the *Thathanabaing* in council as the head of the Church keeps within his jurisdiction and does nothing contrary to law, it is not for the Courts to question the correctness of either his orders or proceedings in ecclesiastical matters.[40]

I have discovered very few records of the last thathanabaingship— for Taunggwin was fated to be the last of his line. May Oung refers to the *thathanabaing*'s consultation of his Sangha-Nayaka (chief of the Order) "in all matters relating to religion, but all disputes are settled

38. Chan Htoon 1899–1902, 1:326–337.
39. Chan Htoon 1899–1902, 1:337.
40. Chan Htoon 1899–1902, 1:326–337.

and decided by eight Sudhamma [Thudhamma] *Sayadaw*s who form his Council and are appointed by him."[41] He goes on to say:

At the present day [1914], there is a regular constituted hierarchy of officials appointed by the Thathanabaing. In and for the city of Mandalay there are four Thana [*htana*]-gyok Sayadaws, one for each of the Divisions, Northern, Southern, Eastern and Western. Below these, there is one Taik-ok for each Kyaungdaik. Outside Mandalay, there is one Gaing-dauk in charge of each group of twenty or more monasteries, one Gaing-ok over three Gaing-dauk, and one Gaing-gyok over three Gaing-ok. All these have jurisdiction in matters relating to religious usages and institutions, subject to the control of the Sudhamma Council.   [1914:202]

The surviving lay secretary to the last *thathanabaing,* mentioned above, told me that the records were destroyed during the war and that he only had a faint memory of the structure of the primate's office. He opined that there was, as in the old days, a *mahadanwun,* that is, an officer responsible for census work and the regulation of movements of monks.[42] There were two kinds of Thudhamma Council *sayadaw*s: first-class and second-class councillors, their rank depending on the kind of cases settled by each. The Thudhamma Council did not travel on circuit: its members were mostly Mandalay monks who remained in that city. There were eight *sayadaw*s of the first class in the first council, and no limit to numbers in the second.[43]

There were four members of the first council still alive in 1959: the Sankyaung Sayadaw, AMP,[44] the Khemathiwun Sayadaw, AMP, the Weluwun Sayadaw, AMP, and the Payagyi Taikthit Sayadaw. As noted earlier, I interviewed the first of these, who confirmed the existence of two councils but stated that there were eight members in each. He said

41. The role of the council as an ecclesiastical court seems stronger at this point in history than it had been in the past hundred years. Disputes had, it would seem, been traditionally settled by a series of referrals and appeals to individual officials within whatever hierarchy existed at the time, with the council acting as more of a learned theological debating society than an official monastic supreme court. Under a really powerless *thathanabaing,* the council seems to have assumed a greater role, J. F.

42. The Simla Document (Tin Tut 1943) denies this, but Smith (1965:54) mentions a *mahadanwun* appointment for 1921 with reference only to Vinaya and ecclesiastical law offences.

43. The Masoyein Sayadaw was said to have been a member of one of the councils.

44. A title awarded to honor a monk. See Glossary.

there was also one advisory *Sayadaw,* an older man. Some cases were delegated from the first to the second council, mainly those dealing with disputes over monastery or pagoda ownership. He gave an estimate for all of Burma of 800 *dauks,* 600 *oks,* 400 *gyoks,* but if we were to follow May Oung's proportions (see above) and take the Sankyaung's estimate of 800 *dauks* as a basis, this would give us only 26 *oks* and 89 *gyoks* for the higher ranks. Appointments seem to have been related to size and density of territories. Both informants stated that, under the primate, appointments to the Thudhamma Councils had been for life. After the death of the Taunggwin Sayadaw in the spring of 1938, the council continued under an appointed president, until the Japanese occupation.[45] It was interrupted during the Japanese occupation (1942–1945) but resumed with the same cast when the British returned. The council's functions were minimal, and it was suspended on national independence in 1948. Before then, however, the civil courts had undermined the whole system.

By the mid-thirties there had been a major change in British policy regarding ecclesiastical authority, after a gradual increase in the control of civil courts since the granting of the sanad in 1903, for in 1935 a Rangoon court decision radically changed the nature of the *thathana-baing*'s office. Between 1903 and 1935 the primate's jurisdiction seems to have extended over only Upper Burma, with a council and provincial officials as in royal days, but with very few, if any, lay officials to help him and minimal backing from the central political authority. Without this backing, as a study made in World War II concluded, the primate "ceased to be an effective force in the maintenance of order among the monks and he did not in latter years make any attempt in that direction."[46] "The Thathanabaingship," the text continues, "had in fact become largely a high distinction," and the same is true of the councillors and provincial officials. The hierarchy did, however, continue to intervene in quarrels among monks and between monks and laymen in regard to property alleged to be dedicated to religious purposes.

But the 1935 ruling affected even such mild exertion of authority. The decision held that the "Buddhist Community in Burma has no constitutional or legal status, and is in the same position as any other re-

45. Stewart 1949:7.
46. Simla Document, Tin Tut 1943:14.

ligious body not established by the state."[47] No member of the hierarchy therefore had any jurisdiction to determine disputes of a civil nature whether among monks or between monks and laymen. This had always been true of Lower Burma, but misapprehension regarding civil backing of the *thathanabaing*'s decisions had arisen in Upper Burma from the 1893 *U Teza v. U Pynnya* case[48] onward, all relevant cases being now reversed. The court held further that there was no primacy jurisdiction granted to the ecclesiastical hierarchy in the ceremonies undergone by monks at their ordination and, indeed, that such would be contrary to Vinaya procedure. The following is a quotation from the account of the case in Dunkley:

The office, functions and jurisdiction of the *Thathanabaing* before the British annexation cannot be ascertained with certainty. The Thathanabaings were appointed to prevent corruption of the Buddhist scriptures and to purge the Order of undesirable characters. In course of time they claimed and were sometimes permitted to decide not only questions relating to dogma and discipline, but also disputes concerning civil matters that arose between members of the Order, as well as between such persons and laymen. In the regulation establishing the civil Courts in Upper Burma the tribunals of the Thathanabaing are not mentioned, and no jurisdiction of any sort or kind has been conferred upon the Thathanabaing by any authority competent in that behalf. The recognition of the Taunggwin sayadaw as Thathanabaing by the Lieutenant Governor under the sanad of 1903 had no legal operation. The Thathanabaing's authority has prevailed only in Upper Burma; the Lower Burma Buddhists do not recognize his jurisdiction. There is no "consensual" jurisdiction conferred upon him by the bhikkhus [monks] themselves at their ordination. Neither the Thathanabaing nor the hierarchy set up by him are mentioned in the Vinaya, which comprises the 227 rules by which the Sanghas are governed. The bhikkhu at his ordination undertakes to observe these rules of conduct, but he does not expressly or impliedly give any undertaking to obey the Thathanabaing or to abide by his decisions or of his tribunals. Such an undertaking would run counter to the rules laid down in the Vinaya for the settlement of disputes among members of the Sangha. U Teza v. U Pynnya, and other cases following that case, overruled. [1941:102][49]

Thus the reversal of a decision in a Pakokku property dispute re-

47. Mootham 1939:123.
48. The 1893 case discussed earlier in the chapter, in which the *thathanabaing*'s authority was backed by the court.
49. See Harvey 1946:29.

established, with a vengeance, the purity of Vinaya regulations in Burma. Ironically, it confirmed to some extent the view which I hold of the nature of the Sangha in Burma, though it would challenge the institutions a number of Theravada countries had evolved to cope with politicoreligious relations. The desire of the British at the time must have been less to re-establish a pure model of the Buddhist Order than to assert some degree of control over an undisciplined monkhood. It is beyond the scope of this study to inquire in detail into the British government's reasons for this, though we can make one or two suppositions. Owing to their first fundamental misunderstanding of the place of the primacy, the British had undermined it, in any case, by the sanad of 1903. An undermined Order meant trouble on the disciplinary front. We will see how the monkhood took the lead in the nationalist movement of the 1930s and it will then be clear why the Order could no longer be left to its own devices outside the jurisdiction of the civil courts of the land.[50]

Monastic Resistance to Lay Control

The 1935 judgment caused considerable public concern in Burma because it virtually nullified the positions of *thathanabaing* and the Buddhist hierarchy. Interpretation of the Buddhist canon in matters of faith and doctrine was still left to the Buddhist elders, but this counted for little since everyone was traditionally supposed to make up his own mind on such matters. Thus the death of the last primate in 1939 created a vacuum which, under the circumstances, neither the public nor the monkhood was eager to fill.[51]

50. At issue here also is the unwillingness to allow uncodified Burmese religious traditions to be supreme over Western notions of law in written, rationalized form, subject to challenges by "rights" of individuals, who, in effect, become unwitting agents of religious change. The 1935 decision struck at the heart of the religious system, which as an *ideal* system did not define and codify its need for royal purification efforts and control. The Vinaya defines the ideal, eternal Sangha, not the actual means whereby the state should promote the faith. Because the religious role of the Burmese state was not written, legal, or codified did not mean necessarily that it did not exist as a vital cultural pattern for both the Sangha and the society. To objectify the Sangha's perpetual weaknesses and its dependency would be fatal to its symbolic function as an ideal. British "misunderstanding" of the nature of the Sangha can also be interpreted as a malevolent ignorance and assumed innocence under which Burmese religious culture was "legally" undermined. J. F.

51. For two other views of the matter, see Smith (1965:55–57), who notes

In this vacuum, various attempts were made to legislate civil laws to control the Sangha. As early as 1928 three politicians attempted to promote such control but they were defeated at a meeting led by the Aletawya Sayadaw in Rangoon,[52] and the political leader Sir Joseph Maung Gyi unsuccessfully tried in 1934 to get a bill passed that would have given definite civil jurisdiction to ecclesiastical tribunals in cases involving decisions based on interpretations of Vinaya.[53] After the 1935 case, Sir Joseph once again placed his bill before the Buddhist Order and the public. There was considerable public support for the bill. However, the majority of the monkhood, according to Tin Tut (1943:102), held the following view:

The enactment of the Bill would be an acknowledgement that lay authority has power to legislate in matters which are regulated by the *Vinaya,* and that apart from the desirability or otherwise of the enactment, the monkhood could not acknowledge such power. The orthodox took their stand on the point that Buddha intended the *Vinaya* to be the sole guide in regard to the settlement of disputes within the monkhood and that irrespective of whether the decisions of ecclesiastical tribunals could be enforced in the civil courts or not, they were not prepared to go beyond what is laid down in the *Vinaya.* There was probably also a fear that the proposed Act would become a precedent for the enactment of lay legislation to control the monkhood. Orthodox opinion was so strong that those who favoured the Bill did not press the proposals and Sir Joseph Maung Gyi made no further attempts to revive his Bill.[54]

We see here the emergence of an argument which was to play a very important role in the Sangha's reaction to ecclesiastical jurisdiction for the rest of the period covered by this book.[55] Briefly, the orthodox Sangha appears to have felt that civil authority should be given no opportunity to pass any law that in any way bound the monks to certain procedures outside their own strict Vinaya behavior. This attitude can be seen in a number of different lights, though it is often difficult to judge these matters because information as to which monks were speaking at the time is not always available. The monkhood does not seem to

---

the British leaning on the primate against the political monks, and von der Mehden (1963:125).

52. Pyinnyaramikamaha Sayadaw 1958:22–25.
53. Simla Document, Tin Tut 1943:10.
54. Simla Document, Tin Tut 1943:11.
55. Cady (1958:364–365) places the whole matter in its political context with additional sources.

have opposed the sanad granted to the Taunggwin Sayadaw, but, influenced by the obviously declining power of this primate, clinched by the civil courts' supremacy established in 1935, the Sangha determined to have nothing further to do with the heathen lay authority. In other words, after a period of uncertainty in which the monkhood hoped that the role played by the British would not be very different from that of the Burmese kings, it had finally accepted the evidence that the British were not sympathetic to Buddhism and it had thus adopted a policy of withdrawal from any form of lay control. No doubt this is part of the story, and indeed it may have been one of the factors which impelled some monks to join forces with and assume the leadership of the nationalist cause.

But there is something else. The scanty documentation on the history of the Burmese Sangha suggests that, whereas some elements in the Order were always ready to compromise with the lay authority and thereby assume positions of power, other elements, largely in what I have called in Chapter 2 the "passive" Sangha, were content to remain within the rather anarchic framework of pure Vinaya, outside the lay world altogether. Perhaps we can see the "active" Sangha as those who were sympathetic to the interpretation of ecclesiastical jurisdiction in Dhammathat (Burmese customary law) terms, whereas the "passive" faction always insisted on nothing but pure Vinaya. Thus the British were not the only ones who were divided over whether or not such things as the primacy were allowed by Vinaya, for the conflict also arose within the Sangha. Recall that the *thathanabaing* was never regarded by the whole, fundamentally ungovernable, Sangha as its head and that documentation is meager on the general monkish reaction to the British recognition of the primacy. Perhaps the British annexation caused no real interruption but merely helped to confirm a trend already present in the Burmese situation by further weakening the power of the primacy, thus allowing the "passive" Sangha its head.

Thus there are two possible clues to the Sangha's reaction to the events of a troublesome century. On the one hand, as discussed earlier, from Mindon's time onward certain "active" groups within the Sangha reacted by taking their own fate in their hands and forming miniature Sanghas with their own strict discipline based largely on an increasingly strict observance of Vinaya rules. These groups, we know, did not react well to the British backing of a Thudhamma primate and to the assumption, never wholly abandoned by the British, that Burmese Buddhism was one and that sects could on the whole be disregarded. Indeed, the sects seldom allowed their affairs to come into the primate's sphere of interest. The "passive" Sangha's situation is of the same nature in regard to Vinaya but does not entail self-defence by internal reorganization. It is, of course, more difficult to document, but large numbers of monks apparently continued to live within the Vinaya, their disputes being settled locally, and they paid less and less attention to the primacy. Thus there was either little enthusiasm for naming a new primate after the death of the Taunggwin or more passive resistance to the idea (when the Sangha was at all consulted). Still another factor may have added body to the passivity of the Sangha. Many monks must have realized by the 1930s that they would have difficulty in retaining their Vinaya purity without giving up some of their freedom to civil control. Rather than submit to lay direction, however, many Burmese monks just sat on the fence and waited. A majority of the monks must have done just this, and this factor must never be forgotten when discussing the numerically smaller groups of the "active" Sangha. Both these reactions will be reconsidered in a later chapter in terms of developments under the AFPFL regime.

The Option of Lay Buddhist Organizations

While the majority of the Sangha may well have been on the fence waiting, an active few eventually became involved in a new Burmese phenomenon born of the nationalist fervor of the first decades in this century. I refer to the birth of lay Buddhist associations that may have started with religious motives as paramount but which eventually became deeply involved in the politics of seeking freedom from colonial rule.

A number of factors appear to have prompted the formation of lay societies concerned with Buddhism as early as the final years of the nineteenth century; one of them, significantly enough, was the feeling among Western-educated intellectuals that there was no hope for progress in Burma in the traditional thinking of the Sangha. This element of the story will be important right up to recent times: a degree of anti-clericalism on the part of these Western-educated laymen is sometimes expressed, particularly when the contrary pull of the desire to uphold

Burmese ways is felt, in the ambiguous view that only missionary monks should be given a modern education, while ordinary monks should remain in their place with old, sanctified learning. In 1897 the Moulmein Sasanadara Society for educational and social "uplift" started an Anglo-vernacular high school to be financed by curtailing expenditures on life-cycle ceremonies, including the *shinbyu* (novice initiation rite). The Buddha Kalayama Meikta Athin, first of Myingyan, later of Mandalay, founded the Buddha Thana Noggaha [Sasana Nuggaha] School for Buddhist instruction and the observance of Buddhist *ubone* or holy days. Around 1904, a similar Asoka Society was formed in Bassein with the aid of a European monk, while the Rangoon College Buddhist Association began to hold meetings at about the same time. The documents available on these lay movements do not name any monks, though there were doubtless some monastic advisers.[56]

Best known among these associations was the Young Men's Buddhist Association (YMBA), founded in 1906 on the model of the YMCA. It began as a students' group devoted to the discussion of religious subjects, later expanding to include plans for reviving Burmese arts and literature. Around 1910, according to the official biography of the nationalist monk U Ottama, members U Hmon and U May Aung were sent around the districts to promote district branches, mainly in urban centers. In 1917 the YMBA opened itself to affiliation with similar societies, including the Sasanadara Society of Moulmein, which acted as host to the first united conference.[57] Though the names of these participating organizations are not clear, this united group called itself the General Council of Buddhist Associations until about 1920, when it changed its name to the General Council of Burmese Associations (GCBA).

The importance of these associations is manifest in such nationalistic issues as the famous "shoe question," which involved heated debate over British refusal to remove shoes at sacred places. Monks were necessarily involved in such expressions of popular political consciousness. According to Cady, the issue had been raised unsuccessfully in 1901 and 1912, but in 1916 U Thein Maung, then a budding lawyer from Prome, deleted the words "except to Europeans and Americans" after the words "Footwearing Prohibited" on a board outside the Toungoo Shwesandaw

56. Maung Maung Pye 1951 (?):3–4.
57. Cady 1958: 179–180; Maung Maung Pye 1951 (?):4–5.

Pagoda, of which he was a trustee. The test came some six months later when the British district commissioner failed to persuade Thein Maung to take down the notice on the occasion of the viceroy's visit and the noble lord had to cancel his visit to the monument. According to the *Golden Jubilee Number of the YMBA,* the magazine from which I take this account, Thein Maung sought support from the *thathanabaing,* from whom he received an elusive reply. The advisers to the primate, who were consulted next, quoted a passage of scripture deploring all contention and quarreling. Thein Maung then took the matter to the YMBA, which failed to act until 1918, when Governor Sir Reginald Craddock decided to visit the famous Shwemawdaw Pagoda at Pegu. An emergency meeting in Jubilee Hall saw the case put brilliantly by Thein Maung, with May Aung in the chair.[58] Most of the local branches of the YMBA joined the agitation, and the government finally decided that the monk in charge of each pagoda could decide the question for himself. As late as 1919, associations were still asking the government to enact a law on the subject.[59] While most British residents ceased visiting the Shwedagon Pagoda in Rangoon until World War II, some authors bemoaned the foolishness of the situation and swore that Burmese monks of their acquaintance had never fussed about the subject at all.[60]

We need not follow here the YMBA missions abroad nor the details of the split in the association in which a moderate or "elder" wing formed the "Twenty-One Party," but Furnivall's analysis of the significance of the split is relevant:

This marked a definite stage in the progress of nationalism: the severance, if only formal, of politics from religion. Hitherto Nationalists had been linked together, nominally at least, on the basis of their common Buddhism, but the manifesto of the Twenty-One Party was Nationalist, not Buddhist; political, not religious.

In the more extreme nationalist party some Buddhist monks were prominent; there remained a close tie between Nationalism and Religion, and Nationalism still drew much of its strength from Buddhist sentiment; but

58. *Golden Jubilee Number of the Y.M.B.A.* 1956: 22–23, English Language Section.

59. Cady 1958:189–190. Remember that the Dwaya Okpo Sayadaw was involved with the Ledi Sayadaw on this footwear issue. The Okpo seems to have adopted the "British" viewpoint for some reason of his own. Smith (1965:88) mentions the Ledi's 1920 book on the pro-"Burmese" side of the subject and the attack by monks on Europeans at the Endawya Pagoda in 1919.

60. Brown 1925:169–170; Foucar 1956:18; Collis 1953:56.

the new policy made a wider appeal, potentially embracing all peoples in the country instead of only Buddhists.   [1948:143–144]

A Nationalist Monk: U Ottama

Thus, in the first of a long series of moves on the part of moderates toward British colonial administrative posts and British honors in education and government, the leadership of the nationalists was left to the younger party, headed by such men as Chit Hlaing, Thein Maung, and Ba Pe. These nationalists were much closer to the people than the moderates and ready to collaborate with monks. The Wunthanu Athins,[61] local branches of the lay political group known as the GCBA, were formed in Burma in 1921–1923. They soon were complemented by corresponding organizations for political purposes in the Sangha, in the form of branches of the General Council of the Sangha Samettgyi (GCSS). The latter appears to have been founded in 1921, but splits soon occurred.[62] The exact relation between the lay GCBA and the monastic GCSS is difficult to determine, though the latter most likely split along lines defined by the former. Cady tells us that "the *pongyi* agitators appear to have attracted a very considerable personal following among the women of the villages. They captured control of many of the G.C.B.A. sponsored village *Athins*" (1958:231). Further, commenting on the monastic nationalist hero U Ottama and his following, he writes:

U Ottama did for nationalism in Burma part of what Ghandhi did for it in India by transforming an essentially political problem into a religious one. But the approach was more crude. Buddhism was allegedly being attacked; the monks were being mistreated by police and courts; the dignity and pride of the Burman nation was, therefore, being outraged. . . . The political *pongyi*s as a rule used prophesies and magic as well as direct agitation to turn the hatred of the people against the foreign government, the police and courts, the tax collector and even the village headman. The weapon of boycott was also widely advocated. Pious monks faithful to their vows could do little to deter the extremists, who themselves achieved control over the

61. *Wunthanu* means "protector of national interest" (Cady 1958:649). *Athin* is a widely used Burmese term for many kinds of organizations. These public-spirited village groups sought to interest the rural population in national political issues, often in defiance of the authority of traditional village headmen. See Cady 1958: 223, 234–235.
62. For different dates, see Leach 1937:33; Stewart 1949:7–8; Cady 1958:232; Smith 1965:106; Pyinnyaramikamaha Sayadaw 1958:82; Sandawara, n.d. (1956?: 83); and Ba Yin, n.d.:138.

General Council of *Sangha Sametggi* (Associations), organized in 1922. The G.C.S.S. was used to direct the *pongyi* political program. *Pongyi* methods carried relatively little appeal to the less radical Westernized intelligentsia within the Y.M.B.A. and G.C.B.A. . . . In contrast with the situation in India . . . Burma had no such indigenous middle class. If nationalist politicians in Burma wanted popular backing, they had little choice but to line up with the political *pongyis*, who alone swayed the village *Wunthanu Athins*. . . . At the village level, where the headmen were forbidden, as officials and presumably allies of government, to participate in politics or to stand for election even to a circle board post, the political *pongyi* stepped in to fill the vacuum of leadership. In 1922 it was the Sangha Sametggi which cooperated with the G.C.B.A. to boycott the Burma visit of the Prince of Wales. . . .

Governor Craddock's caustic rejoinder that the yellow robe was losing its colour and that the *pongyis* were sacrificing "the veneration of the ages for the nine days' applause of a gaping multitude" was as impolitic as it was ineffective.   [1958:232–233]

At this point consideration in greater detail of the upbringing of U Ottama will be informative. A quasi-official biography, written by U Ba Yin of the newspaper *Bama Khit,* follows a fairly widespread hagiographical tendency on the part of Burmese authors to upgrade the sanctity of their nationalist monks, though this in itself can be a valuable antidote to the "political agitators in yellow robes" approach. Furthermore, the book contains much information which has not yet found its way into the literature in English.[63]

U Ottama was born as Paw Htun Aung in Rupa village near Akyab, Arakan, in 1879. He was the son of traders and had a younger brother and sister. The biography lays considerable stress on the boy's initiative in attempting to gain a Western education, thus illustrating the cultural conflict between generations which must have prevailed in those days, when the *min,* or Westernized intellectual class, was forming. Around 1888, U Ottama persuaded his parents to send him to an Anglo-Burmese school, and thus he went, with his brother, to the primary school in Akyab. By dint of much effort he passed the fifth-standard examination after two years. He is described as having missed the first prize owing to visit to the toilet in the middle of the examination and as having torn up his second prize certificate on the way home. An English clergyman wanted to adopt the boys and send them to Calcutta and England, but

---

63. Ba Yin, n.d. Von der Mehden (1963:134ff.) has made use of this source, and Smith (1965:95ff.) has followed von der Mehden.

their mother refused. While pregnant with her first child, she had dreamed that her son would become a monk. Despite Ottama's efforts (he stole household money to run away from home), she withdrew both sons from school, claiming that the education they were receiving there would virtually oblige them to become government officials. Ottama then began to work for his uncle with the aim of saving up to go to Calcutta, but the uncle did not wish him to leave either and appropriated his savings. At this point, Ottama seems to have fallen in with his parents' wishes out of desperation and to have gone to the scholarly Shwezedi Sayadaw of Akyab, who persuaded him to become a *pothudaw* (lay mendicant) while awaiting sponsorship into the Sangha as a novice. Ottama's aim was to escape from his parents' orbit. The mother continued her delaying tactics and asked him to wait a year so that she could weave his yellow robes herself according to an Arakanese tradition of their class.

At fifteen, Ottama became a novice with his brother. Hearing of a certain "Yesagyo Tutorial Group" in Pakokku, Ottama aimed to reach it by traveling with the Dahkaung Sayadaw. He went to Maubin, then to Toungoo, where he took first prize in an examination for novices and gained the attention of a wealthy Shan woman. She agreed to send him to Calcutta, where he arrived at the age of sixteen; there he studied for three years up to a successful tenth-standard examination. Thence he returned to the Pakokku group, where an agent of the Bombay-Burma Company, a family friend, acted as his lay supporter.

Obsessed with the idea of acquiring and spreading knowledge, he soon returned to Calcutta, where he was involved in the Bengal anti-British agitations of 1904 and their aftermath, and he was asked to teach Buddhism and Pali at the National College set up by the Indians. Here he learned a number of old and contemporary Indian languages. He appears to have made several attempts to visit a certain *arahant* he had heard of in Tibet with the aim of spreading Buddhism in India; these efforts were unsuccessful, and he went instead on a tour of India, Egypt, France, and other European countries. Ottama seems to have felt that France was the only European country then competing with England for new overseas territories and that a new alliance with the French could be formed. At this time, however, he heard of the great Japanese victory in the Russo-Japanese war, which the biography views as amazing for several revealing reasons (it is not clear whether these were Ottama's):

the Japanese were smaller in stature than the Russians, they ate rice instead of wheat, and they were Buddhists, a religion, according to Europeans, of the lower rungs of humanity.

Reversing his direction, Ottama returned to Rangoon in 1907 and went on to Yokohama in March via Singapore. Finding that he could not obtain his customary *hsoon* (alms food) and other monastic necessities there, he wrote to the chaplain of the Buddhist College in Tokyo, a Reverend Ottani (Ōtani?), who told him to learn Japanese at the latter's expense. Eventually Ottama was offered a professorship of Pali and Sanskrit, though he refused to accept any salary.

While in Japan, Ottama learned of the arrival in that country of the maharaja of Baroda (Western India)—seemingly through one of the three hundred or so Indian taxi drivers of Tokyo who knew of him and respected him as a great nationalist. Ottama persuaded the Japanese Ministry of Industry to hold a royal party for the maharajah. He also met Sun Yat Sen and advised him to get the Chinese to abandon old customs, including "wearing pigtails which enabled imperialists the better to tie Chinese together before throwing them in bunches into the river." Ottama left Japan in 1910 to travel through Korea, Manchuria, Port Arthur, China, Annam, Cambodia, Siam, Ceylon, and India. He met the (self-exiled?) Burmese Mingun prince in Saigon. In India, he eluded police efforts to trail him by meeting both Baroda and Thibaw in French-administered territory. Ottama returned to Burma in 1911, when the YMBA was forming its district branches, and he seems to have made his first contacts with Ba Pe and Hla Pe, publishers of the *Thuriya* (*Sun*) paper, and with U Kyaw Yan, of Mandalay, who gave him publicity in his paper *Burma Star*. At the request of Dr. Htun Aung Gyaw of the Rangoon General Hospital and U San Shwe, a headmaster at Prome, he wrote a book on Japan which was eventually published by the Thuriya Press. Shadowed by the police, Ottama toured Burma before leaving again for Japan, taking with him his sister and three young men to whom he wished to offer an education.

On his return from Japan in 1919, Ottama was to be seen mostly in the Thuriya Press offices on Sule Pagoda Road. Ottama contributed many articles to the *Thuriya,* and possibly to other papers such as *Myanma Alin* and *Pyinnya Alin.* He wrote and spoke about the *wunthanu rekkhita taya*[64]—the points of law to be observed by nationalists

64. *Wunthanu: vamsanu* (P): the race, family, lineage; *rekkhita: rakkhati* (P):

—including the wearing of homemade cloth and the boycott of tinned and other foriegn foods. The *Thuriya* appears to have worked hard for the "younger party" within the nationalist movement, and, just before the Eighth Conference of the GCBA at Prome in the course of which the GCSS was first mooted, the newspaper published Ottama's advice on the need for a rapprochement between the Sangha and politicians. The *Thuriya* also published a letter from Ottama to Governor Craddock telling him to leave Burma. He told his readers not to fear government officials, who were no more than public servants before whom no one should quake.

Prior to the agitation that led to his arrest, Ottama traveled to and from Calcutta, where, in December 1920, he heard of the Rangoon University student strike. Chatterjie (1956?:1) tells us that he himself was then employed in the Rangoon Telegraph Office and received a message from Ottama to the strikers. Orders from higher up came to suppress the message, whereupon Chatterjie insisted that the sender should be informed and reimbursed. Ottama, informed in this manner, published his message and its fate in the Calcutta papers. U Ottama then rushed to Rangoon to inspire the students with the agressiveness and anticolonialist experience of the Indian Congress Party leadership which, under Gandhi, was later to win independence for India.

Other published sources disagree regarding the dates of the events that followed, but clearly the imprisonment of U Ottama and the founding of the GCSS were closely connected and were, in turn, related to the split between "older" and "younger" GCBA. The mass meeting in Jubilee Hall in August 1919 may or may not have been addressed by U Ottama; the data are not clear. But at the "annual" conference of the GCBA in 1920 a resolution was passed that the Sangha should in the future be consulted by GCBA leadership. For some writers it is at this point that the General Council of Buddhist Associations became the General Council of Burmese Associations. Next came the arrest, trial, and first imprisonment of U Ottama. Cady (1958:231–232) writes of a ten-month sentence in 1921 and Ottama's release in 1922, at which point the GCSS was founded. U Ba U, who rarely provides dates, writes of a two-year sentence, with release in the early part of 1921. Ottama's

---

to guard, protect, preserve; *taya* (B): law; hence the law that preserves and guards the village Burmese (against their enemies).

biography gives 1920 at one point, 1922 at another. Cady's reading is probably the most reliable.[65]

Even though doubt exists as to the date on which the General Council of the Sangha Samettgyi (GCSS) was founded, there can be little doubt that Ottama was in fact the guiding force behind the organization.[66] Other well-known monks were also involved in its leadership, such as the Bame Sayadaw (president?), the Aletawya Sayadaw (also president once?), the Shwegyin U Dhammadaraka (executive secretary), U Wepullaka (executive secretary), U Wisara (lecturer), and the Bagaya Sayadaw (lecturer).[67] Perhaps there were splits early in the history of the GCSS that followed GCBA rivalries. In these shifts, Ottama stayed with factions that did not seek any rapprochement with the government, as in his opposition to payment of taxes.[68] In 1924 he was invited to Mandalay, at which time a serious disturbance took place.

The biography, as usual, has its own version of events. A large crowd is said to have gathered on hearing that Ottama was arriving at Shanzu Station. Ottama was driven in a car with large numbers of monks and laymen in front and behind. The opposing group appealed to the police not to allow the Ottama procession along a certain route where they were holding a meeting. The crowd disobeyed the police and was assaulted with stones and bottles. "Guessing the direction of the missiles," the crowd then stoned the other group's meeting. In the ensuing melee, one monk was killed. Various Ottama leaders were imprisoned, and Ottama himself was dispatched to Rangoon that very night. Ottama "decided" that he should go to prison again and, within a month, asked Tharrawaddy U Pu (his opponent!) to hold a meeting in a Lanmadaw cinema. Ottama made a speech there and was arrested seven days afterward, in October 1924. At his trial the monks did not stand up when the judge entered the courtroom; therefore, their chairs were pulled from under them by the police guards.[69] Ottama was given three years

65. For an account of the trial, see Ba U 1959:79–80, and Ba Yin, n.d.:41–46. Smith (1965:98) writes of arrest in 1921 with a twenty-month sentence, later reduced to one year.

66. Pyinnyaramikamaha Sayadaw 1958: 82–83.

67. There is disagreement over who were the leaders and over the allegiance of the Aletawya. See Pyinnyaramikamaha Sayadaw 1958:82–83; Ba Yin, n.d.:42, 62; Maung Maung Pye 1951(?):15; and Cady 1958:232.

68. Cady 1958:252–253.

69. Cady 1958:253, n.40.

but was enabled by the respectful jailkeeper to evade hard labor. He chose cane-work and spent the rest of the time in meditation. Thus concludes the biographical account, citing a Jataka and noting that the imprisonment amounted to little more than throwing a turtle back into its lake.[70]

Various rivalries between laymen and monks in 1924–1925 brought to an end the nationalist unity between the urban and rural groups and between Westernized and traditionalist Burmese. Sangha influence is said to have died down somewhat owing to Ottama's imprisonment until 1927,[71] but on his release, Ottama joined U Soe Thein's branch of the General Council of Burmese Associations (GCBA), and it is said that at the Pyinmana conference of that branch a very secret committee was formed, with Saya San at its head, for the purpose of selecting rebel leaders. Shortly after, Ottama was denied permission to go to Russia and Europe (his aim had been to obtain arms and ammunition); instead he went to Sagaing. As a monk, he was unwilling to break Vinaya rules by obtaining arms himself, but it was believed by many that he wished to show GCBA local branch leaders how to make contact with foreign powers.

Subsequent events broadened the scope of Sangha involvement in the Ottama tradition. A group of political monks started a Burmese news-paper, the *Wunthanu,* at this time. In 1927 the government had to outlaw a pamphlet that exhorted all Buddhists and GCSS monks to stage mass religious meetings in towns, to pledge remembrance of English lawlessness, and to meditate on the impermanence of all things (includ-ing, it must be presumed, the British Raj). Its author was one U Wimalasara of Tharrawaddy. At the same time, traditionalist rebellions of the *setkyamin* type arose in Tavoy, Shwebo, and Pegu. Nationalist feeling heightened also when the monk U Wisara made violent anti-government speeches and began a hunger strike in jail which killed him in 1929.[72] For reasons which are not clear, the Soe Thein GCBA boy-cotted his cremation in 1930.[73] Cady (1958:261) mentions the final arrest and imprisonment of U Ottama in 1928, which are not recorded

70. Ba Yin, n.d.:77ff.
71. Cady 1958:255.
72. Cady 1958:260–261; von der Mehden 1963: 130.
73. Cady 1958:290.

in the biography.[74] By late 1930 the Soe Thein faction of GCSS was pursuing secret political plans of its own. In the same year Sangha agitation against missionary schools and teaching of Christianity to Buddhist children added fuel to antiforeign sentiment.[75]

The story of U Ottama should make clear the degree to which certain elements of the Sangha became involved in the nationalist movements. Quite certainly he was more ardent and aggressive than the other nationalist monks, but the causes he espoused were taken up by many others in the Sangha.

A Nationalist Ex-monk: Saya San

These complex events form the background for the Saya San rebellion, which broke out in 1930. This native movement captured the attention and spirit of the Burmese people through its use of traditional forms of royal and religious symbolism which were directed at real grievances held by the people. The brave but total defeat of the patriots, the trial of Saya San, and the legends that grew out of the affair have made the rebellion famous in the history of Burma. Cady (1958:311) finds that "most of the organizers under Saya San were political *pongyis* who worked through the local *Wunthanu Athins*" (GCBA branches), and there is indeed evidence to show that many leaders were as he describes them.[76] I have some doubts about the word "most" and would point out again that there is here a case to be made for nonmonastic "*sayas*" as well; also, some of the monks were unconventional "*saya*" monks not affiliated with the political Athins.[77]

Some evidence indicates that within the Saya San rebellion itself there were bickering factions traceable to rivalries within the GCBA and GCSS, although local groups may not always have carried out the central office's wishes. We have shown that the Soe Thein GCBA is said by the Ottama biography to have participated in the rebellion, and his disclaimer of involvement must be taken with a large pinch of salt.[78] In

74. See also Smith 1965:98. He appears to have stayed in prison until his death in 1939.
75. Cady 1958:306–307.
76. Ba Yin, n.d.:4, 7, 8, 18, 23, 24, 26, 28–30, 32, 35.
77. Burma 1934:8, 12–14, 20, 34–36.
78. Burma 1932:65. Cf. Cady 1958:315, n. 85: "Although U Soe Thein ap-

the government's files on the rebellion is a special notice to local branches from the Soe Thein GCBA indicating alarm at the violent methods of Saya San and stating that "these quacks are not recognized nor encouraged by the U Soe Thein G.C.B.A. controlled by the Thetpan *Sayadaw* . . . [nor by] the famous *Sayadaw* U Ottama" (Burma 1934:18). On the other hand, evidence exists that Soe Thein GCBA monks participated in Henzada and Yamethin outbreaks, and elsewhere a monk suggests to a potential revolutionary that he become affiliated to the Soe Thein instead of the rival U Su branch of the GCBA (Burma 1934:18). Clearly there was constant competition for allegiance among the factions, and there is some evidence for thinking that Saya San and other leaders may have tried to build up their own organizations (the Galon Athins) out of Wunthanu Athin groups and to transfer allegiance from the factions to their own persons. The available government reports of the rebellion were not really concerned with the political organization problems of the Burmese side, but evidence exists of rivalries between individual rebels.[79]

One fact, extremely important in understanding why it is difficult to tie the rebellion to a particular faction, has not been mentioned in analyses of this revolt. Simply, it is that Saya San was only one of the "kings" involved; there were, according to the government report, three or four in all. The implication is that this was not a case of a Burma fighting against the British for independence; this was not even a united "grassroots" nationalist movement fighting for the same cause. Rather it was a series of personal uprisings, using and being used by the local Wunthanu Athins, any one of which, had it been successful, would probably have gone on to take over and absorb all other factions into its own private army. Aung Hla of Dedaye is a case in point. He was sixty years old, an elder of Htandaw, and president of a local circle of nationalist organizations (there being some thirty in all in Dedaye township). His wife was head of the local Women's Nationalist Association. Aung Hla had considerable local influence and used the local Athins in his preparations for revolution. There is little doubt that he was considered the head of the movement and would have become "king" if

---

parently at first tried to halt the rebellion, his G.C.B.A. later enrolled volunteers for it."

79. Burma 1934:18.

successful: he is quoted as saying, "From now on I am king indeed. My sons will be crown princes" (Burma 1934:3–4).

"Kings" were not necessarily seeking to be kings simultaneously with each other and Saya San's way was opened, or let us say enlarged, by the defeat of Aung Hla. However, at his trial Saya San went back upon his "royal" proclivities: it was "for the economic progress of Rahan [monk] and inhabitant, so also in the interest of the religion of Our Lord" that he had to declare war. He had been a member of the Soe Thein GCBA many years, the chairman of a committee to report on *thathameda* taxes, and the founder of the Galon Athin, which had been formed to resist the illegal depredations of the authorities, offer civil resistance against the forest laws whereby villagers had to pay for bamboo and wood, and oppose the separation of Burma from India. The title of the organization, he said, had merely referred to the "Great Galon bird of the Letpan tree;"[80] he had lost control of the movement on the twenty-second of December and was not responsible for its acts of violence (Burma 1934: 10).

During my stay in Burma, one informant described Saya San as one of the last great *nat*-men. He was said to have claimed magic powers such as flying through the air so that when the citizens of Rangoon were to start rebelling he would arrive by air in Rangoon. Another informant thought of Saya San as head of a *weikza* type of organization that gave its members such great confidence and strength to face death that even their opponents respected and admired them. Saya San was said not only to have claimed to be the *setkyamin,* or world emperor, but also to have powers such as stamping on an airplane's shadow and making it crash. It was even said that the man arrested, brought to Rangoon, tried, and executed was not the real Saya San. The real Saya San had gone into the jungles and was biding his time. Thus the rebellion was becoming mixed with the traditions and themes of Burmese culture found in the *Glass Palace Chronicle* and its oral traditions.

The same pattern was found elsewhere. A Galon Athin was founded

---

80. The Letpan, or silk cotton, tree was the home of the mythical Galon in Jataka tale no. 543 in Cowell (1895, 6:93). It is interesting that in the story this the bird is so strong that in its pursuit of its eternal enemy (the naga serpents), it innocently causes considerable damage to noncombatants (it carries an entire banyon tree into the sky). No demerit accrues to the bird, however: "If he did it not knowing what he did, it was only ignorance, not a sin." Saya San's use of the Jataka is obvious in terms of his own defense at the trial. J. F.

at Taungbyat in November 1937, its members being told that Saya San was president and that the *athin* was called the Thupa Galon Raja Athin (Burma 1934:14). A more sinister note was struck by the maniacal document seized in a Henzada monastery condemning meat, opium, and other "foreign" products and stating that people were killed in such parts for using those products (Burma 1934:34). The author was one Dewa Thiba Aung Mya Yatana, president of a Maha Thathanapyu Ahpwe.[81] A Tagaung monastery was selected as the headquarters of another movement on the grounds that the first Burmese dynasty had appeared there. In this case the inspiration came not from Saya San but apparently from U Okkantha, *sayadaw* of Taungdwingyi, Magwe District, who was said to have been capable of granting power against the British (Burma 1934:36–37). The impression grows that there was never any real question of central control of the Saya San rebellion from the outside. This conclusion has an important implication which must be borne in mind below: whatever they may have done as local organizers, the monks of the various factions of the GCSS never appeared to have a national scope for their endeavors, any more than their corresponding lay factions had. Monks, however, were instrumental in putting an end to much fighting with an amnesty offer, the Aletawya Sayadaw and other reputable Rangoon monks touring the country to make these offers.[82]

Activist Political Groups from the Sangha

The years after the Saya San rebellion were marked by the extremely complicated minuet danced by the various Burmese factions around the theme of separation from India. In the process the initiative in leadership was transferred from activist monks to the native politicians in the national Legislative Council and government.[83] In the 1932 elections monks cried that Buddhism was in danger from Anglican interests, and the "spurious" issue was successful as a campaign tactic.[84] According to

81. The name of the *ahpwe* probably refers literally to "the great purification of the religion." *Thathanapyu* is a term that traditionally was used to describe the purification of the Sangha by monks appointed specially by the king to banish unorthodoxy. This *ahpwe* would seem to be promoting a political purge in the old tradition. J. F.
82. Cady 1958:314.
83. Human Relations Area Files 1956:979ff.
84. Cady 1958:338.

Cady, however, "the boycotting technique was now discredited along with Saya San's revolutionary tactics, and the actual exercise of popular political influence would henceforth center in that portion of the elected council leadership which was willing to stay on good terms with the *pongyis*. Dr. Ba Maw exploited the new situation with consummate skill (1958:339). For more than one writer, 1932 was the date of the real entry of the Sangha into politics.[85] By 1934, when J. A. Maung Gyi, generally recognized as a devout man, tried for the second time to win passage of his proposal to put legal power behind ecclesiastical decisions, monks seeking freedom from lay control took over the gallery of the Legislative Council en masse to defeat his proposal. Even though some of the leading *sayadaw*s of Rangoon supported the proposal, the motion was lost. Only five Burman councillors dared to defy the monks in the gallery and vote for the bill.[86] Between 1933 and the 1936 election, factional disputes can be traced in the GCBA that involved monks, such as the Mingalun and Thetpan Sayadaws, the latter's followers opposed to Ba Maw. In the 1936 election, U Ba Pe's Ngabwinsaing Party was born in the monastery of U Pyinnyathami of Mandalay, with monks such as the Shweman Sayadaw present. The use of monasteries, monks, and pagodas for political meetings and organizational focus became common in this period.

A review of the material collected during the governmental investigations of the serious 1938 riots against Muslims, Indians, and police helps to clarify the types of prewar organizations formed by monks. The monastic group referred to most often is the GCTMYSA, or General Council of the Thathana Mamaka Young Sanghas' Association of Rangoon. Active on this council were such monks as the Thadu Sayadaw (U Pyinnyathami of Kemmendine), U Withoukda, U Kumara, U Teza, and U Nyeya, some of whom were speakers at the Shwedagon Pagoda just before the riot. Branches of this organization were located at such Rangoon *taik*s as the Thayettaw and the Bagaya, the latter the center of Ba Maw supporters (Burma 1939a:49–50, 53). The organization would get behind issues such as the furor over *The Abode of a Nat,* a novel by Htin Baw, insignificant in itself, to which had been attached in an appendix anti-Buddhist statements by a Muslim, Maung Shwe Hpi, from

---

85. Hobbs 1951:363; Simla Document, Tin Tut 1943. On the influence of the Sangha in general during this time, see Harvey 1946:28; and Christian 1945:72.
86. Cady 1958:364–365. Ba Yin, n.d.:78–79.

a book written in 1931. The novel appeared on July 14, 1938, and 1,350 copies were sold in ten days. Papers like *The Sun,* the *New Light of Burma,* and *New Burma,* which had maintained an anti-Indian attitude since 1933, were the vehicles of monastic protest (Burma 1939b: 34–35). On July 16, *The Sun* (owned by the tempestuous U Saw) published a letter by U Sandawuntha of Thayettaw Monastery on the sufferings of Burmese women married to Muslims, a theme used by the monkhood in appealing to the people throughout the period in question. Between this date and July 26, a variety of monks connected with the GCTMYSA summoned the author, Htin Baw, to give them copies of his book, and a rumor, discounted by the government's Committee of Inquiry, had it that the monks had obliged the author to add the anti-Buddhist passages by the Muslim Shwe Hpi. On July 19, *The Sun* published an article directed at the book by Ledi U Withokdasara of the Theingyi Monastery, Shwedagon precinct, in which he called for urgent action against the enemies of Buddhism (Burma 1939a:6–7). On the twenty-first, U Kettima of the Thayettaw Taik and U Paduma of the Publicity Bureau of the GCTMYSA joined in the fray. On the same day, a meeting of the General Council determined on a mass gathering at the Shwedagon Pagoda. The agenda included vigorous action against all concerned with the Shwe Hpi book, protective legislation for Burmese women married to foreigners, and reopening of an old sore: "To take vigorous action against the granting of permission to enter pagodas, *kyaung*s and *wuttagan*[87] lands with shoes on, on certain conditions" (Burma 1939a:6, 7, 8, app. 1). On July 22, the *New Light of Burma* published evidence of a letter of discontent addressed to the nation's prime minister by one U Nagainda of Bonpyan Monastery, Bahan Taik. Up to the twenty-sixth a succession of inflammatory letters and articles continued to appear in these papers, some warning that trouble could be expected to arise from the great Shwedagon meeting on the twenty-sixth (Burma 1939a:9–11).

The meeting on the twenty-sixth is said to have been attended by some 10,000 people of whom 1,500 were monks—a figure representing greater Sangha participation in lay activities than heretofore. The meeting, addressed by the above-mentioned monks, "developed in a crescendo of vituperation and abuse against Muslims in general," and "it was notice-

87. *Wu myei tagan* (B): sacred ground or precincts.

able that, throughout, the speeches dwelt upon the Burmese-Muslim marriage question." A procession, whipped up by a few organizers, started with about 500 laymen and 500 monks. At the crucial point, there were some 500 people, mostly monks. Along the way, members of the procession armed themselves, and monks with sticks were seen assaulting Muslims. A police force eventually charged, and several monks were injured. Much was made of police behavior in the Burmese popular press because of police irresponsibility in handling injuries (which it reported as killings) and because of consequent outbreaks outside Rangoon in the next days. In the evening of the twenty-sixth, the police had to interfere with monks of the Thayettaw Taik, who, together with laymen, were using the monastery as a fort. This was the first example of misuse of monasteries, which was so strongly to impress the government's Inquiry Committee (Burma 1939a:13–15, 23, 32). In subsequent days rumors spread to the districts to the effect that the Sule Pagoda had been destroyed and monks murdered, and that the Shwedagon was in imminent danger of attack (Burma 1939b:19). In some places police strength or the influence of sensible elders prevented trouble; in other places, riots ensued with armed monks among the leaders (Burma 1939a:45). Cady mentions 132 "specifically authenticated cases of misuse of the yellow robe in acts of incitation to violence, actual assaults, looting, arson and murder" (1958:395).

Summarizing the part played by certain monks in the riots, the Final Report of the government's investigators first states that a larger majority of monks than suspected had nothing whatsoever to do with them, or deplored them (Burma 1939a:276–278). There is, on the other hand, ample evidence of trouble caused by younger elements, and we find that Cady's figure of 132 cases is derived from a committee report:

We have in the course of our investigation taken specific evidence in which we have been told that in nearly fifty cases armed *pongyi*s were among the crowds, in an equal number of such cases *pongyi*s themselves were seen to commit assault, in nearly twenty cases *pongyi*s were found looting, in eight cases they were found commiting arson, and in four committed murder. We must not be taken to mean that all these cases have been judicially proved before us. On the other hand they are only those of which we have received specific evidence or to which there is a reference in official records. They are, we think, only a few of the cases which actually occurred. [Burma 1939a:278]

Another great cause of concern to the committee was the frequency with which monasteries were used as forts, tattooing places, publication centers, and loot-safes, exploiting the virtual immunity monastic centers have from the police. The Thayettaw, in Rangoon, was one example; there were many others: the Payagyi in Wakema; monasteries in Paungde and Rangoon and Mandalay; the Paya in Toungoo; and the Thumpayagyi in Pegu. The committee felt that the notion that monasteries are inviolable must be dispelled in order that political capital of the sort made out of the Pakokku search incident (an unfortunate one in that two monasteries were confused and the wrong one searched) would be no longer possible. On this and similar counts the committee felt impelled to advise a reconsideration of the problem of ecclesiastical law (Burma 1939a:278–280, 132ff., 297).

The committee came to the conclusion that the riots were political and not religious. Summarizing their views on the Sangha's role in them, the committee stated:

But, in recent years, a great change has spread through Burma and many of the young generation of *pongyi*s have turned to politics. And the same traditional reverence which they enjoyed . . . has made them also in the new regime the greatest political force in Burma. The danger is obvious both to Burma and to the Religion itself in Burma. We think the former is widely realized but the latter certainly is not. It is a commonplace of politics in Burma to find every politician supported by "his own" local or particular *pongyi*s or Associations of *pongyi*s. We find some of them acting as election agents, in substance if not in form. Many *kyaungdaik*s and many *kyaung*s have become centres of political intrigue and even Pagodas (the Shwedagon itself is an outstanding example) themselves are used as platforms for political meetings and political propaganda. . . . In the aftermath of unrest and indiscipline which the riots left behind, their influence is just as marked. They cannot be excluded from the "means employed" or from the category of agents of disorder. We cannot too strongly say, as friends of Burma and of her Religion, that the danger to both from the degeneration of the *Sangha* which has set in is great. [Burma 1939a:291–292]

World War II, the Japanese invasion, and the rise of the Thakin movement, which was finally to win independence from Britain, to a considerable extent negated these forebodings. However, political monks of one brand or another continued to appear up to the war. U Saw, who eclipsed Ba Maw as the leading political figure until his arrest and imprisonment by the British in Africa, held the support of an All-Burma Pongyis' Council, a branch of the old GCBA.[88] Other politicians, including Ba Maw, continued to use monk presidents at their political meetings.[89] The rising Thakin group had Sangha supporters within their national organizations, the Dobama Asiayon and the All-Burma Youth League, but their political programs tended on the whole to be carried out without the benefit of Sangha attendance. It is significant that fairly recently published reminiscences of the Rangoon University strike of 1936 bear no mention of any monks.[90]

Literary Satire of the Modern Monk

In addition to incidents involving Sangha initiative, there were also factors which rose directly out of the lay world. One such was the attitude which large sections of the sophisticated, urban laity began to adopt toward the Sangha, and we may ask whether such attitudes represented real or potential danger to the survival of the monkhood as a viable organization.[91] No field material to date can compete effectively with the extraordinary material available in the famous novel *Tet Pongyi,* written in 1937 by Thein Pe Myint, an analysis of which does not appear to have been attempted before. I may be forgiven, then, for spending some time on it here.[92]

---

88. Cady 1958:403.
89. Cady 1958:417.
90. Tha Hla 1958.
91. For more on the modern monk, see Spiro 1970:354–377.
92. The first edition, published by the New Light of Burma Press, Rangoon, sported a six-page preface by Maung Nu (later to be U Nu, prime minister) discussing the different nature of fables and novels and apologizing for certain minor failings in the author's writing; an eight-page humble justification by Nu to the monks of Burma explaining the motives of the novel; and a six-page preface by the author Thein Pe Myint explaining the word *tet,* the didactic nature of the book, and the resolution of Sangha problems since Independence. The preface to my edition, printed in the fifties, describes a series of events which begin with Thein Pe Myint coming to pay respects to U Okkata of Taungdwingyi (who later wrote *Lu The Lu Pyit*) at the Shin Ardeissawuntha Taik, Rangoon. After praising Thein Pe, U Okkata asks him why he is not reprinting his novel. Thein Pe replies that the matter concerns monks only. The monk opines that, despite the Sangayana whitewashing operation, the Sangha gets worse and worse (a reference to the Mahamuni episode in which monks shot at each other); therefore he should reprint. It is said that Thein Pe prefers not to. The monk then asks for a copy of the book, and Thein Pe presents it to the *taik,* asking that his youthful mistakes in

There are two skillfully interwoven plots, the principal one dealing with an apprentice *katika* (a preaching monk) and the second one presenting the affairs of a rich old maid and her less prosperous, nationalist nephew. These plots—as far as available—will be taken in order by chapters, beginning with the apprentice's adventures. (Page numbers in my Burmese edition are given in parentheses.)

Chap. 1. The book opens with a *sayadaw* (Mr. Parrot) teaching a *katika* [preacher] novice how to preach. Parrot refers the young man to books providing scriptural explanations; stresses the need for elegance, refinement, sweetness of voice; urges the use of double entendre in pleasing women listeners; suggests dwelling on old maids' problems in sermons to flatter them; and recommends imitating the great actors such as Po Sein.[93] (1–12)

Chap. 2. The personnel of the monastery (monks and nuns) are described, as well as the important panderer, the *kappiya* (lay steward). The hero, novice U Thudaza, sees the private goods and furniture of *Sayadaw* Parrot and envies them, just as a Rangoonite envies *mohinga*[94] dishes. (13–22)

Chap. 3. A *katika* Thudaza admires and models himself upon calls to read an exchange of letters between himself and a woman. The *katika* answers the woman, telling her that, in the age of cars and planes, lovers should not dally. He makes fun of naive student letters to women and tells Thudaza that monks have easy access to women since they are not suspect and since discontented laymen dare not accuse monks—the most they can do is refrain from sending food. The jealousy of monks for *sayadaw*s who have all the women is explored. (22–38)

Chap. 6. Thudaza confesses his love for the youngest nun to the *kappiya,* who is taking his notes to her. The *kappiya* advises Thudaza to dare a visit while Sayadaw Parrot is away. Thudaza comments on the *sayadaw*'s greed (he takes half of any offering, leaving the other half to his five

---

not stressing the existence of good monks be rectified. Then the preface reveals that U Nu refused reprint rights on the original preface, saying that circumstances had changed.

U Pinnyazawta reprinted my edition of the book at the Gyobyu Press, Rangoon. The edition was very soon seized by the police. Because of the difficulty of sending texts out of Burma after a certain time, the last fifty pages of the book in translation never reached me.

I thank Mrs. Anna Allott, Department of Burmese, School of Oriental and African Studies, for considerable gracious help in connection with this text.

93. Throughout the book, much of Thein Pe Myint's art in fact consists of exposition and criticism of such techniques: an excellent, and humorous, way of having his say about literature.

94. A popular Burmese dish made with fermented rice noodles.

monks) but the *kappiya* tells him that he is greedy himself—for the nun. (59–65)

Chap. 7. Thudaza woos the nun through subtle discourse on the scriptures. The nun wavers between Thudaza and the *sayadaw*—"Pon-pon" (presumably from *pongyi*)—to whom she feels indebted. Thudaza wins the nun; she asks him to take off his robe before making love. Thudaza is called Maung Paya (darling monk), and the nun, interestingly enough, has Thudhamma prefixed to her name by her lover when he begs her to "decide his case."[95] (65–73)

Chap. 8. Thudaza, however, thinks more of success than of love. He comes up against closed-shop techniques among Rangoon *katika*s. His mentor, the love-letter writer, invites him to co-preach with him at Prome and "gain practice in the outbacks." As Thudaza is preaching to his nun, the citizens of Prome learn about the forthcoming sermons. (73–80)

Chap. 10. Thudaza makes up for his sermon and dons a silk robe for the first time. After initial difficulties, in the course of which he gains the audience's sympathy, he preaches by means of a popular song. This catches on; he is invited back and becomes known as "Popular-song U Thudaza."[96] (90–102)

Chap. 12. Thudaza has achieved fame; his portrait is in all the papers. He has preached at the Shwedagon, the Kemmendine Kotatgyi, the Kammayut Military Academy, and in Pazundaung. He is waiting to go higher still. The *kappiya* warns him against making his nun pregnant. Thudaza answers in a way that seems to refer to contraception. There follows a long and traumatic discovery of the lovers by Sayadaw Parrot. The nun cravenly accuses Thudaza and the *kappiya* of seduction. The next day the the latter are thrown out. Thudaza announces diplomatically that he is going to tour the country for the benefit of all beings. (120–126)

Chap. 13. Thudaza is on tour with the *kappiya* as his fall-man at Thonze, Tharrawaddy, Minhla, Letpadan, Gyobingauk, Mattalin, Paungde. He deliberately adds Tharrawaddy U Nyeyya's nationalism (which he sees as a needed ingredient) to his repertoire. A magistrate warns him, however, that he will offend policemen and officials, who will cease to honor him, so he promptly stops. In Minhla, politicians fight for his favors, and one even quits his party for him. At Paungde, he fails to receive the welcome he expects and, like a prima donna, he refuses to preach. (127–139)

95. Probably a reference to the Thudhamma *sayadaw*s of the *thathanabaing*'s courts.

96. A kind of parody of the way in which a monk acquires his title. The popular song *Laba laba Ma Kyi ye* (Come along, come along Ma Kyi) which he used is combined with his name to get "Ma Kyi's U Thudaza," for short. There is also an obscure reference to the Mohnyin Sayadaw, a famous preacher, at this point. A little later the famous Tharrawaddy U Nyeyya Sayadaw is mentioned. (Pagination and chapter headings become a little unreliable in the translation after chapter 10.)

Chap. 14. Thudaza sets off one place against another and also solicits resolutions on the part of laymen so that they will offer goods for the sake of their own *kamma*[97] and at the same time gain publicity for their own goods. He announces that he is going to talk about the five hints in politics and about curative medicine, but he deals, as usual, with sex.[98] His discourse corrupts the audience in various ways. (140–154)

Chap. 15. Thudaza visits the old maid who has become his chief pupil. One day they are left alone together, and Thudaza offers to preach to her about her personal needs. He says she requires a husband and, after a long disquisition, concludes that all good men are in the Sangha. He criticizes girls who spend so much time making up that they are irritated by monks who arrive to collect food. (155–165)[99]

So much for the principal plot. The subsidiary plot involves the old maid and her nephew. Parts of it eventually join up with the main plot, but it can be more speedily dealt with:

Chap. 4. A portrait is presented of an educated, avaricious, wealthy old maid of forty who cannot get married because she is still hankering after an ideal man. (38–46)

Chap. 5. There is a scene between the old maid and her nephew (TS). She is bent on making him find out about a widower she has heard of, while he is scheming on how to get her to send him to the university. The university strikes are touched upon. They are at cross purposes. (46–59)

Chap. 9. The nephew (TS) and his mother visit the old maid, who refuses to help. TS's dreams collapse: his ambitions run parallel to the monk's. When, at this point, TS is asked if he will attend the monk's sermons, he lashes out at lascivious monks. His aunt calls him a potential Dhammantaraya.[100] (80–90)

Chap. 11. TS passes his exams but finds that only the rich can get into the university. He reveals himself as a nationalist who will not kowtow to the British. With the help of friends he starts a shop. Another visit to his aunt provides the occasion for another tirade against the monks and the laity who support them.

The construction of the novel leaves room for both explicit and implicit criticism of the monkhood and the laity. The nephew's two speeches are probably the most explicit. In the first he accuses the monks

97. The record of one's deeds in terms of merit and demerit.
98. The five here are nationalists, Ba Pe, Maung Gyi, Ba U, Ba Si, and Ba Swe. A little later, the fall-man jokes about U Ottama.
99. The translation available to me ends at this point.
100. *Dhammantaraya:* "Buddhism in Danger." He is, thus, a potential danger to Buddhism. This term was used in the first army regime's campaign against communism, 1958–1959.

of wakening rather than dampening the lusts of their audiences, of keeping women, making Burmans sentimental and soft, yearning for a role in politics, taking bribes, and fighting over lands and monasteries, and he laments the fact that there is no Burmese king to disrobe such *parajika*[101] monks. The criticism[102] is underlined by the meanness of the old maid, who can afford to support the monks but not the worthy nephew. A political note is sounded: "Things always turn out this poorly when one who has no money associates with one who has." TS's jealousy and frustration, which are legitimate, contrast with the monk Thudaza's, which are not. The second attack is more openly nationalistic. It takes the form of a discussion between aunt and nephew, so that TS's anger is given full vent by his aunt's questions. At the same time, we no longer have just an angry young man; rather, we are faced by an educated (he knows his Pali) and sophisticated nationalist who can see all sides of a question and knows that bad behavior on the part of monks is usually an exaggerated form of what was originally reasonable behavior. Most politicians—he names Ba Maw and U Saw—powder themselves; in monks' sermons, together with the singsong which exceeds the requirement that the Dhamma should be made pleasant to hear, there are other excesses. TS then attacks gifts in excess of need and formal "necessities": trunks, brass cots, lace curtains, sofas, chairs. By such gifts to a passive Sangha, the monks are drawn into sensual enjoyment and grad-

---

101. *Parajita* (P): defeat or downfall of a monk caused by four temptations: (1) theft, (2) sex, (3) killing, and (4) false claims to supernatural powers.

102. Such criticisms are not new. Mrs. Allott has drawn my attention to a *myittaza*, a sort of rhymed letter, sent by the famous Burmese monk-author U Pon Nya (?1807–1866) to a friend from whom he had heard rumors about his own behavior. The monk explains that he had gone once to the house of a layman to ask for medicine for an illness. "A certain fellow, an ox, an oaf with his arse where his mouth should be," had gone about saying that the monk had been courting, and the whole town had believed it. The allegations are totally untrue. Rather disconcertingly, however, the poet continues: "And if I were interested in the sort of thing that creature suggested (I can tell you this because you are my true friend), there are girls, pretty and tender, not too small or too tall, just well proportioned, slim and slender, tender buds not too full or too skinny (let us say like creamy coconut, soft to the spoon's caress or, if not soft, then firmer but yielding to the knife's thrust)—just the right sort for *pongyis* and kings and quite unsuitable for the young lads of the town—girls who come, far too many of them, to visit my monastery; young things with their hair still cut short or else just tossing their locks. I even have to take a cane and whip them to drive them away." (Translation by Mrs. Allott)

ually begin to hanker for more and to ask for it in sermons. The gifts, furthermore, are made so publicly that one must suspect the laity of giving for the sake of acquiring a name and publicity. It is because of this form of charity that the Burmese have become poor, TS argues. The aunt counters this with the notion that the less one gives the worse one's *kamma,* or balance of merit, becomes; the worse it becomes, the less one is able to give. TS replies with the view that true charity pays attention to the need of the recipient: what possible need is met when, for instance, fortunes are spent on monks' funerals? Finally, not bad monks but those monks of good *sila* (i.e., those who observe the precepts) should be given to; in this way good behavior will be reinforced, and the good will triumph (pp. 112–118).

Thus TS makes a critique of the laymen as well as of the monks and does not attack monks as such, as has often been maintained. This is a rational, informed, fair-minded attack on the whole Sangha-laity relationship in its degenerate form. The notion of the Sangha as a "field of merit"—the Abhidhamma-inspired view that it is the frame of mind involved in giving that matters and not the character of the recipient—is forgotten. One should scarcely expect it here.

The implicit criticism of the monkhood is contained in Thein Pe Myint's account of the way of life his characters lead. Thus six monks in Thudaza's monastery not only failed to go out for food but paid the *sayadaw* some 8 *kyat*s for the rice they needed. Among the nuns attracted to this "earthly paradise," the eldest, a widow of forty, reacted to Parrot's *payoga* (magical powers) by renunciation—of the flesh of of widowhood one is left to guess. It is implied that the nuns, who feed the *sayadaw,* are at his tender mercies in more ways than one. Finally, the *kappiya* (lay steward) doubles as a trader: selling flowers from the gardens each morning at the bazaar and being subjected to grumbling and criticism over his spending, his cooking, etc. (pp. 12–17). Throughout the novel, monks are portrayed as living extremely well, with constant disregard for the Vinaya. The case is made all the stronger since biting satire alternates with compassion and understanding: we are not dealing with puppets only. Thus, the declaration of love scene is quite touching, and Thudaza takes, momentarily at any rate, moral responsibility for his deed (pp. 70–71). Sayadaw Parrot is obviously very moved and upset when he discovers his beloved in Thudaza's arms, and there is some compassion in the author's description of him (pp. 124–127). Throughout the book, the hero has moments of clear-sightedness: he sees the Shwedagon and his thoughts are purified; elsewhere he momentarily remembers the true meaning of what he is saying. Other characters even comment upon the action: as noted above the pandering *kappiya* reminds Thudaza, who is accusing Parrot of greed, that he himself is greedy, and so on.

So far, however, we have only touched the surface. It is the progressive degradation of the hero and his calling that must have been truly frightening to the Burmese reader and perhaps accounts for the novel's impact. There is, first, a personal degradation: this monk cannot concentrate. The scene before his first sermon is instructive: he cannot remember his speech; he can only see himself and his audience in his mind; he cannot listen to what his preceptor is telling him; on the dais him mind blurs. He has to work himself into his sermon rather like a revivalist preacher (the "spirit of the chair" seizes him), and he ingratiates himself with his audience by telling them that this is his first sermon (pp. 94–96). It is not only here—vagueness would be excusable in a first sermon—but also many times later that he is overtaken by the same inability to think of anything but his glory, his conquests, his triumphs with women, and so forth. A monk who cannot concentrate is not a monk: furthermore he endangers the Law itself, the very scriptures he is supposed to expound.

There is also degradation of the Sangha. The attack is made so subtly by Thein Pe Myint that one might overlook it: the implications are far greater than TS's rather superficial criticism allows for, though the presence of TS and his ambitions running parallel to the hero's, serve to underline the real theme. The Order has been degraded from the Sangha into merely another profession. The preachers compete with one another. There is a closed shop in Rangoon. There are hierarchies, with degrees of fame and rewards. All the more terrible for being (in human terms) rather touching is the professional attitude taken by the lovers: Thudaza's nun wants to be the first to hear him preach; their love-play is blasphemously conducted in professional terms: the monk preaches to the nun, who dresses as a lay woman before sleeping with him (pp. 74, 77). The implication is that these people not only lack ideals and consistency (the monk's political dealings show this) but also pervert the basic educational function of the Sangha. Such criticisms are implied by the words *tet pongyi,* which in 1937 meant a modern, up-to-date, or advanced monk. The slang phrase "with it" captures the flavor of the Burmese term that so upset the Buddhists of the day.

The political and economic allegations inherent in Thein Pe Myint's critique, as pointed up by the plight of the author's mouthpiece, TS, are basically that the money spent on these worthless monks could better have been spent on citizens in real need. As I stated above, I do not think, as some have, that *Tet Pongyi* was an outright attack on the Sangha as a whole, but we must note that the author's accusations were in keeping with statements of brave young nationalist politicians, to the effect that pagoda gold should be used for hospitals and schools, and with criticism of such aims leveled by religious-minded people against "enemies of Buddhism."[103] As I pointed out in the last chapter, I do not feel that the Burmese spend that much on the Sangha itself, but *Tet Pongyi* is a good example of the opinions of an important segment of the urban laity in the prewar period. The book shocked the prewar Burmans, but it also hit home.

The Philosophy of a Buddhist Nationalist Monk

If we ask who really were the "modern" monks (if there can ever be such), we think perhaps of U Ottama, who did not live to see World War II. Was he modern enough, or too modern? He died in Rangoon Hospital in September 1939, after a long illness during which there were some signs of mental instability. The data on his last days are confusing, but there is evidence that he was lonely toward the end, as he had been at the beginning of his career. Chatterjie tells us that nationalist politicians such as Tharrawaddy U Pu and Sir Paw Tun were extremely reluctant to contribute to the funeral. He obviously had made many enemies. Eventually, however, he was recognized as a national hero, and he is so treated in Burma today.[104] What is the significance of his life?

U Ottama's career should be viewed in terms of the nationalistic dynamics that have been discussed in this chapter. When U Ottama first

103. It should be noted that Thein Pe Myint has been one of Burma's most vocal and persistent communists, a charter member of the 1939 cell in Rangoon. To sully the nation's religious ideal by reducing *sayadaws* and monks to lovers in a novel can also be seen as the usual Marxist deflation of religion, as much as any desire to reform and promote an institution cherished by Thein Pe Myint. J. F.

104. Chatterjie 1956(?):3; Cady 1958:332; Ba Yin, n.d.:85–87.

appeared on the scene, he was barely recognized by the Sangha and was barely given asylum in monasteries because of his political interests and his alleged violations of Vinaya.[105] His curious brand of traditionalism mixed with Gandhian boycotting and noncooperation methods eventually gave a basically political problem the strongest religious and cultural coloring. By the time of his imprisonment he had formed a following of extremist Sangha leaders who took control of the GCSS and greatly influenced the policy of their affiliated GCBA organizations. What was the philosophy behind his actions?

His biography provides access to some of the ideas that illuminated this "agitator in yellow robes," with which phrase so many Western observers are content to dismiss him. There is constant stress on the theme of "nationalism as a service to others," which burns in Ottama's breast. He writes to his brother from Calcutta: "My younger brother, you have been born as a human being—is it only for your own benefit or is it for the benefit and progress of all human beings? Do consider this deeply and see if you can put it to good use in your life."[106] His brother does not understand until he hears the Jataka of the monkey king who sacrificed himself to keep his enemy alive. On more than one occasion in the book, there is an implicit comparison of Ottama's deeds with acts of the Buddha, as embryo Buddhas of the past are said to have always sacrificed self for the benefit of their tribe or country, there being no value in coming into the world if it is for one's own benefit alone.[107] No occasion is lost to show that, whenever interrupted by adversity in his labors, Ottama devoted himself—in prison especially—to meditation and religious self-improvement. He is absolved of any violence, of heaping up money for himself, or of charges that he kept a wife in Calcutta.[108] At his death he left 20,000 yen in a Yokohama bank reserved by him for spreading the teachings of the Buddha abroad, which sum was untouched by his relatives after his death. He wrote in a book about how a rich man had asked him to marry his daughter but that, since he had discarded the pleasures of touch since his boyhood, he had refused the girl. Though he had a reputation for roughness of speech,

105. Maung Maung Pye 1951(?):14; Ba Yin, n.d.:37.
106. Ba Yin, n.d.: 26–27.
107. Ba Yin, n.d.:45, 49, 59.
108. Ba Yin, n.d.: 84–86.

several examples of his kindness and refusal to hector people are adduced. He is credited with democratic sentiments, and his Jubilee Hall speech is cited as a text on learning how to agree to differ and see the other party's point of view.[109]

Ottama's optimism may seem naive or uninformed to some, but it appears to have been closely related to his hope and pride in his country and countrymen. He does seem to have thought that France or America would intervene on Burma's side, but his main emphasis was on self-help. A speech made in 1922 in Mandalay is quoted from a newspaper of the time. In this he accuses foreigners of having hypnotized the Burmese into believing that they are an inferior race: foreigners have, quite wrongly, debased accounts of Burmese royalty and thus cut Burmese off from their own culture. England is presented as one of the great homes of liberty in the past, now decadent owing to too much blood-sucking in the colonies. Figures are cited to prove that too many Christians are favored in schools, too many members of the "imported Sasana" (i.e., Christians) favored everywhere in Burma. Because of both the ideals of Buddhism and the strength of Britain, the way of violence must not be espoused: Burmese must live simply, on home products, and improve themselves in every way they know. The British can stay in Burma if they cut down their ambitions and their oppression. The future must be faced with optimism, for the doctrine of *kamma* forbids one to cry over the past. In all this, the monks are presented as being and having to be in the forefront of home rule agitation.[110] In another speech, Ottama declares that England has reconnoitered the Bhamo-Myitkyina area in northern Burma in order to put England's great number of unemployed to work there. This leads to a survey of races which have been chased out of their homes by Europeans: the Australians, the Maori, the Red Indians, the Congolese, and other Africans.[111]

This is certainly not what we have referred to earlier as "royal revivalism," with its use of magic and the occult.[112] How far U Ottama was involved in such traditionalism is uncertain. There is very little evidence of it in the biography. This is not the place to review the *gaing* element in later nationalism, but, in comparison to the Saya San case,

109. Ba Yin, n.d.:54–58.
110. Ba Yin, n.d.: 63–71.
111. Ba Yin, n.d.:71–73.
112. Cady 1958:310.

there seems to be little of it by the time of the 1938 anti-Indian Riots.[113] Instead, Ottama's position seems to have been Buddhist, shaped by a nationalistic end which selected his means. His was looking forward, instead of looking backward with the more traditional rebel monks with whom we began the chapter.

The Mindon Sects' Responses to Modern Society

If the general theory of the Sangha which has been hypothesized in this book is correct, then we would expect to find that during this nationalistic period the sects introduced earlier were busy organizing, expanding, disciplining, and defining themselves as a defense against possible lay control by either the British colonialists or the Burmese politicians in the government. Such indeed was the response of the major sects to the nationalistic movements we have reviewed.

As noted above, the Shwegyin Sayadaw never cooperated with the Taungdaw but went his own way. He was not recognized by the British after 1885. We do know that his fame spread to Ceylon and Thailand and that he was effective in Lower Burma. In 1893, he is said to have met U Thila of the Tawya *gaing,* founder of the famous Shwehintha Tawya Taik discussed above. The latter monk had been very successful in building monasteries in Rangoon, Pegu, Nyaunglebin, Shwegyin, Kyaikhto, Thaton, and Moulmein, and he was reputed to be an *arahant.* The Shwegyin Sayadaw is said to have listened to U Thila preach and to have been so impressed that the Shwegyin and Tawya *gaing*s decided to amalgamate, "the reason being that their aims and objects were identical and, as both stressed the observance of *Vinaya,* it was like the mixing of the waters of the Ganges with those of the Yamuna: the Shwegyin spreading in Lower Burma and the Tawya spreading in Upper Burma."[114] *The Present Religious Events* informs us that in the years 1897–1898 the Shwegyin and Dwaya sects separated over the manner of recitation of certain *paritta*s, or protective charms. Can we infer that Shwegyin hoped to compensate for the impending loss of the Lower

---

113. Cf., however, Burma 1939a:210.

114. Panditta 1955:1–4. The "forest" theme in the very name of the Tawya order should be carefully noted. The Report of the All-Shwegyin Conference of 1936 indicates that the *next* in line after the Shwegyin Sayadaw, the 1st Mahawithudarama Sayadaw, effected the merger.

Burma Dwaya contingent by making an alliance with the Tawya *gaing*?[115] Though much research still needs to be done into the early history of these sects, the splitting of the country by British conquest was clearly connected in some way with their divisions, and the alliances formed were in part inspired by the desire for all-Burma coverage, however much the rhetoric of union may have been phrased in terms of common attitudes to monastic discipline. This is not to deny that the unsettled nature of the times called for just this stress on Vinaya. In this same year, 1893, the Shwegyin Sayadaw died, and the cremation ceremonies were said to have been restrained.

A listing of the Shwegyin leaders who followed him (see Appendix E) shows that as late as 1920 there were still separate heads for Upper and Lower Burma, and we might also note the fact that the Kyaungdawya Sayadaw is always listed among the "original" *sayadaw*s immediately after the founder of the sect, although he apparently was never a "supreme president." Does the fact that the Kyaungdawya was a Lower Burma man and the head of Rangoon's prime *taik* indicate that the integration of Shwegyin and Tawya groups took longer than many would care to have admitted? The question needs further research.

The Vinaya emphasis of such sects as the Shwegyin has remained a distinguishing characteristic. During my stay in Burma, I inspected a contemporary document known as the "Thathana Thuddhi Saok" (Shwegyin sect's membership book), which is to all intents and purposes a monastic passport. Each Shwegyin group (here: *ahpwe*) must keep a register of such books as they are issued to individual monks and must record the serial numbers of same. This register must be submitted annually with the Lent statistical lists to the sect's Central Headquarters. Each monastery head must personally hand such a book to a new novice or monk and record in it the details of the new member's place of origin, ordination, and any subsequent residences. Each monk must carry his book with him wherever he goes. If lost, reapplication must be made to the original master. New books must record the reason why the old book was lost. If the monk disrobes, the book must be surrendered, and a full account of the reasons, together with the day, hour, and minute at which the disrobing took place, must be recorded in it; thereafter it must be carefully kept at the monastery

115. Pyinnyaramikamaha Sayadaw 1958: 69.

where the monk's original master resides. If one is disrobed for *parajika*[116] offienses, the reasons, must be recorded in the book after consultation with the supreme president, and the disrobing must be carried out by the relevant Winido (Vinaya) department. No monk can be received by any monastery unless he has his book with him. Provision is made for the recording of ten changes of residence (mostly during student days) with entries by the *sayadaw* who is being left and the *sayadaw* who is receiving. There are twelve pages devoted to good or bad conduct records. In addition there are a number of pages devoted to a summary of the rules of monkhood in their strict Shwegyin version.

A review of the 1936 report on business before the Shwegyin Central Mandalay Council confirms the Vinaya emphasis and sect discipline in the areas of monastic schools, Pali exams, cooperation with other sects in approaching the British government of Burma, and attention to texts written by the "original" *sayadaw*s. Other resolutions contain reminders that no expensive and festive cremations of Shwegyin monks are to be allowed, that no monks are to attend *pwe*s (festivals), accept money, wear chemically dyed robes, and so on. Throughout there is great stress on the need for constant attention to rules, and there appears at times to be a call for the creation of "rules and regulations" committees (which hardly would be left with much new to say!). Likewise, in very Burmese fashion, the monks are constantly exhorted to make their points calmly, to see their opponents' point of view, to respect the "original" *sayadaw*s, and to remember that, because of them, they are all as "brothers and near relatives one to another." Exhortations on these themes, indeed, take up much of the report.

To administer this system of discipline, the Shwegyin developed during the colonial period the fairly definite organization and hierarchy we reviewed in the last chapter. This structure is still the basis of the sect's existence. Quite clearly the Shwegyin hold themselves up to more exacting standards as a defense against the times. For example, rank is apparently achieved through seniority, as elsewhere in the monkhood, but the membership booklet points out that not five but seven full rainy seasons (*wa*) spent as a monk, with considerable other attainments, are necessary in order to become a master and reside alone, while ten rainy seasons must be passed before one can become a presiding monk or

116. See n. 101, above.

abbot of a monastery. Furthermore, the sect has developed, in addition to the hierarchy, a system of centralized control that apparently holds considerable power. A Supreme Council under the supreme president resides in Mandalay, and all important decisions concerning the sect must be referred to it. Officers of this body are said in the 1936 report to be elected by the conferences of representatives of the entire sect, but the highest offices clearly are filled for life.

The Mandalay leadership supervises the hierarchy below and promotes a two-way flow of information and directives. Officials at the sect centers (*htana*) and district (*gaing*) levels come themselves or send deputies to the sect's conferences and thus have some say in the election of superior officers. The rules and regulations formulated at the conferences are copied and taken back to the centers and districts, and the results of local discussions are then passed on to Mandalay. However, the Supreme Council clearly has the last say. An analysis of committee membership shows that there is considerable duplication of staffing so that the Supreme Council members extend their influence into such bodies as the Welcoming Committee and the Public Relations and Information Committee. Also, there has been in the Shwegyin sect an effort to retain power in the hands of Upper Burma monks. A glance at the list of presidents in Appendix E shows that numbers 1, 2, 3, 5, 6, 7, 9, 10, 11 or a total of nine out of eleven, were Upper Burma men. This centralizing tendency is noticed even in accounts of the meetings of the Supreme Council, where most topics get short shrift indeed, suggesting that the council had firmly decided to reach its decisions by itself in places where minutes would not be taken. There is, basically, a fairly clear pattern of organizational statuses with titles, but deference to age or monastery ownership factors may encumber the power structure with anomalies that blur the lines of organizational authority.

Thus, the importance of the strong central group of senior monks is considerable. The efforts made by these older *sayadaw*s to retain control of the sect as it grew larger by evolving a solid district-based organization have been amply repaid by the great respect paid to Shwegyin in Burma and by the freedom the sect has attained. Because of such success the AFPFL reform of the Sangha program met difficulties because sects like the Shwegyin wished to remain aloof and resisted being drawn back into the Sangha as a whole by a commonality of rules.

The Dwaya sect, presents quite similar patterns of organizational activity and disciplinary emphasis. In terms of the structure of authority developed in the colonial period and continued to the modern era, the head of the Dwaya is called the *maha nayaka* (great leader), a post later given national status in 1952 when the government recognized a Dwaya *rattaguru*.[117] Next in line are the *anu nayaka*s, who appear to be the heads of great monasteries that "serve" various townships, their ecclesiastical business aided by *gana* and *anu rakkhaka*[118] monks, who act as "protectors" and "secretaries." Under this system a monk may have one title in his capacity at the monastery and another title for his sectarian role, as can be seen in Appendix F, where the venerated "ancestor" *sayadaw*s of the Dwaya are listed. The strict line of succession, however, is not so easy to determine, as a glance at the appendix confirms. This sect also developed a hierarchical organization, as did the Shwegyin.

The Dwaya, of course, likewise stressed their Vinaya purity. A number of informants told me that Dwaya monks made quite a fuss about eating and living with others, in contrast to Shwegyin, who made much less. In Paungde, where Dwaya once predominated, this used to be the case (Prome, Henzada, and Tharrawaddy are now said to be Dwaya headquarters). A Shwegyin leader held that Shwegyin mixed with others much more than Dwaya did. All this supports the data indicating that the Shwegyin tried to persuade the Dwaya sect to join Nu's Sangayana (see Chapter 5), although both sects had rejected King Mindon's bid to participate in his Fifth Buddhist Council. On the other hand, both sects opposed ecclesiastical courts after national independence, and Dwaya were to be found among the activist Sangha Party, but not Shwegyin. The explanation for the latter phenomenon may be that given by a Ministry of Religious Affairs officer, who told me that Upper Burmans referred to the Dwaya sect as "Dwayaw" (mixed), because, from an inferiority complex at being so few, the Dwaya often pretended to be Thudhamma or Shwegyin. In the crucial matter of registration of monks (which will be discussed later), Dwaya tried to issue its own cards, but the army refused permission.[119] Their success in creating a separate re-

---

117. *Rattaguru:* an honorary title given to sect leaders by the U Nu government in the 1950s. See Chapter 5, below.

118. *Gana* (P): chapter of monks. *Anu rakkhaka: anu:* district (?); *rakkhati* (P): to protect.

119. *The Nation,* May 27, June 11, 1959.

spected identity seems at times to have been less impressive than the Shwegyin efforts.

By 1935 the Hngetwin sect had about a hundred monasteries in its growing organization. The second leader, U Zawtikadaza, was still alive in 1938, when he formed a Satubumika Mahathatipatan Sangha Association (Ahpwe) in "systematic style," with two *gana dipati* officials (the highest rank), four *gana pamukkha*s, eight *gana sariya*s, sixteen *gana nayaka*s, a number of *gana katika*s, three *ganeithara*s (?), and six hundred monks.[120] Thus the sect organized itself along familiar lines, assigning its own honorary titles to positions in its hierarchy. After U Zawtikadaza died in 1944 at the Paramisan Monastery, two *dipati sayadaw*s seem to have been at the top of the hierarchy. By national independence in 1948 there were somewhere between 170 and 200 monasteries, with 1,400 monks and 100,000 reputed followers. The sect's three main centers were at Kungyangon, Thaton, and Mandalay. Despite the importance of the last location, three out of the four *pamukkha*s and most *sariya*s (see above titles) were Lower Burma monks.

A similar pattern of sect organization is found in a 1954 history of the Weluwun sect.[121] The document I discovered provides some information on Weluwun organization, though here as elsewhere the reader's primary interest is manifestly expected to be in the biographical details of the lives of the *sayadaw*s. At one point reference is made to 3,000 monks. A very vague list of functions of two supervisory bodies—the Mahanayaka Ahpwe and the Anu Nayaka Ahpwe—is offered: they are to meet every six months or yearly to advise both monks and lay followers. Disputes are to be settled personally by a visit of the *anu nayaka* officials concerned. It appears that the *anu nayaka*s are responsible for sending information to headquarters from the districts, including letters of introduction for monks changing monasteries, Lent lists of resident monks in the various monasteries, names of monasteries joining the sect, and so forth. Rules for presiding *sayadaw*s of monasteries and basic "academic" qualifications are very similar to those of the stricter "Mindon" sects. The *maha nayaka*s (great leaders) are listed as 16 in number [Myanaung, 3; Henzada, 1; Kyangin, 2; Inpin, 1; Bassein, 4; Thaton, 1; Minhla, 1; Rangoon, 1 (Bahan); Prome, 2] and the *anu nayaka*s number 23

---

120. The significance of the Pali terms for these titles is not clear.
121. Cover ripped off; no bibliographic details available.

[Myanaung, 4; Henzada, 3; Kyangin, 3; Shwegyin, 1; Inpin, 1; Kyonpyaw, 2; Bassein, 3; Thaton, 1; Prome, 3; Rangoon, 1 (Kemmendine); Htaintaw (Tharrawaddy District), 1]. Note that they are all Lower Burma men.

The Weluwun rules resemble those of the Shwegyin and Dwaya sects. Regulations are cited concerning the proper way of visiting lay inhabitations; refraining from the use of sandals and sunshades; abstaining from tobacco and betel after midday; avoiding witnessing shows, dances, and horse races; not attending pagoda and *pongyi-byan pwes*:[122] not handling money without a lay steward; not accumulating or lending money; not trading or stocking vegetable products or breeding cattle; avoiding alchemy, talismans, charms, amulets, *mantras*,[123] doctoring, and fortune-telling; and not postponing burial of a monk, whatever his rank, more than seven days. All these rules have been noted before for other sects, and they provide a good picture—from the inside—of what lax monks are alleged to do. In addition there are other miscellaneous rules of interest, some of which are doubtless shared with other strict sects. All monks must be able to recite the 227 basic Vinaya rules by heart, must refrain from living with any monk who is awaiting the result of an ecclesiastical court ruling, and must not initiate novices who do not know their texts. If under suspicion of transgression of Vinaya, one must abide by one's superiors whether the suspicion is correct or not; one must visit one's *maha nayaka* (sect leader) at least once a year and hold a prayer meeting once a day. Relations with laymen must be very restrained and careful: should one be unable to prevent pwes from being held in one's monastery, one must remain unperturbed in one's room and refrain from witnessing the *pwes*; one must refrain from shopping with lay donors or leading or guiding them and bargaining for them—even if with one's master or parents; one may not, unless ill, ride in carts, rickshaws, trishaws, or any other vehicle; one may not paint, carve, or sculpt unseemly figures or cause others to produce them. Above all, one is not to interfere in political affairs or to consult anyone but one's own sect leaders in the settlement of any dispute.

122. *Pongyi-byan pwes* (B): not unhappy social gatherings at a monk's funeral.
123. *Mantra* (SK): recitation of scripture as a spell.

A Modern Shan Reformist Sect

Such are the organizational and Vinaya patterns of the orthodox Mindon sects. It is helpful to compare these with the modern development of a nonorthodox sect, the Zawti, a "Paramat" sect of the type discussed earlier in this book. By following a clue in Scott's writings on a group known as the Mans, I was able in the Shan States to find some Zawti sectarians and to elicit some information from them. They can be considered as also showing a defensive pattern of organization and disciplinary severity, but using, of course, a unique way of their own—a layman's reformation of sorts.

I found this material in Kyaukme, in the Northern Shan States, where I had gone to witness a cremation with a well-known Shwegyin *sayadaw*. I quote from my field notes:

The Shwegyin *sayadaw* arranged his food with the *taga*s (lay donors) and asked them to summon an expert on Yun and Zawti for the next morning. At the time of our visit to the Zawti village, he said that these people were very strict and would not go to any monks but theirs. He thought they were about 300–400 years old and that they had been chased out of Burma by the kings. I asked him whether Zawti were Paramat. "Yes, from the point of view of Thudhamma and Shwegyin, Dwaya, Zawti, Yun and Hnget are Paramat."

The next morning, I found an old gentleman waiting to see me at the monastery. His account of Shan sectarianism was revealing:

The word Zawti is from the Pali word for radiance: *joti*. The Zawti are very strict and do not mix with other monks because they control their mouths; actually they are always controlling the 6 *indriya:* Eye, Ear, Nose, Tongue, Body, Mind. They are extremists in meditation. The avoidance of the ten *ducarita,* or evil forms of conduct, and the following of the ten *kusala kammapattha,* or good courses of conduct, are enjoined on *taga*s and *tagama*s [female donors], who are strictly subordinated to monks. Any sinner is threatened with boycott and has to entreat the monk with 3 *kadaw pwe* offerings[124] to the head of the sect, then 5, 7, even 14 until satisfaction is obtained. Otherwise it is possible for the head to throw out a member of the sect.

The monks use the Pali Tipitaka in Shan, and wear the yellow robe. There

124. Offerings in a bowl to honor monks (coconut, banana, etc.—ingredients somewhat the same as those offered to a *nat* or spirit).

are few monks: about one hundred in the Northern Shan States. I don't know about other parts. The Zawti live mostly in Momeik (Mong Mit), Hsenwi States, and Namkham. In all places but the headquarters, there are many Zawti *kyaungs*, but these do not have monks. Laymen look after the buildings and wait for rare monk visits. The head layman looks after funerals. On holy days laymen observe precepts before a pagoda while the head layman reads from a book.

That very afternoon, we visited a small Zawti monastery a few minutes' drive away, on the outskirts of Kyaukme. I quote from my notes again:

We talked to various lay people inside the monastery. They said the sect had been in existence for about one hundred years, but I could not obtain the succession or lineage of monks. One woman said she had known four: the first died in Namkham, the second in Maikhe(?) (Hsipaw State), the third in Momeik, and the fourth, now about seventy, lives in Mohnyin, above Katha. He is called Keithidhamma Sayadaw, which the Shan pronounce Tikidhamma, and lives with some twenty-four monks. He travels about, staying in a place for three to five years, and people go to him wherever he happens to be. Monks come to villages only under invitation, and no monk has come here since the foundation. Children go to Mohnyin for the *shinbyu* (novice initiation).

The next-door Zawti Kun village has been inhabited for about six years. Some of its people came from Momeik, some from Kohkang. All are Zawti: there are about 42 households with 200 people. Everyone speaks Shan—and, indeed our informants looked like typical Shan, with knee-thigh and forearm tatoos. The move was made because a livelihood was easier in Kyaukme. Some of the people are traders, some gardeners, some cultivators; Zawti, though eating meat, do not keep animals or fowl and have no fishermen or butchers.

They did not know the total number of Zawti, but they estimated that, at the last triannual all-Burma *shinbyu* at Mohnyin, 20,000 people were present.

Katthein (robe-weaving ceremony) is also performed each year for the *sayadaw*. Boys stay one year with the *sayadaw* before becoming *koyins* (novices) and then stay as long as he wishes them to.

During Lent, people observe the eight precepts without the aid of a monk. They claimed to call their local sect leaders *pandaka*, which they said was the same term as *paya taga* (pagoda donor) in Burmese. I was unable to obtain an answer to the question "Why are there so few monks in Zawti?"

The monastery, as well as a pagoda built for a Mandalay stone image, is of simple design, in wood, with many Shan appurtenances: a banner with four-square decorations, many robe-wrapped Buddha images, a fish-shaped trough used at the water festival with a sprinkler (I saw a similar thing in

Namkham) and very tall bamboo poles with streamers on whirling wooden fish weathervanes.

The village was very pretty and tidy, and I had a glimpse of pineapple and vegetable fields.

Although there is no space here to give further historical data on this reformist sect, the Zawti appear to have been a late eighteenth-century sect that survived, after being chased out of Burma proper to the Shan States in the northwest. A number of Shan Buddhist customs appear to have been adopted, with Shan texts and Shan iconography. Beliefs retain some Paramat traits, insofar as we can derive these from the very vague literature on the subject, especially in terms of their worship of the mysterious Nyan-daw ("wisdom as pillar of fire")[125] and their strict attention to personal religious discipline. The most interesting factor remains the concentration of Zawti laymen in a few villages and the one-monastery and headquarters concept of leadership. The Shan landscape does not permit easy access from monastery to monastery, and the Shans may have had to make do with relatively few monks. Also, apart from any hypothetical Zawti theory of single leadership, the migration to the Shan States may have influenced the Zawti monks' decision to retain one center of control. The movements from place to place, unexplained by informants may have arisen out of a natural desire to be within easy reach of different Zawti villages at different times. While little can be said about the relations between monks and laymen in the sect, they do not seem to be marked by anticlericalism, though naturally much stress should be placed on the assumption of responsibility and discipline in the personal religious life of monkless lay villagers. A further factor in what must appear as a fight for survival among the Zawti, who number some 20,000 people with no more than 30–40 monks, may be the general laxness of Shan monks in other sects. An important lead that should be followed up by scholars is the probability that the Shan States provided a refuge for many centuries to sects chased out of Burma proper for "heretical" beliefs.

In terms of sectarian behavior in the nationalist period, the Zawti, like the more orthodox sects, showed the same defensive tendency toward self-organization and self-imposed discipline, both being very effective means of warding off more powerful political forces which would use the

125. See Chapter 2 for Paramat worship of Nyan-daw as described by Scott.

existence of disorder and poor behavior as excuses for social control. The other possible strategy, of course, was for monks to enter the political area and seek to control the forces that threatened the religion to begin with. By and large all the Mindon sects avoided the latter route.

Nationalist Leadership and Supporting Monks

A review of the role of the entire Sangha in the nationalist period suggests that an intimate knowledge of the family structure of particular leading political and religious individuals would tell us more about the country than anything else. Here we can only begin to talk of certain classes of families associated with a particular set of vested interests and a particular outlook on the world. Nevertheless three broad groups need to be isolated for the purpose of commenting on politicoreligious developments. The first "class" comprised the Westernized intelligentsia, who were as deeply involved in the process of government as any class of Burmese nationals could be at the time: as government officials, professional men, jurists, merchants, and landholders. They can be called the *"min"* class, and their primary roles were as officials and administrators. The *min*'s detached attitude to the whole course of nationalism finds expression in such works as Mi Mi Khaing's *Burmese Family* (1945) or U Ba U's *My Burma: The Autobiography of a President* (1959). It seems fairly clear that this *min* class also had its monks, in the persons of *sayadaws* like the Aletawya and the Shweman. At the opposite pole is the third class, the rural peasantry and proletariat, composed, as far as this model is concerned, of leaders of local Wunthanu Athins and the majority of the "political *pongyis*," the latter described by one observer as "an intellectual proletariat with little to lose from rebellion and activism." In the middle, in the "second class," are a group of men whom I shall refer to as the nationalists proper. Their main characteristic is that they sought to bridge the gap between the first and third classes in an effort to provide a wide backing for the nationalist movement. While a thorough analysis of their social background is still needed, we can venture to say that many of them issued from the *min* class. Ottama himself had a *min*-style education. During the period we have been reviewing, the plums of political office offered by the British were a constant temptation, so that a movement back toward the *min*s can be seen as a constant feature of the behavior of these nationalists, with new groups of younger and more radical nationalists filling the place of the "officialized" older ones. The group of nationalists which, through the hazards of history, happened to be ready to take over the government of independent Burma from the British-affiliated (or Japanese-affiliated) and therefore disgraced *mins*, was, of course, the younger Thakin group of U Nu, Aung San, and others. It is interesting to note that, once "officialized," these new *mins* did not behave so differently from their predecessors.

The position of the nationalists was thus open to every kind of ambiguity. On the one hand they were aspiring to freedom for Burma under their own government; they had an interest in what that government would be and in its programs, which would turn out eventually to be little more than liberalized and socialized versions of programs already worked out by the British Raj. On the other hand, in order to gain popular backing for themselves, they had to keep contact with the rural leaders and especially with the rural Sangha leaders, without allowing these traditionalists to undermine their own liberal and socialist programs in favor of some return to a "Golden Burma" of the past. The monks can thus be said to have been made use of, rather than helped to create a viable twentieth-century Sangha. There does appear to have been a time when the monk leaders perceived the possibility of attempting some form of social control dominated by themselves, but their attempts at such were undermined and rendered ineffective by inadequate organization at the national level.

Clearly, the large majority of the passive Sangha continued about its Buddhist business. There is nothing in the admittedly somewhat sparse data to suggest that the activist minority ever really tried to control the whole Sangha, still less that it could have done so had it tried. Forces in the country, and in the Sangha particularly, strongly resisted a politicized monkhood. To this day the belief persists among Burmese that Burmese Buddhism is the finest flower of the culture, that monks are its culture's repository, and that Burma is nothing without Buddhism or its monks. Like many nations at the crossroads, Burma wishes both to preserve the best in its past and to open up a freeway to the future. Inevitably the question of the monkhood's role had to be raised early. Would it lose its sanctity if it participated in political events? The answer was not only conditioned by fear of Sangha rivalry and of any form of theocracy. It was also conditioned by the strong feeling that any extensive Sangha role in lay affairs would doom its sanctity.

5. The Sangha and the Independent State: The Revival

The struggle for "sanctity," if one wishes to view the Sangha's relationship with the state in such a light, becomes most intense during the years after Independence was achieved in 1948. In this chapter the emphasis will be upon those events leading up to and culminating in the important U Nu period of the fifties. In Chapter 4 we reviewed the spectrum of the Sangha's reactions to nationalist politics up to the 1940s, and we shall begin this chapter with a very brief review of the relations between the Sangha and secular power during the complex events of World War II.

Political Use of Monks in World War II

The Japanese made much of their common Buddhist cause with the Burmans, and there are many accounts of monks welcoming their armed forces to Burma, thus incurring the enmity of British and Chinese troops.[1] The Japanese had great hopes for using the Sangha as an instrument of state, as religion had been so used in Japan.[2] The Intelligence Bureau at Simla, India, referred to a Tokyo broadcast in 1942 saying, "If we control the Pongyis in Burma our task is complete."[3] In their effort to use religion the Japanese even told the predominantly Christian Chins, for example, that there were many Christians in Japan. Some members of the Sangha definitely cooperated with the Japanese.[4] It has been said that some of the ardent prewar nationalist monks became pro-Japanese when independence was promised by Japan to the Burmans: "U Muneinda and U Tilawkanyana organized a scheme to send young pongyis and students to Japan apparently for cultural purposes but possibly,

1. Cady 1958:436–443.
2. See Guyot 1969:62. J. F.
3. Burma 1943, 1:28.
4. Tun Pe 1949:10–11.

though by no means certainly, to form the nucleus of the later Burma Independence Army."[5] In October 1942, a first Japanese attempt to sponsor an all-Burma Sangha organization to "carry out a positive religious program of benefit to the Burmese People" was stillborn. Equally unsuccessful was the Burma Buddhist League, with its headquarters in Rangoon and two-hundred branches; its strength was said to be 60,000 monks, of whom 2,000 had special training and were to be sent round Burma to "de-Europeanize" the minds of the Burmans. This report was based on a radio message broadcast in various languages but, significantly, not in Burmese![6] A Greater Asia Buddhist Conference convened in Tokyo in July 1943 did not impress Burma as it was hoped it would.[7] The Japanese also had plans to allow only one monk and one novice to live in each monastery—an unrealistic program, to say the least.

While some monks in the Sangha did cooperate with the Japanese, the conqueror's behavior soon alienated most village monks and their lay supporters, according to Thein Pe,[8] who wrote from India:

Our *pongyi*s are the hardest hit victims of Japanese barbarism. In Zigon *pongyi*s were told by the Japanese to climb a mango tree to cut down branches for their horses. It was with difficulty that I could persuade them to do the climbing themselves. The *pongyi*s of Mingon *kyaung* in Kyaukse were forced to wash the clothes of the Japanese and draw water for them. Many make trousers out of the yellow robes. Monasteries usually top the Japanese programme of plunder.[9]

Ba Maw, as Burmese head of state, was somewhat more successful in dealing with the Sangha. His Sinyetha ("Poor Man's") Party of the late 1930s was amalgamated with the younger Thakin nationalist group into what was known as the Dobama Sinyetha Asiayon (We Burmans Poor Man's Society). One of the four branches of this party was the Dobama Sinyetha Sangha Asiayon, where politically minded monks could unite under Ba Maw as the *adipadi,* or supreme leader.[10] In September 1943

5. Pearn 1943:13.
6. Burma 1943, 1:28.
7. Cady 1958:449–450.
8. Thein Pe: Thein Pe Myint, author of *Tet Pongyi* (see Chapter 4). [The communist position was, of course, violently antifascist, and communist Thein Pe Myint was stirring up anti-Japanese feelings to promote his underground resistance forces in Burma. J. F.]
9. Thein Pe 1943:53–54. See also Tun Pe 1949:20, and Burma 1943, 1:16.
10. Maung Maung Pye 1951 (?):82; Hobbs 1951:368; Burma 1943, 1:29.

Ba Maw is supposed to have declared that he wished to train Burma's "250,000 idle *pongyis*" in technical subjects so as to make use of monastic schools.[11] Attempts on his part to found a united Sangha body appear to have begun in May 1943, in the shape of the Maha Sangha Ahpwe, or Great Sangha Association. Leaders of several rival monk factions converged on Rangoon for a stormy twelve-day session which, according to the Simla Document, ended with agreement on July 28. The Maha Sangha Ahpwe was to be controlled through a national council of *sayadaw*s, each with thirty years' standing, aided by district *sayadaw*s with twenty years' standing, all to be elected by the monks. Cady (1958:464) writes of a Lower Burma, pro-government faction winning a tentative victory and electing the Aletawya Sayadaw as head of the council. The victory was presumably won against the Upper Burma faction led by the Nyaungyan Sayadaw, mentioned by Hobbs (1951: 358).[12] It is not clear what the disagreements were about.[13]

The Maha Sangha Ahpwe (MSA) was supposed to unite the Order. Hobbs (1951:368) mentions four sects existing at the time: Thudhamma, Shwegyin, Dwaya, and Kan.[14] I, of course, would add the others traced in previous chapters. All the sects were to unite and work for the "new order" in Burma and to promote friendly relations between Burmese and the Japanese. In late 1943, according to Hobbs, the MSA made a public proclamation to the effect that the war was a holy one for Burma. By early 1944, some districts were organized, and monk spokesmen went among the people defending the policy of the MSA council of *sayadaw*s. The Japanese and Ba Maw, as the puppet national leader, were, of course, quick to use the MSA for propaganda purposes.

11. Burma 1943, 1:42.

12. See also von der Mehden (1963:151), who sees the Aletawya's opposition as the Thadu Sayadaw of Rangoon, leader of a "Thathana Asiayon," and the Nyaungyan Sayadaw of Mandalay, leader of the "Thathana Pyu Aphwe." Von der Mehden records that a onetime minister of religion remembered almost the entire Sangha entering the Maha Sangha Ahpwe. [See Guyot (1969:55–63) for evidence that the Maha Sangha Ahpwe was primarily a Thudhamma effort, which was boycotted officially by the sects such as the Shwegyin. J. F.]

13. Maung Maung Pye [1951(?):87] shows the Aletawya Sayadaw (head of Ba Maw's Maha Sangha) greeting the British liberator, Lord Mountbatten, on his return to Burma.

14. Hobbs probably took the names from earlier literature, for the presence of the "Kan" sect is anachronistic. Cf. Cady (1958:464), who also mentions "four main sects."

Cady (1958:464) notes, however, that because of the transparency of the uses to which the MSA was put, the effect was not unity but an intensification of "the religious rift" in the Sangha. In effect monks followed their own ends and took little interest in the social welfare work of the Circle Army or the East Asia Youth League.[15] The attitude of the nationalist Thakins toward Ba Maw's policies is a complex matter, but it is noteworthy that U Nu expressed contempt for Ba Maw's use of the *pongyis*, whose sensibilities some said the latter was too willing to accommodate.[16]

In any case, the Sangha seems to have been equally indifferent, eventually, to both the imperialist aims of the Japanese and the extremes of Ba Maw's political ambitions. During the war, for example, Pali candidates continued to take Patamabyan examinations (see Glossary) as though the Buddha's world were timeless.[17] After the war, there was no unified Sangha, nor any disciplined and well-honed organization primed to do the will of the country's politicians. In short, the Sangha seems to have emerged from the war in basically the same state as it entered the war. Had Aung San, the war-time leader of independent Burma, not been assassinated but lived to put his sometimes severe visions into reality, the Sangha might indeed have faced major changes, but, as things worked out, national independence found the Sangha facing, not a revolutionary approach such as Aung San's, but a series of halting and hardly definitive attempts to meet the well-worn problems of Sangha discipline, state support of monastic higher learning, and the future of the monastery school for youngsters. These became the issues of early Independence.

Proposed Sangha Control through Monastic Courts

As shown in the last chapter, the 1935 court decision destroyed the remaining legal bases of the *thathanabaing*'s ability to solve Sangha disputes, and no monk was appointed to the Taunggwin Sayadaw's position when he died in 1938. After the war, in independent Burma, a

15. Also known as the National Service Association (1942), formed to encourage youth to do civic philanthropy. It was Ba Maw's indigenous version of the East Asia Youth League, a popular youth civic service group originated by the Japanese and later taken over by the Burmese.

16. Nu 1954:90–91. See also Cady 1958:464–465.

17. Burma 1943, 1:45.

legislative approach was taken toward disciplinary matters, resulting in the Vinicchaya-Htana Act of 1949, which attempted to return religious disputes from civil courts to the monkhood for solution.[18] The act provided for the establishment of ecclesiastical courts in all sections of the country that began at the township level and then progressed to appellate district courts and finally to union courts with final jurisdiction.

The Ministry of Religious Affairs was to be responsible for the maintenance of Sangha electoral rolls in all townships, to be corrected and brought up to date every three years, and local lists were to be kept with each deputy commissioner. Any monk in good standing who had spent the rainy season of the previous year in the Sangha and had been continuously residing for six months prior to the election in the township concerned was to be included in these rolls. Such monks were to elect two classes of *sayadaws*: Vinayadhara (Burmese: Winido) *sayadaws* and Ovadacariya *sayadaws* (see Glossary). Vinayadhara *sayadaws* were to hear and decide cases dealing with Vinaya matters, and there were to be such judges at each level of the system. The minimum requirements for judges at the township level included twenty years in the Order; a position as presiding monk, *taik-ok, taik-kyat,* or lecturer of a teaching monastery; and a reputation as a scrupulous and knowledgeable person. The Ovadacariya *sayadaws*, whose function was to help and advise the Vinayadharas in matters of doctrinal interpretation, were required to have spent at least thirty years in the Sangha. There was also an "election *sayadaw,*" to be responsible for getting the township *sayadaws* together in order that they might vote for district and union court judges. Throughout the system, monks were envisioned as voting for the personnel at the next higher level. Furthermore, the Vinayadhara *sayadaws* were to pass a single judgment in each case based on a majority opinion among them.

This 1949 act was followed by the Provisional Vinicchaya-Htana Act of 1951, which was passed, according to a Ministry of Religious Affairs spokesman, "in order to enable the Sangha to solve their disputes where no proper elections of the two classes of *sayadaws* could be made on account of the unsettled conditions in the country." For each provisional court so established, the president of the Union of Burma was to appoint

18. The Vinicchaya-Htana and Vinicchaya Tribunal Act of 1949 and the Provisional Vinicchaya-Htana Act of 1951 (published in 1959). This version builds the important "amendment act" of 1954 into the original act of 1949.

up to ten Vinayadhara *sayadaw*s. To all intents and purposes the provisional courts were the same in status as the township courts and were responsible to the union courts. Ovadacariya *sayadaw*s were not mentioned. Quite obviously, this act attempted to substitute executive political initiative for missing Sangha support of these attempts to involve the monks in a religious legal system modeled after a secular one.

In 1954 the original act was considerably modified by the passage of the Vinicchaya-Htana Amendment Act, which stressed not ecclesiastical courts but tribunals that could bypass the original township courts if both parties in the dispute so wished. Under this act Vinayadhara judges were to be chosen, by mutual agreement, to compose a tribunal. If the plaintiff and defendant failed to agree, the local civil court came into play and could refer them to either an ecclesiastical court or a tribunal. If the latter was not acceptable, the civil court issued letters to the plaintiff and defendant as well as to certain Vinayadhara *sayadaw*s requesting them to form a tribunal for which the civil court was responsible. If there was still no agreement, the civil court appointed a tribunal from a roster of qualified *sayadaw*s prepared by the Ministry of Religious Affairs, and this tribunal judged the case in the presence or absence of plaintiff and defendant, the judgment being enforceable and filable in the civil court. The judgment given there was final and binding on all parties and could not fall under the jurisdiction of an ecclesiastical court.

An explanation for the shift in emphasis from courts to tribunals may have to do with the problem of sects. The act of 1949, provided that, "with regard to the religious sects whose members form a minority of the *Sangha* . . . the Shwegyin Sect in Upper Burma shall elect one Union *Vinayadhara Sayadaw* and one Union *Ovadacarya Sayadaw,* and . . . in Lower Burma, the Shwegyin Sect and the Dvara [Dwaya] Sect shall each elect one Union *Vinayadhara Sayadaw* and one Union *Ovadacarya Sayadaw. . . .*" This is all that is said about sects, but the amendment act of 1954 places the problem of sects in the foreground. It should be noted that " 'Sect' means the *Sudhamma* [Thudhamma] Sect, or the *Shwegyin* Sect or the *Dvara* Sect"; other sects are apparently not recognized. In the panels of the tribunal *sayadaw*s to be prepared by the Ministry of Religious Affairs, "the *sayadaw*s belonging to the *Sudhamma, Shwegyin* and *Dvara* Sects shall be listed according to their respective Sects, and the *Sayadaw*s who do not belong to any of those Sects, shall be listed separately." The civil court was to take into consideration the sects of the plaintiff and the defendants: if their sect was insufficiently represented on the local roster, they were to use the roster of an adjoining district. Finally, "in the matter of constituting the Ecclesiastical Tribunal under this section, if the plaintiff and the defendant are members of the same sect, all the *Vinayadhara Sayadaw*s . . . shall belong to that sect. If the plaintiff and the defendant belong to different sects, *Vinayadhara Sayadaw*s shall be chosen each from their respective sects, and the Umpire *Vinayadhara Sayadaw* shall be a *Sayadaw* chosen from the sect to which neither of the parties belong, or a *Sayadaw* chosen by the *Vinayadhara Sayadaw*s of the Ecclesiastical Tribunal."[19] Quite possibly the amendment act of 1954 was written to deal with the factor of sects, which had been insufficiently considered in the original act of 1949.

On the question of difficulties arising in both courts and tribunals, most of my informants in 1958–1959 were in agreement. Trouble arose from the fact that only the most politically minded monks bothered with the courts and became judges, and where they were acting, there was trouble. Most monks, well versed in Vinaya though they might be, were ignorant of the finer points of civil law and legal behavior. A majority of disputes arose from worldly matters such as inheritance of monastic property. Parties and sides were taken, and sometimes judges were approached by powerful factions. There was corruption. In some cases judges could not enforce their orders. Civil courts had to be brought in, thus causing dissatisfaction among the purists. There were cases in which orders were passed without written judgments, others in which judgments were written, learned about by one party before being issued, and subsequently changed by the judge under pressure. Everyone complained of too much personal interpretation. While the 1954 amendment tribunals may have favored a better articulation between ecclesiastical and civil authorities, the interference of the civil power often upset the purist monks. And since Shwegyin and Dwaya were the purist sects, their allegiance to even the amendment act was always subject to variation. Virtually all court judges were Thudhamma monks, since the "Mindon sects" remained aloof from the 1949 act. Furthermore, court and tribunal monks tended to be the same *sayadaw*s.

The problem was placed in better perspective when my *kappiya* (lay

19. Burma 1959d: 4, 17, 20, 23.

steward) informant linked the whole question of ecclesiastical courts, with the attempt of the government to create a Sangha Parliament which was to bring democratic self-government to the monks. In his view, the majority of monks were against these plans because they smacked of governmental control, whether in the form of a Sangha Parliament or a court system. In the old days, before any of these laws were passed, the monks had been accustomed to deciding their quarrels among themselves. The 1949 ecclesiastical courts act had put an end to this and had vested judgment powers in monks whom the politicians in power always found some means of influencing. In this light, the 1954 amendment act had been a throwback to the old precourts system and had naturally been favored by the more disciplinarian Shwegyin and Dwaya sects. In the *kappiya*'s opinion, the monks in favor of the 1949 act would, by and large, turn out to be those in favor of the Sangha Parliament and would thus be opposed to the amendment act. This view was confirmed by a prominent Supreme Court judge and constitutional adviser who told me that he had attempted to keep clear of involvement in the formulation of the 1949 courts act, with which he had never agreed. He had, on the other hand, been instrumental in passing the amendment act to reverse the trend toward lay political control. Another prominent layman with similar views stated that, for all the talk about the ecclesiastical courts, they had not yet really been set up. He stressed that, unless a monk confessed of his own free will, it was very difficult to punish him in any way. Young monks relied on the democratic principle in Vinaya to combat the establishment of authority over them by older monks. The monastic hierarchy involved in setting up ecclesiastical courts thus provoked as much trouble as the Thudhamma Council had caused in the previous period of the kings.

Data obtained from the Ministry of Religious Affairs in Rangoon in 1959 indicates that there were 2 union courts in operation, 20 district courts, and 134 township courts, with about 3,000 monks involved, all told. While some informants argued that none of these courts, except those in Rangoon and Mandalay, really operated, this official picture shows courts being set up even *after* the Vinicchaya-Htana Amendment Act of 1954 which, of course, was supposed to establish tribunals. The effectiveness of such courts is questionable, and further research might perhaps reveal them to have been government "show-courts" rather than fully operative judicial bodies. That the process continued, however, is evident from figures provided by a late-1961 source; it lists 2 union courts with 36 monks (the figure should probably be 72), 21 district courts with 552 monks, and 114 township courts with 2,280 monks.[20] These slightly different figures may cover permanent courts only, since there was evidence in earlier data that provisional courts sometimes became permanent courts. Finally, a 1960 army source speaks of 16 permanent courts and 9 provisional courts being established during the first army regime (1958–1960), with 448 *sayadaws* nominated to them (Burma 1960:465).

Actually, the ecclesiastical courts issue, like many such problems, became deeply involved in the political rivalries that led to and surrounded the split in the postwar coalition party, AFPFL (Anti-Fascist People's Freedom League), headed eventually by U Nu after the assassination of Aung San. In 1958, when the AFPFL government split into a Nu-Tin "Clean" faction and a Swe-Nyein "Stable" faction, the political monks divided accordingly.

This political rupture of the fragile unity that characterized the AFPFL in the postwar years was to set the stage for an even deeper division in Burmese politics that still exists as this book is being completed (1975). In retrospect, it is clear that this 1958 split symbolized the struggle between U Nu and his dreams of a democratic socialist state and General Ne Win with his conviction that only the army could wield sufficient authority to create the socialist society. The "Clean" faction basically represented the Nu proponents, and the Swe-Nyein "Stable" faction evolved rapidly into the Ne Win power bloc and its army supporters. The political monks thus, in essence, divided on the issues of Nu's dream of parliamentary government and Ne Win's vision of a militarist state.

There were basically two Thudhamma groups involved. One, the Yahan Byo Ahpwe (YBA), or Young Monks' Association, generally supported the Swe-Nyein Stable AFPFL faction which would become pro-army, while the Kyaungtaik Sayadaw Ahpwe (KSA), or Presiding Sayadaws' Association, supported the Nu-Tin faction. The latter group seems to have supported the 1949 courts act, with the YBA for it at first but switching to opposition. If we consider the amendment act of

20. *International Buddhist News Forum*, 1, no. 2 (Nov. 1961):35. (The report could have have been written earlier.)

1954 as a retreat from the 1949 act, then we can understand YBA support of the more traditionalist 1954 amendment position. Such a position left the YBA closer to the sects such as the Shwegyin and Dwaya that did not want *any* civil control but saw the 1954 act as the lesser of evils. When the YBA moved closer to army support, it also provided the army with a more direct approach to the reformist elements in the Sangha, as will be noted later. The important point here is that the ecclesiastical court plan was identified with the Nu government, but it was received by even the normally supportive Thudhamma monks with less than enthusiasm.

State Proposals for Monastic Universities

A similar reception awaited another program of the Nu government, the Pali University plan to support monastic learning of sacred texts by means of state aid to a university system created for that purpose. Some remarks made by U Win will serve as an introduction to the topic. Speaking at the inaugural meeting of the soon-to-be-important Buddha Sasana Council in 1951, Minister for Home and Religious Affairs U Win told how, after the fall of King Thibaw, the Burmese went on caring for the religion on their own without the material support of the British government, acting as "the real Promoters of the Faith in the absence of the Faithful Ruler." Speaking more specifically of the Pali University project, he stated:

Pali is the language of the *Tipitaka*s and as such has been studied most assiduously throughout the centuries by the *Bhikkhu*s [monks] and learned men in all the Buddhist countries. In Burma it was a compulsory subject in all the schools throughout the country during the days of the Burmese kings. In the Constitution of the Union of Burma it has been laid down as a directive principle of State policy to encourage the study of Pali which "shall enjoy the protection and support of the State." In 1947 the Committee for enquiring into the project for establishing a Pali University submitted its report to the Government recommending the establishment of a Pali University in Burma. Again in 1948 another Committee submitted a report in the same year. Again the matter was referred to a larger Committee which finally recommended a report recommending a Pali University and giving support to Dhammacariyas [exams on Pali texts]. It was this report which led in 1950 to the introduction of the 1950 Act.[21]

21. *Light of the Dhamma*, 1, no. 1 (Jan. 1953):25–27. Cf. Cady 1958:422, n. 110.

There is evidence of examinations held by kings since the reign of King Thalun (1629–1648), when the candidates were brought to the palace in decorated chariots and gilded palanquins, and viva voce tests were conducted.[22] These continued until the British occupation but were then interrupted until the question of reinstituting them was raised in 1891. The government decided to hold annual examinations from 1895 (or 1896) on, and these continued until 1941, when the war interrupted them; they were resumed in 1946. It can be seen, then, that the government of Burma did not leave the matter of the survival of Pali entirely in the hands of the "faithful people."

A number of committees were created throughout the period to evaluate the success of the program, and one of these published a very helpful report in 1941 (Burma 1941). It notes that, as early as 1912, Duroiselle, then professor of Pali at Government College, Rangoon, suggested a Pali College, either at Rangoon or at Mandalay, on the model of those in Colombo, Ceylon. It should teach all branches of Pali studies as well as the elements of Sanskrit and should be run by a small board of sayadaws appointed by the government, who would send out ecclesiastical censors (mahadanwun) to other monasteries. Duroiselle also thought that the board and professors of the college should be aided with robes, rice, and other necessities on a yearly basis. Later, in a "Memorandum on Vernacular Schools of 1924," the then Director of Public Instruction recalled Duroiselle's suggestion and deemed government support of the Patamabyan Pali examinations insufficient. In 1937, before the Patamabyan Examination Enquiry Committee, U Pe Maung Tin, principal of the University College, Rangoon, proposed a Pali University at Mandalay under the management of the Buddhist clergy. The renascence of interest in Buddhist studies all over the world was also mentioned, and already at this early date the "unique position" occupied by Burma as "the present spiritual home of the religion" was deemed to require the prompt establishment of a Pali University. It was clear that Pali education and the national interest were not long to remain unrelated.

After explaining that Pali is taught in both monastic and lay schools with varying degrees of emphasis, the committee notes that no scheme of improving Pali scholarship will be successful unless the government

22. Taw Sein Ko 1913:248–249.

takes into account carefully the nature of the monastic establishments in the forefront of Pali instruction—the teaching monasteries, or larger *taik*s. The committee sees the latter as forming a cluster of several individual monasteries, up to twenty or more (Burma 1941:17). The size of these establishments is due to the instruction they offer and to the presence of famous lecturers. Students vary in numbers from twenty to several hundred. The organization of such establishments is briefly reviewed: the *sayadaw*—head of the *taik* by virtue of age and usually also of erudition; the *taik-ok*—chief administrator and master of discipline; a *taik-kyat*—assistant to the *taik-ok* in larger *taiks;* the *kyaung pongyi*—resident head of a member monastery by virtue of age rather than erudition in many cases; and finally the lecturer *sayadaw*s, who are Pali scholars. There may be very few such lecturers, so their classes can include up to five hundred students, in all but advanced subjects. Different masters are followed on different subjects; it is unnecessary to follow one master throughout.

Lectures at such monastic "universities" are given at fixed hours, usually at the rate of three to four sessions a day and one or two in the evenings, averaging four daily, for a total of eight hours. They begin around 7:30 A.M. and end around 10:00 P.M. The work of the lecturers is said to be onerous. Effective supervision and control of students' work is difficult and usually impracticable: the preparation of lectures takes too long, and the lecturers themselves have little recreation and rest. Pupils are therefore left to themselves in matters of attendance, preparation of lessons, lecture notes, independent reading, and so on. Only a few places can maintain regular routines. On the other hand, general monastic discipline in these schools is often of a high order. Admission is difficult and unlikely without personal guarantees from members of the *taik* or persons connected with it. It is admitted that regard or lack of it for "house rules" depends entirely on the character of the leaders, the local atmosphere, the moral tone of the *taik,* and its traditions. From this brief sketch, the committee concludes that the largest, at any rate, of these establishments "are already Colleges in themselves and form part of a framework, only the rivetting of which is required to erect a Pali University for Burma" (Burma 1941:19).

By the time a discussion of the type of university to be proposed is begun, it is clear that "encouragement rather than reform of indigenous systems" is the path to be chosen. After carefully weighing the advantages of a teaching university of a Western type, the committee concludes that conditions in Burma are not favorable. (Already, at the very beginning of the committee's labors, it had been interrupted by serious discontent among prominent monks in Mandalay, who had heard rumors that the committee had already made up its mind on such a university and favored a particular kind of institution as its core [Burma 1941: 4, 20]). It is argued that a new university in Rangoon would be prohibitively expensive. Furthermore, it is felt that old, established institutions will not lightly give up their reputations and traditions and that famous monks will not wish to break lifelong ties with lay followers in their own home districts to take up posts elsewhere and uproot themselves for the sake of a new institution.

Such *sayadaws*, the report continues, would view with alarm the possibility of a diversion of students away from their own monasteries into government establishments. At present the large old *taiks* are suffering only from lack of funds and a paucity of patrons. Their buildings are often magnificent as well as hallowed by age; the life of the monks is a hard one, and their needs are few. Thus, it is difficult to escape the conclusion that a university of the affiliating type, with some forty ready-made "colleges" that could join immediately, would prevent jealousy, encourage emulation, and cost the government little beyond help with equipment and grants of rice and basic necessities.

More significant than any other argument, the committee reports, is the fact than an overwhelming number of *sayadaws* consulted favor this scheme. The country-famous Mahawithudarama Taik of Pakokku, said to command the allegiance of over eighty *taiks* and several times that number of single monasteries all over the country, is unanimously in favor (Burma 1941:22). The Shwegyin sect, led by the Withokdayama and Abayarama Taiks in Mandalay, and most Thudhamma monks interviewed are also said to be in favor. A sop to the central university idea is the suggestion that a central "model college" should be created by the government, staffed by younger *sayadaws*, with the main purpose of setting Western standards of scholarship, but this is said to be not necessary to the affiliating type of university and should be set up only when and if funds permit.

This early lukewarmness on the matter of a central college should be noted in view of later arguments over the idea for a central university. A careful reading of this committee report also indicates that the *saya-*

daws interviewed looked askance at any proposed government interference in the appointing of lecturers, although they might admit a role for government in supporting minimum standards of scholarship and a need for material support if it did not conflict with the Vinaya. *Sayadaws* also seemed wary of letting lay committees become too powerful in Pali scholarship support: they wanted "active encouragement" rather than "control." Furthermore, the committee itself seemed to take the conservative position regarding the curriculum needed: "Ancient lore shines best in its traditional environment and goes ill together in company with ultra-modern learning." A little later in the report, the committee concludes, somewhat contradictorily: "But we consider that the study of Pali on sound linguistic lines by modern methods and the introduction of critical methods of Western scholarship in the study of Sacred Literature should be among the improvements towards which the efforts of the University should be directed from the outset" (Burma 1941:29). One wonders if Western methods would not automatically bring in some of the *content* the committee previously rejected? This duality regarding Western education existed in Burma during my stay there and paralyzed many of the government's efforts in the ecclesiastical education field.

Much of the thinking in the 1941 report seems to have helped to shape the Pali University and Dhammacariya Act of 1950 which provided for the establishment of a "Pali University for the propagation and promotion of the Pariyatti Sasana [religious scholarship] and to support lecturing *Dhammacariya Sayadaws* [monks teaching for the Pali exams] with the object of relieving them of anxiety concerning four priestly requisites" (Burma 1959c:1). The system of affiliation allowed monasteries with at least ten Pali students involved in lectureship classes to join. Smaller monasteries could combine with others in order to qualify, and those monasteries depleted by students' "graduation" were allowed time to recruit new scholars. Students had to reside eight months per year in the teaching monastery and attend 60 percent of their classes, and scholars who were not officially enrolled in the "Pali University," could apply to take the examinations if they met certain conditions (Burma 1959c:1–2, secs. 4–6).

A central council was set up mainly to recognize and inspect monasteries seeking affiliation and to hold exams and reward successful scholars with funds (government monies included) collected and distributed according to Vinaya rules. The composition of the council was as follows: a representative *sayadaw* from each affiliated monastery; *nayaka* (master) *sayadaw*s of nonaffiliated monasteries nominated by the government at the instance of the affiliated monks; and two *sayadaw*s elected by the *nayaka sayadaw*s of the Union Pali Education Board, all of these or their representatives to hold office for three years. This council was supposed to be the supreme authority of the Pali University, supplanting the Executive Committee if necessary.

A very important section of the 1950 act placed the university under the wing of the Ministry of Social Services and Religious Affairs by stipulating that "the President [of the Union] may, with the previous approval of the Central Council, appoint a layman whom he may think fit to be the Chief Administrative Officer of the Pali University and *Dhammacariya* Department," such an officer to have a staff at his disposal. Section 14 ensured the appointment from the same source of a treasurer. Thus, in practice, the Pali University became a department of the ministry, with an executive officer at its head.

All these proposals for new forms of monastic universities represented potential threats to the independence of the traditional system of monastic learning that had evolved over the centuries in Burma. As I have suggested earlier in this book, however, the centers of traditional Pali education (the large university *taik*s) had been the very targets of royal attempts to influence the Sangha in the previous century. The Nu government, so often stepping to a royal refrain, appears to have attempted the same path.

Government Interest in Monastic Examinations

Further government influence, of course, could be exerted through the grants to the Sangha program to support the Patamabyan Pali exam system that since royal times had enabled a probationary monk to achieve the full grade of *pongyi*.[23] The "results grants" concept had awarded cash payments yearly to the heads of monasteries that presented successful candidates. The 1941 committee was critical of that system, however:

It is based on the assumption that the successful candidates are resident students of the schools from which they are presented to the examinations and that they pursue their studies under the lecturers residing in the same

23. Scott and Hardiman 1900, 1:78.

institutions. In actual fact, however, there are numerous instances in which the pupils reside in one monastery but attend classes held by noted lecturers who reside in other monasteries. In general practice all such students give the names of their resident monasteries as those presenting them to the examination. The result is that when *sunsandaw* [government aid] is offered for successful attempts, the benefits go to the successful candidates and the heads of their resident monasteries. The lecturers who have contributed most to their success go unrewarded for their strenuous work and painstaking labours and we are told that many a lecturer of learning and repute are having a lean time for all their meritorious efforts.   [Burma 1941:35]

The 1941 report therefore recommended the system which was eventually followed in the 1950 act and suggested that the "results" system might be changed also in the case of the Patamabyan exams, though conceding that for some years neither the latter nor the Pali University system would have the registration capacity to switch principles. Did the change in the system discourage "resident" monasteries in any way from putting forward candidates for examinations? There is no evidence either way, but the rising figures of examination enrollment suggest that the advantages of government degrees combined with a strong tradition of learning in the Sangha counterbalanced any such tendency as may have existed. As for the 1950 act, the second schedule under section 23 provided for the following grants: "rice-grant" of 720 *kyat*s per annum for each Dhammacariya[24] and each non-Dhammacariya principal of an affiliated monastery; 960 *kyat*s per annum for each Dhammacariya principal; and a donation of 500 *kyat*s per annum for miscellaneous expenses to each affiliated monastery.

The awards in the Patamabyan system were as follows: A lower-grade candidate obtained 50 *kyat*s, with an additional 15 if he answered in Pali, and a copy of *Yamaka,* while his lecturer received 12 *kyat*s. A middle-grade candidate got 75 *kyat*s (plus 20 for Pali) and copies of *Patthana, Abhidhana,* and *Alankara;* his lecturer received 24 *kyat*s. In the higher grade, a *pathamagyaw* (top scholar) received 150 *kyat*s,

24. Literally, one who observes righteousness (for derivation, see Glossary). The term is used here to denote a monk who has passed the exam and/or is a member of the Pali University system, under the terms of the Pali University and Dhammacariya Act of 1950. *Dhammacariya* is also the name of the difficult written examination in Pali on the Tipitaka. Those who pass it are often honored and supported for life by such lay associations as the Zedi Yingana Pariyatti Athin (if they reside in Rangoon) or the Setkyathiha Society (in Mandalay).

others 100 (plus 25 for Pali) with copies of *Parajika Atthakatha* (2 volumes), *Silakkandha Atthakatha,* and *Dhammasangani Atthakatha.* The lecturer received 36 *kyats.* These gift books,[25] designed to help a candidate pass on to the next grade, are edited and published by the Buddha Sasana Council[26] according to texts agreed upon at the Sixth Buddhist Council.

By the mid-fifties, it is not at all clear what size awards were given to Dhammacariya scholars. The *Sangayana Souvenir* account of April–May 1954 reports that each pass candidate received 300 *kyats,* while an honors candidate received 1,000 *kyats* (25 extra for Pali), teachers obtaining 400 *kyats.* The Buddha Sasana Council report of 1954 states that a pass was worth 300 *kyats* and an honors pass 500 *kyats.* The 1956 report raises the latter figure to 600. The 1958 report lists awards of 100 *kyats* for each honors subject passed. A candidate who offered one honors subject in Pali got a special title and a cash award of 500 *kyats.* In all these latter texts there is no mention of the *siromani,* or highest-honors category, but an account received from the Ministry of Religious Affairs in 1958 states that the *dhaja* or honors title went only to those who passed all honors tests; the *dhaja* monks also were awarded 600 *kyats.*

There seems to be recognition by the government of the desire of some institutions and individual monks to abstain from such cash incentives. Certain lay associations promoting Pali scholarship apparently did not wish to join the Pali University system, but the 1950 act leaves the door open for them to send students. It also notes that certain high institutions such as Pakokku and Monywa have not been presenting any appreciable number of candidates for even the lower Patamabyan examinations, and the door is left ajar for their students for two years in case they wish to join the Pali University plan (Burma 1941:33). The act makes it clear that the government still desires to offer incentives (and these incentives are in the last resort monetary) for monks to join its own program, but it recognizes that there will always be monks who do not wish to join it. The 1950 act even has a provision whereby nonparticipating Dhammacariya lecturers can receive government aid:

25. For the significance of the prize books mentioned in this paragraph, see Appendix G.
26. As we will see, the BSC was controlled by Nu supporters and thus can be viewed as an instrument of his political aims for the Sangha.

The Government shall select qualified lecturing *dhammacariya*s who are not lecturing *dhammacariya*s of the Pali University in accordance with the rules contained in the Third Schedule of this Act and make grants to them at such rates as are prescribed therein. The President of the Union may, from time to time, revise such rules and rates; provided that such rates shall at all times be one-half of the rates at which grants are made to lecturing *dhammacariya*s of the Pali University. [1959c:sec. 26]

The schedule then makes it clear that, since ten students was the minimum required for affiliation and, since monasteries could amalgamate for that purpose, these arrangements covered those who *would not* rather than those who could not join the government program. The government was to form a *"Dhammacariya* Selection Board composed of the Deputy Commissioner and Inspector of Schools concerned and the Chairman or his representative of the Religious Association, if any, of the place concerned." Lecturers selected by the board were to be delivering lectures twice a day to a required number of students: at least thirty monks in each Mandalay monastery and numbers decreasing to fifteen, but not below, in smaller centers. The English translation of the act states that the board was to find out from "three other locally prominent head *Sayadaw*s of the *sect"* (my italics) whether the monk in question should receive the 30-*kyat*s-per-month grant.[27] This mention of sect may afford a clue to the nature of some of the opposition to the government scheme.

One can see the entire government plan in a clearer light if it is understood that exams for sacred scholarship have been institutionalized in Burma since royal times and supported by powerful lay associations. The Zedi Yingana Pariyatti Athin, for example, is such an organization run by the trustees of the Shwedagon Pagoda, and their Dhammacariya exams have been held on the pagoda platform. In Mandalay, the Setkyathiha Society performs the same function.[28] Four levels of exams are given: the *patamange* (low), *patamalat* (middle), *patamagyi* (high), and the *dhammacariya* (pass and honors).[29] Before 1926 there were

27. Burma 1959c:10, sec. 6. The words used in the Burmese text are *ganasarya gana-pamukkha,* which have a local more than a sectarian connotation.

28. There are also Vinaya exams given by monasteries and "dara" exams given by the Paripatti Sasana Nogaha Society (more difficult and less popular than the Patama exams outlined in Appendix G).

29. For brief review of the basic works of sacred literature upon which these exams are based see Appendix G.

apparently no *Dhammacariya* exams. By sponsoring and holding exams and by giving incentives and awards, the government was thereby in a sense competing with the established lay Buddhist system. When the Pali Education Board was set up to supervise the government's exam system, members of the lay associations were included, as well as representatives of such other concerned groups as the Faculty of Pali at Rangoon University, the Ministry of Religious Affairs, the Ministry of Finance, and the Public Service Commission (Burma 1952a). But the lay associations were not the only vested interest in this important area, and the government had to deal also with the large established monastic "universities."

State Attention to Established Monastic Universities

The most important of these large teaching *taik*s is the Pakokku system, which we have dealt with as a sect, even though the monks concerned do not so identify themselves. The 1941 report mentions the system as "the powerful organization of great numerical strength led by the famous Mahawithudarama Taik of Pakokku, which commands the allegiance of over eighty *kyaungtaik*s [*taik*s] and several times that number of individual *kyaung*s scattered all over the country" (Burma 1941:22). The figures for lecturers and pupils cited by the report are slightly higher than those I obtained in 1959; it stated that the Central Taik had 15 lecturers and 950 pupils; the East Taik 15 lecturers and 500 pupils; and the Mandalay *taik* 8 lecturers and 125–150 pupils. In Pakokku, I was told that the Central Taik boasted 500–600 monks, some of whom were Shwegyin and Dwaya, while at the East Taik the figure of 342 monks and 93 novices was cited, including 30 Shwegyin and 15 Dwaya.[30]

Some kind of compromise appears to have been effected between cooperation and independence, for by the late fifties Pakokku monas-

---

30. A reference by a YBA leader (a politically active monastic group; see Chapter 6) in 1959 to the effect that his organization was painfully making some progress in "Shewegyin" Pakokku indicates (1) that the toughness and self-centeredness of Shwegyin were recognized as present among Pakokku men, and (2) that YBA people preferred to find euphemisms for their KSA opponents. His explanation was revealing: "Well, the top *sayadaw*s follow the same rules as Shwegyin within their monasteries; only in public do they behave as Thudhamma." (To anyone not seeing them as a sect, Pakokku monks are, of course, Thudhamma.)

teries were offering both their own training and training for government examinations. At the East Taik, I was told that 60 monks were taking the Pali University examinations and that the *taik* functioned as a constituent college of the government system. This led to a government subsidy of 495 rupees monthly. The old stress on the local form of education persists, however, and I was told at the Central Taik that the Pakokku education is a hard, all-round one, not just a preparation for set texts and examinations. Many prominent monks of all sects had come to study in Pakokku. In the Rangoon Payagyi Taik, I was told that government Dhammacariyas were still looked down on as minor intellectuals, and there too the two systems of examinations were carried on side by side.

The more I became familiar with Sangha organization in Burma, the more I began to see a relationship between the Pakokku Taik and the Rangoon Payagyi Taik that transcended the obvious fact that both were highly respected "university" *taiks*. Early in my stay, my attention was was directed to the large Chauktagyi (six-storey) Monastery known as the Payagi Taik,[31] named after a huge statue of Buddha in the *parinibbana* attitude[32] which had been destroyed after some misguided European criticism as to its lack of realism. The truth is that the extraordinary image was a triumph of the Burmese folk style, floating most improbably but with a stunning effect above the monastery buildings far below it; similar statues can still be seen in Prome and elsewhere. The prime minister and many religious worthies started a fund and attempted to persuade apparently reluctant Rangoonites that small contributions made one the equivalent of a *paya taga,* or donor of an entire pagoda. But it was in a different context that I began to see the Payagyi Taik when it turned out that it was the headquarters of the Presiding Sayadaws' Association (KSA), the large body of pro-Nu monks organized to combat the Stable AFPFL's forces, that is, the powerful Yahan Byo Ahpwe (YBA) of Mandalay, which supported the Swe-Nyein faction of the AFPFL. Frequent meetings of the highest religious officials and the Buddha Sasana Council people took place at the Payagyi Taik, and it was obvious that the Payagyi monks, the Presiding Sayadaws' Association (KSA), and the whole policy of the Nu government were very closely intertwined.

31. Payagyi (B): great holy one (lord, god, or pagoda).
32. Buddha in a reclining posture as he was at his death or when passing into Nibbana (Nirvana).

Clearly there was a strong link between the Pakokku sect and the Payagyi, even if, as some made out, the former did not actually rule the latter. A prominent printer in Rangoon, who was responsible for preparing a *kammawa* (ordination text) used by the Pakokku sect, told us that the Payagyi had two daughter branches in Rangoon, the Kemmendine Bagaya Taik and a *taik* in Campbell Road. These three *taik*s coordinated activities with Pakokku *taik*s but were not ruled by them. Once a year there was a meeting at Pakokku with homage given to the leading Pakokku sayadaw. At the time of my first visit to the *taik*, the Payagyi sect was mourning the Pakokku Sayadaw, U Nandawuntha, and the Payagyi Taik Sayadaw, U Kondanna, who had both died at about the same time. Large envelopes bearing the names of both monks and containing texts written or edited by them were being given out to visitors. On my second visit, in July 1958, the relics of U Kondanna were being taken to Pakokku, and that Lent, at the lay visitors' ceremonies, large photographs of both *sayadaw*s were exhibited in the great hall of the monastery.

The Payagyi Taik is also most interesting as a scholastic institution. It appears to have been built in 1930 by the Honorable Sir U Po Tha, a member of the Upper House in British times and a great *paya taga*.[33] It is said to have started with 18 monks. Since 1935, it has usually had about 500 pupils, though at times—as during the Japanese occupation—its numbers have risen to 700 with the influx of monks from the districts. The 1941 report of the Pali University Enquiry Committee lists it as the largest university monastery the committee visited in Rangoon, with over 500 pupils and 8 lecturers. In 1958 it had about 505 monks and 41 novices, with 12 recognized teachers. There were 30 separate buildings, one of them sleeping a hundred monks. All houses were run on a dormitory principle, and each teacher was in charge of a house. Monks rose at 4:00 A.M. during the monsoon, at 4:30 in other seasons; and there were lessons every day at the following times: 6:00-8:00 A.M., 12:00-1:45 P.M., 1:45-3:00, 3:30-5:00, and 8:00-9:00 P.M. From 6:30 to 7:30 P.M. there was group homage in the *taik*'s ordination hall. All monks ate together in a large hall, only the teachers eating in their own monasteries. Different scriptures were taught

33. The Payagyi statue itself was apparently built around the turn of the century.

in the different member monasteries, with some degree of choice of lecturers. Examinations only were prepared for—there is, for instance, no special meditational activity in such a place—and there was one examination per year for each level, held on the same day throughout Burma. The *taik* had eight thousand books. All in all, the impression was one of concentrated work of a kind rarely found in Burma. Certainly the hushed, scholarly, and tidy atmosphere of the Payagyi recalled the spacious Pakokku buildings, and their attitudes toward education appeared to be similar.

In such an atmosphere, then, I was curious as to why government influence was so intense at the Payagyi Taik. I suspect that the favors showered upon the Pakokku and Payagyi monks in terms of tithes and support were in some way related to the Pakokku sect's reluctance to join in the government's Pali educational plans—a reluctance which, coming from such a senior body in the field of ecclesiastical academics, could scarcely have boded well for the program as a whole. A reluctant but definite Pakokku move in the direction of the government's Pali University program in the late fifties tended to confirm my suspicions.

Monastery Schools Re-examined by the State

The government, of course, after Independence also tried to approach another educational problem that involved the Sangha deeply—that of the monastic schools, the earlier history of which has been traced in previous chapters. In this connection, the report of a committee set up in 1940, published in Burmese only in 1948, just before Independence, is instructive. The foreword states that task of the Committee on National Education in Buddhist Monasteries, composed of laymen with a board of advisory *sayadaw*s, was to offer suggestions as to the best ways to approach monks to obtain their participation in the primary education program and to indicate how regulations concerning the establishment, recognition, and running of monastic schools could best be laid down in conformity with the rules of Vinaya. While the committee was to pay attention to previous regulations, codes, and reports, the problem was said to be so urgent that they should have freedom of choice as to whom to interview and be free of all pressure from any quarter whatsoever. The government claimed to be fully aware of the long-drawn-out conflict between church and state, and every care would be taken not to offend the monks. Above all, the foreword warned, the large number of unrecognized monastic schools waiting to be of service to the country should be borne in mind.

The president's report opened with the usual regrets concerning the decline of morals in Burma and the assigning of cause to the decline of monastic schools. The monks were treated throughout as very prickly people to deal with. The government's intention, it was stated, was to ask the monks to accept pupils out of pure *metta;*[34] there was no intention whatsoever of forcing them to accept any rule or regulation. Nor were any children to be forced to attend monastic schools; rather, measures should be taken to inspire their parents to send them there. The monastic schools would not interfere with the development of lay schools; for the monastic schools, offering mainly primary education, would become training grounds for children wishing to go on to lay schools for their secondary and final education. A warning was sounded that monks should decide soon in order to benefit from the Primary School Education Bill. Should they allow too many lay schools to spring up and then find it necessary for their own prestige to teach, they might find that they had made their decision too late in the day. The effort to be made here was a serious one.

As usual, it was taken for granted that everything had been for the best in the best of traditional worlds. This view had an amazing permanence, for it played an important part in the national Buddhist Revival under U Nu. Virtually the whole blame for the British failure to incorporate monastic schools into national education was placed on the fact that the advisers who were consulted were unacquainted with the ways of the monks and with Vinaya rules. Prejudice against monastic schools on the part of school boards set up after 1916 was noted, though it was admitted that such boards had little revenue with which to recognize new schools in any case. Stress was placed on the failure of officials to appreciate that monks should be treated as very special beings (Burma 1948:24, 27–28). A further point was made with regard to unrecognized schools: the drift of children away from monastic education caused hardship to certain monks insofar as children no longer attended to the needs of their masters, and certain monks were reduced to coaxing and obliging children to remain in monastery schools. There is little doubt in my mind that, while this factor, as such, was not stressed to the

34. (P): benevolence, love for all beings.

laity by monks themselves, it played an important part in the Sangha's realization that education was a field to be regained (a more important motive, I suggest, than the political ideals, which most monks were content to leave to laymen).

The reasons given for the decline of monastic schools are also noteworthy, since they constitute a Burmese critique of the British educational system. First, it was said that no position of importance in society could be obtained by those knowing only Burmese; therefore, any parent who could afford it would send his child to British schools. Second, the influx of alien races (such as Indians) coming into Burma in order to compete economically with the Burmese had made it imperative for the latter to equip themselves with modern knowledge. Only after these two points had been made did the report recognize the fact that monastic education was outdated and the implications of the fact that only poor children were sent to monastic schools. As a result of all this, the government said it had decided to make primary education compulsory and to bring the monks into the system.

Despite its recognition of an outdated system, the report held to such virtues and verities as learning in the monastic environment, preserving the moral atmosphere of the monastery, retaining honorifics in dealing with monks, hoping that government aid would be handled for the monks by lay stewards, believing that non-Buddhists can use a Buddhist education to get along well with their neighbors, and stressing the foolishness of teaching ideas contrary to Buddhist views (such as the earth is round, etc.). The report did, however, suggest that Pali was too difficult for the primary level, and it did recognize that, since English would not be taught in such schools, the use of Burmese should be promoted in courts and offices of local administration, and the Burmese language should become an avenue of promotion in the society as a whole. Published very shortly before Independence, no doubt with the agreement of both the British and future Burmese leaders, this report pointed to the kind of policy to be followed by an independent Burma and, characteristically, placed the blame for previous failures on British ignorance of the ways of monks and laymen.

After Independence was gained, monastic schools fell into the province of the Mass Education Council. The idea for this body is said to have started at a meeting of "Old Boys" of the Myoma Coeducational

High School in 1948, with a plan for Old Boys' summer courses in better citizenship. U Nu saw here an idea which could be applied to the whole country, and it was coordinated with U Tun Pe's program of social education. The Mass Education Council Act was placed on the statute book in 1948, creating the Mass Education Fund, into which annual government grants were channeled. At first the council operated under the Ministry of Education, but, with "the stress that has increasingly come to be laid on the sociological aspects of the movement," it was later brought under the wing of the Ministry of Social Welfare. The major aim of the council was to revive the village, which had "sunk deep in the mire of centuries-old sloth and neglect."[35]

Apparently the monastic school problem was entrusted to the Mass Education Council in 1952. I quote U Than Aung, the education minister: "With effect from this year [1952], the Mass Education Council will be undertaking with the consent of the Presiding Monks,[36] to provide necessary books, equipment and furniture to 1,000 monastery schools. And the scheme will be extended to other monastery schools in future years at the same rate. I would therefore appeal respectfully to the venerable monks to assist education by giving their co-operation" (Burma 1952b:99). The plan was to use the cooperation of the monks to combat illiteracy, since the government did not have the money to pay for the needed work to be done. If a *sayadaw* was willing to register his monastic school, the ministry would donate to him the Teacher's Guide Book, various other books, and furniture. It was hoped that, without infringing upon Vinaya rules, monks could educate the illiterate by working in their "spare time." The monastic pupils were to take government exams and, if successful at the fourth-standard level, go on to secular schools to continue their education. In 1953–1954 only 96 registered monastic schools sent in any pupils for such exams, but by 1957–1958 the number had climbed to 479. But since there were 5,545 registered monastic schools at that time (the target had been 8,000), the mass education plan was moving at a snail's pace.

A second four-year plan was announced at a press conference held by Premier U Ba Swe in July 1956. Again the extension of compulsory education to the whole Union of Burma was said to be delayed by the

35. Mass Education Council 1956:7–10.
36. KSA, the pro-Nu monks' association.

paucity of state primary schools; again it had to be recognized that monastic schools were essential. Sixty-two education executives were selected and given a three months' training course. Ten of them then went out to undertake divisional duties, while the other fifty-two were apportioned between the districts. A certain amount of familiar re-shuffling was effected, and the social service program was implemented through the monastic schools—children, it was hoped, eventually teaching parents—because of the shortage of mass education officers in general.

Since the Mass Education Council was one of U Nu's favorite projects, little was heard of it after the first takeover by General Ne Win in 1958. The official account of the Ne Win government's accomplishments—*Is Trust Vindicated?*—made no reference to the council or to monastic schools. In contrast, religious instruction with examinations was said to have been implemented for the first time in *state* schools, and various activities regarding social welfare (some of them at Chawdwingon Camp, an old headquarters of the Mass Education Council) had been supported by the military. Otherwise, the monastic school program had disappeared from the account of both the Ministry of Education and the Ministry of Social Welfare and Religious Affairs. In October 1959, I was told by Mass Education people that it had become the Rural Welfare Division of the Directorate of Social Welfare. They claimed to have established registered monastic schools only where there were no other schools. They organized training seminars of as much as two months' duration for monks. Not competition but complementariness was the spirit, and an effort was to be made to do something for even the poorest children.

The entire monastic school program can be seen as part of the total pattern of government interest in Buddhism, which included the eccle-siastical court scheme, the state-supported Pali university plan, and state aid for the Pali examinations. No matter how these government ventures were described by the promoters, they basically represented an attempt to influence the Sangha. I have tried to suggest that there was a quiet but firm resistance on the part of many in the Sangha to such initiatives on the part of the state. On the other hand, most Burmans have a genuine concern with monastic discipline and education and they wish

37. See also *Light of the Dhamma*, 6, no. 4 (Oct. 1959):5.

them both to continue in a healthy state, particularly in modern circumstances which have weakened the monkhood. Most Burmans, even those opposed to the monkhood on political or scientific principles, also feel that monastic culture has been the major vehicle of Burmese culture itself. The independent government of the Union of Burma clearly tried to infuse new life into this aspect of culture, but by so doing the government also sought to bring the monkhood under a greater degree of lay control, and more precisely under its own control. For, ultimately, beneath these different manifestations of concern for the monkhood, is the paramount goal of discovering who the Burmese monks are, counting them, and thus bringing them once and for all within the orbit of the state's control.

U Nu and His Plans for a Buddhist Revival

The political leader who most expressed his independent country's concern for the religious dimension was, of course, U Nu, although he was by no means the only leader to do so. As premier of Burma for most of the years between 1947 and 1958, his plans and schemes dominated the stage, including the period of my field work in Burma. To think of U Nu as politically a Thakin may be historically correct, but such a term does not capture the essence of his attitude toward religion. Actually Nu's attitude can be profitably contrasted with the basic Thakin position.

The Thakin movement, which originated in nationalist student agitation in the thirities and successfully accomplished the task of creating an independent Burma, was not, at its inception, much interested in religion. A practical socialist program was much more to the taste of the majority of the Thakins, and they saw themselves first and foremost as the supplanters of the older, turn-of-the-century revolutionary monks as leaders of the people. Much has been said, more or less unofficially, about the attitudes of Aung San, their leader, toward the Sangha. Most of this indicates that he was thoroughly unsympathetic to any political role whatsoever being played by members of the Order, and there are some indications that he wanted to limit recruitment to the Sangha and control it very severely. I have heard it claimed by reliable observers that he would probably have imposed a *thathanabaing* on the Order as a whole and carried out a number of measures such as registration of monks to keep the Sangha under strict AFPFL control. It is reasonably certain

that Aung San, a hero in his own right (and not too religiously motivated, as was U Nu), would not have needed the monks' support which
other politicians, before and after him, believed they needed. As will be
shown, U Nu's attitude toward Buddhism, and the Sangha in particular,
was quite different.

While U Nu's abiding interest in old Burmese culture and religion
showed itself early in his personal life, from the time he wrote the
preface to Thein Pe Myint's *Tet Pongyi,* the early policy of his government was not particularly dominated by religious issues, and his key-
note speeches of the late 1940s make little mention of religion.[38] At the
time of national independence, the future Ministry of Religious Affairs
was in a rudimentary state, and its minister, U Win, a very staunch
supporter of U Nu in his later campaigns, occupied a rather low place
in the official hierarchy (Burma 1949:19). The beginnings of Nu's swing
toward an official interest in religion are not easy to pinpoint, though
clearly unofficial interest was there from the beginning, as stated above.
Perhaps the key moment was the splitting of the AFPFL, when the
extreme left wing left the party and began insurrections outside the
government, a process that left Nu free to develop more conservative
and traditional approaches to achieving national unity. Brohm has an
interesting suggestion—that Pandit Nehru, whom Nu visited in 1949,
may have pointed out to Nu the failure of the leftist's dream of unity
and suggested a new concept of "Buddhist unity." Certainly Nehru later
showed much support for the Burmese concept of a Revival (Brohm
1957:375–376).

The Revival, as the term will be used here, represents the government-promoted plans and official acts to give new life to Buddhism in
Burma. The range of efforts to accomplish such a goal included state
support of Buddhist education, attempts at improving Sangha discipline
and unity, Buddhist social service projects, encouragement of meditation for monks and laity, dreams of a state religion, and, most importantly, plans for a Sixth Buddhist Council or Sangayana to recapture
and revitalize the accomplishments and glory of Mindon's efforts in that
regard.

Certainly the Revival is vital to an understanding of Sangha-state

38. Brohm 1957:369–372. It would be repetitious to study U Nu's religious
career in detail here; several volumes of speeches are easily available, as are a
number of studies. The material is most recently summarized in Butwell 1963.

relations in independent Burma under U Nu. To see its rise and fall as a politicoreligious phenomenon, it is necessary to grasp that the Revival was first and foremost a program, that it had a beginning and an end, however many repercussions it may still have in the personal religious life of many Burmese. It coincided broadly with the major part of the career of U Nu as prime minister of Burma and as an international figure of some standing from 1947 on, and it ended with his fall from power at the hands of the army regime in 1958. From the ideological point of view it can be seen as the moral aspect of Pyidawtha, U Nu's vision of the ideal state in which people and government live in happy cooperation.[39] Because of the extent to which Nu and his followers used the Revival in their speeches, their tours of the country, and their electoral programs, it became, in effect, a religious model of the state itself. From the point of view of practical politics, it was the essential contribution of the Nu wing of the AFPFL to the Burmese scene, while Nu's opponents, led by Ba Swe and Kyaw Nyein, concerned themselves with the more practical, materialistic side of socialism. Thus, as the Revival programs developed, they became subjects of debate between the opposing factions of the AFPFL, and the Revival itself became one of the major causes of the AFPFL split.

Internal rivalries also existed inside even the small groups of men responsible for the Revival. These rivalries never appeared on the surface of united Ministry of Religious Affairs bulletins and reports, yet they were evident to me during my field work. Institutionally speaking, the rivalries amounted to a familiar situation in Burmese politics: the hiving off, if not the deliberate creation, of independent agencies within government ministries and departments which then served as fiefs of particular individuals or small groups of individuals. Dominating the whole pattern, Nu's Revival itself can be seen as the greatest "fief" of them all.

In Brohm's excellent but still unpublished thesis he makes a most important contention, for which there is considerable evidence: that U Nu's new course was adopted very gradually in a manner which could lead him to claim that it was a response to public demand. He guided

---

39. Pyidawtha (B): literally, "pleasant royal country"; usually translated as "welfare state" or "cooperation between people and government for the happiness of the country," particularly as outlined in 1952 speeches by U Nu. See Cady 1958:616, 647.

himself "by the moves which urban religious devotees had made on their own." The Nu government gradually took cues and assumed the leadership of programs which had already been initiated elsewhere either by others in government or by groups of devotees acting informally. As shown earlier in this chapter, the ecclesiastical courts and the Pali education problem dealt with ideas that stemmed from prewar reports, and the government took over, in the case of the Pali University, ideas and practices which great lay societies like the Zedi Yingana Pariyatti Athin had been applying for many years. The discussion that follows supports Brohm's view and, in particular, shows how the Buddha Sasana Council arrogated the task of centralizing and choosing among the various programs initiated by outside agencies. What usually happens in such a centralizing process is that a number of people initiate very similar ideas at more or less the same time, after which a powerful, government-backed agency takes the lead in implementing the idea while the less powerful and resourceful agencies wilt. However, "wilting" does not imply disappearance. The scene is littered with the remnants of small societies and agencies which would lose too much face if allowed to disappear. They hang on with rudimentary duties and purposes. In the Burmese context this may have a more positive function than is implied above: one informant stated that "we have a multitude of little proliferating groups so that no one is ever controlled entirely by anybody else"! In the agencies that will be examined with regard to the Sangayana, or Sixth Buddhist Council, certain personalities bridged the gap between the wilting agency and the prospering one: the major case involved was the transformation of the Buddha Sasana Nuggaha Ahpwe into the Buddha Sasana Council.

Lay Buddhist Committees to Promote the Revival

Accounts of the foundation of the Buddha Sasana Nuggaha Ahpwe (BSNA) describe how U Nu, just before national independence, went on a nine-day religious retreat in the neighborhood of Kelasa Hill, Thaton, and on his return to Rangoon founded the BSNA in November 1947, together with nine other Buddhists, including "the Great Richman," Sir U Thwin, its first president.[40]

40. *Sangayana Monthly Bulletin,* 1, no. 6 (Oct. 1953):10; *Pyedaungsu Myanma Naingandaw Buddha Thathana Nuggaha Ahpwe* 1958:7–17. Others were U San

The aims of the organization were (1) to work for the progress, expansion, and stability of Buddhism; (2) to help in the progress of *pariyatti* and *patipatti*,[41] and (3) to set up a great Pitaka *taik*[42] where the Buddhist scriptures could be enshrined.[43] Among the qualifications for membership were the following rules: no alcohol, no gambling or betting of any kind, and the observance of "sabbath" or *ubone* days—not very different from a great many other Buddhist societies in Burma, though out of this one unprecedented things were to grow.

Shortly after its inception, Sir U Thwin donated land, and a prestigious Buildings Committee was formed. Before long they had constructed a monastery, four meditation monasteries, a preaching hall, and an ordination hall. Also added were a clinic and a residence for Sir U Thwin. These buildings were the headquarters of all BSNA and later all Buddha Sasana Council activities until the buildings for the Sixth Buddhist Council were constructed at Kaba Aye, Rangoon.

From the start, the BSNA promoted activities that were central to the Revival and the Sangayana. With great excitement and effort, it sought and discovered a *tipitakadhara,* a monk who could recite the entire Pali Tipitaka from memory: in February 1954, some three months before the opening of the Sangayana, the venerable monk U Vicittasarabhivamsa conquered the last of the texts and became capable of acting as "replier" during the purifying of the Pali texts at the Sixth Buddhist Council meetings.[44] The passionate interest of highly placed ministers and officials in these examinations reflects one of the more striking purely religious aspects of the Sangayana which has not been sufficiently stressed in previous accounts of this event. The *tipitakadhara* quest should be seen as vital to Burmese belief in the value of memorizing the scriptures as the epitome of education, and we probably should

---

Thein (commissioner of income tax) as secretary; U Ohn Saing (a merchant) as treasurer; U Ba Khin (commissioner, general auditor) as auditor; and committee members U Nu, U Tha Det (mill owner), Henzada U Mya (minister of trade and commerce), U Tin Bwa (a merchant), U Tin (minister of finance and revenue).

41. *Pariyatti* (P): the scholarship and theory of Buddhism. *Patipatti* (P): the practice of Buddhism; also meditation.

42. A building to house the sacred books of the Tipitaka (the Vinaya, Sutta, and Abhidhamma).

43. *Sangayana Monthly Bulletin,* 1, no. 6 (Oct. 1953):10: "An International Buddhist Library."

44. Ibid., no. 11 (Mar. 1954):2; 2, no. 2 (June 1954):22.

see the government as seeking to show that such religious feats heralded an age of new prosperity for Buddhism, in order to counter the older concept of the growing decadence of Buddhism as men became further away from the days when the Buddha gave all beings his teachings. The two-thousand five hundredth anniversary of Buddhism was thus to be held on a note of optimism.

In such a spirit, the BSNA also promoted the Burma Hill Tracts Buddhist Mission (TTA), an organization founded to "bring about unity and cooperation between the peoples of the Plains and the People of the Hills."[45] This group seems to have developed out of the Maha Sangha Ahpwe at the end of the war, as an attempt to missionize potentially refractory minorities in outlying areas of Burma, with the Nyaungyan, Sandayon, Mahawithudarama, and Payagyi Taik Sayadaws involved in its founding and early administration. Two of these monks were part of the Pakokku-Payagyi pattern we noted above as being vital in the Nu-Tin faction of the politicized Sangha.[46] This missionary effort was to be financed at first with GCBA funds but then by the BSNA. By 1952, another governmental group, the Buddha Sasana Council (BSC), promoted not only the missionary efforts for the hill peoples but also efforts for other non-Buddhist Burmese and for conversion efforts in foreign countries. These lay groups of Buddhist politicians and liberal donors believed in the Revival concept that the rest of the world was in such a state that it really needed a missionary message from pure Buddhism, kept over the centuries by the Burmese as custodians, so to speak.

In still another area did the work of the BSNA contribute toward the Revival and the Sangayana—through the promotion of lay meditation and the sponsoring of centers for its practice. As a result of inquiries made all over Burma, the Mahasi Sayadaw was chosen to administer the showplace Thathana Yeiktha meditation center in Rangoon.[47] The

45. *Pyedaungsu* 1958:101–115.
46. The Nyaungyan Sayadaw has previously been discussed as the Upper Burma Maha Sangha Ahpwe leader during the war (see above Chapter 5, n. 12); the Mahawithudarama Sayadaw is from Pakokku (for that *taik*'s role and for the Payagyi's connections with U Nu's political monks, see above in this chapter). It is also noteworthy that the Burma Hill Tracts Buddhist Mission foundation meeting took place at the Chauktatgyi Pagoda nearby, the site of the Chauktatgyi Monastery, which is also known as the Payagyi Taik, the focal point of KSA, pro-Nu activities. For more on the TTA, see Chapter 6.
47. *Sangayana Monthly Bulletin*, 1, no. 6 (Oct. 1953):10.

Mahasi was a *dhammacariya* scholar, a widely respected instructor in the *vipassana*, or mindfulness school of meditation, and a recipient of the A.M.P. title. Later he became a member of the Supreme Sangha Council (to be discussed below) and the questioner in the Pali text revision process at the Sangayana. Scarely a foreigner passed through Rangoon without visiting his Thathana Yeiktha center, which served for a model for many others throughout Burma. The meditation movement will be discussed in more detail later, but it is introduced here to show how the BSNA fathered it and other key programs that were to become central to the Nu Revival. Certain monks and monastic centers, as noted above, were to play very important roles.

Actually it was at the Mahasi Sayadaw's Thathana Yeiktha that the first two founders' meetings of the important Buddha Sasana Council (BSC) took place in 1950, and a draft of its provisions was presented at the same place to a hundred or so monks.[48] They were mostly Union Ovadacariya or Vinayadhara (Winido) judges (see above, in this chapter), who tended to be pro-government. At this same meeting, the Nyaungyan Sayadaw exclaimed that the founding of the BSC was "a real boon to the *Sasana*," i.e., the Buddha's religion. After a third Mandalay meeting, a significant editorial reported that Attorney General Chan Htoon had taken an important part in the planning,[49] and his speech before Parliament supporting a bill to give legal basis to the BSC is worth study.

U Chan Htoon opened his address with the claim that he was "one of the persons who originally conceived the idea of the Bill and drafted it." He claimed that the bill arose from two situations, one international and the other national. The world had suffered from two vast wars and was in danger of facing a third. The World Fellowship of Buddhists, held in Ceylon in 1950, had noted an interest in Buddhism and expressed the hope that the peoples of the West might be won over, not so much to Buddhism itself, as to the principles of leading the righteous life inherent in Buddhism. In addition to the west, which was "longing for Buddhism now," Dr. Ambedkar and Pandit Nehru had both considered that it was time for a Buddhist revival in India. In Burma Buddhism was the religion of the people and the noblest jewel of the culture, yet the Burmese did not live up to it. "In fact when we went to the World Conference," said

48. *Light of the Dhamma*, 1, no. 1 (1952):30–34.
49. *Sangayana Monthly Bulletin*, 1, no. 5 (Sept. 1953):4.

Chan Htoon, "I was rather afraid that someone there might ask me why in spite of the fact that Buddhism was flourishing in Burma there should be such widespread disorder and ruthless killing." Chan Htoon's references to dacoity, insurrections, increasing crime, and the "cruelty towards one another of the people" were followed by a denunciation of the hatred, greed, and delusion which, for example, made the price of consumer goods so high in Burma compared with Ceylon.

Inquiring into the causes of this discrepancy and ignoring the fact that the same had happened to Ceylon, U Chan Htoon went on to blame foreign domination for the decline in morals. Now that Burma was independent again, a democratic constitution could be implemented only if the people lived up to what was truest in their ideology. If the 90–95 percent of the population that was Buddhist would live up to this, the minorities would have no cause for fear; if the 5 percent non-Buddhists also lived up to the Dhamma (Buddha's teachings), there would be everlasting peace in Burma. Thus there was no question of infringing upon the rights of Burmese minorities: "The establishment of the Buddha Sasana Council will not in any way affect or infringe the rights of other religions or the interests of followers of other faiths." On two occasions in the latter part of his speech, U Chan Htoon referred to the conception and drafting of the BSC bill by U Nu and himself only.[50]

Speaking on the same date, U Nu welcomed the creation of an organization representative of the whole of Burma, the main aims of which would be the spreading of the Dhamma abroad and its proper foundation in Burma. Missionaries would now be sent with confidence into other countries. True representatives of Burma could now be selected for attendance at international Buddhist conferences. The Burmese would cease merely visiting pagodas and would pay attention to the main aim of Buddhism: the attainment of Nibbana (Nirvana). The BSC would combat the enemies of Buddhism in the intellectual field, especially those who pretended that "Lord Buddha was a lesser man than Karl Marx." The organization would also fight the enemies of Buddhism on a practical level. One such effort would be the establishment of Buddhist centers of learning, and, above all, the translation of the Pali scriptures into good Burmese so that the man in the street could really understand what Buddhism was about. U Nu ended, like U Chan

50. *Light of the Dhamma,* 1, no. 1 (1952):23–24.

Htoon, by giving assurances that the religious freedom of other faiths would remain unimpaired.[51]

These two speeches give us a good overview of the thinking that influenced the Revival movement. The specific view of the Ministry of Religious Affairs, which was to play a central role in the Revival, is found in another speech, made by Minister of Religion U Win at Rangoon University for the inaugural meeting of the BSC in 1951. He drew a picture of the decline of religion and morals in the sixty-year interval between the end of the reign of Thibaw and the beginning of national independence:

When we were denied freedom, what was the state of our Religion? Sanghas split up into different sects; contact between the Sanghas and laymen were few and far between; there was a dearth of learned men; religious practice was neglected and darkness gradually fell on our Sasana [religion]. . . . While in the past every Buddhist child got his rudiments of Buddhist religious education thanks to our wonderful monastic schools, our children were gradually kept away from them during the alien regime. Thus an ever-widening gulf crept in between the Sanghas and the laymen; the old Sangha organization lost its former cohesion and the Sangha eventually came under the aegis of lay courts of law. With this decline in the structure of Sangha society came the deterioration in the Sangha's code of conduct. Lay morality also declined in consequence. With this general deterioration in human morality, breaches of law became rampant. In fact the present insurrection in our country is attributable to this decline in human morality.

In spite of this dark picture, some, said U Win, had refused to stoop:

Those good-intentioned people carried on this noble work [of building, feeding monks, examining scriptures] for over 60 years without the material support of the then Government. They were the real Promoters of the Faith in the absence of the Faithful Ruler. Now the circumstances have changed. Independence is once more restored and the Government is duly elected by the people according to the constitution. It is but inevitable that the Government becomes the Promoter of the Faith on behalf of the people who elect it. The Government thus elected cannot merely look on indifferently at the religious structure which had been disintegrating during the last sixty years.

The Supreme Goal of the Revival: The Sangayana

Thus did U Win introduce the AFPFL's religious mandate, which was designed to "promote Buddhism in a concrete manner" but was to be

51. *Burma Weekly Bulletin*, 137 (Oct. 1, 1950):3–4; *Light of the Dhamma*, 1, no. 1 (Nov. 1952):31–32.

"in no way connected with politics nor . . . sectarian."[52] The task of holding the Sangayana, however, was handed over to the Executive Council of the BSC in 1951, and the government's minister for religious affairs was made a member of that council. Other government-connected members of the council were Justice U Thein Maung (Vice President of the BSC); Justice U On Pe; Sithu U San Nyun; Commissioner of Income Tax U San Thein; Director of Religious Affairs Patamagyaw U Kyi Pe: Director of Fire Services U Hla Pe; Deputy Director of Religious Affairs (Mandalay) Justice U Chan Htoon (Honorary General Secretary); and representative from the Ministry of Religious Affairs U Ba Swe.[53] Many of the key members of the Executive Council of the BSC, such as Sir U Thwin, who was its president, were the same men who had directed the BSNA, except that the younger U Chan Htoon provided much energetic leadership as old age diminished the ability of Sir U Thwin to keep up the pace.

As the Sangayana got under way, the younger man chafed impatiently under the president of the BSC Executive Council and in fact took over a good deal of control, although restrained all the time by the moderate U Thein Maung. Minister of Religious Affairs U Win, while only one minister in a crowd, nevertheless had several points of contact with the Executive Council in the persons of religious affairs officers serving on it. By and large, the authority of older men predominated, and especially the authority of lawyers who, under U Thein Maung and U Chan Htoon, were the government people who most avidly and repeatedly paid their respects at Buddhist ceremonies and public holidays. These older men stood out among the younger Thakin ministers as old-time nationalists who had been fighting for Burmese independence in the days before the Thakins were born and had assumed office, in most cases without seeking it, under the Japanese, where they were in close collaboration with U Nu in Ba Maw's government. These were men whose education and training in the law had been British and whose horizons were wider than those of the Thakins but who had mellowed with age and returned to the traditions and modes of behavior of their youths. In the religious sense they were probably the best material U Nu

52. *Light of the Dhamma*, 1, no. 1 (1952): 24–29; *Burma Weekly Bulletin*, n.s., 2, no. 2 (Apr. 22, 1953):12.
53. *Sangayana Monthly Bulletin*, 2, no. 5 (Sept. 1954):2–3, 11.

could find to mold and control his Revival program; in a political sense it can no doubt be argued that, in giving them power, U Nu was recognizing the *min,* or Westernized class, and keeping the right wing in Burmese politics happy, while the socialists busied themselves with the socialist state proper. The influence of these men must not be underestimated in Burmese political history: they were to be called upon once again, if only as figureheads, when the army regime wanted Cabinet ministers untainted by Thakin affiliations.

These men exerted their power in the smaller Executive Council of the BSC, for the general and larger BSC council did not really have much say. The regional representatives from geographic areas of the Union who represented the many existing lay Buddhist associations looked impressive on paper in the official BSC act of 1950 (Burma 1959a), but these area representatives were outvoted at the Executive Council level, and the latter body held the real power to initiate and control events. Ecclesiastical court monks also played the role of advisers to the Executive Council, although not sitting on the council formally. It was therefore this council that really planned and guided the great Sangayana.

Beyond its potency as a symbol of the Revival, which was great enough to impress foreign as well as home observers, the Sangayana was undoubtedly an impressive achievement in a very young country still involved in civil war caused by hill tribe and communist insurrections. Taken entirely by itself, the Sangayana is little more than a symbol, for there are very few senses in which it achieved what it set out to do, perhaps because it was not even really necessary from the scriptural-purification point of view.

Perhaps the best way to understand the symbolic aspects of the Sangayana is to begin with the story of the origins of the Kaba Aye Pagoda (the Peace Pagoda at the site of the Sangayana), as told by U Ohn Ghine (David Maurice), an Australian Buddhist:

One day, in the year 1948 a devout layman Saya Htay was practicing *Vipassana* [meditation] under a tree in the forest of Shinma Taung at the foot of the hill of that name, seven miles from the town of Pakokku [N.B.] which is 310 miles north of Rangoon, when an old man, a religieux, came down from the hill to Saya Htay and giving him a bamboo staff on which were engraved the words *Siri Mangala* in Pali (and it is to be noted that this means: "Glorious Prosperity") requested him to present the staff to the

Prime Minister U Nu. The Holy Man, who was dressed in pure white clothes, spoke on various spiritual matters and told Saya Htay to beg U Nu to lay the foundation of the Buddha Sasana and to build a Pagoda. The crowning of the pagoda, the final ceremony, should be over, he said, before the end of the year 1952. Great buildings would grow up round the site of the pagoda. If this were done, there would be Peace in the country and Peace in the World.

Saya Htay was so impressed with the bearing and manner of the religieux that he hastened to Rangoon and contacted U Ba Gyan (then Judicial Minister).

Burma was, at the time, facing her darkest hour since after obtaining her independence but a year before, a serious Communist insurrection was endangering the whole country.

Nevertheless, in spite of dangers and fears it was felt that the Prime Minister should be told of the mysterious visit of the holy man and of his present and his request.

U Nu was also most impressed by the account and suggested that a search be made for a suitable site for a Pagoda. U Hla Gyaw [director of fire services] was requested to help find a place and some twenty six days later saw that a most suitable site was a hillock some three miles north of the famous Shwedagon, and near the village of Yegu.

He called in several other Elders, they all saw and liked the place and decided to build the Pagoda there. When they found that the hill had a name, and that it was called Siri Mangala they were sure they were right. [1953:44–45][54]

A number of fascinating themes emerge in this story. One, which we cannot explore here at length, is the significance of the staff given to Saya Htay in terms of the rituals of messianic Buddhism, which I have explored elsewhere: 1963c, 1964. The Kaba Aye Pagoda was undoubtedly related to a "vibrational" ideology according to which numbers, letters, cardinal directions, and such are placed in relation, by magic ritual, with the attainment of certain worldly aims (however sophisticated). Much nativistic, "right-wing" nationalism was connected, for example, with "vibrational" forces designed to make the British leave Burma. In the case of the Kaba Aye, the stated aim was world peace but there was clearly an element of "Peace for Burma" in the wished-for result. It will be noticed that the message of the mysterious "religieux" is intimately related with the idea of a Sangayana insofar as it prophesied the erection of large buildings around the pagoda and specified the date

54. Cf. Brohm 1957: 395–396.

of the pagoda's construction. U Nu is presented, as in the BSNA material, less as an initiator than as a man governed by forces greater than himself at whose command he places himself. There is little doubt, however, that Nu was responsible for the Kaba Aye, and it may well have been his specific contribution to the initiation of the Sangayana. One unfortunate rumor should be recorded, if only to show the nature of some of the opposition to the whole Sangayana question: it was said in Burma that U Hla Gyaw, in the twenty-six-day interval between the beginning of his mission and the finding of the site, promptly acquired leases for the land on which the Sangayana eventually stood. We have already seen that he was a member of the BSC; he was also on the Building Committee responsible for organizing the contract work in connection with the Yegu structures.

Work on the Kaba Aye Pagoda—a curious structure not very happily wedding a circular, Western-inspired "pukka" type of block to a typical Burmese pagoda spire—began in 1950. The work was finished in March 1952, and a *hti,* or finial-hoisting ceremony, began with a procession from the Botataung Pagoda in Rangoon which conveyed the *seinbu* (diamond-bud) of the pagoda and the relics of Sariputta and Moggallana, the Buddha's great disciples, to the Yegu site. In a pageant "reminiscent of the days of the Defender of the Faith, King Mindon," U Win, Sir U Thwin, and U Nu, dressed in "traditional Burmese costume," conveyed the relics to their new home. The hoisting of the *hti* was performed in seven stages, U Nu taking a turn at the pulleys on the third day. The famous Mohnyin Sayadaw preached at the pagoda, and free *pwes* were held for a record attendance; the latter included amusements and also some propaganda in the medical and social welfare fields. A Withaka[55] association of which U Nu's wife was president fed a thousand monks. A number of foreigners attended the event, including the president of the Maha Bodhi Society of India.[56] Brohm contends that the Botataung Pagoda suffered at the expense of the Kaba Aye, the construction of which was rushed ahead, while reconstruction work on the Botataung was ignored (1957:397). The official report speaks of "relics" going

55. From Visakha (P): a famous female lay disciple of the Buddha who fed and supported the Sangha.

56. *Burma Weekly Bulletin,* 211 (Mar. 8, 1952):2, 212; 212 (Mar. 15, 1952):2–3; *Sangayana Monthly Bulletin,* 1, no. 1 (May 1953): 1; *Burma,* 3, no. 2 (Jan. 1952): 83.

back to the Botataung Pagoda in March, though apparently the main ones remained permanently at Kaba Aye.[57] The first Kaba Aye "Pagoda Anniversary Festival" was made the occasion for large celebrations, with a national holiday declared throughout the Union.[58] Only after the pagoda was built was work started on the other buildings for the Sangayana. Its central role as the key symbol of the Sangayana is clear, and it is clearly related to U Nu's personal quest.

One must also see the Kaba Aye Pagoda as symbolic of a broad emphasis during the Sangayana upon pagoda repair and a concern for Buddhist relics, both in Burma and elsewhere. The Shwemawdaw Pagoda in Pegu was an early target of government efforts, and its earthquake-shaken rubble was finally rebuilt by 1954, with the aid of many members of the BSC.[59] In the same year, the famous Kalyani ordination site of the fifteenth-century King Dhammaceti was restored.[60] As early as 1949 efforts were made to begin the rebuilding of the Botataung Pagoda, which had been leveled by British bombing in World War II, and its finial was raised anew by late 1953, although, as noted above, work on it suffered from the attention paid to the Kaba Aye.[61] The restorations mentioned are only three out of many accounts of U Nu flying here and there to lay foundation stones for restoration of Burma's historic pagodas and Buddhist sites.[62]

Closely connected with the pagoda projects were the many efforts to collect relics and symbols of Burma's history. The return of the Lion Throne of King Thibaw from Lord Mountbatten after the war was, of course, an extremely important beginning for the Burmese (Burma

57. *Burma Weekly Bulletin*, 212 (Mar. 15, 1952): 2–3.

58. Ibid., n.s., 1, no. 48 (Mar. 4, 1953):2.

59. Ibid., 211 (Mar. 3, 1952):6; n.s., 1, no. 30 (Oct. 29, 1952):4; n.s., 2, no. 44 (Feb. 3, 1954):346; n.s., 3, no. 2–3 (Apr. 21, 1954):9. See also *New Times of Burma*, July 1, 18, 1950, Apr. 21, 1951; and *Sangayana Monthly Bulletin*, 2, no. 10 (Feb. 1955):8.

60. *Burma Weekly Bulletin*, n.s., 2, no. 13 (July 1, 1953): 102; n.s., 3, 16 (July 21, 1954): 116.

61. *Light of the Dhamma*, 1, no. 2 (Jan. 1953):5–7; *Burma*, 2d Anniv. Ed. (1950):143; Brohm 1957:397; *Burma Weekly Bulletin*, n.s., 2, no. 33 (Nov. 18, 1953): 263; n.s., 2, no. 40 (Dec. 30, 1953):306; and n.s., 1, no. 45 (Feb. 11, 1953):3.

62. We have already mentioned the destruction of the Payagyi statue of the Buddha. A new stone for its reconstruction was laid in 1958 by U Nu. See *Burma Weekly Bulletin*, n.s., 7, no. 17 (Aug. 7, 1958); n.s., 8, no. 51 (Apr. 2, 1959):426.

1949:57). Ceylon and India sent relics on loan to Burma in the early fifties to help the country "in its time of trial."[63] Bo trees, remains of Buddhist saints, archaeological treasures, tablets, royal objects, rare texts, and many similar treasures moved about from foreign countries to Burma and then around Burma itself as part of the campaign to revive Buddhism. When, for example, Pagan relics were brought to Kaba Aye, the Weluwun Sayadaw and BSC officials were there to honor the occasion and to focus public interest on it.[64] The enlistment of foreign support had particular importance in justifying the Sangayana itself.

In planning the Sangayana, the Burmese seem to have associated two events which did not necessarily fit together logically and historically: the attainment of their own Independence and the Revival. In traditional Theravada Buddhism no reason is in fact given for the belief that the 2,500th anniversary of the Buddha would see a revival in the Doctrine. On the contrary, the traditional feeling had always been that the Doctrine would inevitably decay and be forgotten, that man would become more and more debased as a result of the loss of the Doctrine, and that only after a great destruction of the existing world would a new Golden Age come with a new Buddha, the Maitreya, to begin the teaching all over again. In Burmese history, roughly from the time of King Bodawpaya onward, we can observe the interplay of two contradicting beliefs: one in the inevitable decline, and another in the nativistic and revivalistic forces that a messianic dispensation would be granted much sooner than the texts would have it. The interplay of these beliefs can be seen also in the AFPFL program.

Hopes for Foreign Sangha Support

The Burmese planners had also to face the fact that many foreign orthodox Theravada Buddhists did not necessarily hold with the Burmese view of the Sangayana, or even the need for such. Since a genuine Sangayana, many believed, was supposed to bring together the monks from all quarters of the earth to purify the scriptures by oral chanting, international cooperation was vital. Such Buddhists objected to Burmese pretensions and required much persuasion by the Burmese. The Fifth

---

63. *Burma Weekly Bulletin,* 104 (Feb. 11, 1950):1; 107 (Mar. 4, 1950):1–2; and 121 (June 17, 1950):16. For the return of the relics, see *Burma,* 1, no. 2 (Jan. 1951): 110–111.

64. *Burma Weekly Bulletin,* n.s., 2, no. 31 (Nov. 4, 1953):242.

Buddhist Council of Mindon had never been regarded in Asia as orthodox: to non-Burmese it was purely a Burmese affair.[65] The very notion of a Sixth Buddhist Council was highly questionable. As we shall see, the Burmese had to exert themselves to their utmost, during the years of emphasis upon the Relic Program in the councils of the World Fellowship of Buddhists and in the travels of monastic missions which preceded the Sangayana, to bring off some semblance of international cooperation. In fact, as I shall argue, the Sangayana remained a Burmese affair despite all efforts to hide this fact. The Burmese obtained from other countries a token acceptance of the idea and the participation of small foreign missions, but that was all. Other countries accepted Burma's need for the Revival and the Sangayana and allowed her to play out her "great show," but the suspicion remained with them that it was mainly a political event, and as such it did not have their entire allegiance. When U Nu gave his first public description of the Sangayana program in 1951, while in India, he stated that there was a difference between this and other Sangayanas in that not only Pali but also Burmese and possibly English Tipitakas would be produced and that these would serve as authorized versions in the whole Buddhist world.[66]

The major focus of the Sangayana was to be upon the textual purification of the Tipitakas. The Great Cave at Kaba Aye, which would seat 5,000 clergy and 10,000 laymen, the four hostels to accommodate 1,000 monks, the refectory to feed 1,500 monks, the International Buddhist Library, the hospital, the press building, the BSC administrative buildings, and the Asia Foundation's printing presses were all, in essence, designed to provide the means whereby monks could purify the Pali canon and spread the Dhamma thereafter. From the Sangayana's opening on May 17, 1954, to the final closing of the fourth Commentary Session in March 1960, the emphasis would be on such matters. Foreign support was deemed crucial.

After some preliminary contacts, more definite appeals were made. In 1953, a most important Burmese mission traveled in Ceylon. No less an aged prelate than the Nyaungyan Sayadaw accompanied U Win and the

---

65. **Pyinnyaramikamaha Sayadaw 1958:83.** The same source notes that the Fourth Buddhist Council was not accepted by all Buddhists either. Interviews with monks during my stay also confirmed the existence of foreign resistance to the Sixth Buddhist Council, the Sangayana.

66. *Burma Weekly Bulletin,* 192 (Oct. 27, 1951).

Mahasi and Anisekhan Sayadaws to confer with the Sinhalese authorities and to hand over "prerevised" texts for comparison with scriptures available in Ceylon. Here was laid the basis of Sinhalese cooperation in the Sangayana, the only impressive non-Burmese participation eventually granted to the AFPFL religious program.[67] In 1953, the Cambodian *sangharaja* and his small suite visited Burma for about two weeks.[68] A return visit to Cambodia was paid by U Kelasa of the Dhammadhuta College and an official of the BSC. In the same year a Laotian mission came to Rangoon for two weeks for an exchange of presents: there does not seem to have been even a pretence of setting up a Laotian editing mission.[69] A Thai mission led by the deputy *sangharaja* spent the same length of time in Burma.[70] All these missions were taken to visit prominent members of Nu's party and what I am tempted to call "government pagodas and monasteries." They were also duly shown the stone slabs on which the texts from Mindon's Fifth Council were engraved, and pictures were taken of them "comparing" texts.

In fairness it must be said that the textual program from the start had implied a low degree of participation from other countries: if it was difficult to prove the necessity for a Sangayana at all and for revision of the Burmese texts, it was still more difficult to work out acceptable reasons for foreign participation which would transcend normal jealousies between small nations and their unwillingness to spend money on what would enhance a rival nation's prestige.

The "Burma" text used as a basis for revisions appears to have consisted of a partial text issued under the auspices of the YMBA by some Mandalay *sayadaw*s and the stone-slab inscriptions of Mindon's Fifth Council. This text was supposed to be compared with a number of commentaries and subcommentaries and with the "foreign" texts in order to produce a final authoritative version. A typical report on the

67. Ibid., n.s., 1, no. 42 (Jan. 21, 1953):3; n.s., 1, no. 44 (Feb. 4, 1953):1; n.s., 1, no. 45 (Feb. 11, 1953):3.
68. Ibid., n.s., 1, no. 51 (Mar. 25, 1953); n.s., 1, no. 52 (Apr. 1, 1953):3; n.s., 2, no. 1 (Apr. 8, 1953): 7; *Sangayana Monthly Bulletin*, 1, no. 9 (Jan. 1954):4; *Sangayana Souvenir* 1954:6–7.
69. *Burma Weekly Bulletin*, n.s., 2, no. 2–3 (Apr. 22, 1953):12; n.s., 2, no. 4 (Apr. 29, 1953):4.
70. Ibid., n.s., 2, no. 9 (June 3, 1953):69; n.s., 2, no. 10 (June 10, 1953):76; *Sangayana Souvenir* 1954: 7, 11.

nature of the foreign texts, leaving out Ceylon for the moment, reads as follows:

As regards Thailand, the Head of the *Sangha* of Thailand handed over to the O.S.N.C.[71] of the Union of Burma, the Chulalongkorn text, i.e. the text recently [sic] published by King Cullalankara, commonly known as Chulalongkorn of Thailand, in the form of the text obtained as a result of editing and re-editing by a separate group of Thai monks on a national level.

This Pali text known as Chulalongkorn text is that of the Scriptures printed and published by H.M. the King of Thailand and re-edited collectively by Thai *Pitakattayaseka Pitakovida Mahatheras*, proficient and well versed in the Scriptures.

As for Cambodia, the Head of the Buddhist Order of that country sent the text of the Pali Scriptures which is being published after he had personally supervised and edited it, as the text obtained as a result of editing and re-editing by a separate group of Cambodian monks on a national level.

Furthermore was included for collation, the text published in Roman characters by the Pali Text Society of London, which has been in existence for the past 80 years or so and functioning in this line, having been edited and re-edited by distinguished Pali scholars of the whole world. [Burma 1956a:64]

Such an account itself is not very convincing because there is little evidence that a genuine scholarly comparison took place. In effect many of the early plans connected with the scriptures had to be revised or abandoned, and the program of comparison was more ritual than real. In a 1953 speech the chief executive officer of the BSC revealed what amounted to virtual nonparticipation on the part of the Sanghas in Laos and Cambodia: "As previously arranged, Ceylon, Thailand, Cambodia, and Laos were to send a representative each to work in cooperation with the Text Re-editing groups of Burma. The learned *Theras* and *Mahatheras* of Cambodia and Laos were unable to send their representatives, but gave their assent to the decisions to be arrived at by the *Mahatheras* of the remaining *Theravada* countries."[72]

The best the BSC could do after this was to name one of the five sessions of the Sangayana the Cambodia-Laos Session, for reasons of international prestige. As for texts in languages other than those of the

71. Ovadacariya Sangha Nayaka Committee, an advisory board for the Sangayana, reporting to the Supreme Sangha Council (SSC).
72. *Sangayana Monthly Bulletin,* 1, no. 6 (Oct. 1953):7.

five main Theravada countries, the report on them shortly before the opening of the Sangayana was as follows:

It has been considered most essential to have a Hindi translation of the Tipitakas for the benefit of the people of India, which is the country where Buddhism originated. Therefore the work of translating the *Tipitaka*s into Hindi will also be undertaken soon after the completion of the *Sangayana*.

It was intended to have an English version of *Tipitaka* texts also ready for consideration and adoption at the *Chattra*[73] *Sangayana*. But this also has to be postponed till after the Great Council for various reasons.[74]

There was more cooperation from the Thai and Sinhalese Sanghas. In 1953 a Thai "editing mission" of three monks arrived in Rangoon, where they met with the Ceylon mission, which arrived at the same time. The Thai group later proceeded to Mandalay, where two Thai monks scrutinized texts for a period of a month. They returned to Rangoon, lived at the Thathana Yeiktha with the Mahasi Sayadaw for a while, and then returned to their country after a visit of just over five months. The Ceylon "editing missions" were the most serious, for Ceylon was the only country of the "Five" to set up a revising system at home similar, though smaller in scale, to the Burmese. In 1952 a committee was appointed to advise the minister of home affairs on the best way for Ceylon to help in the Sangayana. Subsequently a central board of sixteen leading monks was formed, together with a number of groups of monks in different parts of Ceylon, to scrutinize different texts. A body of lay members was formed to back up this activity, with a hundred members who undertook to collect funds for a special commemorative building at Kaba Aye. Ceylon was honored by having five Ceylonese monks nominated by the Burmese to Sangayana committees.[75]

Revised texts were brought to Burma in successive waves by Ceylon editing missions. The first brought the Vinaya and *Samyutta* (part of the Sutta Tipitaka) texts in early 1953. The leader of this mission remained in Burma until early 1954, receiving the title of A.M.P.[76] Other texts were brought in late 1953 by a second Sinhalese mission consisting of three monks from the Siam, Shwegyin, and Amarapura sects.[77] A

73. *Chattha* (P): sixth.

74. *Burma*, 4, no. 2 Jan. 1954):4.

75. *Sangayana Monthly Bulletin*, 1, no. 8 (Dec. 1953): 2–3, 6–7.

76. *Burma Weekly Bulletin*, n.s., 2, no. 17 (July 29, 1953):131; *Sangayana Monthly Bulletin*, 1, no. 4 (Aug. 1953:5; 1, no. 9 (Jan. 1954):12.

77. *Sangayana Souvenir*, 1, no. 12 (Apr. 1954): 11–12.

third group of texts was brought by yet another mission in early 1954.[78]

Despite this outside advice and help, the Sangayana's final product seems to be a Burmese reading of the Pali texts. However, it is valuable because it is apparently carefully published and because much of what has been previously available to Western scholars, at least, has been Pali Text Society versions based upon Sinhalese readings. Also of use are the *tikas* or various subcommentaries which the Pali Text Society had not published. Nonetheless, my overall verdict is that, although the Sangayana text may be of use to Burmese scholars and ecclesiastics, its contributions to international Buddhist scholarship are modest in the extreme. The final texts were in Burmanized Pali for Burmese readers. We thus turn to the impact of the texts on Burma.

Text Publication and Gifts to the Sangha

The report of the Asia Foundation in Burma for 1957–1958 opens with a survey of the publications program it so strongly supported:

Few *Theravada* countries possessed sufficient copies of the *Tipitaka* to serve the requirements of their monasteries, monks and lay scholars. In Burma, editions of the Scriptures in Burmese Pali were in great demand since existing volumes were in poor condition and very costly. Translation into Burmese text[s] entirely free of Pali words had never been accomplished; even partial translations were scarce. Somewhat similar conditions prevailed in respect to the canon of other countries. Thus, a major aim of the Synod becomes the publication of up-to-date yet moderately priced editions of the *Tipitaka.*[79]

The presses, therefore, began in 1953 to print, as their first venture, a Pali *Parajika,* which, significantly, is that part of the Vinaya dealing with the four rules (sex, stealing, killing, and superhuman powers) that, if violated, require a monk's expulsion from the Sangha. Then followed a Pali Tipitaka, a Burmese Tipitaka, *Sangayana Questions and Answers,* Commentaries, and a souvenir album. The foundation report discusses these achievements: "[The] Principal work of the Publishing house has been the 40-volume edition of the Pali *Tipitaka* in Burmese script. . . . Of this first edition 2,500 sets were presented to monasteries where *thera*s participated in the *Chattha Sangayana.* The Ministry of Religious

---

78. Ibid., p. 12.

79. Asia Foundation 1958:7. Much of what follows is based on this report and on original documents obtained from the BSC.

Affairs recently ordered a second printing of 11,000 sets (440,000 volumes) intended as gifts for all monasteries engaged in *Dhamma* work [i.e. teaching the Buddha's words]."

The report goes on to mention sets given to foreign monks, an ambitious program of translation into English, Shan, Hindi, "and other important languages," as well as finishing the publication of the Burmese Tipitaka in 45 volumes[80] (7 issued), a complete Pali Commentaries and a complete Pali Sub-Commentaries, each of 50 volumes, a 60-volume Pali-Burmese dictionary, a life of Buddha in 50 volumes—in short an estimated thirty years of full-capacity publishing work. Among other achievements mentioned are sets of *Sangayana Questions and Answers*, offering "valuable guidance from the Buddha's Teachings for the every-day problems of the Buddhist," as well as the same texts on phonograph records.

A detailed study of the printing and sales figures has shown that no more than 25 percent of the books were sold by 1958, and, since income figures are often below what would have been brought in by sale of only paperback editions, I conclude that gifts are involved. In the marketing report for the Pali Tipitaka, 2,431 sets were said to have been "given" away, but money for them is listed in the sales figures, suggesting that the BSC was thereby paying for what it had produced to give away! The overwhelming impression is that the books were published and produced mainly to be given away. The emphasis on Pali texts suggests that it was the Sangha for whom the massive publication effort was mounted. Taking all the facts into consideration, I conclude that the Buddha Sasana Council publication program was designed not for the people as a whole, very much less for the Buddhist world as a whole, but rather as a kind of return gift to the Sangha for giving Burma prestige by accepting the onerous burden of holding a Sangayana. Also, since the number of monks participating in the Sangayana was relatively small, it was an opportunity to reward monks who had a favorable attitude toward the government and its programs, to suggest to monks the advantages of taking government examinations, and to impress upon the Sangha generally the AFPFL's good intentions toward it. As for the public in general, they liked to offer sets, when they could afford it, to their favorite *sayadaw*s, sets which in many an informant's experience re-

80. Forty would appear to be the correct figure.

mained boxed or cased in public view and virtually untouched. The elements of show and political action both at home and abroad are inextricably mixed and, with them, the genius of one man for turning popular notions about authority to his advantage.

Difficulties in Identifying Government Monks

Identifying those monks whom the government so earnestly wooed is a considerable task. The monkhood that figures in the great majority, if not the totality, of writings on Burma in foreign languages is faceless. From time to time, the names of one or two monks make the political headlines—one thinks of U Ottama and U Wisara—or a scholar like the Ledi Sayadaw achieves a certain fame among Europeans, but apart from these few the Sangha is completely unknown. If it is true that it represents part of the intellectual elite of Burma, it seems curious at first sight that no one has attempted to study its leading individuals, to provide biographies of the great monks such as we have for leading politicians.

A finer pen than mine would be needed to do justice to the great wealth of character found in the Burmese monkhood. Besides, and here I feel a twinge of regret, that is not the purpose of this work. If I mention names at all rather than reduce all individuals to types in a pattern of political behavior, it is because the appearance of individual *sayadaws* in the documentation enables us to fix certain party affiliations which are necessary to this analysis and which can be obtained in no other way. The absence of ecclesiastical history and sociology in Burma— the fact that we simply do not know what groupings members of the Sangha fall into and cannot take anything for granted in this field— obliges the researcher to fall back on the only documentation there is. This usually amounts to lists of monks present at certain functions, in certain contexts, which permit some very tentative generalizations about the cross-influences of Sangha and laity. In order to fix some points of reference for any future scholar wishing to work at length with Burmese sources, I have and will mention whenever possible the names of leading *sayadaws*.

The evidence must be pieced together laboriously, like a jigsaw puzzle. The humblest signs have to be taken into account: reports of which monks were fed at which function; which monks gave the Five Precepts to whom; which monks ordained others, presided over examinations, or consecrated such and such an ecclesiastical building. Nor is it always easy to pin down a particular monk. A monk can be identified by his Pali name, his *sayadaw* title (if he has one), his address (i.e., the monastery he lives in), and occasionally his office or rank in a certain organization. Frequently, however, only one item of identification is given. It may be the Pali name, but many monks bear the same Pali name; therefore, this is often insufficient. The *sayadaw* name alone may also be insufficient, for it does not distinguish an individual from his predecessor or his successor. More often than not, just when we would like to know which monks were present at a particular ceremony, the source gives a general description such as "the Ovadacariya," or "the *nayaka" sayadaw*s. Accepting these limitations, let us look at the Sangayana and try to answer two important questions: who exactly, in the Order, was involved in the Revival, and why were they involved?

The Nu Sects and Cooperating Monks

We might best begin with the matter of titles. As noted before, the British began awarding the AMP title in 1915, and the U Nu government continued the custom, awarding the honor in a special 1953 ceremony at which, significantly, a new title was also given: that of *rattaguru*. The creation of *rattaguru*s was the nearest the AFPFL got to nominating one or more *thathanabaings*. A committee of *sayadaw*s and laymen took some time in the fifties to compile a report on titles, and their recommendations were accepted by the government only with some emendations. The records of the proceedings of this committee were unavailable to me, but it has been said in Burma that its attempts to obtain a more authoritarian Sangha structure failed, owing to too much wavering on the part of U Nu, who could not bring himself to force the Sangha too fast. It appears that the government merely acknowledged seniority in the Order in nominating the *rattaguru*s and gave them no more powers in law than they already had, if indeed they had any, at the hands of their own sects. The title carried an award of 1,000 *kyat*s and the right to use special insignia.

The government's apparent recognition that a single *thathanabaing* was no longer possible strongly substantiates my argument that the sects represented a major obstacle to any unification of the Sangha under the leadership of a state-sponsored head. Possibly U Nu wanted to create a supreme council of *rattaguru*s, one from each sect, but there is no evidence that he succeeded in doing so. The Dwaya's refusal to join the Sangayana is an example of the barriers he faced.

Appointed *rattaguru* of the Thudhamma monks was the Nyaungyan Sayadaw, U Revata, from the Mogaung Taik in Mandalay. This famous Upper Burma leader had represented a sizable group of monks within the Maha Sangha Ahpwe during and after World War II.[81] Like the Aletawya Sayadaw and others, after Independence the Nyaungyan carried over his Maha Sangha Ahpwe activities into political realms, as we have noted elsewhere in this chapter. He promoted the 1946 Burma Hill Tracts Buddhist Mission concept, which can be seen as an early monastic effort that later gave rise to similar plans during the Sangayana years. He favored the founding of the Buddha Sasana Council, and he was a member of the Supreme Sangha Council, the group of monks who had the most to say about the running of the Sangayana. To promote the Sangayana, he traveled to India with U Win, and he presided over the planning session for the event itself, becoming the president of the formal Sixth Buddhist Council to revise the scriptures and thus the monk most involved with all the activities of the Sangayana. The Thudhamma loyalties of this monk, however, are clearly shown in his inviting the head of the Dwaya sect to a 160-dish meal that only strengthened the Dwaya's refusal to join the Sangayana activities. His stature was such that he brought prestige to the Sangayana, but there are those who were critical of such Sangha involvement in government affairs. Such critics noted that at his funeral in the mid 1950s, after a splendid lying in state, the coffin should have reposed for a time on each of three towers, but machinery failed. Also, a complicated cremation, using electrically charged metal balls, failed because the current passed too high between them. Previously his great float had caught in a wire and overturned. Ordinary cremation had to follow. One could, and some did, see these funeral complications as the predictable result of a political monk's overextension of his proper role, not just as unfortunate happenstance.

After the death of the Nyaungyan Sayadaw, the Masoyein Sayadaw, U Thuriya, was appointed Thudhamma *rattaguru* in 1956. This monk,

---

81. The organization is also known as the Thathana Pyu Ahpwe. The Nyaungyan's role in the founding of the Maha Sangha Ahpwe in 1943 was discussed earlier in this chapter.

from the Masoyein Taik in Mandalay, was also an Upper Burma man from the traditional center of Sangha prestige. He had previously been awarded the AMP title and had been a member of the Supreme Sangha Council of the Sangayana, as were the Nyaungyan and most politically important monks in the Nu program. The Masoyein appeared with other key monks at the ordination hall dedication for the government-promoted Thathana Yeiktha meditation center in 1953, and he became an editor of the Sangayana texts, as did two other monks from his *taik,* U Kosalla and U Visuddha (the Pathan Sayadaw). The range of his support of government programs can be seen in his chairmanship of the 1956 Sangha Parahita Ahpwegyok (SPA), the social service organization effort to involve the Sangha in such projects as running orphanages or establishing schools for the blind. In recognition of such a wide range of helpfulness, when U Nu offered *hsoon* (alms food) to 118 monks at Mandalay, he chose the Masoyein Sayadaw to preside over all. The grant of the prestigious title of *rattaguru* can also be seen as a recognition of loyalty to government plans for the Sangha.

While the Thudhamma presence in Sangayana affairs was overwhelming, the other, more established sects' commitment was earnestly sought if not achieved. For example, the Shwegyin monk U Sanda, the Sankin Sayadaw[82] from the Vipassana Gandharama, Sagaing Hill, was appointed Shwegyin *rattaguru* in 1953, at the age of eighty-three, apparently on the basis of seniority, but I could find no record of his having participated in any government programs or having attended any Nu functions. Neither could I find any such commitment on the part of his *taik-ok.* A similar pattern is involved with the awarding of the title of Dwaya *rattaguru* to U Saridathaba, the Payagyi Sayadaw of the Payagyi Taik in Henzada.[83] He was eighty-six at the time of his appointment in 1953, and he can be considered the head of the Dwaya sect then, but neither he nor any other leaders of his sect would participate in the Sangayana, as noted before, nor are there records of their involvement in the usual Nu projects. At the death of U Saridathaba, the title was awarded in 1958 to U Kelathawuntha, the Yetankhun Sayadaw of the Yetankhun

---

82. Sometimes spelled Sangin. This may be the U Sanda who was one of the serial heads of the Shwegyin Withudayon Taik in Mandalay in the 1930s. See Appendix E.

83. This Payagyi Taik should not be confused with the Payagyi taiks in Rangoon and Mandalay, both of which were very actively pro-Nu. J. F.

Taik in Henzada.[84] No political activity is recorded for him or members of his *taik*.

The patterns evident in the Mindon era resemble those of the Nu government as it sought entrance to the Sangha at large by sponsorship of selected sects, just as Mindon did with the Shwegyin. Thus considerable significance can be seen in the award of the *rattaguru* title to a Pakokku monk, U Zawana, the Ashe (Eastern) Taik Sayadaw from the Mahawizayarama Ashe *taikthit* ("daughter *taik*") in Pakokku.[85] U Zawana was a pupil of the Yesagyo Sayadaw,[86] the founder of the Central or Mahawithudarama Taik in Pakokku, but the leadership of the Mahawithudarama had passed among three other of the Yesagyo's pupils: U Pinnya, U Nandawuntha, and U Thundara. By the time of my visit to Pakokku, U Pinnya had died; U Nandawuntha has taken over as "Pakokku Sayadaw," had served on the Supreme Sangha Council, and had received the AMP award in 1953.[87] At the latter's death in or shortly before 1958,[88] U Thundara took over both his position at the Supreme Sangha Council and his leadership of the Central Taik. Meanwhile U Zawana had left Pakokku to return to his native place, Natheyauk in Nyaung-U township, but was recalled to the Mahawizayarama Ashe *taikthit* some time before his appointment as *rattaguru* in 1956. The only record found of government connections was the award of the AMP title to U Zawana in 1927, but at his funeral in 1959 it was announced that the president of the Union, many ministers, and a large group of "Stable" AFPFL politicians led by Kyaw Nyein would attend. The BSC announced it would offer eighty-two sets of scriptures in his honor.[89] Both wings of the AFPFL (the Stable and the Clean) apparently wished to be seen honoring the Pakokku Taik leader.

84. Also spelled Yetagun. The residence of U Thiri Tilawka Thaba and Sanda Thiri, the latter in some sources said to come from the Payagyi Taik. The two *rattaguru*s may thus come from the same Henzada Payagyi Taik. See Appendix F. J. F.

85. This U Zawana is also not to be confused with the monk of the same name from Thaton who was YBA president in 1952. J. F.

86. See Chapter 2 and Appendix D.

87. Significantly, the Payagyi (Rangoon) Taik's U Kondanna was awarded an AMP title in the same year. *Burma Weekly Bulletin*, n.s., 2, no. 17 (July 27, 1953).

88. The fact that the Payagyi and Pakokku taiks jointly mourned the deaths of U Nandawuntha and U Kondanna (n. 87 above) was discussed earlier in this chapter.

89. *The Nation*, Jan. 13, 1959.

After U Zawana's death, U Thundara, the last of the Yesagyo's pupils, seemingly was by 1959 in charge of the Mahawithudarama Taik and looked after the Eastern Taik as well, along with four *taik-ok*s nominated by the late U Zawana. He also had been awarded an AMP title, and he was on the Executive Committee of the Burma Hill Tracts Buddhist Mission group. I had heard that he was on the Supreme Sangha Council, but I was not able to find him so listed in the literature. It is interesting that the earlier Pakokku leader, U Pinnya was much more politically active, having been a Maha Sangha Ahpwe member in 1946, a moving force in the Burma Hill Tracts Buddhist Mission group, and one of the leaders at the Sangayana opening ceremonies. The early Pakokku leadership had supported the Pali University concept, according to a 1941 committee report (Burma 1941), and we have speculated earlier in this chapter that the government's attention to this group of monks was related to such educational support. While the Pakokku monks claimed on my questionnaire (described in Chapter 3) to be Thudhamma (except for one Dwaya!), and although others would not speak to me of themselves as a sect, the Nu government clearly considered them a sect because it put them on an equal footing with the Thudhamma, Shwegyin, or Dwaya sects in terms of the *rattaguru* title.[90] Perhaps it is significant that the Hngetwin and Weluwun sects were *not* so honored. The Weluwun sect appears to have had to wait for proper recognition until 1958, when the Sandayon Sayadaw,[91] its aged head, was made AMP, as was the Bahan Weluwun Sayadaw. The Hngetwin was not so honored at all.

The Weluwun sect's Sandayon Sayadaw U Acinna, from Thaton, who became head of the sect after the death of U Puntawuntha, the original Weluwun Sayadaw,[92] had shown an early interest in government plans by becoming president of the Burma Hill Tracts Buddhist Mission organization in 1946, but I found no evidence of later involvement on his part. The Bahan (Rangoon) Weluwun Sayadaw, U Kemasara (Khemacara), however, was more active, joining the Burma Hill Tracts

90. The title was also given to a number of foreign monks who helped with the Sangayana.

91. The history of the Weluwun sect and the Sandayon's leadership role in it were discussed above, in Chapter 2.

92. This monk, basically from Rangoon, should not be confused with U Adeissa, the Weluwun Sayadaw from Mandalay, who is Thudhamma.

Buddhist Mission group, attending the ordination hall dedication at the government-sponsored Thathana Yeiktha meditation center, joining the BSNA, serving on the executive committee at the KSA in 1957, acting in 1959 as vice-president of the Rangoon Executive Committee of the KSA, greeting the Pagan relics when they were brought to Kaba Aye, and making two trips to Japan to promote Buddhism. He was granted his AMP title in 1958, the same year the Sandayon Sayadaw received his, presumably in recognition of all his effort, but one still wonders why the Weluwun Sayadaw was given titles so much later than the other sect leaders. One clue is that the Bahan Weluwun Sayadaw took an anti-amendment stance in the ecclesiastical courts issue (see above, this chapter) that may have been more anti-Dwaya than anything else. Another clue is the Bahan Weluwun's appearance at a June 1959 meeting of the Rangoon Central Solidarity Association at which he gave a very strong speech in favor of the army's Dhammantaraya campaign.[93] There may have been, therefore, less specifically pro-Nu loyalty and more support for Sangha independence in the Weluwun sect than one might think at first. The Bahan Weluwun's frequent association with the Bagaya Sayadaw also suggests more conservative inclinations deriving from earlier nationalistic days in GCSS.[94] Furthermore, it may be that quiet disciplinary-meditational sects of the Weluwun and Hngetwin types, by their very reluctance to participate in public affairs, discouraged the political powers from furthering such advancement. My impression is that they spare the government the need to court them and that they fill the few positions they *are* offered out of a sense of duty and by a system based on seniority among their monks.

In contrast, the Payagyi complex in Rangoon reveals a much more politically active group of monks who were in closer contact with the Nu government. The leader, the Payagyi Taik Sayadaw, was U Kondanna, also known as the Chauktagyi Sayadaw.[95] The first meeting of the Burma

93. *The Nation,* June 7, 1959. *Dhammantaraya:* Buddhism in danger (from communism). For *dhammantaraya,* which I interpret as the army regime's alternate to the Buddhist Revival, see Smith 1965:131–136.

94. The Weluwun Sayadaw of Kemmendine (at the other Weluwun branch in Rangoon), present at the Thathana Yeiktha dedication for the BSNA and an officer of the KSA in 1955 and 1957, participated in Sangayana activities to some degree, but he was given no government titles.

95. There are also Payagyi establishments in the Henzada area: the Payagyigon Monastery, the Payagyi Monastery, and the Payagyi Ledi Monastery, all Dwaya

Hill Tracts Buddhist Mission group was held at the Chauktagyi Pagoda, and the Payagyi Taik Sayadaw was its first president. He was part of the court system as a Union Ovadacariya judge. A member of the Supreme Sangha Council, he was also president of the KSA in 1955. His participation in the Sangayana was extensive: he helped to select the *tipitakadhara* (the monk who could recite the whole of the scriptures), he helped to plan the Sangayana through the Supreme Sangha Council, and he was one of the five chief text editors in the Tipitaka publishing process. He not only contributed his own effort but also provided monks from his *taik:* U Aseinda (KSA president in 1957 and Sangayana editor), U Pannajota (Sangayana editor), and U Javana from Payagyi West (Sangayana editor). Four Payagyi Taik monks, for example, attended the ordination hall dedication at the Thathana Yeiktha with the Payagyi Sayadaw. If we look at other institutions connected with this *taik,* the contribution of this group of monks to the Nu programs is even more obvious.

The Payagyi Taik, discussed earlier, was built by Sir U Po Tha, who also built the Chauktagyi Pagoda, the reclining Buddha statue, and the Mahawizayarama Taik, all in Rangoon, while Po Tha's relatives built the Payapyu Taik in the Pazundaung section of Rangoon. The Mahawizayarama Taik, which I visited, contains complete replicas of the Mandalay Mindon Tipitaka texts on stone. The monastery was built for U Kumara, who had been the monk who recited the entire Tipitaka for King Mindon at the Fifth Buddhist Council. The symbolic significance of this *taik* for the Sangayana is obvious.[96] The Payapyu Taik in Pazundaung, built by Po Tha's father and mother-in-law, became famous as a Vinaya exam center, with obvious import for the government's exam promotion efforts. The Payapyu Sayadaw was on the Ovadacariya Sangha Nayaka Committee (OSNC) composed of various titled monks,

---

centers. It will be remembered that the Dwaya *Rattaguru* U Saridathaba was also called the Payagyi Sayadaw. There is a Payagyi Taik in Mandalay, which contains the Hanthawaddy Monastery and Sayadaw, as well as U Okkantha. Both monks are KSA, AMP, and Supreme Sangha Council; in addition the Hanthawaddy was a Sangayana editor and U Okkantha was a Union Vinayadhara. The connection between Rangoon and Mandalay Payagyi monks' activities may be more than coincidental. It is also interesting that the Sandayon Sayadaw (Weluwun) studied at the Mandalay Payagyi Monastery.

96. The *taik* at which King Mindon's chief advisers for the Fifth Council lived was the Mahawizitarama Taik in Mandalay. J. F.

ecclesiastical judges, and SSC members. An earlier (?) Payapyu Sayadaw was also the author of one of the major chronicles used in Chapter 1 of this book, the *Thathana Bahu Thuttapakathani.*[97] The scholastic significance of all these establishments suggests a vital aspect of the Sangayana as envisioned by the government.

Also connected with the Payagyi Taik is the Kemmendine Bagaya Taik, as noted above. The head monk of that *taik,* the Bagaya Sayadaw, U Paduma, was one of the most active political monks in the Sangha during nationalist times. As early as 1922 the Bagaya Sayadaw had been a lecturer for the nationalist General Council of the Sangha Samettgyi (GCSS), and he reputedly joined the political scene to prevent extremism.[98] By the 1930s he took a strong stand against separation from India, and by the time of the Round Table discussions with the British on future independence for Burma, his stature was such that he was consulted by participants before the negotiators left for England. He was deeply involved in arguing issues involving monastic courts in 1928, and in 1935 he led a determined group of monks to excommunicate U Ardeissawuntha of Pazundaung for his book recommending admission of women to the Order.[99] At this excommunication we find him leading a group of Rangoon *taik*s that acted together often on political matters. The immediate neighbors of the Bagaya Taik are as follows: the Salin, Thadu, Weluwun, Zeyawaddy, Linlun, Uyin, and Kyaunggyi taiks. They seem to have been a powerful political group under the Bagaya's leadership.

The Kemmendine Bagaya Taik also is the residence of a later but almost equally active monk, U Tiloka, who was listed as a member of the Supreme Sangha Council, who held a *pariyatti dhammacariya* position, and who was one of the editors for the Sangayana. This *taik* can be linked to the activities of the Bagaya-Tawya Sayadaw, U Nagawuntha. He seems to have participated in most of the government-sponsored or -promoted projects already noted: the ordination hall dedication at the BSNA Thathana Yeiktha meditation center, the AMP group award in 1956, membership in the Supreme Sangha Council, promotion of the Pali University plan by serving on its education board and council, and attain-

97. Payapyu Sayadaw 1928.
98. This information was gained from informants in Rangoon, 1958–1959.
99. Rangoon *Gazette,* Sept. 10, 1935. I first discovered this reference in the excellent historical files of Dr. R. L. Soni, Mandalay.

ment of the *pariyatti dhammacariya* award for scholarship. It is such monks that formed the foundation for government programs involving the Sangha, and we can see therefore how the Payagyi complex played a central role.

If we consider the Payagyi group of *taik*s as part of the larger Pakokku system, we can better understand why the title of *rattaguru* was offered not to the Weluwun or the Hngetwin but to the Pakokku Sayadaw, for by so doing the government promoted its monks and its programs in both Upper and Lower Burma. Nu did not succeed in deeply involving such "Mindon" sects as the Shwegyin and Dwaya, but like Mindon he tried to promote his own monks and, in effect, to create a bellwether sect in his effort to control the Sangha. The refusal of the Pakokku to admit to a sectarian, non-Thudhamma nature does not erase the significance of the actual existence of a Pakokku *rattaguru*. But Nu's ability to control the Pakokku was just as tenuous as Mindon's ability to control the reformist and Vinaya-based sectarians in the Sangha of his time. To put on the spectacle of a Sangayana is one thing, but to get monks to agree to lay control over the Sangha through courts or registration is quite another matter.

The Sangayana was predominantly a Thudhamma affair, and before we leave the subject of the individuals involved we might note a few other important Thudhamma monks. One major figure is certainly the Aletawya Sayadaw (mentioned at the beginning of this chapter), who was head of the Maha Sangha Ahpwe in 1943 and yet greeted Mountbatten on his return to Burma. He gave to Ba Maw the Lower Burma position on Sangha matters, in contrast to the Nyaungyan's Upper Burma view. After Ottama's arrest, he was an active president of the GCSS, often in alliance with the Shweman Sayadaw. He led a drive for amnesty and nonviolence in the rebellions of the 1930s and was a somewhat conservative force, being the first to go to America on the Moral Rearmament campaign and using his influence in a pro-army way during the Dhammantaraya campaign. From his highly respected position, he spoke out at a 1959 meeting on the laxity of monks who go to shows and entertainments and he joined with the Hnitkyaikshitsu and Singapore Sayadaws in the same year to promote monastic primary education. From his massive protest meeting of 10,000 in 1928 against lay control of the Sangha (i.e., the Vinayadhara Bill) to his outspokenness at KSA meetings in the late 1950s, the Aletawya Sayadaw was a powerful force in Sangha politics. He was involved in the Burma Hill Tracts Buddhist Mission program, the dedication of the Thathana Yeiktha, and the events of the Sangayana itself. He is one of the most frequently mentioned Sangha leaders in the literature on the Sangayana.

Another major Thudhamma monk is the Hnitkyaikshitsu Sayadaw, U Nyanika, of the Hnitkyaikshitsu Monastery in Rangoon, which is part of the Thayettaw Taik. His involvement fits a now familiar pattern: Hill Tracts Mission group, Thathana Yeiktha dedication, Supreme Sangha Council, AMP in 1956, vice-president of the KSA in 1957, Ovadacariya monk in 1955, promoter of monastic education, Sangayana editor, and 1963 president of the All-Burma KSA. His *taik,* of course, has been famous in Burma since early nationalist days as a source of political monks of all shades. Like the Payagyi Sayadaw, the Hnitkyaikshitsu is often found in the company of other Thayettaw Taik members who support government projects: U Parama (from Hmangin Monastery), U Thawbana, U Thibatha, U Thuriya (the Pitakataikthit Sayadaw, member of the Executive Committee of KSA), and U Nandathami (the Thathanalankara Sayadaw, KSA Executive Committee member and Union Vinayadhara). In the late fifties, the Thayettaw Taik had its disagreements with the army over efforts to remove "squatters" from its premises.

Many other monks could be mentioned if there were space; the "missionary" monks, for example, also played a role in the Sangayana promotion. The famous U Thittila, from Rangoon University, traveled to such places as London to talk about Buddhism and Burma's efforts. A member of the Rangoon University's Pali Department, he was well known as an Abhidhamma lecturer. He promoted such causes also as the Tiger School, a Burmese social service project of considerable fame and success (see Chapter 6). Also willing to travel and promote Burmese Buddhism was the famous Mahasi Sayadaw, U Thawbana, whose Thathana Yeiktha meditation center in Rangoon has been mentioned many times. He even established a center in Ceylon. Other missionary monks such as U Pyinnyadipa and U Kowida also worked as missionaries, but U Thittila and the Mahasi Sayadaw are the best known.

This brief introduction of some of the individual members of the Sangha who epitomize the "political monks" of the Nu government era illustrates the type of involvement and commitment that characterized politics and the Sangha during the period of the Sangayana's preparation and presentation. Basically the Nu government seems to have attempted to work through the Pakokku sect, just as Mindon created and then tried to use the Shwegyin. We can also see that the Thudhamma monks were courted by both Mindon and Nu at the same time that overtures were made all the while to the reformist sects. Unlike the royal days, however, the 1950s saw the full flowering of organized Sangha pressure groups or task-centered groups never dreamed of in the Vinaya, as the Sangha became involved with the innumerable councils and committees spawned by modern politics. A portrait of the Sangha's involvement with the Sangayana would not be complete without a review of the two basic organizations in which the Sangha most actively participated in response to government hopes.

The State Monks in Council

Many of the monks just discussed were members of the SSC, or Supreme Sangha Council.[100] This group of twenty-six monks, drawn from the whole of Burma, had charge of the ecclesiastical arrangements for the Sangayana. The SSC was apparently formed in 1951 by a group of Ovadacariya ecclesiastical judges, who, in essence, had been created by the government in the Vinicchaya Htana Act of 1949. A 1952 report confirms the nature of the group then planning the Sangayana. This highly important role of government judges appears to have eluded investigators to date, and yet the Sangayana can barely be understood without it: "The *Bhikkhus* [monks] attending the conference were the Union *Ovadacarya Maha Theras* and the Union *Vinayadhara Maha Theras* appointed under the *Vinicchaya Thana* Act [Ecclesiastical Courts Act] and *Agga Maha Pandita Maha Theras* [the monks on whom the title AMP. had been conferred for their learning]."[101]

AMP monks were therefore consulted along with ecclesiastical court monks in the Sangayana organization proceedings, and while it is true that the title was granted to monks for their learning on many occasions, the needs of the SSC and the government generally were not forgotten. Thus, if we look at the monks who were members of the SSC at one time or another, we find that out of twenty-six monks eighteen held the

100. Also known as the Bharanittharaka Mahatheras or the Council of Wunh-saung Sayadaws.
101. *Sangayana Monthly Bulletin*, 1, no. 1 (May 1953):11; *Sangayana Souvenir*, 1, no. 12 (1954):4–5; *Burma*, 4, no. 2 (Jan. 1954):1–4.

title of AMP, two of them being *rattagurus*. There appear to have been
two major awards ceremonies to grant AMP's, in 1953 and again in
1956, both of which can be linked to the needs of the SSC. The first
provided the SSC with eight monks; the second with four: a total of
twelve of the eighteen AMP's. Besides providing for the SSC, the 1953
awards also gave three AMP's to the Pali Education Board, two to the
Pali University Council, and two to the four-man committee appointed
to study the teaching of Buddhism in schools. The 1956 awards gave the
SSC its energetic secretary and joint secretary as well as two members to
the Pali Education Board and two members, including a secretary, to
the Pali University Council. Of the other main awards made during the
time of the Sangayana, that of 1955 seems to have been devoted mainly
to learning in that it provided no one for the SSC but gave two AMP's to
the Education Board and three to the Pali University Council.

The government manifestly tried hard to include the sects. Out of the
twenty-six monks on the SSC, sixteen were Thudhamma; as many as
seven were Shwegyin, including the vice president of that sect, U
Nyanawuntha, the energetic joint secretary U Withudda and the person-
able, English-speaking Anisekhan Sayadaw; one was Dwaya; and
Pakokku was represented by the Mahawithudarama Sayadaw and the
powerful Payagyi Taik Sayadaw of Rangoon. We must, however, realize
that the SSC was itself superseded by the Ovadacariya Sangha Nayaka
Committee (OSNC), which acted as an executive committee, much as
the Buddha Sasana Council was a symbolic or public body while real
power was held by its Executive Committee. I was not able to find a list
of the original members of the OSNC, but I believe they were quite
similar to those in the SSC: that is, AMP's, Union ecclesiastical judges,
and monks elected by the SSC from the following areas: two monks
each from North and South Shan States; three learned Burmese monks;
five monks each from Ceylon and Thailand; three from Cambodia; and
two from Laos. It was the OSNC that was to advise both the Supreme
Sangha Council and the government, and it was their task to select the
Sangayana editors and provide the four requisites for their maintenance.

At a 1951 planning session of the OSNC, presided over by the
Nyaungyan Sayadaw, the crucial decision was made on the number of
monks to be invited to the Sixth Council. Here it was laid down that
2,000 Burmese monks and 500 foreign monks from four Theravada
countries would be invited, the total symbolizing the 2,500th anniversary

of Buddhism. There would be five two-year councils minus the *wa* (Lent) and *katthein* (robe presentation) periods, when presumably the monks would return to their monasteries. At each session 425 Burmese monks and 75 foreigners would chant the texts.

There are signs that the government was not able to have its own way entirely in the matter of inviting even the Burmese monks, though such signs are rarely allowed to appear in the official reports. A number of famous scholars do not appear in the lists, and I know from personal contact with them that they did not wish to leave the monasteries for this arduous work. It was evidently not always easy for *sayadaw*s to get away. In a radio announcement of 1954, a rather curious passage appears:

> In the combined conference of the *Ovadacariya Sangha Nayaka Maha-theras* [OSNC] and *Bharanittharaka Mahatheras* [SSC] held recently at the Thathana Yeiktha, it was decided that all the Burmese *Bhikkhus* [monks] who have not yet participated in the preparations for the holding of the *Chattha Sangayana* [Sixth Council] and who are competent to take part in the proceedings be chosen, and a *Bhikkhu* from each such centre be invited to the Great Council. Pursuant to this resolution, requests have been made to 15 centres for nominating a competent *Bhikkhu* each, and so far only a few replies have been received. I hereby humbly request that the remaining centres will kindly send in the names of the *Bhikkhu*s they desire to select for the purpose of taking part in the proceedings of the Sixth Great Buddhist Council.
>
> The Deputy Commissioners, Regional Representatives of the B.S.C. and the various Township Officials have been requested to send in the names of those *Bhikkhu*s who are competent to participate in the proceedings of the Sixth G.B.C. As the time for holding of the *Chattha Sangayana* is drawing near, I would request that the officers concerned would kindly expedite despatch of the names of competent *Bhikkhus*.[102]

The same bulletin reports that some 700 Mandalay and up-country monks would come from Mandalay, while 200 would come to Rangoon from Pakokku, Nyaung-U, Yenangyaung, and Thayetmyo, and 60 from Prome. This leaves the figure of 1,040 monks for Lower Burma. The emphasis is significant in terms of the Upper Burmese Sangha's partici-pation. If U Nu had had his way, the Sangayana would have lasted a full ten years, and these monks would have made quite a migration By my visit in 1958, however, the proceedings at the Sangayana were being held in such a desultory fashion that it was difficult indeed to

102. *Sangayana Souvenir*, 1, no. 12 (1954):33.

visualize the flourish and promise of the great opening. As the other government projects in the Buddhist Revival and the political rivalries represented by the YBA and KSA are reviewed in next chapter, it should be recalled that when a government representative spoke at the opening of the new Kalyani ordination hall at Kaba Aye in 1954 he said that he hoped it would reunite the Sangha in Burma as its namesake had done in days of old.[103] Such indeed was the idealism of both the Revival and the Sangayana.

The Ultimate Quest for Autonomy

To review, in this chapter we have seen how the Buddha Sasana Council grew out of the association founded in 1947 known as the Buddha Sasana Nuggaha Ahpwe, and how it came to dominate the whole religious scene in Burma, entrusted as it was with the virtual management of the Sangayana. It originated in the midst of a relatively small group of persons, men whom one could describe as British-educated, right-wing gentlemen of the old school, members of the important families which had assumed or received office under the British regime and had been to a large extent dispossessed of office by the younger Thakins who led the 1936 university strike. The Buddha Sasana Nuggaha Ahpwe originally differed little from other lay societies and associations of its type, but the government eventually established a dominating association by monopolizing little by little the whole field of lay organized religious behavior and by gradually giving it a national coloring through its control of governmental religious programs. It became tied in with other instruments of governmental policy—such as the ecclesiastical courts—and, by patronizing and furthering those already in authority through those instruments, it seems to have tried to take over the functions of the *thathanabaing* in the old royal system. In short, the process appears to have been one of ascribing supreme power to monks while in effect keeping control over them: the Sangayana caused the monks to shine on a stage that was theirs and theirs only, but it was the BSC that chose the actors, invited the audience, and made the most of the play's box-office value, within the country and with the help of outside visitors.

103. *New Times of Burma,* July 17, 1954. Here Kalyani refers to the famous fifteenth-century site in Burma which was the center of King Dhammaceti's Sangha reforms. See Chapter 1.

My concern is not so much with the international aspirations of the creators of the Sangayana nor with its history but rather with the BSC as an agency of the government, operating within the framework of a ministry which in many ways was superseded by its offspring. The BSC had considerable impact upon the Sangha, much as Mindon had a hundred years before. My principal aim here, as so often in this book, has been to support the thesis that Burma is led, when it can be said to be led at all, by very small groups that have, for a time, triumphed over other, very similar, small groups—the triumph being mainly one of persons rather than policies, though the Cold War had by the 1950s begun to bring policies in with a vengeance. The triumph, however, is of such a nature that the vanquished groups rarely vanish but rather carry on side by side with the winning group, performing more or less the same tasks as that group, until they die out or merge with their most successful competitors. In such a world, where personalities and charismatic leadership are all-important, the victorious group in turn splits up, and the process begins again. Because it is more important for a Burman to achieve his own ends than to prevent another from achieving his—in that it is also important to appear to honor or actually to honor a nonviolent ethic and to safeguard the rights of the vanquished—the defeated groups tend to persist for a very long time without apparently fulfilling any very rich social functions. Perhaps, though, this is the function they fulfill: to allow each one his quest for personal autonomy. In the words of an informant cited above, "Thus no individual ever comes to be completely controlled by one group." Certainly the Burmese Sangha can be said to have learned that lesson well.

6. The Sangha and the Politics of Revivalism

So far we have concentrated upon the religious aspects of the Revival, and thus we have tended to emphasize the Sangayana. There is no doubt that it was the high point of the whole Revival effort, but by no means was it the only one. In this chapter, we will review some of the other efforts of the Nu government to promote Buddhism. As usual, particular attention will be paid to the relationships between the state and the Sangha. Politics become extremely important in the final days of the Revival because the Nu government's proposals for Buddhism and the Sangha became embroiled in potentially explosive national and international rivalries.

American Foundations and Notions of Sangha Education

One such proposal that caused considerable debate and concern was the Institute for Advanced Buddhist Studies, which was a relatively late addition to the Ministry of Religion's domain. The Institute should be seen as a continuation of the government's long-standing interest in education, as evident in the Pali University concept (with its accompanying exams) and in concern for the welfare of the Pakokku and Payagyi "university" *taik*s. A brief history of the Institute will illustrate the government's position. In early 1953 a representative of the Ford Foundation arrived in Burma to consult about plans for an international Pali university.[1] In late 1953 an agreement about this was signed between Ford and the Ministry of National Planning and Religious Affairs,[2] and in 1954 a special four-month course in library science and museology was held at the United States Information Service Library for future employees of the university.[3] The foundation stone for the Institute was

1. *Burma Weekly Bulletin,* n.s., 1, no. 51 (Mar. 25, 1953):3.
2. *Burma,* 8, no. 2 (Jan. 1958):66.
3. *Burma Weekly Bulletin,* n.s., 3, no. 19 (Aug. 11, 1954):138–139.

laid by U Nu in 1954 in the neighborhood of the Great Cave assembly hall of the Sangayana at Kaba Aye, and, under the direction of Niharranjan Ray, consultant, the Institute began buying its first books and collecting its first sets of gifts, both books and other objects.[4] In the meantime, Hpe Aung, Lecturer in Philosophy, University of Rangoon, and Hla Maung, Lecturer in Burmese at Moulmein College, were studying library science at Columbia University under the auspices of the Institute of International Education and Cecil Hobbs of the Library of Congress; they subsequently toured oriental institutes in London, Paris, and Leiden.[5] The Institute for Advanced Buddhist Studies started functioning in 1955, and the two travelers took up the posts of director and deputy director in that same year.[6] In 1956 the buildings being unfinished, the offices of the Institute were shifted from the Apparagawyana Buildings to the Buddha Sasana Council (BSC), where they were still uneasily situated in 1958–1959. In 1956 the Institute was transferred from the Ministry of Union Culture to the Ministry of Religious Affairs, and in 1957 Hpe Aung was appointed head of a separate department at the ministry.[7] These are the bare facts of the Institute's founding and development, but the issues behind these details are important and complex, for they involve basic conflicts between the West and Burma over concepts of religion, and they reveal disagreements within Burma as to the function of the Sangha in a modern world. We will begin with the roles of the foundation and the government in terms of the idea of converting the Sangayana site into the Institute for Advanced Buddhist Studies, since the Sangayana would come to a close eventually.

The direction in which the Ford Foundation and, perhaps at first, the government seemed to be going is indicated in a paper dated November 10, 1955, by the above-mentioned Niharranjan Ray, an Indian scholar known for his studies on Burmese Buddhist history, who was appointed adviser on cultural affairs to the Union of Burma under the Ford program. His short paper begins with much praise of Burmese Buddhism and introduces its proposals in a very diplomatic fashion. Buddhism being "another name for essential humanism," it is hoped that, besides

4. Ibid., no. 1 (April 7, 1954):1, 8.
5. Ibid., no. 26 (Sept. 29, 1954):195.
6. *Burma*, 8, no. 2 (Jan. 1958): 81; *Burma Weekly Bulletin*, n.s., 4, no. 37 (Nov. 15, 1955):296.
7. *Burma*, 8, no. 2 (Jan. 1958):63–66.

Buddhism itself, the important humanities may find a place at the proposed university at Kaba Aye. The author opines that such a university's aims and ideals are best served by a residential type of organization: the buildings at Kaba Aye for the Sangayana, the site itself, its distance from the city center, and the fact that Rangoon University is not residential all give weight to this proposal. The difficulties of establishing another rival university within five miles of that of Rangoon are only glanced at: the facts that the existing Rangoon University serves general academic purposes while the proposed Institute's structure will be specialized, for the Buddhist clergy, and Parliament's omnipotence in legislating necessary charters, are mentioned but not stressed. These difficulties are of great importance, however, as will be shown.[8]

Previous government studies on improving Pali education had always resisted the idea of a model college which would inspire the organization and curricula of the existing affiliated monasteries. However, in Ray's paper the idea is resurrected in a more powerful form. The state-supported Pali *taik*s are defined as the traditional educational system of the Buddhist clergy, and that system is to be left untouched. Nonetheless, he writes, some monks feel the need for a wider ecclesiastical education, embracing not only Pali and Buddhism but also allied languages and religious systems, the history of Buddhism in various parts of the world, the history and geography of East, Southeast, and South Asia, as well as the rudiments of such subjects as sociology or elementary science: "This would go a long way to give the venerable monks a wider background and make them better and more useful leaders of their religion and society, and also better preachers of the pristine doctrines of the Lord Buddha." Such proposed change was a much discussed point in Burma! But the author continues: "At the same time the proposed University should not, in my humble opinion, be closed to lay members of the Buddhist society of Burma and her neighbouring countries and to other willing entrants of non-Buddhist faiths and climes." A mixture of lay and ecclesiastical elements is necessary to combat the traditional, static, and perhaps obscurantist tendencies found in purely monastic organizations. A mixture of secular and religious subjects was encour-

8. Ray is briefly referred to in *Burma*, 8, no. 2 (Jan. 1958):61. There is also a text on Ray and U Hpe Aung in *Burma*, 7, no. 1 (Oct. 1956):51. The quotes here are from a paper provided by the Ministry of Religious Affairs; I am not completely certain that this was written by Ray.

aged in the ancient universities of the Buddhist world, and the Western divinity schools are also encouraging such bilateral approaches.

The rest of the paper deals with a modernized curriculum, the undergraduate division, the role of the institute in providing doctorates and master's degrees as a part of the new "university," the plans for the administration, and the hope that the institution will take root in the soil of the people. It is said that Parliament and the Buddha Sasana Council are committed to a Buddhist residential university as well as to an institute. The latter is halfway to completion; the former has hardly been thought of. The author expresses hope that his proposals may speed this process.

I noticed during my stay that the University of Rangoon made little effort to embrace the plan, and I concluded that the University of Rangoon must have felt secure in the knowledge that the oldest Burmese traditions in effect guaranteed the plan's failure by virtually forbidding the Sangha and laity to be educated together. There was constant disagreement over habitation rights in the Sangayana hostels at Kaba Aye, with a traditionalist party, mainly centered in the Buddha Sasana Council, refusing to allow lay people to live in buildings which had, during the Sangayana, served as monasteries. (One of the first suggestions put to me by the director of the Institute was that I should ask to live in the hostels as a test case against such traditionalists.) Thus, when Ray confuses the question of lay and ecclesiastical participation in the university with that of a mixture of secular and religious subjects in its curriculum, he is either being overly diplomatic or failing to grasp the most important cancer at the very heart of his scheme. That aspect of Burmese ecclesiastical-lay relationships involved a reluctance to allow the monk to participate in advanced education, perhaps to keep down ecclesiastical participation in the country's affairs. This was a very strong, if not always explicit, tradition.

Another serious difficulty was that the plan called for a rector of the Institute and university who would by definition have to be a Westerner, and yet the BSC was supposed to agree to not only the appointment but also the whole organization in advance. Here we have the elements of a stalemate which was to dog the two Ministry of Religious Affairs agencies until the military government of General Ne Win virtually put an end to both their aspirations. During my whole stay in Burma, the

Institute and the BSC were at daggers drawn over the matter of the university, thus effectively preventing any progress whatsoever in this direction. And the conflict raged mainly over the expected topic: the BSC wished to make of its own Dhammadhuta College (established in 1952) the undergraduate core of the proposed new Buddhist university, while the Institute was obliged to support a rival body known as the Sangha University.

The prospectus of the Institute's Sangha University sets forth an astonishingly heterogeneous but very familiar set of aims that can be summarized as follows: (1) to produce missionary monks capable of preaching to the modern world, both at home and abroad, in a modern manner, fully equipped with mundane knowledge; (2) to give vocational guidance to young people, based on Buddhist principles; (3) to forestall the imminent decline of monastic prestige resulting from monks attending private secular schools run by laymen; (4) to establish a special Sangha University with high standards; (5) to provide adequate instruction for foreign monks and laymen coming to Burma for Buddhist studies; (6) to correct errors of interpretation in foreign translations of Buddhist texts and to foster the purest form of Buddhism: (7) to conduct extensive research and pilgrimage tours within and outside of Burma; (8) to conduct seminars at the university or other suitable places; (9) to offer classes in subjects bearing on missionary work; (10) to practice meditation at suitable centers and in turn to disseminate teaching based on *vipassana;*[9] (11) to send qualified graduates of the university abroad and inland; (12) to assist other like-minded bodies; (13) to aid in construction of pagodas, shrines, monasteries, and other sanctuaries; (14) to contact established universities in other countries for the purpose of educational exchange; and (15) to give above all unstinted devotion to the cause of Buddhism so that it may spread through the whole world.

The entrance qualifications laid down were that those monks shall be admitted who have passed a *dhammacariya* examination or a matriculation examination, or were visiting monks from other countries. In effect the entrance requirements restricted the students to a small number of very intelligent monks. The subjects listed as taught were as follows: missionary methods, Pali literature, Abhidhamma, Buddhist literature,

9. *Vipassana* (P): insight. A method of meditation.

Burmese, English,[10] mathematics, geography, history, general science, logic, philosophy and ethics, psychology, and comparative religion.

When I attended a ceremony of the Sangha University and heard the formal speeches, I was struck by the emphasis upon missionary efforts in the English-speaking world. The burden of virtually all the speeches was the need for learning English as a universal language and as the key to understanding the peoples missionaries would work among. The principle *sayadaw* in his talk humorously noted that the Buddhist missionary monk no longer had to deal with clownish ignoramuses but instead faced redoubtable enemies as well as very perceptive friends. The director *sayadaw* also referred to his visit to England and concentrated his fire on Christian apologetics, stressing the need for redressing the balance in this field. The keynotes were learning English and missionizing the West. After the meeting a nonsympathetic layman, in rebuttal to the director's promotion of modernization of the Sangha, said to me, "But, you see, the whole system of traditional education depends on this learning by rote, on using the memory. The whole system is upset and disrupted by Western methods. Critical methods if you like. Take Ceylon. Errors have crept into the texts, respect for monks is on the decline. People do not take off their shoes and bow to the monks in the proper way." This is the vital issue—Burmese versus Western notions of education—and such tensions are involved with Dhammadhuta College as well.

Backed by the BSC, Dhammadhuta College started in 1952. It seems to have had a relationship with the Payagyi Taik through its second head administrator. Its growth was not impressive; a 1958 BSC report on the college states that enrollment grew from 16 monks in 1952 to 38 in 1958, including 11 Burmese, 13 Japanese, 12 Laotians, and 2 Cambodian monks. Requirements for admission were successful completion of the *dhammacariya* examination or an equivalent foreign standard and a keen desire to do missionary work. Students were selected by the Education Subcommittee of the BSC and then had "to sign a bond with the Union Buddha Sasana Council which undertakes to provide food,

10. At the director's request, I volunteered to teach some 12–15 sessions of English classes, ostensibly to the entire student body of about eighty but really to the thirty or so who actually came regularly. My teaching, I am afraid, was extremely haphazard, but I must record the students' warm and touching gratitude for anything I could teach them, and I found them to be a handful of obviously intelligent and active students.

lodging, yellow robes, medical aid, and other contingent expenses for all the selected students" (Burma 1958:14–15).

The curriculum involved such expected items as the Abhidhamma and the history and essence of Buddhism, but also psychology, comparative religion, and English, not to mention a detailed English curriculum where lectures in English by U Nu and U Chan Htoon figured side by side with abridged versions of *As You Like It* and *David Copperfield.*

By the time of my stay it was generally known that many at the college were in a state of despair and felt as if they had been completely abandoned by the college's political sponsors. The lack of teachers was desperate, particularly in English-language courses. Tensions between the Sangha University and Dhammadhuta College existed even though the institutions at times shared the same *sayadaw* lecturers!

Apparently the BSC position was that they had been first on the scene: those who had used the Sangayana hostels during the Sixth Council should be allowed to use them for *the* university, which they obviously felt they had founded in the form of Dhammadhuta College. The BSC viewed the appearance of the Institute and its Sangha University with no enthusiasm whatsoever. This situation, influenced by invisible manipulation on the part of foundations and the two educational institutions, continued for the greater part of my stay. There is some evidence that the director of the Institute, while a very good friend of Prime Minister U Nu, on the one hand, also had good standing with the army. He lectured frequently to army officers, and, during the first army administration, the Sangha University acquired its own building at Kaba Aye. Evidence in the documents indicates that the army was prepared to favor the Institute at the expense of the BSC. Thus, in a 1959 document (Burma 1959b:64–66), the Institute was featured, the BSC not mentioned at all. In a later publication (Burma 1960:465), the Institute was used in startling manner to show how efficient the army was.[11]

Also, while the original plan for the Institute assumed a Western approach, the form that eventually triumphed was Burmese in essence and in personnel. Thus the director and deputy-director were Burmans, and visiting professors from abroad became their subordinates rather than their equals. Likewise lower in the scale, two foreign "local re-

11. The BSC is mentioned very briefly in the 1960 report.

search" scholars were under the charge of not a Westerner with the usual self-flattering view of his own potentiality to help but of a "special research scholar," who was eventually to obtain a scholarship himself to the United States and thus supplement and supplant the foreigners. The process of "Burmanization" could not have been carried further. Even so, the total effect of the Institute and the competing college and university is debatable. Some of the monks involved, such as the leader of one of the two competing educational institutions, were close to despair, but fortunately the number of monks so influenced was small indeed. The impact upon the Sangha of some of the ideas concerned was, however, a more important matter. One such "idea" was the social service and missionary ideal promoted by internationally oriented Buddhists and many Western foundation people, in particular.

Missionary Monks and Social Service

As already noted in Chapter 5 the BSNA (Buddha Sasana Nuggaha Ahpwe) had a great interest in the Burma Hill Tracts Buddhist Mission, and many government monks played key roles in its formation, such as the Nyaungyan, Sandayon, Mahawithudarama (Pakokku), and the Payagyi Taik Sayadaws. The government had closely watched the progress of the BSNA and had quickly seen the importance of its propagation work and effectiveness. Whether this was anything more than U Nu watching U Nu is hard to say. We are told that the government had set aside money for the support of the four great religions of Burma and that, in view of the impressive progress of the BSNA, the funds earmarked for Buddhism had been handed over in part to this organization. One of the first actions of the BSNA at its fourth executive meeting in 1948 was to decide to give help to the Burma Hill Tracts Buddhist Mission. From a religious budget of 400,000 *kyat*s, a sum of 250,000 was allocated to the Hills, while 100,000 was reserved for use in Burma and 50,000 for use in foreign countries.

Buddhist mission schools were apparently established in the Chin Hills, Naga Hills, Kachin Hills, and other non-Buddhist areas. As early as 1951 a group of social-service–minded monks through their Sangha Parahita Ahpwegyok (SPA) organization is said to have reorganized and given support to thirteen monasteries in the Kayah State. The usual pattern of activity would seem to be the establishment of first a monastery, then monastic or lay schools, with accompanying distribution of clothes and medicine. In 1951 sixty-five monks were sent out "to those Hill areas and up to now over 52,000 people of those areas have embraced Buddhism; over 4,000 people also have been given education." The Buddha Sasana Council's 1954 report refers to support of the All-Burma Blind Welfare School of Pakokku, an establishment with some forty-five pupils created in 1937 and run by a monk; reference is made as well to the Assam Hill Tracts Mission and the Bengal Buddhist Association of Calcutta.[12] The BSC's 1956 report (Burma 1956b:25) states tersely that there were by then 95 mission centers all over Burma with 95 Buddhist missionaries, "the children in these regions" being "trained in Burmese and Buddhist literature and 38 lay teachers [being] engaged for that purpose." The 1958 report does not mention the Hill Tract Missions at all.

Behind the figures is a story of diminishing returns—a few Buddhist converts and a few *shinbyu*s (initiation ceremonies for novices) held by Burmese monks and local leaders who had found it convenient to "choose" Buddhism; these compensated little for the failure of adequate programs for the Hill populations as a whole. The *shinbyu*s appear to have been held mainly in the Kachin Myitkyina area, which has a sizable population of ethnic Burmans.[13] I was not able to visit any BSC mission, but I was several times given to understand that only the greatest devotion born of personal choice led monks into remote areas where less than customary attention was paid to them and where consequently sustenance was more of a problem. Many "council" monks appear to have become discouraged under such circumstances.[14]

Nor do Buddha Sasana Council adventures in the missionary field

12. *International Buddhist News Forum*, 2, no. 12 (Dec. 1962):22; Burma 1954:3.

13. *Sangayana Souvenir* 1954:39.

14. F. K. Lehman (personal communication, 1973) offers a contrasting view: "Between 1957 and 1961, my years in the Chin Hills, the Buddhist missions were truly beginning to take hold at Haka, Mindat and Matupi, at least. In the Kayah state, unevenly also. I care little for the 1958 report's failure to mention the hill missions, because I saw them going on actively." Lehman thus takes issue with my evaluation of the missionary movement and the modernization of the Sangha efforts. Perhaps if and when research is possible in these areas again, matters such as these can be clarified.

abroad appear to have had much success. A considerable number of visits to and from other Buddhist countries, largely in connection with the Sangayana, have already been mentioned, but those were different from missionary work proper. In the latter field, the following cases may be mentioned. One Burmese monk was sent to Phnom Penh at the request of the head of the Cambodian Order and was reportedly "daily teaching Burmese to a class of 200 pupils, comprising Burmese and Cambodian people." In Bangkok, two Burmese monks held Abhidhamma and *vipassana* classes. The English-speaking lecturer in Abhidhamma at the University of Rangoon, president of both the Dhammadhuta College and the Sangha University, was invited by both England and Australia, and this monk did visit the latter on occasion. But the most ambitious venture, in which the prime minister was most interested personally, concerned Japan. As the Burmese view has it, certain Japanese during the war and also during visits to the Sangayana as observers and to the Third World Fellowship of Buddhists meeting in Rangoon at the time of the Sangayana, had become interested in the "pristine" teaching and the possibility of introducing it into Japan.[15]

Early contacts between the Burmese and Japanese Buddhists were undoubtedly enthusiastic. Missions were sent, societies formed, teaching centers founded, monks trained in Japanese culture, and ground broken for new pagodas. Efforts at Dhammadhuta College were hardly adequate, however, no matter how ambitious, and by the time of my visit in 1958, the Japanese I interviewed showed little enthusiasm for the program and were planning to rejoin their own sects after returning to Japan.

To one at all familiar with the very large number of alternative forms of religious allegiance open to the modern Japanese and also with the effervescence of "New Religions" in that country, it would not seem unlikely that some Japanese might have taken a passing fancy to the Burmese version of Buddhism. Perhaps political and economic considerations were also involved, though the Japanese official role appears to have been small. It is doubtful whether many Japanese could take seriously the Burmese claim to possessing the "pristine" teaching. More likely an urge to travel and to acquire a free education were, as they so often are in Asia, the main motivations, whatever purpose the Japanese visits may have served in the minds of the BSC personnel.

15. Burma 1954:21; 1956b:22.

While there are few successes to report in its missionary efforts, the BSC seems to have done slightly better with its social service projects. Insofar as the Buddhist monastery had always been a source of education and advice in the society, sporadic acts of social service no doubt have always characterized Buddhist organizations in traditional Burma. Though no statistics were found on the subject, a number of orphans and mistreated and abandoned children probably found their way, in the villages, into the care of the monks, there to be brought up and educated—as likely as not, perhaps, to become monks in their turn. Very little organized service of this kind, however, was manifest before World War II. When social service did become manifest in the formation of formal organizations, the causes appear to have been threefold. To begin with, during the war a great number of displaced persons and orphans took refuge with monks, and when the war ended an embarrassing number of these, especially children, stayed on. We know from other accounts that education and the social services were among the things most disorganized by the war in Burma. Following close on this immediate reason for action came increased competition with other religious bodies after national independence had been achieved. Third, we have seen that, during the period of my visit, certain monks came to be understandably worried about the recruitment problem and to realize that if most youths sought a modern, lay education, the monasteries would soon be depopulated and the Sangha could not continue its work. Against this background the social service movement within the Order can best be examined.[16]

The ideological background of the formation of a social service organization for the Sangha needs some exposition. Despite the occasional acts of social service customary for monasteries in royal Burma, the feeling has always been in that country that the principal aim of monks should be their own search for enlightenment and that they should not be distracted from this by any worldly pursuits albeit of the most charitable kind. Thus, acts of social service are not traditionally performed as a matter of course or in consonance with any Buddhist theory on the subject, but rather are the natural outcome of usually good and ethically minded Burmans living, with some freedom, among their respectful and grateful fellow-countrymen. A point closely tied to this concerns the general nature of lay gifts to the Sangha and the religion. It was already

16. Cf. Spiro 1970:284–290.

apparent to me, before going to Burma, that the whole nature of Burmese society might well be changed if Burmese changed their views about what actions constituted meritorious deeds. Overwhelmingly, these have consisted in gifts to the Sangha, primarily of food but also of buildings and various facilities and basic requirements. In Western terms this is hardly to be viewed as social service, nor can water jars set up by the roadside for passing thirsts be valued greatly in this respect. The whole atmosphere of the Buddhist Revival taken together with the socialist programs instituted by U Nu's government did perhaps suggest that Buddhism and socialism could be conjugated to the extent of making social service a part of the acquisition of merit.

There was, of course, opposition to the melding of Buddhism and socialism particularly in terms of involving the monks in organized social service work. Perhaps the clearest expression of the dissenting viewpoint is from the Australian Buddhist U Ohn Ghine (David Maurice), who remained within the orthodox framework as editor of the BSC *Light of the Dhamma* and yet spoke out as few cared to do:

Your [editorial] leader of today's date [Jan. 20, 1959] seems to envisage the breaking of the 227 rules of *Vinaya* of the *Sangha* and hails as encouraging the news that an association of American theists has persuaded a section of the *Sangha* to undertake social service training.
May I beg to differ?
The *Bhikkhu*s [monks] . . . have their work, work that is even above social service. Please note the key-word "even" as social service is a high and worthy avocation. But another key-word is "above."[17]

The author went on to argue that the Sangha has the highest possible task of teaching the preachings of the Buddha and of providing a cure for the world's ills. The task of the Sangha is not merely to offer a palliative in a world growing more and more degenerate, even if, as the leader contended, the Sangha itself is also degenerating in many quarters. Ohn Ghine argued from the *Digha Nikaya* text that the word *parahita* (the welfare of others) has nothing whatsoever to do with "social service" and suggested that, if monks wish to devote themselves to what is indeed a fine ideal for Buddhist *laymen*, they should leave the robe. He had a few words also for the American foundation involved: "If the foreign association financing the show will stick to its original purpose

17. *Light of the Dhamma,* 6, no. 1 (Jan. 1959).

of fighting communism and lay off its desire to change our religion, so much the better for all concerned."[18]

Those who wished to rebut the above position cited passages of the Buddhist scriptures, the exemplary competitors in Burma's Christian missions, or the respected Ramakrishna groups, but perhaps the best way to understand those who favored monastic social service is to look at the Tiger School, which is where the first Sangha social service organization, the Sangha Parahita Ahpwegyok, began. The school was founded by U Pinnyazawta in 1920 as a monastery school, just a few miles outside Rangoon. The place became the Tiger Monastery when two rich Chinese brothers, who had made their fortune out of a popular medicine known as Tiger Balm, dedicated a school with buildings and furniture in 1924.[19] At this time the government recognized the primary school and began to make grants in aid. In 1925 the government made the Tiger Monastery a middle school and also opened a primary teachers' training school on the same premises. The "Tiger Balm brothers" went on contributing heavily until 1942, when the monastery was taken over by its present leader, U Nyaneinda. Under the Japanese, the Japanese language was forcibly added to the curriculum. When the British returned, the Tiger Anglo-Vernacular School was the first educational establishment to begin functioning again in the Insein district.

In 1945 some elderly refugees approached the *sayadaw* of the Tiger Monastery on the subject of starting a vocational school there to teach needed skills to orphans and displaced children. A provisional body was formed which began giving charity shows and collecting funds. Thus the Tiger Orphans' Vocational School opened in 1946 and soon acquired a full governing body. The school opened with 28 boys and went through three years of hardship, mitigated a little by union government grants but mostly by an opportune visit from the Tiger Balm brothers in 1950. By 1953, however, the place was a high school with over 1,000 students, many from the surrounding quarter, and with a full staff of teachers, the monks being spared from this activity.[20]

18. *New Times of Burma*, Jan. 21, 1959. Cf. *The Nation*, Jan. 20, 1959. On *parahita*, see Davids and Davids 1921:224.

19. I am very much indebted for much of the following information to Maung Sein Myint's "A Study of the Tiger Orphans' Vocational School" (Sein Myint 1957).

20. The twelfth Annual Report claims an enrollment of 2,200, including kindergarten pupils. night-school students, "5 deformed and 2 blind."

The present plant consists of an area of some seven acres on which are found sixteen monasteries, three hostels for residents, school buildings for the primary, middle, and high schools, a kitchen, a dining room, a shrine room, and an artesian well supplying both the complex and the neighborhood. The vocational facilities were initiated with a building donated in 1948 by the local agent of the Eveready Flashlight Company. Various individuals donated machines, and three more came from the Directorate of Education together with the pledge of an annual grant. In 1949 the Ministry of Industry intervened with two machines and some Japanese reparation funds fed to the school by U Nu and Finance Minister U Tin. The Tiger Balm millionaires stepped in shortly afterward with another 50,000 *kyats*. Similar charitable acts financed everything from the hostels and monks' dining hall and kitchen to a complete brass band. At the same time, it was stated that the school had always made it a policy not to depend on grants but to work toward self-sufficiency through the sale of its products, even though advertising was prohibited because of Vinaya scruples. U Nyaneinda once stated that, while foreign aid is fine, one cannot always exist "by breathing through another's nose."

All monks, members of the governing body, and a medical officer gave their services free. In 1958 the Tiger monasteries housed twenty monks and five novices. The four vocational staff teachers were paid by the monastery, while the thirty teachers of the government schools in the complex were paid by the Education Department. A give-and-take arrangement satisfactory to everybody seemed to exist: the monasteries had state schools on their premises; in return for this their orphans could go to the schools and could be supported at night schools and provided with further education by the surrounding population.

In organizations involving the Sangha, success frequently depends on the initiative and persuasive powers of the monk in charge, together with a favorable *taga* (lay supporter) situation (as in the case of the Tiger Balm brothers). The old saw about the success of success, however, is also applicable here: government agencies were apparently glad to help organizations which were already doing well by themselves, especially in cases where good school facilities were available on monastic premises. This kind of bias had been built into the Burmese situation with the "criteria for recognition" of the British educational authorities. The pattern continued into modern times, for it is clear that social service support funds went to establishments already doing well by themselves instead of the backward institutions most in need of help.

The initiative for the formal foundation of the Sangha Parahita Ahpwegyok (SPA), the Sangha social service group, came from U Nyaneinda of the Tiger School, backed by U Pawara of the Mandalay orphanage and other leading *sayadaws*. In 1956, a meeting was convened at the Tiger School. In the course of this, five permanent leaders were appointed: U Thittila, AMP, of Rangoon University and four *sayadaws* from other successful orphanages and vocational schools.

By 1956 there were 28 schools in the SPA organization caring for a total of 1,367 children, while a 1957 source records 37 schools with 2,650 children plus a total of some 17,000 day students. As the SPA progressed, it began to prefer "the enhancement of the efficiency standard of existing branches to the increase of such branches," and it thus instituted fairly rigorous screening procedures. The SPA, at its inception, appears to have received the support of a number of famous monks. A meeting was held at Mandalay in 1956 or 1957 chaired by noted monks, such as the Masoyein and Hanthawaddy Sayadaws, as well as by the eminent Shwegyin author and disciplinarian, the Mahagandayon Sayadaw U Zanakabiwuntha. The Shweman Sayadaw gave the concluding address. In a personal conversation with U Zanakabiwuntha, however, I was told that, while he did not disapprove of the SPA, he would not join himself as he did not feel that it fitted with his own very strict concept of Vinaya. Most of the names above indicate that the SPA was not unfriendly to the government.

In 1959, after a previous experiment with some 30 monks, the SPA held a six-week seminar at the Tiger School for 68 monks from all over Burma as well as for some laymen associated with the orphanages. Leading Sangayana monks, professional social workers, teachers, and government officials gave lectures and demonstrations, and discussions were held on a seminar basis to share the personal experiences of individual participants. Stress was laid on contemporary concepts of social welfare work, the importance of vocational training, the health and care of the child, and his integration into the community after departure from the school, as well as more modern methods of finance and administration, selection and training of teachers, and public relations with the community at large. An American foundation granted $5,000 to this seminar, filmed some of the seminars for distribution among SPA member schools, contributed toward travel expenses, and provided lecturers. Influenced by these seminars, the SPA began to plan expansion in the fields of general social service, including the problems of the blind, the aged, the criminal, and the disabled. The monks were keen, from the inception of the SPA, to contact the Social Service Department, the Mass Education Council, and the Burma Hill Tracts Buddist Mission for help and cooperation. The government should be encouraged, they thought, to open schools on monastery grounds. It should also be asked to look favorably on job applications by orphans and other school personnel. Some monks immediately requested interchange of facilities between orphanages and even interchange of children, but this was opposed by a number of independent-minded monks. Thus, there was no shortage of ideas in the SPA.

Clearly some members of the Sangha enthusiastically supported the social service concept which the Nu government also encouraged. Within monasteries motivation was strongly increased by reasonable fears of recruitment problems and a desire to find more students for the vital monastic schools. A competitive urge vis-à-vis Christianity and other Western forces also may have motivated some monks. Quite obviously many also felt a genuine need to change some of the Sangha's traditional roles in society. The issue was debated during my stay and likely will not be resolved in any hurry. Interestingly, the social service organizations were some of the more successful Revival projects in which the government showed interest.

State Promotion of Meditation

Another well-known but perhaps not as successful aspect of the Buddhist Revival was the meditation center program.[21] As usual, one has to wonder if the government really initiated and developed it or merely joined and then attempted to control an already popular movement. The actual practice of Buddhism for the sophisticated urbanites involved in the Revival meant mainly the practice of meditation. Adopting the time-honored "recognition and subsidizing'" processes with which we have become very familiar, the BSC made itself responsible for the upkeep of existing meditation centers, provided they fulfilled BSC requirements. The first step taken was to divide meditation centers into four classes, each receiving government grants: class A, with more than 50 trainees (500 *kyat*s per annum); class B, with 30–50 students (300

21. Discussed briefly above, in Chapter 5. Cf. Spiro 1970:48–56, 273.

kyats); class C, with 10–30 students (200 *kyats*); and class D, "meditation centers not falling under any of the above classes" (100 *kyats*).[22]

The BSC report for 1954 goes on to say that "many virtuous *Mahatheras* [respected monks] who have vast experience in teaching *Vipassana* [insight meditation] to their disciples, have been recognized and appointed by the Council as *Kammatthana* [meditation subjects] teachers, and their Meditation Centers are classified as Class A." Among the seven-seventeen sayadaws so listed were ones of such countrywide fame as the Mohnyin Sayadaw of Monywa, U Neikbeinda of Prome, the Webu Sayadaw of Shwebo, a *sayadaw* of the Myingyan Sunlun group, and, of course the Mahasi Sayadaw of the BSC Thathana Yeiktha Center at the Buddha Sasana Nuggaha Ahpwe headquarters in Rangoon.[23]

The documents available suggest that the queries made by the BSC before recognizing and subsidizing centers aroused some opposition because of the opinion that meditation above all was a field in which control by one organization, however well meaning, was undesirable. As near as I can make out, a list of 216 likely centers was made out by the council, and a seventeen-point questionnaire was then sent to them.[24] The questionnaire items are listed here (with quotation marks for direct quotes) as a prime example of the government's efforts:

1. Name of center.
2. Area.
3. Location.
4. "In what sections of *Kammatthana* [meditation subjects] is the training given?" (see note x)
5. History of the center.
6. Constitution.
7. Method of training. (see note xx)
8. a. Name of presiding teacher and of his teacher.
   b. Names and qualifications of monk or lay assistants.
9. "Describe the different classes of people taking training in the Centre (Whether aged persons, youths, well-to-do persons, influential persons, or workmen should be definitely stated)."
10. Optimum time required for satisfactory training in system, and average time taken.

22. Burma 1954: addendum, p. 1; 1956b:21; 1958:17.
23. Burma 1954: addendum, p. 2. A list of recognized centers is found in *Sangayana Monthly Bulletin*, 2, no. 2 (June 1954):4–5.
24. *Sangayana Monthly Bulletin*, 2, no. 2 (June 1954):5. *Report on the Situation of Buddhism in Burma* (Burma 1956b:21) lists 14 points; I received a similar list from the Ministry of Religious Affairs.

11. Number of trainees who have completed the course.
12. Idem for period Jan. 1–Dec. 31, 1953.
13. Value of buildings and capacity.
14. Names of Managing Committee members and their status.
15. Present financial standing of center.
16. "Whether the Centre is progressing or declining (Full particulars in support of this statement must be given)."
17. List of the "yogins [trainees] a) who took training for some days, and b) who permanently reside in the Centre and practice meditation, during the past 12 months. (Note: The list of those yogins who take training by hours need not be given.)"

Notes:

x "In *Maha Satipatthāna Sutta,* there are 6 pabbas (sections) namely, 1) In and Out Breathing; 2) Considering the 4 Postures; 3) Attentiveness and Clearness of Consciousness; 4) Reflections on Loathsomeness of the body; 5) Analysis of the 4 physical elements; and 6) 9 Cemetery meditations. State from which section a yogin is first trained to become established in *samadhi* [concentration] and then trained to practice *Vipassana.*"

xx "In describing the method of training, mention how a yogin is trained to attain the higher stages of *Vipassana,* except those relating to the Paths of Sainthood." [25]

The questions in the 17-point list can, from one point of view, be taken as perfectly reasonable inquiries into the respectability of the candidates for recognition. Another point of view, however, leads us directly into the politics of meditation and Revivalism.

Foreign visitors to Burma intent on glimpsing the process of meditation soon realized that the BSC's official center, the Thathana Yeiktha, in Kokine Road, was not only the most logical place to stay but also that to which much advice naturally led him. The Mahasi Sayadaw was a most powerful figure, as noted in Chapter 5. It follows that this teacher, in charge of his own much-favored center, with branches scattered throughout the country and even in Ceylon, may have had some say in the matter of the recognition of other centers, depending on whether or not he approved of their system of teaching. In the 1956 and 1958 BSC reports, "training in Rangoon" is made part of the qualifications for grant support, and such preparation would most likely take place at the Mahasi Sayadaw's institution.

25. *Sangayana Monthly Bulletin,* 2, no. 2 (June 1954):5.

Resistance to such control and to such bureaucratic baroque as the questionnaire quoted above can be seen in the following government report on the success of the effort:

Seventeen questions relating to the working of the Meditation Centres have been sent to 121 Centres of all classes which have been subsidized by the Council last year, for the purpose of allowing double rate of the present grant to those Centres which satisfy the necessary conditions. These replies in the nature of Reports have to be submitted to the Council [BSC] through the Regional Representatives who scrutinize them before forwarding them to the Council.

Replies were received from 45 Centres out of these 121 Centres and, of these, 10 had to be returned as they did not bear the remarks of the Regional Representative concerned.[26]

Such evidence indicates that the government was less than successful in using the carrot and stick approach to that part of the Sangha and the lay Buddhist world which had developed meditation groups. It should be noted that some meditation masters acquired rather large followings and were able to construct impressive centers, the Mohnyin Sayadaw's amazing complex at Monywa, which I visited, being a case in point. In one lonely Shan village I was even told of the latest *gaing* of them all— the Vipassana Gaing, an unsophisticated reference to the various incipient organizations based upon the teachings of such *sayadaw*s as the Mohnyin, the Wissudhimagga *pontawgyi*,[27] or the Mahasi himself. The government (i.e., the BSC) can be seen as alert to identify and, under the disguise of support, to control, in its self-appointed role as *thathanabaing,* any potential schisms or sectarian movements within the Sangha. It is doubtful whether instruments such as questionnaires, however, would serve the ends for which they were designed.

We might note in passing that the BSC was inspired, partly because of writings considered overly candid in Burma, to make certain requirements of foreign visitors who were interested in meditation. Such persons have never been very numerous: only eleven persons are listed in the 1956 report (Burma 1956b:22). A 1958 BSC prospectus suggests that personal details of birth, sex, marital status, parentage, education, profession, religion, extent of Buddhist knowledge, language capabilities,

26. Ibid.
27. (B): head monk of a monastery.

and physical health, together with two references from persons "of some standing" and a letter of recommendation from the Burmese embassy or legation concerned, should be sent to the BSC well in advance. Candidates will be "accommodated at a Meditation Centre selected by the . . . Council and the course at this Centre will vary from a minimum of six weeks to ten weeks, depending on the progress of the pupil." During their stay, candidates must observe the following rules: (1) keeping the Eight Precepts; (2) following unconditionally their preceptor's instructions; (3) spending all but six hours out of twenty-four in *vipassana-bhavana* (insight meditation), with reading, writing, purposeless talking, and visitors to be avoided; and (4) undertaking to practice such discipline for a minimum of six weeks. Those desirious of joining the Sangha must undergo a period of probation as laymen while they learn the seventy-five novicehood rules, and a further period as a novice learning the 227 Vinaya rules. Finally the report states: "Both in the case of those practicing Meditation and those who join the Noble Order of *Bhikkhu*s, they must promise that they will not write and speak on Buddhism mentioning the name of the . . . Council without the prior consent of the Council. Those who, in the opinion of the Council, have made sufficient progress will, naturally, be helped and encouraged to preach the *Dhamma*."[28]

The volume of uninformed writing on Buddhism by Westerners after short periods of study is such that the above rules and regulations are perfectly understandable. Likewise the rules for meditation practice are certainly in the practitioner's interest. It should also be said that, to my knowledge, nothing stood in the way of a foreigner's meditating or joining the Sangha privately without BSC sponsorship if he so wished. Nevertheless certain of the regulations outlined above represented a departure, in my opinion, from the leisurely life and tolerance of Burmese Buddhism and suggest the layman's pride rather than detachment from same.[29]

Two Major Political Action Groups in the Sangha

This chapter has dealt so far with rather indirect government influence upon the Sangha, but there are two important Sangha groups that were

28. *Light of the Dhamma*, 5, no. 3 (July 1958):36.
29. For some foreign writing on BSC hospitality, see, among others, Mannin 1955, Shattock 1958, and Byles 1962.

openly political in terms of the rise and fall of the Revival and were deeply involved with internal rivalries of the government. One group, the YBA, evolved to be monastic spokesmen for the army point of view; the other, the KSA, developed to promote basically the policies of the Nu government, although there were some deviations in the case of both sides. The older of the two groups is the Yahan Byo Ahpwe, the YBA, which was discussed in Chapter 4 under the name of the General Council of the Thathana Mamaka Young Sanghas Association of Rangoon. It was this group that was so active in the anti-Indian Riots of 1938, and its leading *sayadaws* then were the Thayettaw and Bagaya, both of whom (or their successors) were politically active twenty years later.[30]

A quotation from a Rangoon newspaper of a later date, from an explanation of a photograph of "Monks on the March," gives us a vivid picture of the early YBA:

This picture was taken in 1938, the year of revolution in Burma. Students led the clamour for national independence and the peasants marched from the fields, the oil workers from the wells. The monks joined and led the march. Buddhism required the monks to isolate themselves from earthly things, but the times did not permit such aloofness. In Mandalay the "Young Monks" went round the town chastising by memorable methods those young Burmese ladies who dared to wear transparent voile imported from abroad. They waited at street corners and got the young men to shave their heads and rid themselves of Western style hair crops as a gesture of contempt for Western rule. Odd things they were, but those were the gestures that gave life to the national movement. Mandalay is the city of monks, and thus it was that in Mandalay many monks rose to martyrdom when mass demonstrations were fired on by the Government in that fateful year 1938. Monks in those days swayed legislative council elections. They were nationalistic to the marrow of their bones and yet they were not without their snobbery. They liked to be approached by people like Dr. Ba Maw who, with a knowing wink to his Jesus, would go and *shiko* the monks and woo their influence for his votes. Many of the Mandalay monks liked Dr. Ba Maw for his good looks and the way he spoke Burmese with his version of the Cambridge-Bordeaux accent. Even Aung San who was known to be brutally blunt at times, did not ignore the monks. As a soldier he would say audibly in public that the monks should be pressed into the Army—and there was no pressing necessary for the monks were only too keen to leave their monasteries for the barracks—but Aung San the politician would never go to Mandalay

---

30. Both *sayadaws* are discussed at the end of Chapter 5. Before the AFPFL split, many political monks (who were later to be divided into Nu and anti-Nu factions) followed the party leadership under U Nu.

without going to *shiko* the right monks at the right time which was election time. This time, some elements of the monkhood in Mandalay were roused, presumably by the opposition parties, to anger over a fight between two citizens. Those elements went round the streets and caned one or both the fighters. However, they spared U Kyaw Nyein and U Tin and other Ministers who flew up to Mandalay to *shiko* the right monk, though a trifle too late to prevent the trouble. The elderly *Sangha* and the Young Monks too threw their weight on the scale of calm and peace and U Kyaw Nyein and his colleagues were able to return to Rangoon un-caned, their Western hair styles intact.[31]

I have quoted this at length not only to give some idea of the history of those times but also to indicate something of the nationalistic, not to say patriotic and quasi-militaristic, fervor in which the YBA grew up and which it still possessed in the time I knew it.[32]

The YBA attained great prestige in 1950 by taking over the administration of the sacred Mandalay Hill and other Buddhist centers founded by U Khanti. The Shweman Sayadaw told the story as follows: U Khanti, a monk who had given up the Order and become a *yathe* (hermit) in order to build pagodas and shrines, died in 1949 and left the administration of the Mandalay Hill shrines to two Thudhamma *sayadaw*s, the Weluwun and the Atumashi, whose monasteries were close to the hill. The workers and maintainers of the shrines were paid only when big donations were made, and debts accumulated, which the *sayadaw*s could not handle. They consulted the YBA's U Zawtika, who consulted the Shweman. The latter advised an immediate takeover to prevent Mandalay Hill getting into the hands of "rotters." The committee, created under the patronage of the *rataguru* Nyaungyan Sayadaw,[33] accordingly handed over the running of the hill to the Mandalay Hill Association, with the consent of leading Mandalay *sayadaw*s and the AFPFL president in that city, the late U Ba Din, a silk merchant. Accordingly, in 1954, a new constitution of the Mandalay Hill Association was promulgated.

The constitution set up various executive officers on the same pattern as the YBA's organization and promulgated stringent rules about

31. *The Guardian*, Apr. 10, 1956.
32. See Spiro 1970:386–389 for more on the YBA (YMA).
33. Again, it should be noted that this incident took place in the days before the "split," when ostensibly there was one AFPFL for monks to relate to, and U Nu was its leader.

the collection, banking, and administration of the moneys involved, according to strict rules of Vinaya. The text made it clear that the YBA was in control, and I was told that the YBA president was also the Hill Association president, while a yearly shuffling of executives is arranged between the two associations. With the Mandalay Hill Association, the forty-six other establishments founded by U Khanti, whether standing by themselves or within other ecclesiastical lands, fell under YBA control. Twelve of these are situated in Mandalay township, six in Yamethin, four in Thaton, three in Minbu, two each in Maymyo, Sagaing, and Pegu, and one each in Namtu, Thibaw, Mogaung, Taunggyi, Pintaya, Pyinmana, Lewe, Moulmein, Belugyun, Mount Popa, Kyaukse, Mogok and Ava. It is interesting to note that two of the Mandalay pagodas involved are the famous Taungbyon shrines where the greatest *nat* festivals of Burma are annually carried out. When I attended this festival in 1959, I observed discreet visits by YBA officials and can scarcely doubt that rich funds swelled the treasury of the Hill Association in those parts. The YBA's position was that they were restoring the occasion from a *nat* ritual to its proper state—that is, a *pagoda* festival![34]

The YBA worked harder than any other known Sangha association for the acquisition of funds. On inquiring once why my garage manager was unavailable for three days one week, I found that all engineers in the township sympathetic to the YBA had been asked to help in the Mandalay Hill annual festival. Drawn by such novelties as a motorcycle race and the Modelers' Association of Central Burma airplane display, crowds of young people otherwise unattracted by pagoda *pwe*s came, brought their parents, and left money. Two other clues to the care devoted to fund-raising occur in the 1958 Supreme Executive Report: the Mandalay Hill report is found to be wanting in details; accordingly strict injunctions are given for the next year; and on another page the organization of the Taungbyon festivals is put into the hands of the supreme president and supreme secretary.

The constitution of the YBA, drawn up in 1954 and published the next year, set up eight departments, including distribution, organization, finance, auditing, education, library, investigation, and coordination. Each YBA group, at any territorial level, was to have a president, a vice-

---

34. See Spiro 1967:113–125 for a full discussion of the festival.

president, a secretary, and an assistant secretary, in addition to one executive officer for each of the departments—all these to be elected annually. The question of Ovadacariya monks was left rather vague. A high official of the YBA informed me that there had at first been a group of these but that they had wielded too much power since all decisions of the executive committees had had to be placed before them. The YBA grew weary of their pressure and dissolved them in 1951, adopting a single patron in the person of a famed nationalist monk, the Shweman Sayadaw. This depreciation of the Ovadacariyas is an interesting contrast to their favored position in the rival KSA (discussed below). As for the annual elections, the usual pattern of frequent re-elections is found: in 1959 the powerful U Zawtika was said to have been president since at least 1956, while a newspaper account dating from 1954 cites him as president.[35] The duties of the various officers were far more minutely laid out than in the KSA documents and included such tasks as the following: eradicating all unorthodox teachings, monks, and shrines from the *sasana* (i.e., the religion); removing all forms of immorality and dangers to the religion; opening classes for teaching the religion and distributing books therein; promoting monasteries in areas at home or abroad where Buddhism is not widespread; providing for monks' needs; defending the rights of Buddhists; proposing correct systems of meditation; caring for all YBA monks taking association examinations or *patamabyan* examinations; cooperating with the Pali University Act; improving teaching in monastic and lay schools; contacting and maintaining contacts with "all the cultural associations of the world"; and of course establishing and provisioning YBA groups at all territorial levels. The rules and regulations affecting group formation, times of meetings, quorums, and so forth were also far more disciplined than those of the KSA. Each monk in the YBA carried a card bearing his photograph, biographical data, and a list of his various attainments and proficiencies.

The familiar tendency for power to be placed in the hands of a frequently re-elected group of monks can be observed in such fragmentary evidence as could be secured. It should also be recorded at this stage that two officers listed were outstanding Vinayadharas in the courts system (see Chapter 5), while no less than nine officers were high-ranking members of the Pali University system. Also the familiar pattern

35. *New Times of Burma,* June 19, 1954.

appears of a recurrence of the names of certain leading *taik*s, such as the Htilin, the Kinwun Mingyi, and the Sagu. All the monks listed belonged to Mandalay establishments, although it is possible, of course, that some of the *sayadaw*s had been brought to Mandalay from other parts.

Despite my repeated questioning, data on recruitment was not forthcoming. U Kuthala, a YBA official I interviewed on this point in Mandalay, stated that individuals rather than whole *taik*s joined the YBA, though from the statement that out of 32 monasteries in the Khinmagan Taik 10 were Yahan Byo one may gather that a monastery would probably go the way of its *sayadaw*. Recruits were made mainly from Thudhamma; Shwegyin people had to be "very secretive" if they enrolled. The YBA had had to work for five years to establish a branch in Pakokku before finally succeeding in 1957. U Kuthala counted Pakokku as a Shwegyin stronghold because "the top *sayadaw*s follow Shwegyin rules inside their monasteries, though in publc they behave as Thudhamma." It wll be remembered that the Pakokku sect was likely to be pro-KSA. One YBA monk interviewed in 1959 said that there were about 100 YBA *ahpwe*s (organizations) in the whole of Burma and something like 16,000 monks. Dissatisfied with these figures, I attempted to get some better statistics and asked for a complete breakdown by area. Unfortunately I was furnished with only the total number of 18,800 monks for the whole of Burma, together with a list of all the organizations, without any breakdown. Analysis of this list leads me to believe there is an Upper Burma emphasis to YBA, with particular concentrations in Yamethin District and in the Lower Chindwin.

Fortunately I was able to make several visits to YBA headquarters, and my first was made in the company of a leading Ministry of Religious Affairs official for Mandalay, who had a healthy respect for the YBA's power at the time. We glimpsed the prosperity of the Mandalay Hill organization and met such leading monks as the Shweman Sayadaw and U Zawtika. In 1959, the garage manager previously referred to was very anxious to introduce us to one U Kuthala, whose power he claimed to be far more extensive than it appeared at first sight: he had been secretary of the All-Burma YBA but was about to become head of the new Press Section and was concerned with the complicated financial affairs of the YBA. On arriving at the "Inquiries Desk," we immediately noticed a difference in efficiency as compared with other Sangha organizations. Young monks looking very businesslike sat about at desks with sheaves of papers before them, and contact was made with U Kuthala over an internal telephone. Groups of army officers came in and out of the building all through our visit. We passed through a room downstairs in which there were a number of printing presses and other machines from British, American, and German manufacturers. It appeared from papers lying about that these presses were publishing a magazine, the *Mya Yatana,* some books on Buddhism, the *Light of Buddha* (a Mandalay lay monthly very similar to the BSC's *Light of the Dhamma*), and some smart green membership cards which turned out to be the new identification papers for members of the Army Security Councils. There were also posters on the walls showing aggressive-looking monks brandishing their beads in the face of bomb-carrying communist insurgents.

In interviews with U Kuthala during the period of the first army regime I was given information in a number of areas. In reference to the touchy matter of registering monks, I was told that in 1953 the YBA had pointed out to the Government the need for a monk census. The reply had been that insurgent conditions[36] made this impossible for the time being but that the YBA should set an example by making lists of its own monks and establishments. There are no indications, to my knowledge, that the YBA opposed governmental census activities, as some monks were doing at this time.

Asked about the proposed Hluttdaw (Sangha Parliament),[37] U Kuthala said that the YBA was adopting a neutral attitude for the time being and that they would act as new situations arose. He claimed that the Stable AFPFL was of the same opinion; General Ne Win as head of the caretaker government did not want a Hluttdaw for the moment, but U Nu was still for it. U Kuthala was diplomatic about the YBA's attitude to the Moral Rearmament campaign[38] in Rangoon and other such matters, claiming with a smile that the YBA found it more important to get rid of communists than to set themselves against other religious groups. On the other hand, he was formal about the Buddha Sasana

36. Conditions referred to include rebellions by Karen insurgents, the Chinese Nationalists troops in Northern Burma, and the usual communist uprisings.
37. The Hluttdaw issue is discussed in detail below.
38. U Nu had been very much involved for some time in the Moral Rearmament movement, as had been a small number of monks.

Council and said that the YBA had nothing whatsoever to do with it. As was not unusual, it was asserted that the YBA had had much to do with the idea of the BSC in the first place.

Although there is little evidence that the YBA stood for any specific political aims or desired any revolutionary innovations within the Sangha (in fact, they were a very conservative force), they were brought clearly into the political field by their acceptance of American aid and by the momentum of the process which led to the AFPFL split and the subsequent army regimes. These are delicate matters, and the proof of some of them is beyond my means to ascertain: all that can be reported here are the claims of the YBA and its enemies alike that it was involved in some of the sensitive issues of the time.

A prominent American foundation operating in scholarly, educational, and social welfare fields during my stay in Burma had first arrived in the country with the clear aim of recruiting anticommunist forces. Its first director was said to have started his operations in an extraordinarily secret manner. Later he put out advertisements that he wished to help people who would be prepared actively to combat the "Red menace." YBA leaders, among others, responded to his call and asked for a printing press. The foundation director wished to keep his advisers away from the Mandalay center, but it was nevertheless discovered that, apart from printing a rather unmonkly magazine, the *Mya Yatana,* the press was also being used for the printing of labels for a Mandalay beer company. The second foundation director, alarmed by various reports such as this, attempted to disengage himself with the aid of U Nu, but U Kuthala is said to have threatened to expose certain matters, and the foundation was advised to seek some compromise. Eventually a foundation adviser managed to convey to U Kuthala that many of his activities were unorthodox enough for him to be in a dangerous position, and something of a stalemate was said to have been reached, with the foundation apparently turning to other activities.

In response to criticism regarding American aid, the YBA at a meeting in 1959 stated that, while it was true that it had accepted a press from the Americans, similar gifts had been received by Rangoon and Mandalay universities, the Buddha Sasana Council, and other bodies. Were all these to be accused of being under American influence? The YBA would in fact receive aid from anyone—the United States, the Soviet Union, or China—provided there were no strings attached.

Finally, it was argued that the Burmese knew well enough that the YBA detested alien ideologies, as they had proved by the leading part they took in the liberation of Mandalay, in the course of which they lost seventeen heroes.[39] Such meetings and speeches did not stop people from believing that, denials to the contrary, the YBA was still receiving American help in 1959.

The political stance of the YBA was clearly pro-Stable AFPFL, pro–Swe-Nyein, but it is difficult to tell how far back in history the Stable allegiance goes. Was it manifest in friendship with the Socialists before the split? This is not certain. A prominent Buddhist layman of Rangoon who had been a high-ranking police officer before going in for Buddhist missionary work and flirting with various independent "third force" parties on neither side of the AFPFL split commented in 1958 that he remembered the YBA having been taken up first by the newspaper *Bama Khit,* which had a reputation for being in favor of the Nu-Tin faction of the AFPFL and pro-American, promoting the roles of American foundations in Burma. My informant stated that later the YBA was supported by both the Socialist leader Bo Khin Maung Gale and the American foundation in Mandalay at about the same time. Though the YBA people had run about in great style in Mandalay (in a car, and smoking the best foreign cigarettes), had been guilty of various misdeeds in the town, and had acquired the management of the prosperous Taungbyon festival, their American sponsors had criticized the handling of their magazine and they had quieted down since the AFPFL split. The informant thought that the YBA might have come under *Bama Khit* influence again, however. A curious item in the press gave further substance to these remarks without clarifying them. It was stated that the police had visited the *Bama Khit* office, interrogated its owner, and taken away two parcels found in the room of U Nyandawbatha, a monk temporarily in residence, who was arrested. His residence was given as the Masoyein Taik,[40] Mandalay—a monastery considered to have been of the KSA persuasion—but he was also said to be a member of the YBA. He had been arrested early in the insurrections and charged under the High Treason Act when arms and ammunitions had been found in

---

39. *Pyidawsoe,* Sept. 2, 1959.
40. See Chapter 5 for an account of the *rattaguru* Masoyein Sayadaw and his activities in support of KSA and Nu government programs.

his possession. He was sentenced to life imprisonment but later released after a successful appeal to the courts.[41]

Visiting the Religious Affairs Office in Mandalay a fortnight later, I obtained some clarification. The monk in question had indeed been a YBA member and had received arms from insurgents which he had kept underground with the authorities' knowledge. For some reason he had quarreled with the YBA. Meanwhile, the YBA's U Kuthala had been friendly both with *Bama Khit,* which had helped him to get a printing press from the Americans, and with U Kyaw Nyein. When the split occurred, the YBA had at first tried to mediate between the Clean and Stable factions; failing in this, it went Stable, breaking the link with *Bama Khit.* Thereupon the newspaper, looking for someone to act against U Kuthala, picked on U Nyandawbatha. The immediate reason for the latter's arrest was said to have been his friendliness with a leading member of the Nu party who was using him as an adviser.

Given this atmosphere, people showed great concern about the deaths of two monks in a controversy over the election of trustees for the Mahamuni Pagoda, the KSA and the YBA each claiming the dead monks as "martyrs."[42] Another case involved the beating of a monk by four other monks armed with iron rods who drove the victim off in a jeep.[43] Some confidential reports I obtained cited examples of YBA members hunting down monks, disrobing them, and tatooing the words "false monks" on their foreheads. It was suggested, indeed, that the ecclesiastical courts were in part set up to put an end to such drastic proceedings. In February 1959, a monk told me that the YBA members were very heavily armed in the districts and organizing swiftly. Other informants told me that monks were armed by both government and the opposition.

I did not personally witness many examples of tough behavior by monks, though one episode may be worth recording. One night in January 1959, I attended a small local *pwe* in Mandalay. While some monks were sitting quietly at the back watching the performance, a few young ones, holding hooked staffs, patrolled the audience with great purposefulness. They shone torches into the audience's faces and inter-

41. *The Nation,* June 10, 1959; *The Guardian,* June 10, 1959.
42. *Htoon,* July 29, 1958; *Mirror,* Nov. 21, 1958.
43. *The Nation,* July 18, 1958.

vened in a number of scuffles apparently started by laymen in the audience, on one occasion handing over a man to some military police-men. They appeared to be collaborating with some laymen who held seating plans. A young university student I talked to commented that they were bad monks, "going up to people and hitting them." When I asked if they were YBA, he seemed very scared and said, "Definitely not," then hastily walked away. When I later asked about this incident, at the Religious Affairs Office, I was told that "people still have a great respect for monks and might well invite them to police a *pwe*. Even the official guardians of the peace would listen to monks, who often had no other outlet. Then again many *sayadaws* protected their monks, going to the very highest authorities and getting Religious Affairs officers into trouble."

I even heard a number of rumors about YBA involvement in the complicated Kuomintang (KMT) affair,[44] the KMT troops being used as a "buffer" between Burma and the looming menace of Red China and the waiting rebel, Bo Zeya. In my interview at YBA headquarters, U Kuthala, the press representative, spoke to me about the KMT as a buffer state although he did not mention YBA involvement. Other in-formants, however, felt sure the monks were involved. I mention these rumors to show the degree to which people began to associate certain sectors of the Sangha with politics; Sangha participation in the Revival reached extremes in such extensions of religious activity—an extension that would and did invite a severe corrective.

While I was fortunate in having good contacts with the YBA, owing partly to the freer atmosphere of Mandalay and partly to the great self-confidence of the YBA, I was not so fortunate with the KSA (Kyaung-taik Sayadaw Ahpwe, or Presiding Sayadaws' Association). Its leaders were very aloof and reluctant to allow me to attend their meetings, one session being lifted bodily into another, inner chamber when I appeared. Much of this was at the instigation of suspicious elder laymen of the Buddha Sasana Council, but even friendly informants among the *saya-daws* were extremely reluctant to discuss their KSA activities.

Since the YBA is considered an older organization, the KSA can be understood as a group triggered by the existence of the YBA in order to

44. The presence in Northern Burma of Nationalist Chinese troops, said to be supplied by American CIA funds and materials. Cf. Cady 1958:621–624.

promote the political policies of the Nu-Tin "Clean" AFPFL faction. I attribute a strong role to lay politicians in its founding, as I see the problem as basically one of a felt need on the politicians' side for ecclesiastical backing.

In Chapter 5 attention was given to certain monks in the wartime Maha Sangha Ahpwe who formed the Burma Hill Tracts Buddhist Mission group in 1946, and it was noted how these monks were often later found in the Supreme Sangha Council, which ran the Sangayana. Many of these monks were also members of the KSA.[45] I was able to obtain a copy of the 1957 constitution, and since the KSA was only founded in 1955 it is a useful document. The structure of the organization follows the familiar territorial lines, rising from village or suburb to township, district, Upper Burma, Lower Burma, and then to the all-Burma or Union level. This as well as the patterns of representation and election procedures follow very closely those found in the ecclesiastical courts enactments, the sects constitutions, and the YBA constitution. There is a very strong suggestion that the KSA pattern was superimposed on two pre-existing organizations of leading monks in Rangoon and Mandalay— a fact confirmed by the Singapore Sayadaw—and it is easy to gather that these two were amalgamated to form the all-Burma executive group that ruled the roost throughout.[46] The usual mention is made of the Shan and Kayah states, though I never found any direct evidence of KSA extension into these parts comparable to lists found for the YBA. There is also the usual department system, in this case presumably copied from the YBA, with Departments of Sasana Affairs, Distribution, Organization, Finance, and Auditing. Of these the second is of special interest as it is concerned with censorship of anti-Buddhist or heterodox publications which can be destroyed after being brought to its notice. This suggests that the powers of the ecclesiastical courts monks were being

45. Analysis of the 57 members of the Burma Hill Tracts Mission group, for example, shows that at least 23 were high-ranking officers in the KSA, including the KSA president, the Payagyi Taik Sayadaw. Eight of the 26 SSC monks came from the Maha Sangha Ahpwe.

46. The Singapore Sayadaw said that Rangoon and Mandalay alternate as Union headquarters. The first president was a Mandalay man, the Khemathiwun Sayadaw; the second a Rangoon man, the Payagyi Sayadaw (Pakokku sect). This seemed to be contradicted by a third presidency held by the new Payagyi Sayadaw (from Rangoon) when his predecessor died and, more definitely, by the Rangoon Hnitkyaikshitsu Sayadaw's presidency in 1959 (see *New Times of Burma*, Mar. 25, 1959).

thought of here rather than those of mere KSA members and, indeed, there were examples of KSA leaders taking legal action against a number of publications actually disliked by the government. Apart from this, the document seems to leave loopholes for inactivity anywhere, and the vague injunctions to monks that they should never offend anyone and should always take the other person's opinion into consideration do no more than repeat the familiar lesson that Burmese monks enjoy the same cultural maxims as the rest of their countrymen.

As far as I could tell, the membership of KSA was fairly small; the best I could do was to interview the general secretary of the KSA, the Singapore Sayadaw, in October 1958. He claimed that there were 5,966 monks in the KSA, from some 641 monasteries. Another source, however, said there were 4,500 KSA monks in Rangoon alone, with "147 branches in the districts."[47] I was able to obtain membership lists only for committees in Rangoon, in my attempt to analyze the kinds of monks involved. The committee executives had familiar affiliations: they were Sangayana executive committee members, AMP's, Union Ovadacariya and Vinayadhara ecclesiastical judges, and judges from ecclesiastical courts at the district and township levels. These limited data on membership suggest that the KSA derives its power from its members' roles in the ecclesiastical courts structure rather than from powers inherent in the KSA itself. The KSA seems to be a rather redundant body of monks, required no doubt to back up the Rangoon leaders' actions with a show of all-Burma unity and to transmit to rural areas some of the policies of these leaders.

The government frequently consulted leading KSA monks on a wide range of issues, from peace-making with rebels to education and the teaching of Buddhism in schools, but my overall impression is that it was almost always the Rangoon leaders (many of them, of course, brought to Rangoon from elsewhere) who were consulted. A review of the issues on which the KSA took a stand or acted reveals a complicated pattern that cannot be reduced entirely to a pro-Nu stance, as we have so far tended to suggest. One factor that confuses matters constantly is the tendency of the KSA and YBA to arrange their positions so that they are conveniently in conflict over most issues. For example, a Ministry of Religious Affairs officer in Mandalay noted that

47. *New Times of Burma*, Feb. 22, 1959.

the YBA had originally agitated more than any other group for the establishment of the 1949 courts, but when it became clear that these courts were staffed largely by monks of the KSA persuasion the YBA took a stand against the courts and for the amendment. Such shifts were apparently not uncommon on either side. With caution, therefore, a review will be attempted of some of the KSA's involvement in the political as opposed to religious aspects of the Revival.

One issue that exercised KSA leaders in 1958 was Thakin Kodaw Hmaing's[48] reputed failure to do the monks' bidding in terms of bringing all insurgents back into the fold in a manner the monks expected from the charge given to his Peace Committee in 1956 to bring unity to the strife-torn country through Buddhist impartiality. The KSA monks here supported strongly the Nu government position on the matter, which was basically that the communists had used a few members of the Sangha to give the false impression that the whole monkhood supported the peace drive.[49]

A month later, the KSA was criticizing the court amendment act and urging a return to the original Vinicchaya-Htana Act of the forties. Here, of course, they were not supporting the government but opposing the YBA's pro-amendment stance.[50] In that same month the KSA was involved as consultant in interworker violence between Nu-Tin and Swe-Nyein supporters, with the monks apparently taking the role of peace-keepers.[51] In these examples, the KSA position fluctuates from active government support to disagreement with its legislation.

On the question of the controversial Hluttdaw, or Sangha Parliament, the KSA publicly supported it but privately admitted that it was passively resisting it,[52] but the YBA in August 1958 was still publicly for it, which

48. A well-known nationalist leader, formerly a monk, journalist, and co-founder of Dobama Asiayon; recipient of the Stalin Peace Prize. See Smith 1965: 200–201.

49. This controversy was widely covered in the press. See, for example, *The Burman*, June 26, Aug 6, 8, 1958; *The Nation*, Aug. 8, 15, 1958; *The Guardian*, Aug. 8, 1958; and *New Times of Burma*, Aug. 8, 1958.

50. *The Guardian*, Sept. 18, 1958; *New Times of Burma*, Sept. 18, 1958; and *Hanthawaddy*, Sept. 17, 1958.

51. *The Nation*, Aug. 28, 1958.

52. This information was obtained in an interview I had with an executive of the KSA. We have previously noted that certain orthodox Buddhist members of the U Nu party were not always in favor of all the AFPFL programs; a case in point is Chan Htoon's support of the amendment of the Ecclesiastical Courts Act.

suggests that, as the major AFPFL political split developed in 1958, the KSA and YBA diverged likewise. Once again, I suggest that the lay world's contests define and perhaps determine those of the political monks more than the other way around. More will have to be said on the Hluttdaw issue later.

Another controversial question was U Nu's plan to establish Buddhism as the state religion, and the KSA at its 1959 meeting took a strong position in favor of the plan. It is worth noting here that the KSA position on this argument was definitely pro-Nu in contrast to the YBA's anti–state religion position, which, of course, was the stance of the army as well.

In the education field, the KSA strongly supported the government's Pali University schemes and worked with the BSC to honor successful monks by helping to award degrees.[53] The KSA also was deeply concerned with the recruitment problems of the Sangha, and they put considerable pressure upon the government, through the Hnitkyaikshitsu, Aletawya, and Singapore Sayadaws, to support monastic primary education programs. The *sayadaws* made it clear that this question for them amounted to the survival of the Sangha itself.[54]

In most of the matters so far reviewed, the KSA leaders were acting as middlemen on behalf of the government or voicing the preoccupations of the monkhood at large. In the issue of censorship, however, they appear to have acted with considerable circumspection, and it is difficult to tell whether they initiated certain moves on the government's behalf or merely waited to be consulted by political leaders. At any rate, one of the prominent issues revolved around a curious personality, Myanma Aye, a self-styled Buddha-*raja* and *setkyamin*,[55] who was one of a long line of millenarian leaders in Burma exploiting certain messianic beliefs for political purposes. Whereas earlier leaders of this sort had some kind of altruistic purpose at heart in keeping with Burmese nationalistic aspirations, Myanma Aye came along at a time when these purposes had been fulfilled, and he acted throughout for his own self-aggrandizement. In February 1959 a news report appeared to the effect that, moved by protests from various official Buddhist sources regarding Myanma Aye's scandalous activities and publications, the

53. *New Light of Burma,* Dec. 10, 1959.
54. *The Nation,* Feb. 4, 8, 1959.
55. World emperor. See Chapter 4 and Glossary for its political connotations.

Ministry of Religious Affairs was about to prosecute and that the discussion would be taken up at the KSA Third Annual Meeting.[56] The Singapore Sayadaw's comments at his press conference in March, however, were very guarded. He limited himself to saying that the KSA had not yet been approached by either the government or Myanma Aye and that the book on which the investigation hinged would be examined at the meeting itself. In actuality, Myanma Aye was arrested around March 5, and any reports of the KSA's consideration of his book at the meeting do not seem to have been published.[57] Some of this KSA reticence on the matter may be explained by the fact that the beliefs held by Myanma Aye were widespread in Burma and were in fact shared by a number of monks. For example, a Burmese press report on one U Kundinnya of Daik-U, speculating on whether or not this monk had attained a high rank in the messianic hierarchy, mentions that he was secretary of the Presiding Sayadaws' Association of Daik-U, an organization possibly linked with the KSA.[58]

In another case, the KSA was consulted about the disrobing of U Okkata and U Wathawa, author and editor respectively of the controversial work *Lu The Lu Pyit,* a month after they had been arrested and imprisoned.[59] In both "censorship" cases, the guilty were apprehended before their cases were put to the KSA, so that here again it seems that the monks ultimately did what political laymen told them to do.

In the area of international events, the KSA sometimes took a stand, such as condemning Chinese aggression in Tibet and supporting the invitation of the Dalai Lama to Burma.[60] The Bahan Weluwun Sayadaw spoke out strongly in 1959 for the army's Dhammantaraya campaign, with its anticommunist message. The KSA, of course, was perfectly capable of saying, as one of its members actually did, that the Dhammantaraya revelations about the communist danger to Buddhism (the Army project) justified the need for making Buddhism the state religion (the Nu project)!

Frequently the KSA remained passive, secure in the knowledge that it was, for long, the Sangha representative of the party in power. The

56. *The Nation,* Feb. 22, 1959.
57. Ibid., Mar. 5, 1959.
58. *The Reporter,* Jan. 27, 1959.
59. *The Guardian,* Sept. 10, 1959.
60. *New Times of Burma,* Apr. 10, 1959; *The Nation,* Apr. 22, 26, 1959.

KSA can, however, be seen as voicing also the educational and self-protective concerns of the monkhood in general; it usually pronounced on the various issues placed before it with due regard to the Vinaya and the dignity of the Order. On occasions, it took its own line and demanded certain securities from the authorities in return. As we shall see, what was asked in return, or what they were told to ask for—the establishment of Buddhism as the state religion—was ostensibly the signal for the downfall of U Nu and the end of the Revival.

Smaller Political Action Groups in the Sangha

While the YBA and KSA were the two major politicized groups in the Sangha, there were many others which, though perhaps smaller or more impermanent, often compensated for such factors by being most vociferous. Most of the information on these smaller groups comes from scattered references in the press and from a few comments made by informants; by and large, these are extremely cursory and general, and the prevailing habit of assuming identical or very similar names, not to speak of recurrent "borrowings" from each others' programs, makes group identification difficult in certain cases.

If the number of press communiqués issued were anything to go by and if sheer outspokenness on many important political issues were the criterion, an organization known as the Sangha Front would have to be considered of greater importance than any other. I visited its headquarters, the Pyinnyaramikamaha Taik on Stockade Road, Rangoon, in August 1958, and acquired there the book *The Present Religious Events* by its leader, U Pyinnyawunthabidaza,[61] but I did not at the time appreciate its importance and unfortunately was unable to return. The buildings were modern, and it was clear that some political activity was in progress.

Asked about this organization called the Sangha Front, the Singapore Sayadaw, secretary of the KSA, stated that its leader had always been a dissenter. In 1949 he had gone against the Ecclesiastical Courts Act and immediately formed an Amendment Group with a twenty-one-member committee, bypassing the Presiding Sayadaws group of Rangoon (not yet organized into the KSA), "who had been there from the beginning," by his appeal directly to the Ministry of Religious Affairs. He had also

61. Alias the Pyinnyaramikamaha Sayadaw 1958.

begun to demonstrate against the Sangha Hluttdaw (monks parliament) as soon as plans for it were announced. The KSA was at that time looking into the matter and had not yet made a decision. When they eventually went against the act, U Pyinnyawunthabidaza of the Sangha Front went to the government and declared himself for it. In 1955 the KSA had taken three days to constitute itself, but U Pyinnyawunthabidaza heard about the proceedings on the second night, and, within one day, he attempted to form a group of his own, though he obtained the votes of only some thirty monasteries. An independent lay informant told me that he doubted the Sangha Front had more than five hundred members, and that most came from Rangoon city. Another informant believed that many of its members were Arakanese, but he may have confused the front with another group. While accusations of imitation and program stealing are familiar in this context, the Sangha Front was by no means led by an imitator and, however small his organization, his was one of the best-articulated critiques of government policy available for the period under review.

The principal activities of the Sangha Front appear to have been in the direction of propaganda through the press, direct appeals on a variety of topics to the Ministry of Religious Affairs, the distribution of its leader's booklet, and the organization of lectures. Present political affairs in relation to Buddhism were clearly the agenda.[62]

A good example of the Sangha Front's style and attitude is its critique of the Sangayana, which is seen in *The Present Religious Events* as just one more example of lamentable lay interference in Sangha affairs. At various points in the book by the Pyinnyaramikamaha Sayadaw, stories of the Sangayanas or councils of the past are told to stress the independence of the monks holding them, their concern with Sangha matters uniquely, and the qualifications of the monks attending. The Fifth Buddhist Council, held by Mindon, is discussed in great detail to show that, despite certain foreign views to the contrary, the king took all the right precautions to legitimate the proceedings. According to the author, only monks who have the particular power of looking back into the past are allowed to hold a Sangayana. These qualifications were satisfied in the Fifth Council. If U Nu and "his sycophants" believed that the marble tablets of Mindon contained inconsistencies and mistakes, they should

---

62. *New Light of Burma,* Oct. 16, 1958.

have smashed these tablets and based a council on their own views. But to copy texts from the marble tablets and at the same time to hold that these contained mistakes was to be in the depths of wicked ignorance. The Pyinnyaramikamaha Sayadaw continues:

> The Sixth Sangayana is not a Synod but a mere swindle for political ends.
>
> Without as much as informing the people, to use the people's funds while letting them starve merely to create a good record for themselves and for their own personal betterment, is an abuse of the people's money.
>
> Because of the Sangayana, which cost more than 5 crores [i.e., 50,000,000] of *kyat*s to convene, the Sasana,[63] far from improving, has become more corrupt. Great caves and monasteries were built; copies were made from great books and cooked rice was recooked. But do not believe that such acts, the loud chanting of young monk students and the bearing of responsibility and burdens by the afflicted people mean that the *Sasana* is in good health. . . . It is to be regretted that the Sasana has to fade because of men who not only slander it but have selfish natures and look forward only to the obtention of their meals. It is because of the Sangayana that the Sangha is neither learning nor teaching but merely eating *hsoon* and sleeping the days away.   [1958:21–22]

More directly, it is claimed that the census figures show that the Sangha had dwindled from some 100,000 in royal times to 80,000 in 1936, 70,000 in 1941, 50,000 in 1948, and 45,000 in 1958.

Another area of the government's Revival program that the Sangha Front author attacks is the Pali University system. The ills resulting from the Pali University were said to be the following. In the first place, salaries to monk lecturers tempted some monks into claiming more students than they really had. Presiding *sayadaw*s of monasteries were making it a condition of acceptance that students should sign agreements to appear for examinations in the name of their monasteries. Crash programs in instruction designed to bring students to examinations within fixed times were detrimental to the old traditions of learning within the Sangha. The claim made on behalf of the Sangayana to the effect that the Mindon tablets contained mistakes had not only reflected poorly on the great Mindon *sayadaw*s but had also undermined the prestige of all religious scholars. Indeed it could be argued that, since ordinations and ordination hall consecrations were now claimed to be incorrect, there was uncertainty as to whether even U Nu's monks were really monks. Jealous of each other's examination results, monks were tempted to

---

63. In this case, the state of Buddhism.

make complaints and to write anonymous letters to officials and to the press. Instead of laymen assisting monks in religious programs, monks were carrying out such programs for the benefit and enjoyment of laymen.

The Sangha Front author, the Pyinnyaramikamaha Sayadaw, also attacks the court system (1958:15–18). According to the author, the courts showed persistent prejudice in favor of *sanghika* claims against owners of *poggalika* monasteries.[64] Thus *sayadaws* of up to thirty-five years' residence in one place "have had their property seized by the courts' police and thrown out into the rain." Many presiding monks had been obliged to leave their monasteries on the representation from young visitors that their premises were really *sanghika*. Bribes, extorted under the pretext that to build a new monastery would be ruinous, are said to have been frequent: "Plentiful as excreta are the experts in Vinaya who have had the nerve to seek this money." Many laymen are only too glad to interfere in monastic cases and use the monks' innocence to draw them into their parties by defending them in the courts. Rumors were rife that "*parajika* godowns"[65] had been opened to feed monks who had fallen from grace in these ways.

U Pyinnyawunthabidaza several times makes it clear how far he considers money to be the root of most evils. He inveighs against the granting of 200 *kyat*s to successful *patamagyi* exam winners and then assigning them to duties at the Sangayana, which he sees as equivalent to disrobing them. As bad as putting arms in the hands of "*pyusawthi pongyis*"—a reference to the Mahamuni Pagoda incident[66]—is the plan made at one time to grant 300 *kyat*s each as a salary to members of the Sangha Hluttdaw. (There had in fact been a public outcry at the time this decision was announced, whereupon Prime Minister U Nu had had to declare that the money would be given only to lay stewards.) But the author saves his most intense ire for the Hluttdaw and registration proposals, both of which will be discussed shortly.

Enough of the Sangha Front's ideas have been illustrated to capture the flavor of a typical, small, political Sangha group. Other groups, pro-

---

64. For a discussion of these categories of Sangha property, see Chapter 3 and the Glossary.

65. Warehouses to feed all the monks who had violated the five basic rules. *Parajika* (P): *Parajita* (P): offenses serious enough to cause a monk's dismissal.

66. I.e., the YBA and KSA dispute over the "martyrs," discussed above in this chapter.

or anti-government, or indeterminate, flashed in and out of the papers with no more than the names of their presidents and secretaries to show for themselves. Such were, for instance, the Thathana Thanshinye under U Zawtika and U Thathana, who supported required monastic registration,[67] and the All-Sanghas Association, led by U Dhammathara and U Medingara, who protested that Buddhist monks were as much entitled as laymen to alternative settlements when the Rangoon Municipality pulled down the certain huts.[68] A Mahathawtuzana Sanghas Party entreated the Rangoon Bus Cooperative Union to allow three monks free on every motor bus but was allowed two.[69] The Thawtuzana Association held a meeting at the Masoyein Taik in Thayetmyo under U Nyanawuntha, U Wipula, U Kawida, and U Thuwunna and condemned Dr. Ba Maw's notorious "psychoanalysis" of U Nu, published shortly before.[70] This list should show fairly clearly why it is easier to speak of "ideas" among the Burmese Sangha than of those who hold them.

There were also regional Sangha associations. Prominent were the Arakanese, who attended a meeting of the Arakan National United Organization at the Arakanese monastery in Stockade Road, Rangoon.[71] An Arakanese Thawtuzana Sangha Association, founded in 1953 and devoted to the racial and religious uplift of the Arakanese, held its annual meeting at the Mingala Thukkha Pali University Taik in 1958 and urged General Ne Win to announce election dates and to settle the matter of Pakistani troop invasions in the following year.[72] An All-Arakan Yekkha-Mandala-Hita Sangha Association, led by U Gawthitayama and U Pyinnyathiri, sought the press out to ask why U Ottama's birthday was not being appropriately celebrated.[73] The Mon Sangha Association claimed to want a Mon state as much as laymen did but encouraged Mon rebels to surrender to the Burma Army.[74] Most of these regional or ethnic associations had very active lay "parishioners" in the city and elsewhere.

67. *The Nation,* June 5, 1959. The Buddha Sasana Purification Committee is probably the same organization (*New Times of Burma,* Mar. 15, 1959).

68. *New Times of Burma,* Jan. 14, 1959.

69. *The Burman,* Sept. 18, 1958.

70. Ibid., Oct. 22, 1959.

71. *The Guardian,* July 13, 1959.

72. *Mirror,* Nov. 10, 1959; *The Nation,* Jan. 13, Oct. 13, 1959.

73. *New Light of Burma,* Sept. 10, 1958.

74. *The Guardian,* July 11, 1958.

Some data were available on communist or fellow-traveling associations of monks. That there were such is indisputable, though the confused and dangerous political situation of 1958–1959 made it extremely difficult to get any worthwhile material about them. One of the very first monasteries I visited in Rangoon was the Shin Ardeissawuntha Taik on Mill Road. At the time of my visit, the presiding *sayadaw* was attending the last day of a World Peace Congress (WPC) celebration held by Thakin Kodaw Hmaing [75] at the Town Hall, and the monastery was virtually deserted. I spoke to the Taungdwingyi Sayadaw, the famous U Okkata, later to be imprisoned for writing the book *Lu The Lu Pyit,* who was preparing to attend the Stockholm meeting of the WPC some ten days later. He dwelt mainly on his desire to stay some six months in France after the meeting and showed me the small French grammar he had always carried about with him since learning the language in Lucknow and Pondicherry.

The *taik* was said to have been built around 1928 and to have always had a liberal reputation: laymen, for instance, are allowed to walk around the grounds with shoes on. It is built on the site of a graveyard which includes a recent tomb of the wife of U Ba Pe, a well-known nationalist who had been good to the monastery. Near the *sayadaw*'s dwelling is a large building which had until recently been a monastery school; the walls were covered with a number of typical left-wing posters, including one of heroic peasants on the march. Another building had contained a now defunct reading club: there were signs everywhere that the *taik* had known better days. The forty-odd monks then inhabiting the place seemed to be very busy scholars: their living quarters were a jumble of books and pamphlets and obviously served as a distribution center. We met three youths who were students at Rangoon University and resided at the monastery.

We were told at the time that it was *Tet Pongyi* Thein Pe Myint (see Chapter 4) who had begun the communist infiltration of the Shin Ardeissawuntha Taik by becoming friendly with one of the monks there. First attempts to send monks to Europe (to a Vienna communist front meeting) had failed when a member of the Buddha Sasana Council, contacted for letters of introduction to European Buddhists, quietly informed the BSC leaders, who had the visas for two up-country monks

75. See above in the chapter for his role as head of Peace Committee. Some felt he too easily espoused communist causes. Cf. Smith 1965:200–201.

quashed. One of these had been U Okkata, but it was thought that he had now obtained his visa for Stockholm because of U Nu's temporary alliance with the NUF[76] and similar parties.

The other monk involved in the Stockholm trip was U Pyinnyazawta, a prominent figure in the Shin Ardeissawuntha Taik. Photographs in the press showed him departing for the 1958 meeting in company with professor U Aung Hla, artist U Ohn Lwin, M.P. U Tin Maung, and other lay men and women.[77] In Peking, the Chinese Buddhist Association referred to the Burmese delegates' stand against "U.S. and British aggression in the Middle East" being in conformity with the teachings of the Buddha, while U Okkata gave a talk on the five precepts.[78] Later the group found itself in Hanoi supporting North Vietnam on the question of reunification and anti-imperialism in Southeast Asia.[79] In 1959, U Pyinnyazawta was still extolling the freedom of religion in the Soviet Union, where he found, "contrary to my expectation," that churches were kept in good repair, rituals frequently performed, and Buddhism adequately taught in "Rubiyatmongolia."[80] *The Nation* did not fail, a few days later, to establish a long letter attacking these statements and publicizing U Pyinnyazawta's links with the recently arrested U Okkata.[81]

References to the attendance of monks at left-wing functions and to the use of monasteries by left-wing parties were frequent in the press. In 1958 the all-Burma conference of the Burma Workers' and Peasants' Party was held in the Theingon Taik on Stockade Road.[82] Near the same time a meeting was held jointly by the People's Communist Party and the Dobama Asiayon to welcome back surrendered insurgents. At this meeting, the monk U Dutthana (a former insurgent) spoke of his fears about AFPFL-contracted debts and the do-nothings in the government, while insisting at the same time that he had abjured politics.[83] A similar meeting was recorded a few days later.[84] As late as January 1959, monks

76. Nationalist Unity Front: a "coalition, including mainly the Burma Workers and Peasants Party and assorted Communists such as Thakin Thein Pe Myint." Cady 1958:640.

77. *The Burman,* July 8, 13, 1958.

78. Ibid., Aug. 5, 1958.

79. *The Nation,* Sept. 4, 1958.

80. *The Burman,* Oct. 16, 1959. Probably a mistake for Buriyat in U.S.S.R.

81. *The Nation,* Oct. 29, 1959.

82. Ibid., Aug. 19, 1959.

83. *The Burman,* May 21, 1958.

84. Ibid., May 25, 1958.

were said to be present at a Youth Front meeting when army and police came to arrest front leaders.[85]

Such evidence, combined with that of the activities of such organizations as the Sangha Front, the KSA, and the YBA, underlines the degree to which certain elements of the Sangha were doing the bidding of lay politicians, no matter how self-motivated one sees the monks as being. Buddhism had become involved in the nation's political life to some degree and thus the active Sangha minority had been "revived" in that sense, but the majority of the Sangha also continued to resist the consequent attempts of laymen to discipline it.

The Plans for Sangha Registration and the Sangha Parliament

One of the major proposals to control the Sangha involved the Hluttaw, or Sangha Parliament of leading monks, but such plans met with very little success during my stay in Burma. The Sangha Parliament problem had two essential aspects not yet clearly distinguished. First, it was questionable whether the Sangha wanted such an organization or not, and it was divided on this point according to political affiliation. Second, before a parliament could be set up, it was necessary for the membership of the Sangha to be properly known, and this could not but involve some kind of registration of potential monastic "voters."

The issue became involved in other complex political forces that produced such chaos in Burma that in October 1958 General Ne Win and the army took over power from U Nu at the latter's request to run a caretaker government until the elections of Febuary 1960, at which time Nu was returned to power, only to be overthrown in a coup by the army under Ne Win in March 1962. The army, faced with social turmoil on all sides, sought to remove the monks from the political scene. Registration and a Sangha Parliament were two options it had inherited in 1958. Whereas the early AFPFL had apparently been treading with the utmost caution in both matters, the army regime soon realized the priority of the registration issue in its goal to discipline political monks, and it attempted to separate registration from the Sangha Parliament issue by connecting the proposed identity cards with national security. The political monks realized the implications of the army registration campaign, however, and attempted to keep the Sangha Parliament and registration united as one issue in the public eye.

85. *The Nation,* Jan. 2, 1959.

The machinery for registration had existed since the passage of the National Registration Act of 1949, and as far back as 1951 we find mention of government plans to register monks.[86] In 1956 a Directorate of Religious Affairs had been set up to deal with the question of a monastic parliament in three stages: (1) the compilation of a census of monks, (2) the formation of a Constitutive Committee to frame a Sangha Parliament bill, and (3) the establishment of machinery to carry out the provisions of the bill once enacted. There is no evidence that work on the census of monks proceeded very fast; we know that it was never completed. This effort does not appear to have been tied to the work of the National Registration Department, such as it was, which was mainly concerned with the registration of aliens. A glance at the official army criticism of AFPFL rule, involving comparative records of census activity between 1952 and October 1958, on the one hand, and November 1958 to January 1960, on the other, is sufficient to prove that progress on the general census was so poor that no Sangha registration could have been efficient.[87]

Under the older AFPFL plan, Sangha registration was probably to be held up until the Sangha Parliament question had been settled, whereas the army regime centralized and focused various government agencies into the national registration campaign and made it a high priority issue.[88] The difficulties the Ministry of Religious Affairs was having during the Nu regime with ecclesiastical courts, already described in part, tend to confirm this analysis. A 1959 report from the army regime tells us that the minister of religious affairs was still looking into complaints over a four-year delay in the issuing of identity cards even to ecclesiastical judges.[89] Complaints had been received that monks appointed and announced as judges in 1955 had not yet received their cards. It was found that 700 cards were ready but not dispatched to the districts, while 800 cards had not even been sent up for signature by the Directorate (Judicial). The head of this Directorate was fired and activities were hastened while I was in Burma.

Sometime between 1956 and 1958 a Constitutive Committee of 118 monks had been formed to draw up a Sangha Parliament bill satisfactory

86. *New Times of Burma,* Oct. 14, 1951.
87. Burma 1960:92–93.
88. Burma 1959b:150–151.
89. *The Nation,* Feb. 22, 1959.

to all sects and groupings. Unfortunately I could not find a list of the committee members, but it is most unlikely that they differed much from those of the monks reviewed as "government monks" in previous chapters. In July 1958 the Sangha Front interviewed U Nu at his house and obtained his promise that the orthodoxy of the Sangha Parliament idea would be publicly debated after research into the relevant scriptures. Should there be no ground for acceptance in the scriptures, a free and fair referendum would be taken in the Sangha on the establishment of such an organization.[90] On August 4, 1958, the Sangha Front warned against census takers who assured monks that their records were unconnected with the parliament question and advised monks not to answer questions unless the census takers produced signed affidavits. These statements reiterated familiar Sangha Front themes, such as the need for royal (as opposed to democratic) justification for Sangha control, the duty of monks not to support laymen in their political squabbles, and so forth.[91] The king of the Spirit-World, entrusted by the Buddha with the care of the religion, the Sangha Front held, was obviously taking his ease with his queens and nodding in his palaces. By August, the Sangha Front, seeing no sign of initiative on U Nu's part, demanded a public debate in September. It also announced its intention to link up with other anti-Sangha Parliament forces and with any political group that would oppose U Nu and his policies in the forthcoming elections.[92]

It was during this period that an army Ministry of Religious Affairs official in Rangoon told me "unofficially" that to all intents and purposes the KSA served as a Sangha Parliament for the time being, presumably because of the preponderance of ecclesiastical judges and *sayadaw*s with seniority in its membership. In April 1959 the same informant told me the Ministry of Religious Affairs had to get control very slowly and gradually, since demonstrations against the government would do no good to anyone. One day, of course, they would get the Sangha Parliament "for full control." My reasonably informed guess is that the army regime had persuaded the Religious Affairs people to go slowly by showing them that the national registration

90. *The Burman,* July 27, 1958; Htoon, Aug. 24, 1958; and Pyinnyaramikamaha Sayadaw 1958.
91. *Candid,* Aug. 5, 1958.
92. *Htoon,* Aug. 24, 1958.

people would do their work for them indirectly. Would the monks be fooled?

It does not seem so. On March 20, 1959, a statement issued by U Pawaya's Central Anti-Hluttdaw Association denounced the Hluttdaw once more and demanded the abolition of the Ministry of Religious Affairs, which had "degenerated into a wasteful political instrument by which the party in power used the cloak of religion for organizing followers." It also stated that "if this registration and the concomitant issue of identity cards to monks would not be made a reason for setting up the *Sangha* Assembly [Parliament], the Committee would agree to submit to registration. But the Committee would first ask the Prime Minister to give a guarantee that registration would not lead to establishment of the *Sangha* Assembly."[93] At about this time, the Sangha Front's disruptive activities caused the Rangoon Police to post men in its own monastery and in the neighboring Mingalayama Taik, which it had attacked. The cause of the fracas was said to be a difference of opinion between anti- and pro-Sangha Parliament factions.[94]

Discussing these matters with an extraordinary scholar and disciplinarian, the abbot of the famous Shwegyin Mahagandayon Taik at Amarapura, I learned that he had been summoned to Rangoon in June for a serious conference on Sangha Parliament preliminaries. While he did not think that the government could run an all-Burma machine as well as one abbot could run a monastery, it was his duty as a *wunhsaung*[95] to give them good advice. An extremely active phase of registration activity was envisaged in 1959 by the army leaders, and the following press report was issued:

Registration of monks, nuns and "koyins," in pursuance of section 2(1) of the National Registration Act, 1959 [sic, 1949] (which was temporarily suspended pending the completion of registration of other sectors of the public) is shortly to be undertaken by the National Registration Department, with the assistance of the Religion Affairs Officers, in all districts.

The purpose of national registration is fourfold: firstly, it furnishes the Government with the correct data on population statistics; secondly, it enables the Government to pick out the criminal elements and distinguish

---

93. *New Times of Burma,* Mar. 20, 1959; *The Nation,* Mar. 20, 1959.
94. *The Nation,* Mar. 1, 1959. For another meeting, see *New Times of Burma,* Mar. 19, 1959.
95. *Wunhsaung* (B): one who carries responsibilities; in this case, a member of the Shwegyin Executive Committee. See Chapter 3, questionnaire results.

them from the law-abiding; thirdly, by requiring voters to produce their National Registration certificates at the polls, it eliminates impersonations in the elections; and fourthly, it helps to trace absconders and offenders at large.

The growing tendency on the part of insurgents to don the yellow robe whenever they are at bay, and the unreserved respect given to members of the religious order by the general public, have shown the effectiveness of impersonating the religious in the insurgents' scheme to intensify subversive activities.

The report continues with claims that insurgents have been sending their men into the Sangha to act as spies all over the country. The home minister, in charge of national registration, asked the assistance of the Religious Affairs minister to extend registration to monks, and the latter instructed Religious Affairs personnel all over Burma to cooperate. At this point, statistics showed there were 60,000 monks and 5,000 nuns in Burma.[96]

Registration under the army regime had no sooner begun than complaints came in from Mandalay in particular that the status of monks was being insulted by their having the same cards as laymen and their being obliged to answer such questions as holder's name, father's name, sex, birth date, birthplace, occupation, marital status, and marks of identification. It was suggested that religious information be asked for and given in the place of this, and Bandoola U Sein promised to broadcast a statement about it very shortly.[97] In May he did so, affirming again that there was no relation between registration and the Sangha Parliament. Laymen, he said, were virtually all registered, and the registration of monks was a matter of principle. Furthermore, communist maneuvers within the Sangha (to mislead novices, incite crime, prevent elections, and so on) were being dealt with in keeping with the army's Dhammantaraya campaign.[98] U Sein also claimed that registration "was in keeping with the requirements of the religious order, which necessitates the maintenance of records of all members of the clergy, incorporating details, such as date of birth, date on which ordained, under which abbot, and names of parents." This neglected the point about which

96. *The Nation*, Apr. 24, 1959.

97. Ibid., May 17, 1959. Bandoola U Sein was Burma's director of religious affairs.

98. It should be noted that the Sangha, including the KSA, by and large cooperated with the army in its Dhammantaraya campaigns.

the monks had been complaining. On the same day the KSA of Pakokku met at the Mahawithudarama Taik to approve of registration.[99] At this point the Dwaya sect offered to print its own cards but was turned down by the government.[100]

Under pressure from many sources, including the U Pawaya of the anti-Hluttdaw group, the commissioner of immigration and national registration, Colonel Chit Myaing, told the press that revised cards had been printed and that registration of monks had been suspended until these blank cards were distributed to the monks. The colonel further expressed regret that certain political monks were dragging in the unrelated Sangha Parliament controversy, and he repeated his arguments about communist infiltration. Registration was said to be proceeding smoothly in several district centers, with 45 percent success so far, though work had not yet begun in Rangoon and Mandalay.[101] Here were signs that the program was running down.

More powerful forces now began to voice doubts. It will be remembered that the KSA showed signs of stress in private conversations. A pro-Nu group of monks, which perhaps represented one side in a possible KSA split, stood out for the plan of making Buddhism the official state religion but took a half-hearted attitude to registration: "N.R. [national registration] of monks should be carried out only with the consent of their superiors."[102] In July a report made it clear that the central KSA had objected to a number of conditions in the registration procedure. First there was the matter of penalties for violations ranging from two years' imprisonment to heavy fines. Colonel Chit Myaing had agreed to revise the wording of these "conditions" "to meet the *Sayadaws*' wishes for a less peremptory tone." In addition, however, two other conditions were displeasing to the KSA. One required any registered monk to inform the ward headman of his intention to be away from his residence for more than one month; another required the monk to see the headman to record changes of address. The KSA considered these clauses "most insulting to the Holy Order," and they wanted them out. No monk, they argued, should ever have to seek leave of a layman

99. *The Nation*, May 20, 1959; *New Times of Burma*, July 7, 1959.

100. *The Nation*, May 27, 1959. Cf. *The Guardian*, June 3, 1959; and *The Nation*, June 11, 1959.

101. *The Nation*, June 11, 1959.

102. Ibid., May 30, 1959.

to move about. The registration chief gave unconvincing replies to this request but stressed that the omission of these two clauses would defeat the whole purpose of the campaign. One has to take with a grain of salt the concluding paragraph to the effect that, "despite these objections . . . it is learnt from official sources that N.R. of monks is progressing satisfactorily."[103]

The KSA eventually named a five-man committee to discuss the offending rules with the Ministry of Religious Affairs people. Meeting them on August 3, Minister of Religious Affairs U Lun Baw explained that Parliament would have to intervene—the Cabinet itself was powerless. At the same time, since this was the last session of Parliament to be held by the army regime, which was now preparing for elections, the matter would have to be postponed. He would, however, prepare a bill for the next government to deal with. In reply the *sayadaws* obtained a promise that monks would not be obliged to register in the meantime, and there the matter seems to have rested.[104] Thus the fears of the monkhood regarding lay control finally had the better of both the Sangha Parliament idea and the registration plan. There was apparently a limit to the cooperation of even the most politicized groups in the Sangha, and it should be remembered that the "Mindon sects" such as the Shwegyin had long before "registered" and governed themselves. The Thudhamma groups in the KSA were seemingly the most afraid of lay discipline.

Mixed Sangha Support for a State Religion

The same attitude, interestingly enough, did not exist regarding the crucial proposal to make Buddhism officially the state religion. Reporting on U Nu's address to the monks at the last session of the Sangayana on February 18, 1962—few people realize how long the Sixth Buddhist Council really lasted!—a writer for the *International Buddhist News Forum*, the organ of the World Fellowship of Buddhists, paraphrased the prime minister's words as follows:

The *Sangayana* has come to a successful conclusion because of the intellectual help received from the *Sangha* and material help from the laity. He hoped that the *Sangha* would help make the second stage *Patipatti Sasana*

103. Ibid., July 7, 1959.
104. *New Times of Burma*, Aug. 23, 1959; *The Guardian*, Aug. 19, 1959. Another meeting seems to have taken place on August 13. See *Guardian Magazine*, Oct. 1959, p. 9.

(meditation) and the third stage *Pativedha Sasana* (penetration or realization of the truth of the *Dhamma*) better success [sic] than they are today. The Union Government having made Buddhism the State Religion of Burma would, U Nu promised, give greater support to the Buddhist religion.[105]

There is evidence that U Nu, during his bid for a return to power, attempted to present his state religion program as the natural outcome of the whole AFPFL effort to bring about a religious revival in Burma. The state religion provisions were introduced at a time when the Revival programs had virtually spent themselves, and U Nu probably pushed the state religion proposals through on behalf of certain lay colleagues and political partners of his, although he was probably aware of the danger and did so with some degree of reluctance. Here the task is to see how the monks reacted, and this is difficult insofar as these events took place after my stay in Burma.

Debate on the state religion issue apparently did not attempt to strike to the heart of contemporary problems of relations between Sangha and state, aspects of which—notably the Sangha Parliament and attendant registration—had caused such heated controversy. It looks as if the monks regarded the proposed State Religion Acts rather in the same light as the Dhammantaraya campaign: as something they could agree to in principle because it did not really concern their own internal organization. In September 1959, not long after the representatives of thirty-three Buddhist associations had met with the Young Men's Buddhist Association in Rangoon to discuss the topic, U Nu made his promise to make Buddhism the state religion in his election address to the conference of the Clean AFPFL Supreme Council.[106] He did his utmost to stress that non-Buddhists' views would be respected and that legislation would not be hasty. The Sangha was not mentioned, though his opponents were quick to point out that, when religion was used in politics, the Sangha was likely to split, thus further confusing the lay devotees. U Nu had to defend himself against these charges. It is true that monks were immediately involved in that the Clean AFPFL had come out with an eleven-point proposal promising, inter alia, the opening of primary schools in monasteries and of separate higher education

---

105. *International Buddhist News Forum*, 2, no. 4 (Apr. 1962):4.
106. *Guardian Magazine*, Oct. 1959, p. 10; *The Nation*, Sept. 27, 1959. Smith (1965) devotes the whole of his seventh chapter to the state religion question. His field work was done during this time.

facilities for the Sangha. The Swe-Nyein Stable party, on the other hand, while accusing Nu of turning people against them, put forward counter-proposals of more or less the same nature.[107]

U Nu was returned to leadership of the country in the elections of February 1960. In May 1960, while his opponents noted that Nu was stalling over the state religion issue, pro-Nu monks, through a body called the United Sangha League,[108] sent him a memorandum pressing him on the point, and the KSA followed this up at its annual conference a few days later. U Nu had previously announced the formation of two committees—one of monks, one lay—to consider the issue; at the first meeting of his new Cabinet, eighteen monks and twenty laymen had been named to what then appeared to be a single committee, the State Religion Enquiry Committee.[109]

At the first meeting of the committee, in April, U Nu had urged the Sangha and lay members to look into the requirements of both Sangha and laymen in the country,[110] but after a number of criticisms had been voiced by the press and by non-Buddhist organizations U Nu found it necessary to declare by July that the state religion issue was decided in principle—the State Religion Enquiry Committee sat only to recommend the best possible means of implementation.[111]

Reviewing a "Month of Trouble" in its editorial for March 1961, the *Guardian Magazine* made a first reference to a phenomenon involving more ominous forms of political behavior on the part of monks—behavior which was to make the state religion negotiations difficult, although in this case the connection was not direct:

The young Buddhist monks were for some time dissatisfied with the manner the authorities had handled the religious *Patamabyan* examination. Malpractice was alleged to have been committed by some of the monk-candidates at the time of the examination and after the holding of the examination the Religious Affairs Department hummed [sic] and hawed over the lists of candidates who should pass and who should fail. The monk-candidates de-

107. *Guardian Magazine,* Jan. 1960, pp. 6–12. Cf. von der Mehden 1963:99–101.
108. Because, other than my own research (1960), virtually no biographical information exists on actual membership of Sangha organizations, I can say nothing about the USL beyond the fact that it was pro-Nu. For its activities see Smith 1965:269–275.
109. *Guardian Magazine,* May 1960, pp. 6–7, 18–19.
110. Ibid., June 1960, p. 11.
111. Ibid., Sept. 1960, p. 12.

manded that those who were found guilty of malpractice be denounced publicly and those who answered well and honestly at the examination should be given their deserts. Finally, the monks felt that their grievance had been ignored and on February 16th afternoon they surrounded the Secretariat building which houses several Ministries and asked the Religious Minister to give them a satisfactory answer. When the Minister was unable to give a firm reply on his own the monks laid siege to the Secretariat. The siege lasted 26 hours and Ministries were immobilised. Clerks and some high officials who could disguise themselves as clerks were let out but three Ministers, police chiefs and several secretaries were trapped inside the Secretariat and "imprisoned." Prime Minister U Nu had to be sent for from his holiday at Ngapali seaside resort. He hurried back to the scene of trouble and placated the monks with words of persuasion but without yielding to the hard demands of the monks. The monks gave way, the majority of them satisfied with the knowledge that now U Nu knew their case and he would talk further with them about the matter.[112]

The months from May to August 1961 were singularly difficult for the Nu government. While U Nu spent forty-five days on Mount Popa (May 12–June 26) on a religious retreat, serious opposition to the state religion issue was gathering in the shape of the National Religious Minorities Alliance, which was attempting to link the issue with the explosive one of federalism.[113] Throughout July, meetings were held between Cabinet members and the State Religion Enquiry Committee and between U Nu and representatives of other religions, in the course of which U Nu stated that provisions suggested by the committee had been considerably toned down.[114] The Constitution (Third Amendment) Act was passed on August 17, 1961, in the Chamber of Deputies and on August 23 in the Chamber of Nationalities: on the twenty-sixth, this constitutional amendment was ratified by both houses and signed by the president.[115] Thus Buddhism became the official state religion of Burma. The constitutional amendment was accompanied by the State Religion

112. Ibid., Mar. 1961, p. 6; May 1961, p. 10.
113. At issue were plans involving a form of autonomy for the Shans, Kachins, Karens, Chins, and Kayahs by establishing states that would compose a national federation. Since many of these groups were non-Buddhist and were in armed rebellion against the central government, the state religion issue became for the non-Buddhists a dangerous threat to their autonomy as states in a predominantly Buddhist nation. J. F.
114. *International Buddhist News Forum*, 1, no. 7 (July 1961):8; 1, no. 8 (Aug. 1961):8.
115. *Guardian Magazine*, Nov. 1961, pp. 9–10; Sept. 1961, p. 6.

Promotion Act, and the two are generally referred to as the State Religion Promotion Act of 1961. The texts are given separately in Burmese sources; they are run together in von der Mehden's account.[116]

What were the provisions affecting the Sangha? Those directly concerned with the monks were very generally worded. In the State Religion Promotion Act, clause 6 states: "In cases where it is proposed to open new State primary schools, preference shall be given for the purpose to those monasteries which can provide suitable and adequate accommodation, and where a sufficient number of pupils is available, and the presiding monk is willing to accept the conditions laid down by the Government."

In the Constitution (Third Amendment) Act, clause 3, envisaging extensions to clause 21 of the constitution, proposes (21A,a) to "promote and maintain Buddhism for its welfare and advancement" in the study and practice of the Teachings and the search for Enlightenment, (21A,b) to "honour the *Tiratana,* namely the Buddha, *Dhamma* and *Sangha,"* and (21A,c) to "protect the said religion . . . from all dangers including insult and false representation, made by words, either spoken or written, or by other means."

Extensions 21B and 21C deal with the maintenance and propagation of the scriptures as recorded by both the Fifth and the Sixth Councils—an interesting measure no doubt connected with criticisms of the Sangayana by opponents of U Nu. Extension 21D provides for at least one annual meeting of *rattaguru,* AMP, Union Ovadacariya, and Vinayadhara *sayadaw*s (the Sangha Parliament question is not mentioned) at which the government is to account for state religion measures. Finally, clause 4, envisaging extensions to clause 43 of the constitution, sees the state as protector of ancient pagodas and temples (43A) and provides for the establishment of separate Sangha hospitals throughout the Union.

The above are the specifically ecclesiastical clauses. We should also note that the general provisions for Buddhist education affected the monks specifically, as was made clear subsequently in the serious agitation over the Nu government's next innovation, the Fourth Amendment Act.

There is little doubt that U Nu took the Sangha by surprise because

116. Von der Mehden 1963:103–107. *International Buddhist News Forum,* 1, no. 7 (July 1961): 21–22; 1, no. 9 (Sept. 1961):19–20. The readings that follow are from von der Mehden.

his leadership produced such rapid enactment of the Constitution (Fourth Amendment) Act, 1961, to protect the rights of religious minorities. A valuable Burmese report on the discussions which led to this allows us a glimpse of the important matters involved.[117] The Cabinet met on August 28, only two days after the final signing of the two previous acts. Explaining the reasons for this proposed measure, Judicial Minister E Maung first drew a difference between Union nationals (the larger political body of Burmese) and Union citizens (of smaller federated states). The latter knew what they were up against in obtaining citizenship in that it was obvious that Buddhism was the majority religion. Among Union nationals, however, there were non-Buddhists, and these had to be protected. The government had had to make quite sure that non-Buddhists were absolutely equal to Buddhists and that neither would see their religious rights as vested in themselves only, without benefit of possible extension to their children, as in communist countries. Hence he explained the importance given to teaching and propagation in the Fourth Amendment. Finally U Nu himself made the point that the non-Buddhists in the smaller federated states had to be thought of very carefully in relation to "the rather strained relations between the States and Burma proper." The issue of federalism was haunting the prime minister.

The new amendment guaranteed to non-Buddhists the right to teach their religion, as well as to practice and profess it, and the right to have their religion protected by the state. U Raschid's[118] addition prohibited minors in school from being taught any other religion than their own without written consent from parent or guardian. At previous Cabinet discussions, U Nu had also called for nominations of non-Buddhists to serve on the Ministry of Religious Affairs Committee, previously restricted to Buddhists.[119]

The Sangha reacted promptly. On September 13, the United Sangha League asked U Nu to defer the Fourth Amendment and to consider very seriously whether it did not amount to recognizing all religions as state religions. On September 17, about one hundred monks demon-

117. *International Buddhist News Forum*, 1, no. 10 (Oct. 1961):13–15.
118. U Raschid was a Moslem member of the Cabinet and as minister of labor and mines was a strong supporter of U Nu.
119. *International Buddhist News Forum*, 1, no. 10 (Oct. 1961):6, 14. *Guardian Magazine*, Dec. 1961, pp. 9–10.

strated outside U Nu's residence demanding withdrawal or postponement but they were not encouraged by the prime minister. On September 21, over five hundred monks of the Sangha Front attacked U Nu at a meeting the Shwedagon Pagoda platform and accused him of reducing Buddhism to the level of spirit-worshipping religions. Protests grew to a climax when on September 25, the day the amendment was to be voted, about 2,000 monks picketed the government building starting at 5:30 A.M. and forced the members of Parliament who tried to go through their lines to sign a pledge to vote against the Fourth Amendment. But U Nu had foiled the monks this time by instructing members of Parliament to come there earlier, at 4:00 A.M., before the picket lines went up. Thus only six legislators were forced to sign by the monks. The rest were safely inside and passed the Fourth Amendment by more than the two-thirds majority needed.[120]

Thus U Nu's leadership triumphed in this battle, but he was not in as strong a position as might appear. The monks appealed to the president of the Union to refuse to sign the new act. None of these moves were of any avail. Much resentment was engendered: monks tore up posters of U Nu and predicted bloodshed; it is also said that extremist groups wished to drum U Nu out of Buddhism altogether.[121]

On October 29, a group of militant monks entered a partially constructed mosque in the new Rangoon overspill suburb of North Okkalapa and took possession of it in protest against the number of mosques being erected there. There was confusion between police and other government authorities, the monks asking to deal directly with U Nu and the government asking for the intercession of influential *sayadaws*. A few weeks later, the monks took matters into their own hands, and in the resulting riots two mosques were destroyed, five lives lost, much property destroyed, and many arrested. There was evidence that the incident had been carefully planned and that the police should have known about it beforehand. On November 17, U Nu, after talks with Muslims and Buddhists, released the laymen and monks except for their ringleaders. Then, on November 18, 1961, over 1,500 monks are said to have met under the auspices of an "Emergency Sanghas Committee" to protest against government "brutality" during the riots. That is the

120. Smith 1965: 276–277.
121. *Guardian Magazine*, Dec. 1961, pp. 9–10; von der Mehden 1963:231.

last one hears of all this in my sources.[122] Not very long after, in March 1962, the army coup d'état put a sudden end to both Nu's political career and the Buddhist Revival.

A Revival Ended and a Silent Sangha

Since this coup, which began the second army regime, took place only six months after U Nu's State Religion Bills were passed in Parliament, we can do little more than talk about U Nu's intentions: the acts themselves barely had a chance to be put into practice. My purpose here is not so much to show how very unoriginal and mild were the measures envisaged as to consider more specifically the Sangha's position in the debate. Two things seem clear. In the first place, U Nu does not appear to have been nearer than before the passage of the two amendments to framing a convincing and efficient body of Sangha legislation. In the second place, the bulk of the Sangha continued to remain passive, while the familiar small action groups protested Nu's conciliatory policy toward Burma's other religions.

Reports emanating from the Buddha Sasana Council and allied bodies during U Nu's last government (1960–1962) confirm the impression that the Revival had spent itself by then. They concern the familiar details of the yearly round of monastic and lay examinations, the progress of the Sangayana, the campaign for Theravada Buddhism in Japan, the visits to pagodas by foreign missions, the work of meditation centers, the travels of relics, and so forth. The frequent reprinting of previous reports suggests the lack of any innovation. The personnel is the same: U Thein Maung,[123] U Chan Htoon, and other stalwarts form the State Religion Enquiry Committee; the same monks (the Masoyein, Aletawya, Hnitkyaikshitsu, Bagaya, and Bahan Weluwun Sayadaws) lead the ceremonies, and the same missionaries (U Thittila, U Pyinnyadipa, U Kowida, and the Mahasi Sayadaw) travel abroad. Pagoda restorations and festivals appear to have received some new impetus. Attempts at matching the army's anticommunist program (Dhammantaraya) appear

122. *Guardian Magazine*, Dec. 1961, pp. 6–7; Jan. 1962, pp. 9–11.
123. He was a well-known lawyer who led the YMBA shoe protest early in this century. He also served as chairman of the Pali University Enquiry Committee, vice president of the BSC executive council in the fifties, chief justice of the Supreme Court, deputy prime minister and minister of religious affairs under the first army regime, chairman of the State Religion Enquiry Committee, and chairman of the BSC as Ne Win took over in 1962.

in efforts to give body to the Five-Precepts Observance Society, in U Nu's directives for the building of magical nine-cubit sand pagodas, and in his attention to state *nat* shrines. In these respects, the story reported of the Revival does not change at all.[124] These activities, however, were not really relevant to the issues that catapulted the Sangha most boldly into the political arena. The government Revival programs that stirred the Sangha were the Sangha Parliament, registration, and state religion schemes—the issues of real concern to the monkhood.

On those issues the self-defense mechanisms of the Sangha can be clearly seen. While the Sangayana served one purpose in terms of Burma's international prestige, its internal function—indeed the function of the whole Revival that included it—was the reassertion of a traditionally defined system of rights and duties toward the Sangha by a lay authority claiming to pick up Burmese history again from where royalty ended. In the old idiom of "purification," the Revival can be understood as basically a disciplinary action on the part of Nu's government, which strove to unify and organize the Sangha through provisions for its political, legal, and educational activities. This operation was unsuccessful ultimately because of the opposition and independence of both the sects and the political associations, including the KSA itself and the YBA, which, instead of bringing unity to the Order, only reflected the disunity, factionalism, and conflict endemic to the lay politics of the times.

While I continued to observe the Sangha from overseas after my departure in 1959, I have arbitrarily put a time limit on this book—the final takeover by General Ne Win in 1962, at which time we find the KSA and YBA were still bickering in fraternal fashion over the familiar issues right up to the final moment. I therefore conclude this book as U Nu and his Buddhist Revival exit from the scene and the Sangha faces a socialist military government determined to put the Sangha to work on observing the Vinaya and to end the Order's role in politics. The silence of the Sangha since 1962 may be due not entirely to the drastic problems in communication and information flow. The story of the effect upon the Sangha of the long army reign has not yet been told.

124. On the Five-Precepts Observance Society, see *International Buddhist News Forum*, 1, no. 10 (Oct. 1961):10; 2, no. 1 (Jan. 1962):21; 2, no. 3 (Mar. 1962):12; 2, no. 4 (Apr. 1962):7; 2, no. 5 (May 1962):18, 22. On the sand pagodas, see ibid., 2, no. 11 (Nov. 1961):27; *Guardian Magazine*, Jan. 1962, p. 12; Feb. 1962, p. 9. On the *nats*, see *International Buddhist News Forum*, 1, no. 12 (Dec. 1961):27; 2, no. 1 (Jan. 1962):21–23.

APPENDIXES, GLOSSARY, BIBLIOGRAPHY, AND INDEX

Combined List of *Thathanabaings*
from Chronicles and Epigraphy

King	Reign dates	Monk-name	Title	Sayadaw-name
Minkyiswasawke	1368–1401			?1. Yakhaing ?2. Amyint
Mingaung I	1401–1422			Pwegyaung Aung Sikhon (A) Pinya Yagyi (?)
(Mohnyinthado)	1427–1440		Dhammasenapati	Pitu
Narapati	1443–1469		Saddhammatthiti	
(Thihathura)	1469–1481	Mahakassapa		
Anaukpetlun	1605–1628	Maharama	Mahasamghanatha	Le-Dat
(Thalun)	1629–1648	Maharama	?1. Mahasamgha-natha	Le-Dat
			?2. Tipitakalam-kara and (?) Ariyalamkara	Taungpila and (?) Dakkhinawun Kyaung
Pindale	1648–1661		Tilokalamkara	
(Taninganwe)	1714–1733	Ukkamsamala		
Mahadhammaya-zadipati	1733–1752	Nanavara		1st Kyaw Aung San Ta
Alaungpaya	1752–1760	Yasa	Maha Atula Yasa DRG	Atula
Naungdawgyi	1760–1763	Nyana	Nanalamkara MDRG	Taungdwingyi Hkingyihpyaw (A) Taungdwingyi
Hsinbyushin	1763–1776	Candovara	Jambudipa Anan-tadhaja MDRG	

King	Reign dates	Monk-name	Title	Sayadaw-name
Singu	1776–1782	Mayavattaka	Gunamunindabhi-sasana DRDRG	Manle
Bodawpaya	1782–1819	Nyana	Nanabhivamsadhamma-senapati MDRDRG	1st Maungdaung
Bagyidaw	1819–1837	Pyinnyasiha	Munindabhisirisa-dhammadhaja MDR DRG	Salin
Tharrawaddy	1837–1846	1. Suriyavamsa	Suriyavamsabhijiri-pavaralamkara-dhammasenapati MDRDRG	1. The-in (died in office)
		2. Nyeyya	Neyyadhammalamkara-bhivamsasiripavara-dhammasenapati MDRDRG	2. 2d Maungdaung
Pagan	1846–1853	Pannajota	Pannajotabhidhaja MDRDRG	2d Bagaya
Mindon	1853–1878	Nyeyya	Neyyadhammabhimu-nivaranakittisi-ridhajasenapati MDRDRG	2d Maungdaung (see above)
Thibaw	1878–1885	?	Malalamkarasasa-nadhajadhammase-napati MDRDRG	Taungdaw and Shwegyin
		Jagara	Jagarabhidhaja-sasanapaladhamma-senapati MDRDRG	

Kings and their reign dates have been standardized from Harvey 1925. Parentheses around a king's name indicate that the information does not appear in the Khemathiwun Sayadaw's mimeographed list or in Tin Tut 1943. See n. 58, Chapter 1.

The sign (A) stands for "alias."

In the titles, the code is as follows: M = *maha* (great); D = Dhamma (teachings of Buddha, the Law); R = *raja* (ruler, king); G = *guru* (teacher).

Monk-names are in Pali, as opposed to the Burmese *sayadaw*-names.

When two monks are listed with Arabic numerals in the same reign, one is believed to have succeeded the other. A question mark indicates uncertainty in the records. If two monks in one reign are joined by *and*, then both held office jointly.

Sayadaws Honored by King Bodawpaya, Including Those on the Sangha Council

Sayadaw names	Royal Title	Builder of monastery	Pali name of monastery	Burmese names of monastery
Min-O	Gunabhilamkara-saddhamma MD-RDRG	chief queen	Jeyyabhumi-viharakitti	La-kham-khum-kha-ram-to (A) Aungmyebontha
Manle	Gunamuninda-dhipati MDR-DRG	Kanni princess	Ramaniya-virama	Marilam-ka-kha-ra-to (A) Bonthaweyan
Hsounda	Tipitaka-sadhammasami-MDRDRG	viceroy's wife	Mangala-dhirama	Khum-ta-kha-ra-to (A) Mingalaweyan
Min-ywa	Nanajambudipa-anantadhaja-MDRDRG	middle queen	Mangala-vasatula	Mam-gam-kha-ra-to (A) Mingalasanlut
*Nyaunggan	Kavindabhisa-ddhammavara-dhaja MDRG	north queen	Mangalabhu-mikitti	No-na-kha-nam-kha-ra-to (A) Mingalabongyaw
Shwedaung	Kavindabhisa-dhammapavara-MDRG	Prome prince	Atulabhumi-vasa	No-no-khe-ram-to (A) Tulutbonsan
Hsinte	Nanalamkarasa-ddhammadhaja-MDRG	minister of interior		Kham-ga-tam-kha-ram-to
Meidhi	Paramasirivam-sadhaja MDRG	Army general		Ma-tih-kha-ram-to
*Lawkahmankin	Kavindasaradha-ja MDRDRG	Minister of justice		Lo-kam-pa-nam-ram-to
1st Bagaya	Tipitakalamka-radhaja MDRG			

Sayadaw names	Royal Title	Builder of monastery	Pali name of monastery	Burmese names of monastery
Kato	Cakkindabhidha-ja MDRG			
Mountaw	Janindabhipava-ra MDRG			
Salin	Mahananabhi-dhaja MDRG			
1st Maungdaung	Nanabhisasana-dhaja MDRG also Nanabhivamsa-dhammasenapati MDRDRG (*thathanabaing*)	king	Ratanabhumikitti (in Asokarama) and Jeyyabhumivihara-kittimangalavira-ma, etc.	

Asterisks indicate monks who were apparently not on the council but who received monasteries from the king.

Pali monastery names are from Pannasami 1861. Burmese names of monasteries are from Pannasami, with the names from Maha Dhamma Thinkyan 1831 below them.

The first four monks listed were appointed as joint heads of the Order and later replaced by the 1st Maungdaung Sayadaw.

Sayadaw names are collated from Maha Dhamma Thinkyan 1831 and Payapyu Sayadaw 1928. The code for titles is the same as in Appendix A.

Parakkama Lineage of the 2d Maungdaung Sayadaw

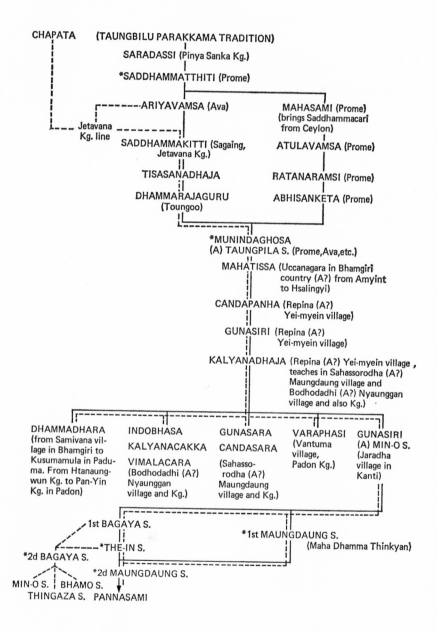

Abbreviations and symbols:

Kg.	= *kyaung:* monastery
A?	= probably the same as, but identification in the chronicles is not direct
———	= Chapata line
*	= *thathanabaing*
S.	= *sayadaw*
A	= alias

Sources: The data here are from Pannasami 1861; Maha Dhamma Thinkyan 1831;. and Payapyu Sayadaw 1928. They all follow a very similar pattern. See also Sandawara 1956(?):52.

It seems that we are really dealing with one line and not with two. The Jetavana Monastery is involved with the Chapata line leading to Saddhammakitti, but this is a very vague filliation and elsewhere we have been told that Ariyavamsa had the Jetavana and passed it on to Tisasanadhaja (Pannasami 1861:107-108; Maha Dhamma Thinkyan 1831:152). Further, the Jetavana was one of the seven monasteries in the Saga chain which gave rise to the Parakkama liné (Pannasami 1861:91; Maha Dhamma Thinkyan 1831:125). Its monks are said to belong to the Ananda line as opposed to the Arahanta Pagan line and thus could be considered Chapata. Another point of interest is that one of the names of the Taungpila Sayadaw's monastery appears to have been Zetawun Shwekyaung. The crucial position of this latter monk in the lineage should be obvious. One wonders whether the name of the monastery of Saradassi in the lineage (Pinya Sanka Kg.) could be related to the Pinya Saga Kyaungs. It may also be worth noting that the monk who is in charge of the first of the Saga Kyaungs is called Suddhamahasami.

Possible Lineages of
Sayadaws of Mindon Sects

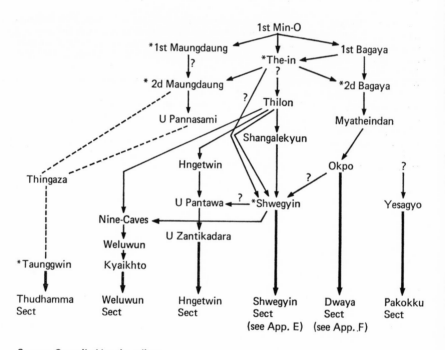

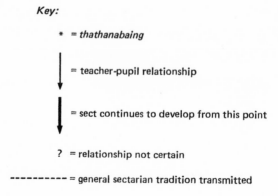

Source: Compiled by the editor.

> Key:
>
> * = *thathanabaing*
>
> | = teacher-pupil relationship
>
> | = sect continues to develop from this point
>
> ? = relationship not certain
>
> ---------- = general sectarian tradition transmitted

Heads of the Shwegyin Sect

No. (a)	Name (b)	*Sayadaw* name (c)	Date of accession (d)	Origin (district) (e)
1.	U Zagara	Shwegyin	?	Hlataw (village)
2.	?	1st Mahawithudayon	?	?
3.	U Nyana	2d Mahawithudayon (Dipeyin)	1920	Shwebo
4.	?	Kyaikkasan	1920	?
5.	U Teiktha	Alon	1927	Monywa
6.	U Zaneinda	Chanthagyi (Hseinmaga)	1929	Mandalay
7.	U Rada	Hlataw	1932	Shwebo
·8	U Kelatha	Kyaiklat Pissimayon	? (in control at 6th Conference, 1935)	Rangoon
9.	U Kawthanla	Withudayon Taik-ok	?	Mandalay
10.	U Sanda	Sankin or Withudayon Taik-kyat	? (*rattaguru,* 1953)	Sagaing
11.	U Egadama	Abayarama	?	Mandalay

Columns c and d are derived from the report of the Sixth Conference. Columns b and e are derived from a list obtained rather hastily at Kaba Aye from Shwegyin monks. This list inserted a Taungdaw Sayadaw between nos. 1 and 2—a curious slip in view of the fact that this was a Thudhamma *thathanabaing;* it omitted no. 4, inverted nos. 5 and 6, and recorded no. 7 U Sanda, Sankin Sayadaw. A later list from the same source follows the report closely.

The origin lists are general and refer to the place of origin at the time of nomination rather than birthplace.

Numbers 3 and 4 ruled concurrently, no. 3 for Upper Burma, no. 4 for Lower Burma. Numbers 7–11 were nominated president and joint-president at the same time and, as one died, the next took over. This is standard Vinaya procedure for monastery leadership carried into the sphere of the whole sect.

Number 11 was the master of two of the most active Shwegyin monks of the Supreme Sangha Council in our time.

Payapyu Sayadaw (1928:191) has the Ingan Mahawithudayon Sayadaw (Visuddhacara-kawidhaja MDRDRG) as Shwegyin head in the time of the Taunggwin *thathanabaing*. Panditta (1955:24) has a Pegu Shwegyin Kyaikkasan Sayadaw, but he seems to have died before 1917(?).

For meaning of *taik-ok* and *taik-kyat,* see Glossary.

The Venerated "Ancestor" Sayadaws of the Dwaya Sect

Name	Monastery	Monastery office	*Gaing* office	Born	Died
1. Okganthamala (Okgansa)	? Okpo, Henzada	? SP	1 MN	1817	1905
2. Mala	Rangoon Kyaung, Henzada	SP		?	?
3. Sandima Lingara Kawidaza	Payagyi Ledi, Henzada	1 SP		1831	1906
4. Buddhanta Thagara Bhodi	Payagyi, Henzada	1 SP		1848	1911
5. Thiri Sanda Zawtiya Thaba	Mahanagawuntha, Salun	? SP		1849	1935
6. Thiri Tilawka Thaba	Yetankhun, Henzada	1 SP	GR	1856	1926
7. Thiri Eindatha Bawara	Dhammayon, Henzada	1 SP	GR	1856	1941
8. Thiri Kawthanla Lingara	Thuddhamazawtikarama, Danubyu	2 SP	AN,AMP	1861	1935
9. Thiri Raseinda	Payagyi Ledi, Henzada	2 SP	4 MN, AMP	1860	1951
10. Nyanawuntha	Nyaungchaung	? SP		1866	1941
11. ?	Thuddhamazawtikarama, Danubyu	3 SP	? MN	1873	1950
12. Sanda Thiri	Yetankhun, Henzada	TO	GR	1885	1956
13. Saridathaba	Payagyi Taik, Henzada	2 SP	5 MN, 1 RATT	?	?
14. Kelathawuntha	Yetankhun, Henzada	3 SP	2 RATT	?	?

Number 1 may represent a telescoping of U Mala with the Okpo Sayadaw (U Okgansa).

Abbreviations: SP: *sayadaw payagyi;* MN: *maha nayaka;* a number preceding these indicates the temporal sequence of heads of monasteries. GR: *gana rakkhaka.* AMP: *agga maha pandita* title. AN: *anu nayaka.* TO: *taik-ok sayadaw.* RATT: *rattaguru.* For meaning of these terms, see the Glossary or Index.

The exact significance of the title of no. 9 is unclear. He may have had to do with the government ecclesiastical courts. This *sayadaw* (an AMP) seems to have played on the Ingapu side the same role as the Thabyebin on the Henzada side in the Dwaya reconciliation.

Burma Weekly Bulletin, 4, no. 49 (Mar. 8, 1956):387, in describing the one hundredth anniversary of the Dwaya sect's foundation, names as head of Dwaya (the *maha nayaka*) the Pandaung Sayadaw.

The last two items (nos. 13, 14) were added to the original list.

Number 13 was appointed in 1953, no. 14 in 1958.

Basic Books Studied
for Pali Examinations

I. *Patamange* exam (lowest grade)
  1. *Bhikkhu Patimokkha:* the basic manual of Vinaya discipline.
  2. *Kaccayana Vyakarana:* a work of grammar.[1]
  3. *Abhidhammattha Sangaha:* a famous twelfth-century Sinhalese compendium of Abhidhamma philosophy, long beloved of the Burmese and popularly known as *Thingyo.*
  4. *Matika:* a portion of the Vinaya.
  5. *Dhatukatha:* the third book of the Abhidhamma, which discusses "the mental elements and their relations to other categories."[2]
  6. *Dhammapada:* a well-known devotional work.[3]
II. *Patamalat* exam (middle grade)
  1. *Dvi-matika* (parts of this are studied): see no. 4 above.
  2. Further parts of nos. 2, 3, and 5 above.
  3. *Yamaka:* the sixth book of the Abhidhamma; psychological in emphasis.
  4. *Jataka Attkatha:* commentaries on the previous lives of the Buddha.
  5. *Dhammapada:* see no. 6 above.[4]
III. *Patamagyi* exam (higher grade)
  1. Further study of the texts for the Patamalat exam.
  2. *Chanda* (unidentified).
  3. *Abhidhana Padipika:* a dictionary of synonyms dealing with "celestial, terrestrial and miscellaneous matters."[5]
  4. *Alankara Nissaya:* a commentary written by a Burmese monk in 1880 on the Sinhalese work in Pali prosody called the *Subodhalankara.*[6]
  5. *Visuddhi Magga:* the legendary compendium of Buddhist doctrine by Buddhaghosa, the fifth-century Sinhalese commentator.
  6. *Patthana Kusalatika:* a commentary on the last and probably the most difficult book of the Abhidhamma.
IV. *Dhammacariya* exam—pass standard
  1. *Parajika-kanda:* the first chapter of the first of the two divisions of the *Sutta Vibhanga* of the Vinaya.
  2. *Silakkhandha-vagga:* the first division (*suttas* 1–13) of the *Digha Nikaya.*
  3. *Dhammasangani:* the first book of the Abhidhamma, dealing with "mental elements or processes."[7]
V. *Dhammacariya* exam—honors (*Siromani*)
  1. *Pacittiya:* Vinaya rules regarding expiation and forfeiture.

1. Malalasekera 1937, 1:479.
2. Thomas 1933:274.
3. For laymen and nuns, longer portions of this work replace the *Patimokkha.*
4. For laymen and nuns, more study of this work replaces the *Dvi-matika.*
5. Malalasekera 1937, 1:140.
6. Ibid., 1:185; 2:1226.
7. Thomas 1933:274.

2. *Patheyya Sutta:* from the *Mahavagga* of the *Digha Nikaya;* legendary accounts of Buddha's lives.[8]
3. *Majjhima Nikaya:* discourses in the Sutta Tipitaka on such subjects as the monk's life; also Buddha's enlightenment and other events in his life.[9]
4. *Samyutta Nikaya:* part of the Sutta Tipitaka on such subjects as the theory of causation, the five *khandas,* the senses, and the Eightfold Path.[10]
5. *Anguttara Nikaya:* part of the Sutta Tipitaka with a strictly numerical criterion for inclusion of material.[11]
6. *Abhidhamma Vibhanga:* second book of the Abhidhamma, dealing with distinction and determination in mental processes.[12]

8. Ibid., p. 269. I surmise that the *Patheyya Sutta* is related to the *Payeyyaka* (Burmese MSS: *Patheyyaka*), but I cannot be sure. See Malalesekera 1937, 2:195.
9. Thomas 1933:270–271.
10. Ibid., p. 271.
11. Ibid.
12. Ibid., p. 274.

Glossary

Compiled by the Editor

Note: Derivations are in brackets. The symbols used are as follows: B = Burmese; P = Pali; B-P = Burmanized Pali; Sk = Sanskrit. The romanization system used for B and B-P is eclectic, resembling most closely the government (1930) and the Grant-Brown system but with no diacritical marks (Okell 1971).

Abhidhamma (P): the more philosophical or metaphysical section of the Tipitaka. Studied avidly by Burmese Buddhists, particularly.

AFPFL: Anti-Fascist People's Freedom League. The wartime and postwar Thakin party of Aung San, Nu, Than Tun, etc., that split into various factions after Independence, including the Nu-Tin Clean and the Swe-Nyein Stable factions.

ahpwe (B): any of various kinds of associations or organizations.

amendment act (of 1954): a revision of the Ecclesiastical Courts Act of 1949 giving more power to sects to regulate disputes apart from centralized controls.

AMP: *Agga Maha Pandita Maha Thera*: [*agga* (P): highest; *maha* (P): great; *pandita* (P): wise man; *thera* (P): elder, monk] title and award for learned and respected *sayadaw*s, instituted by the British and continued by the AFPFL.

Ananda: one of the Chapata monks whose Ceylon orthodoxy started a lineage in Burma in the twelfth century.

Aniruddha: king of Pagan in eleventh century. Reputed to have been a strong proponent of Theravada Buddhism. Extended Upper Burmese sovereignty.

arahant: [*arahanta* (P): a Theravada follower whose nonattachment and holiness qualify him for Nirvana. The highest level of spiritual development possible short of Buddhahood itself.

Arahanta: Shin Arahan: famous Lower Burma monk who is said to have converted King Aniruddha to Theravada Buddhism and to have founded an Upper Burma line of monks.

Ari: In this context, medieval forest monks with a reputation for non-Vinaya behaviour and for Mahayanist or Tantric practices.

athin (B): any of many kinds of organizations or groups.

Atula: famous leader of the one-shoulder monks in the robe controversy.

Aung San: early Thakin leader, leader of independent Burma, and head of first ethnic Burmese army in modern times. Assassinated in 1947.

Ava: former capital city of Burma. Can be used by the British to refer to any royal capital.

Bahan: part of Rangoon between the Royal Lakes and the east side of the Shwedagon Pagoda.

bhikkhu (P): monk.

BSC: Buddha Sasana Council. A lay group that promoted the Sangayana.

BSN: Buddha Sasana Nuggaha Ahpwe. The precursor of the BSC, which promoted the Sangayana.

Burma Hill Tracts Buddhist Mission: an AFPFL project that promoted Buddhist missionary activities among Burma's hill tribes.

Chapata: Burmese monk ordained in Ceylon in twelfth century. Founded Ceylon line of Burmese Sangha.

chronicles: Burmese historical accounts frequently framed in legend and religious lore.

Clean AFPFL: the Nu-Tin faction of the AFPFL after the 1958 split.

Dhamma (P): the Buddha's teachings, doctrine, truth, law.

dhammacariya (P): [*dhamma* (P): doctrine; *acariya* (P): teacher] highest level of Pali examinations and scholarship. Literally, one who observes righteousness. One who lectures on the Dhamma.

Dhammaceti: king of Mon kingdom in fifteenth century. Strong promoter of Theravada Buddhism. Purified Sangha at Kalyani reordination. Author of Kalyani Inscription.

Dhammaduta College: founded and promoted by Buddha Sasana Council.

dhammantaraya campaign: army-sponsored anticommunist campaign under the "Buddhism in Danger" slogan.

Dwaya (B-P): [*dvara* (P): door, entrance] Lower Burma sect founded in nineteenth century by the Okpo Sayadaw. One of the "Mindon sects."

Fifth Buddhist Council: the synod called in the nineteenth century by King Mindon to purify the Theravada scriptures. The Fifth Sangayana.

forest monks: monks who live alone or in groups apart from village or city life, often in order to devote themselves more to meditation with less social involvement in lay affairs. Also called Aranyavasi.

gaing (B): [*gana* (P): chapter of monks] as used in this text, a grouping of *taik*s with incipient sectarian tendencies. Also can mean a faction of monks. As used in earlier Mendelson articles, a group with messianic overtones. Can also be an administrative level of authority above the *taik* level, as in the Shwegyin system.

gaing-dauk (B): ecclesiastical sect position below *gaing-gyok* and *gaing-ok*. Below the *dauk* level are the *taik* heads.

gaing-gyok (B): Sangha official in charge of a district. Under him were *ok*s, *dauk*s, and individual heads of monasteries. Above him were such officers as *htana-gyok*s, sect presidents, or the *thathanabaing*. Somewhat like a Western "bishop."

gaing-ok: ecclesiastical position in a sect, just below that of district *gaing-gyok* and above that of *gaing-dauk*.

galon (B): *garuda* (Sk): *garula* (P): mythical bird which forever seeks its arch enemies, the serpents or *naga*s (the latter being the British in the Saya San use of the symbol).

gana (P): chapter or meeting of monks; Sect. Used in Burma to denote sectarian aspect of an office, as in *gana nikaya,* or sect leader.

GCBA: General Council of Buddhist Associations. Later the General Council of Burmese Associations.

GCSS: General Council of the Sangha Samettgyi. Monastic branch of the GCBA. A politically oriented association.

Hluttdaw (B): the AFPFL plan for a Sangha parliament with a disciplinary function. Formerly, under the kings, a lay executive council of ministers.

Hngetwin (B): a nineteenth-century reformist sect, a "Mindon sect" founded by the Hngetwin Sayadaw.

hsoon (B): the ritual giving of food to monks, usually by inviting monks to a meal at a layman's house or to a neighborhood event.

htana (B-P): [*thana* (P): literally, place, locality: districts] a term used particularly by the Shwegyin sect.

Jatakas: stories about the Buddha's former births, each introduced by a passage relating the events to the time of Gotama's preaching.

Kaba Aye: place and complex of structures where Sixth Buddhist Council (Sangayana) was held (Rangoon).

Kalyani: originally an ordination place in Ceylon where Buddha is said to have bathed. Also a Burmese ordination site for the Sangha reforms of Dhammaceti in the fifteenth century. Used again as site name at Kaba Aye for Sixth Council.

kamma (P): [*kan* (B): *karma* (Sk)] the consequences or "record" of one's deeds from this and previous lives. It affects present action and events.

kan (B): see *kamma* above. As used mainly in this book, the deeds of the body, i.e., actions as contrasted with intent. Can be also a variant term for Mahagandi, or the majority of the Sangha.

kappiya (P): [*kappiya karaka* (P)] a lay steward who handles the secular affairs of the monastery for the monks.

Kemmendine: district of Rangoon, in the northwest sector. Famous for the concentration of monasteries there and the political activity of some of them.

koyin (B): *samanera* (P): a novice in the Sangha. Usually below twenty years of age. Not yet ordained as a monk.

KSA: the Kyaungtaik Sayadaw Ahpwe, or Presiding Sayadaws' Association. A group of politically active monks with a generally pro-U Nu stance.

Kyanzittha: king of Pagan in eleventh-twelfth century. Strong proponent of Theravada Buddhism. Formerly a general. Extended Upper Burmese sovereignty.

kyat (B): basic unit of Burmese money. Worth about 20 U.S. cents in 1975.

kyaung (B): a single monastery.

kyaung-pongyi (B): monk in charge of a monastery.

kyaungtaik (B): a larger complex of buildings than that represented by a single monastery. Called a *taik* in this book. Also used to denote a group of related monasteries (a "mother" monastery with "daughter" branches).

Lent: translator's term for the *wa* (B), or rainy season, when monks are monastery-bound and most men and boys go into the monasteries. A season of more than normal self-denial.

mahadanwun: [*maha* (P): great; *dan* (B): strong; *wun* (B): official] official who carried out disciplinary action for the *thathanabaing*. Supported by power of the king. Kept census and accounts of monks' travels.

Mahagandi (P): [*maha* (P): great; *gana* (P): sect, or *ganthi pada* (P): a text or glossary] a term used to describe the majority of the Sangha in early twentieth and late nineteenth centuries. Precursors of the Thudhamma. Contrasted with Sulagandi.

maha nayaka (P): great leader, master.

Maha Sangha Ahpwe (B-P): literally, great Sangha association; an organization promoted during World War II and for a while after to unite the Sangha, a program of Ba Maw. Thudhamma influence predominated.

mahathera (P): "Great Elder," respected older monk.

Maitreya (Sk): see Metteya.

Maramma: Upper Burmese. Usually refers to the indigenous or non-Ceylonese lineages of monks in Upper Burma. Often rivals of Sihala lineages.

Metteya (P): [*metteyya-natha* (P)] the Buddha who is to come at the end of the present era. Maitreya.

min (B): Westernized class of Burmese with nationalist goals. Often British officials.

Mindon sects: those sects the origins of which seem to be traceable to the Mindon period in the mid-nineteenth century, e.g., Shwegyin, Dwaya, Hngetwin.

Mons: ethnic group in Lower Burma whose kingdoms centered around Thaton and Pegu. Rivals of Upper Burmans.

nat (B): a spirit or god seen by some at the level of "animism" but interpreted in this book as part of Burmese Buddhism seen as a syncretic religious continuum.

nayaka (P): leader, master; head of a sect or *gaing*. Title used particularly for leaders of the Mindon sects.

Nibbana (P): [Nirvana (Sk)] the state in which all attachments are transcended, one is enlightened, and no further births are necessary.

nikaya (P): literally, assemblage, group; as used in this text, a sect. A grouping of *taik*s and possibly *gaing*s under the leadership of a hierarchy of *sayadaw*s.

Ovadacariya *sayadaw*s: [*ovadaka* (P): one who admonishes; *acarya* (P): teacher; *sayadaw:* respected monk] monks, who in the ecclesiastical court system after independence, help and advise higher judges in Vinaya disputes.

pagoda: [*zedi* (B): *cetiya* (P)] stupa.

Pakokku: town in Upper Burma on west bank of the Irrawaddy famous for its seats of monastic learning. Also a sect in the Independence period.

Pali: the sacred language of Burmese Buddhism in which the Tipitaka is written and in which much ritual is expressed.

parahita program: [*parahita* (P): welfare of others] social service projects for the Sangha as part of AFPFL plans.

Parakkama: a monastic lineage of monks that traced its orthodoxy back to Ceylon and down through several nineteenth-century primates.

Paramat (P): [*paramattha* (P): the highest good, ideal in the ultimate sense] a relative term at best, identifying certain Buddhist sectarian groups as on the fringe of orthodoxy. Their emphasis was upon *intent,* not ritual, and their tendency was to de-emphasize the importance of monks in their community roles. On a philosophical level, the term suggests Mahayanist concepts of emptiness.

parampara (P): succession, series; a list of monks in a lineage of teacher-disciple links. Also called *theraparampara*. A highly orthodox lineage.

patamabyan (B): Pali exams at a lower level than the *dhammacariya*s, Honor and grants are given to successful candidates.

Patimokkha (P): that section of the Vinaya dealing with the basic 227 rules of monastic life.

Pitaka: see Tipitaka.

poggalika: [*puggalika* (P): personal, individual] religious property vested in individual monks.

pongyi (B): [*bhikkhu* (P): generally, an ordained monk (literally, in Burmese, great glory or honor)] the term can denote a monk in charge of a monastery, as in *kyaung-pongyi.*

pontawgyi (B): a monk who is usually older than those simply called *pongyi* but not as old as a *sayadaw*. Shwegyin sect's terminology for a monk in charge of monastery but not a *taik.*

primate: the *thathanabaing*, or royally appointed head of the Sangha.

pwe (B): a festival that can have both secular and religious elements, usually featuring dramatic entertainment.

Pyidawtha (B): the socialist state envisioned by U Nu's AFPFL government (literally, pleasant royal country). To some, a welfare state.

rattaguru (B-P): [ratta: *rattha* (P) country; *guru* (P): teacher] honorary positions and titles created by the U Nu government in the 1950s to recognize the one leader with the greatest seniority in most of the major sects. In a fashion, an honorific substitute for the *thathanabaing* concept.

Revival: the political and religious programs in postwar independent Burma designed to revitalize Theravada Buddhism. Promoted particularly by the AFPFL governments.

Sagaing: town and hill west of Mandalay, famous for its forest and meditational monks. An important source of leaders for the "Mindon sects."

Sangayana: [*sangiti* (P): a convocation of the Sangha] the Sixth Buddhist Council in the 1950s, actively promoted by the AFPFL government under U Nu.

Sangha (P): [*Thanga* (B):] Buddhist monkhood, the Order of monks.

sangharaja (P): [*sangha* (P): monkhood; *raja* (P): king] ruler of the Order, or a branch of it, i.e., a *thathanabaing*. Usually used with reference to ecclesiastical organization before the eighteenth century.

Sangha University: an institution supported by the Institute of Advanced Buddhist Studies. For the education of monks.

sanghika (P): religious property belonging to the Sangha as a whole, rather than to individual monks as private possessions.

sasana (P): [*thathana* (B): teaching, order, message, doctrine] religion. In particular, the Buddha's religion.

Sasanavamsa: nineteenth-century Pali religious chronicle of Burmese Buddhism by U Pannasami (1861). Traces Parakkama lineage.

saya (B): a teacher of any kind. Sometimes a reference to those skilled in the more esoteric arts such as curing, astrology, etc.

sayadaw (B): now a term of respect for a monk who has spent ten years or more in the Sangha. Often used in titles with the place name of the monastery of which the monk is the head. Loosely, a term of respect for any ordained monk.

setkyamin: [*setkya* (B-P): celestial wheel; *min* (B): king; *cakravartin* (Sk): *cakkavattin* (P)] the universal monarch who is to come just before Maitreya, the Buddha to come.

shiko (B): give obeisance, bow to honor, pay respect.

shinbyu (B): ceremony of initiation of a novice into the Sangha.

Shwedagon: famous pagoda at Rangoon. In a sense, the national symbol of Buddhism in Burma.

Shwegyin: a Burmese sect founded in the nineteenth century. A "Mindon sect" with reformist characteristics. Strongest in Upper Burma.

Sihala (P): Ceylonese, Sinhalese. That branch of the Sangha in Burma that traced its orthodoxy to Ceylon teachers.

sila: literally, moral practice, code of morality; precepts or religious observances. In a large sense, the word also suggests religious virtue and morality in general.

sima: [*sima* (P)] boundary, limit; ordination site.

Simla Document: secret document prepared during World War II at Simla,

India, by a member of the British-influenced Burmese government in exile. It was a report recommending government policies for the Sangha after the war. See Tin Tut 1943.

Sinhalization: the process whereby reformist elements in the Burmese Sangha used reputed or real connections with the "pure" Buddhism of Ceylon to justify purification efforts.

Sixth Buddhist Council: synod (Sangayana) of the Theravada Sangha in the 1950s at Rangoon. Promoted by the AFPFL, particularly under U Nu's leadership.

SPA: Sangha Parahita Ahpwegyok. An association of monastic organizations with social service functions.

Stable AFPFL: the Swe-Nyein faction of the AFPFL in 1958 split.

Sulaganda: [possibly from *cula* (P): small, minor; *ganthipada* (P): a glossary] the reformist, puritanical opponents of the majority in the Sangha known as Mahagandi in late nineteenth and early twentieth centuries. Precursors of "Mindon sects."

Supreme Sangha Council: the monks who, in conjunction with the BSC, had the most to say about the running of the Sangayana.

taga (B): lay supporter of Buddhism, i.e., of the monks, through food and goods. Monks use this term in addressing all laymen.

tagama (B): female lay donor or supporter of the Sangha.

taik (B): literally, any substantial building. Usually a group of monasteries. Also used for *kyaungtaik* in the sense of a level ecclesiastical organization. Some are large teaching universities.

taik-kyat (B): in Shwegyin ecclesiastical hierarchy, a deputy warden below a *taik-ok*.

taik-ok (B): ecclesiastical officer, below the district *taik-gyok* and above the *taik-dauk*. Performs functions of warden, chief administrator, and discipline officer.

Thakins (B): Burmese nationalists whose agitation helped Burma to gain its independence, many of whom were its early leaders (Aung San, Nu, etc.).

thathanabaing (B-P): one who has authority over the religion. Head of the Sangha appointed by the Burmese king. The primate of the Order. Head of the councils.

Thathana Linkara Sadan: nineteenth-century Burmese religious chronicle by Maha Dhamma Thinkyan, the 1st Maungdaung Sayadaw.

thera (P): respected elder monk.

Theravada Buddhism: the religion of the elders. That form of Hinayana Buddhism that survived in Ceylon, Burma, Thailand, Cambodia, and Laos. It is often contrasted and compared with Mahayana and Tantric Buddhism.

Thudhamma: as used in this text, the majority of the Sangha from which sects split off. Other authors may consider the Thudhamma as a sect itself.

Thudhamma Council: executive council of the Sangha appointed by the *thathanabaing*. Existed at least in the nineteenth and twentieth centuries, perhaps much earlier.

Tipitaka: [*Tipitaka* (P)] Pali canon containing the three "baskets" or collections of Theravada Buddhism: Vinaya, Abhidhamma, and Sutta.

Vinaya (P): one of three parts of the Pali Theravada canon, or Tipitaka. It deals with all rules for the Sangha.

Vinayadhara *sayadaw*s: [Vinaya (P) + *dhara* (P): keeping in mind + *sayadaw* (B)] monks who, as judges in the ecclesiastical court system after Independence, decide Vinaya cases involving Sangha disputes.

vipassana: [*vipassana* (P): insight] mindfulness school of Theravada meditation.

wa (B): the rainy season. *See* Lent.

weikza (B): one supremely adept in messianic Buddhism. In some respects, a wizard who has mastered magic powers or arts, such as astrology, alchemy, cabbalistic signs, *mantra*s, and medicine.

Winido *sayadaw*s: [*Winido* (B): *Vinaya* (P)] same as Vinayadhara *sayadaw*s.

Wunthanu Athin (B): local lay nationalist organizations, usually GCBA.

YBA: Yahan Byo Ahpwe (B): Young Monks Association: a politically oriented group of monks whose final allegiance was anti-Nu and pro-army.

YMBA: Young Men's Buddhist Association.

Yongaing (B): a variant term for that majority in the Sangha from which reformist groups split in the late nineteenth and early twentieth centuries. Basically the same as Mahagandi.

Zawti: [*joti* (P): light, radiance: that is, exalted beyond the others] Shan Paramat sect.

zayat (B): rest house, contributed as act of merit. Sometimes used as place for meditation.

Bibliography of Works Cited

Note: If a date is listed in brackets for an older text, it represents the modern publication year of the edition cited, and the date after the author's name, in such a case, represents the year in which the original text was first released or written.

Ames, Michael. 1963. Ideological and Social Change in Ceylon. Human Organization 22:45–53.

Andrus, J. R. 1948. Burmese Economic Life. Stanford: Stanford University Press.

Asia Foundation. 1958. The Asia Foundation in Burma, 1957–58. Rangoon: Asia Foundation.

Aung Than, U. 1965. Relation between the Sangha and State and Laity. Journal of the Burma Research Society 48:1–7.

Bareau, André. 1955. Les sects bouddhiques du petit véhicule. Saigon: Publications de l'Ecole Française d'Extrême Orient.

Ba U, U. 1959. My Burma: The Autobiography of a President. New York: Taplinger.

Ba Yin, Bama Khit U. n.d. Sayadaw U Ottama. Rangoon: Thamamitta, Djambatam.

Bechert, Heinz. 1966–1973. Buddhismus, Staat und Gesellschaft in den Landern des Theravada-Buddhismus. 3 vols. Wiesbaden: der Schriften des Institutes für Asienkunde in Hamburg, O. Harrassowitz.

———. 1970. Theravada Buddhist Sangha: Some General Observations on Historical and Political Factors in Its Development. Journal of Asian Studies 24:761–778.

Bigandet, P. A. (Bishop). 1858. The Life or Legend of Gaudama the Buddha of the Burmese. Rangoon: Pegu Press.

Bode, Mabel H., trans. 1897. Sasanavamsa. London: Pali Text Society.

———. 1909. The Pali Literature of Burma. London: Royal Asiatic Society.

Brohm, John F. 1957. Burmese Religion and the Burmese Religious Revival. Ph.D. diss. Cornell University.

Brown, R. Grant. 1925. Burma as I Saw It. London: Methuen.

Burma. 1883. Report on the Census of India, 1881, vol. 1. Rangoon: Government Press.

——. 1892. Report on the Census of India, 1891, vol. 9, Burma Report, vol. 1, Operations and Results. Rangoon: Government Press.

——. 1902. Report on the Census of India, 1901, vol. 12, Burma, pt. 1. Rangoon: Supt. of Government Printing.

——. 1912. Report on the Census of India, 1911, vol. 9, Burma, pt. 1, Report. Rangoon: Supt. of Government Printing.

——. 1923. Report on the Census of India, 1921, vol. 10, Burma, pt. 2, tables. Rangoon: Supt. of Government Printing.

——. 1932. Burma Round Table Conference. London: Her Majesty's Stationery Office.

——. 1933. Report on the Census of India, 1931, vol. 11, Burma, pt. 2, tables. Rangoon: Supt. of Government Printing.

——. 1934. The Origin and Cause of the Burma Rebellion. Rangoon: Supt. of Government Printing.

——. 1936. Report on the Provincial Inquiry Committee on Vernacular and Vocational Education (also known as Report of the Vernacular and Vocational Education Reorganization Committee). Rangoon: Supt., of Government Printing.

——. 1939a. Final Report of the Riot Inquiry Committee. Rangoon: Supt., Government Printing and Stationery.

——. 1939b. Interim Report of the Riot Inquiry Committee. Rangoon: Supt., Government Printing and Stationery.

——. 1941. Report of the Pali University Enquiry Committee. Rangoon: Supt., Government Printing and Stationery.

——. 1943–1944. Burma during the Japanese Occupation, 2 vols. Simla, India: Intelligence Bureau, Government of Burma.

——. 1948. Report of the National Education in Buddhist Monasteries Enquiry Committee (also known as Committee on National Education in Buddhist Monasteries). Rangoon: Supt., Government Printing and Stationery.

——. 1949. Burma's Freedom: The First Anniversary. Rangoon: Directorate of Information.

——. 1952a. Pali Education Board Act of 1952 (Act No. 45 of 1952) (in Burmese). Rangoon: Supt., Government Printing and Stationery.

——. 1952b. The Pyidawtha Conference, August 4–17, 1952: Resolutions and Speeches. Rangoon: Ministry of Information.

——. 1954. Report on the Situation of Buddhism in Burma. Rangoon: Buddha Sasana Council.

——. 1956a. Chattha Sangayana. Rangoon: Publicity Sub-Committee of the Chattha Sangayana Central Committee.

——. 1956b. Report on the Situation of Buddhism in Burma. Rangoon: Buddha Sasana Council.

——. 1958. Report on the Situation of Buddhism in Burma. Rangoon: Buddha Sasana Council.

———. 1959a. The Buddha Sasana Council Act 1312 B.E. (Act No. 56 of 1950) (English translation). Rangoon: Supt., Government Printing and Stationery.

———. 1959b. Government in the Union of Burma 1958 Nov.–1959 Feb. Rangoon: Director of Information, Supt., Government Printing and Stationery.

———. 1959c. Pali University and Dhammacariya Act of 1950. Rangoon: Supt., Government Printing and Stationery.

———. 1959d. The Vinicchaya-Htana and Vinicchaya Tribunal Act, 1311 B.E. (Act No. 65 of 1949) and the Provisional Vinicchaya-Htana Act, 1313 B.E. (Act No. 46 of 1951) (English translation). Rangoon: Supt., Government Printing and Stationery.

———. 1960. Is Trust Vindicated? Rangoon: Director of Information.

Butwell, R. 1963. U Nu of Burma. Stanford: Stanford University Press.

Byles, Marie B. 1962. Journey into Burmese Silence. London: Allen and Unwin.

Cady, John F. 1958. A History of Modern Burma. Ithaca, N.Y.: Cornell University Press.

Chan Htoon. 1899–1902. Leading Cases in Buddhist Law. 2 vols. Rangoon: Hanthawaddy Press.

———. 1903. The Principles of Buddhist Law. 2d ed. Rangoon: British Burma Press.

Chatterjie, S. 1956(?). Meeting the Personalities. Rangoon: Rasika Ranjani Press.

Christian, J. 1945. Burma and the Japanese Invader. Bombay: Thacker.

Coedès, G. 1964. The Indianized States of Southeast Asia. Honolulu: East-West Center.

Collis, Maurice. 1953. Into Hidden Burma. London: Faber.

Cowell, E. B., ed. 1895. The Jataka, or Stories of the Buddha's Former Births. 6 vols. London: Pali Text Society.

Davids, T. W. Rhys, trans. 1890, 1894. The Questions of King Milinda. 2 vols. New York: Dover Publications.

Davids, T. W. Rhys, and C. Davids. 1921. Dialogues of the Buddha (Digha Nikaya), vol. 3. Sacred Books of the Buddhists, no. 4. London: Oxford University Press.

Dhammaceti, King. 1476. The Kalyani Inscriptions: Erected by King Dhammaceti at Pegu in 1476 A.D. Trans. Taw Sein Ko. Bangkok: Bangkok Times Press. [1925]

Donnison, F. S. V. 1970. Burma. New York: Praeger.

Dunkley, H. F. 1928. A Digest of Burma Rulings, 1872–1922. Rangoon: Government Printing.

———. 1941. A Digest of Burma Rulings, 1923–1937. Rangoon: Supt., Government Printing and Stationery.

Dupont, Pierre. 1959. L'archeologie mônede dvaravati, vol. 1. Paris: Publications de l'Ecole Française d'Extrême-Orient.

Duroiselle, Charles, ed. 1960. Epigraphia Birmanica, vol. 1, pt. 2. Rangoon: Supt., Government Printing and Stationery.

Dutt, Sukumar. 1962. Buddhist Monks and Monasteries of India. London: George Allen and Unwin.

Foucar, E. C. V. 1946. They Reigned in Mandalay. London: Dobson.

————. 1956. I Lived in Burma. London: Dobson.

Frauwallner, E. 1956. The Earliest Vinaya and the Beginnings of Buddhist Literature. Rome: Instituto Italiano per il Medio ed Estremo Oriente.

Furnivall, John S. 1948. Colonial Policy and Practice. London: Cambridge University Press.

Gaung, U. 1902–1909. Translation of a Digest of the Burmese Buddhist Law . . . 2 vols. Rangoon: Supt., Government Printing.

Geary, Grattan. 1886. Burma after the Conquest: Viewed in Its Political, Social, and Commercial Aspects from Mandalay. London: Low, Marston, Searle, and Revington.

Glass Palace Chronicle of the Kings of Burma. 1829. Trans. Pe Maung Tin and Gordon H. Luce. London: Oxford University Press. [1923]

Godakumbura, C. E. 1966. Relations between Burma and Ceylon. Journal of the Burma Research Society 49:145–162.

Golden Jubilee Number of the Y.M.B.A. 1956. Rangoon: Bamakhit Press.

Griswold, Alexander B. 1961. King Mongkut of Siam. New York: Asia Society.

Guyot, Dorothy. 1969. The Uses of Buddhism in Wartime Burma. Asian Studies 7:50–80.

Harvey, G. E. 1925. History of Burma. London: F. Cass.

————. 1946. British Rule in Burma. London: Faber.

Hitson, H. M., and D. H. Funkenstein. 1959. Family Patterns and Paranoidal Personality Structure in Boston and Burma. International Journal of Social Psychiatry 5: 182–190.

Hobbs, Cecil C. 1951. The Influence of Political Change on the Buddhist Priesthood in Burma. Asia 3:361–371.

Horner, I. B., trans. 1938–1952. The Book of the Discipline: Vinaya-Pitaka. 5 vols. London: Pali Text Society.

Htin Aung, U [Maung]. 1966. Burmese Monk's Tales. New York: Columbia University Press.

————. 1967. A History of Burma. New York: Columbia University Press.

————. 1970. Burmese History before 1287: A Defense of the Chronicles. Oxford: Asoka Society.

Human Relations Area Files. 1956. Burma, HRAF-37. 3 vols. New Haven, Conn.: Human Relations Area Files.

India. 1912. Report on the Census of India, 1911, vol. 9, Burma, pt, 1. Calcutta; Supt., Government Printing.

Judson, Adoniram. 1966. Judson's English and Burmese Dictionary. Un-abridged 10th ed. Rangoon: Baptist Board of Publications.

Kell, G. A. 1959. The Vital Importance of the Donation System for the Burmese. Sociologus n.s. 9:137–138.

Khameinda, U. 1959. Brief Account of the Dwaya Wadi Gaing or Order . . . [In Burmese.] Mimeographed. Report to Assistant Director of Religious Affairs Upper Burma, Deputy Commissioner's Office, Mandalay. July 19, 1959.

Lahiri, Sisir Chandra. 1951. Principles of Modern Burmese Buddhist Law. Calcutta: Eastern Law House.

Lamotte, Etienne. 1958. Histoire du bouddhisme indien. Louvain: Bibliothèque du Muséon.

Leach, Edmund R. 1954. Political Systems of Highland Burma. London: G. Bell.

Leach, F. B. 1937. The Future of Burma. 3d ed. Rangoon: British Burma Press.

Ledi Sayadaw. 1955. Weikzamaggadipani. Rangoon: Thudhammawaddy Press.

Lingat, Robert. 1937. Vinaya et droit laïque. Bulletin de l'Ecole Française d'Extrême-Orient 37:416–477.

———. 1958. La double crise de l'Englise bouddhique au Siam. Neuchatel, Switz.: Editions de la Baconnière.

Luce, Gordon H. 1953. Mons of the Pagan Dynasty. Journal of the Burma Research Society 36:1–19.

———. 1959a. Note on the Peoples of Burma in the 12th–13th Century A.D. Journal of the Burma Research Society 42:52–74.

———. 1959b. Old Kyaukse and the Coming of the Burmans. Journal of the Burma Research Society 42:75–109.

———. 1966. Royal Asiatic Society Gold Medal Lecture. London, mimeo.

———. 1969–1970. Old Burma—Early Pagan, vols. 1–2. Locust Valley, N.Y.: J. J. Augustin.

Luce, Gordon H., and Pe Maung Tin. 1939. Burma Down to the Fall of Pagan. Journal of the Burma Research Society 29:264–284.

Maha Dhamma Thinkyan [Thingyan] [Maungdaung Sayadaw]. 1831. Thathana Linkara Sadan [Sasanalankara]. Rangoon: Hanthawaddy Press. [1956]

Malalasekera, G. 1937. Dictionary of Pali Proper Names, 2 vols. London: Pali Text Society.

Malcolm, Rev. Howard. 1839. Travels in South-Eastern Asia, 2 vols. Boston: Gould, Kendall and Lincoln.

Mannin, E. 1955. Land of the Crested Lion. London: Jarrolds.

Mass Education Council of the Government of the Union of Burma. 1956. Mass Education in Burma. Rangoon: Rangoon Gazette.

Maung Maung Pye. n.d. (1951?) Burma in the Crucible. Rangoon: Khittaya.

Maunghtaung Sayadaw. 1959. Lu The Lu Pyit. Rangoon.

May Oung, U. 1914. A Selection of Leading Cases in Buddhist Law. Rangoon: British Burma Press.

Mendelson, E. M. 1958. La nouvelle birmanie. Critique 128:73–85.

———. 1960. Religion and Authority in Modern Burma. World Today 16: 110–118.

———. 1961a. The King of the Weaving Mountain. Royal Central Asian Journal 48:229–237.

———. 1961b. A Messianic Buddhist Association in Upper Burma. Bulletin of the School of Oriental and African Studies, University of London 24:560–580.

———. 1963a. Buddhism and Politics in Burma. New Society 1:8–10.

———. 1963b. Observations on a Tour in the Region of Mount Popa, Central Burma. France-Asie 179:786–807.

———. 1963c. The Uses of Religious Skepticism in Burma. Diogenes 41:94–116.

———. 1964. Buddhism and the Burmese Establishment. Archieves de sociologie des religions 17:85–95.

———. 1965a. Initiation and the Paradox of Power: A Sociological Approach. In Initiation, ed. C. J. Bleeker. London: E. J. Brill.

———. 1965b. Nationalism and Religion in Southeast Asia. Pacific Affairs 38: 64–68.

Mi Mi Khaing. 1945. Burmese Family. Bloomington: Indiana University Press.

Mootham, O. H. 1939. Burmese Buddhist Law. London: Oxford University Press.

Nash, Manning. 1965. The Golden Road to Modernity. New York: John Wiley.

Nisbet, John. 1901. Burma under British Rule—And Before, 2 vols. Westminster: A. Constable.

Nu, Thakin. 1954. Burma under the Japanese. New York: Macmillan.

Nyanatiloka. 1950. Buddhist Dictionary: Manual of Buddhist Terms and Doctrines. Colombo, Ceylon: Frewin.

Okell, John. 1971. A Guide to the Romanization of Burmese. London: Royal Asiatic Society.

Panditta, Shin. 1955. Shwehintha Tawya Thamaing. Rangoon: Kuthalawaddy Press.

Pannasami, U. 1861. The History of the Buddha's Religion (Sasanavamsa). Trans. Bimala C. Law. London: Luzac. [1952]

Pattamya Sayadaw. 1959. Brief Account of the Shwegyin Gaing. [In Burmese] Mimeographed. Report sent to Office of the Deputy Commissioner, Department of Sasana Affairs, Mandalay.

Payapyu Sayadaw. 1928. Thathana Bahu Thuttapakathani. Rangoon: Dee-dock Press.

Pearn, B. R. 1943. Burma Handbook. Simla: Government of India Press.

Pe Maung Tin. 1964. Buddhist Devotion and Meditation: An Objective Description and Study. London: S.P.C.K.

Pfanner, D. E., and J. Ingersoll. 1962. Theravada Buddhism and Village Economic Behavior. Journal of Asian Studies 21:341–361.

Purser, William C. B., and K. J. Saunders. 1914. Modern Buddhism in Burma: Being an Epitome of Information Received from Missionaries, Officials and Others. Rangoon: Christian Literary Society, Burma Branch.

Pyedaungsu Myanma Naingandaw Buddha Thathana Nuggaha Ahpwe. 1958. Rangoon: Buddha Sasana Nuggaha Ahpwe, Thathana Yeiktha.

Pyinnyaramikamaha Sayadaw. 1958. The Present Religious Events. Rangoon. [Title only in English.]

Rahula, Walpola. 1956. History of Buddhism in Ceylon. Colombo, Ceylon: M. D. Gunasena.

Ray, Niharranjan. 1946. An Introduction to the Study of Theravada Buddhism in Burma. Calcutta: University Press.

Sandawara, Shin. n.d. (1956?) Shweman Sayadaw Payagyi. Mandalay: Ludu Press.

Sangayana Souvenir. 1954. Rangoon: Union Buddha Sasana Council.

Sangermano, Father. 1833. The Burmese Empire a Hundred Years Ago. Westminister, London: Archibald Constable and Co.

Sarkisyanz, E. 1965. Buddhist Backgrounds of the Burmese Revolution. The Hague: Martinus Nijhoff.

Scott, James G. 1909. The Burman: His Life and Notions. New York: W. W. Norton.

———. 1911. Burma: A Handbook. 2d ed. London: A. Moring.

Scott, James G., and J. P. Hardiman. 1900. Gazetteer of Upper Burma and the Shan States. 5 vols. Rangoon: Supt., Government Printing.

Sein Myint, Maung. 1957. A Study of the Tiger Orphans' Vocational School. Master of Social Work thesis, University of Baroda.

Sein Tu, U. 1964. The Psychodynamics of Burmese Personality. Journal of the Burma Research Society 47:263–285.

Shattock, E. H. 1958. An Experiment in Mindfulness. London: Rider.

Shwegyin-taik. n.d. (1956?) Rangoon Myoma hnin Hanthawaddy Insein thon ne paung: Ne hsaingya Shwegyin gaing Winibyan Htana Wazo Thangadawmya Sayingyok . . . Rangoon: Shwelayaung Printing House.

Shweman Sayadaw. 1959. Report to the Department of Sasana Affairs. [In Burmese.] Mimeographed. Written for the Office of the Deputy Commissioner, Mandalay. July 25, 1959.

Smith, Donald E. 1965. Religion and Politics in Burma. Princeton: Princeton University Press.

Spiro, Melford E. 1967. Burmese Supernaturalism. Englewood Cliffs, N.J.: Prentice-Hall.

——. 1970. Buddhism and Society: A Great Tradition and Its Burmese Vicissitudes. New York: Harper.

Stewart, J. A. 1949. Buddhism in Burma. London: University of London, School of Oriental and African Studies (pamphlet).

Symes, Michael. 1800. An Account of an Embassy to the Kingdom of Ava. London: W. Bulmer.

Tambiah, S. J. 1968. The Ideology of Merit and the Social Correlates of Buddhism in a Thai Village. In Dialectic in Practical Religion, ed. Edmund R. Leach. Cambridge: Cambridge University Press.

Taw Sein Ko, trans. 1892. Introduction. In The Kalyani Inscriptions: Erected by King Dhammaceti at Pegu in 1476 A.D. Rangoon: Supt. of Government Printing.

——. 1893. A Preliminary Study of the Po: U: Daung Inscription of S'Inbyuyin, 1774 A.D. Indian Antiquary 22:1–8.

——. 1913. Burmese Sketches, vol. 1. Rangoon: British Burma Press.

Tet Hoot, U. 1961. The Nature of the Burmese Chronicles. In Historians of South-East Asia, ed. D. G. E. Hall. New York: Oxford University Press.

Tha Hla. 1958. The Rangoon University Strikes in 1936. New Burma Weekly 1, nos. 4–6, 8–10 (June 21 to Aug. 2).

Than Tun. 1959a. History of Burma, A.D. 1300–1400. Journal of the Burma Research Society 42:119–133.

——. 1959b. A History of Burma, Chap. 7, Rival Sects of the Religion. New Burma Weekly, Feb. 21, Feb. 28.

——. 1959c. Mahakassapa and His Tradition. Journal of the Burma Research Society 42:99–118.

——. 1959d. Religion in Burma, A.D. 1000–1300. Journal of the Burma Research Society 42:47–69.

——. 1960a. History of Burma, A.D. 1000–1300. Bulletin of the Burma Historical Commission 1:39–57.

——. 1960b. The Influence of Occultism in Burmese History with Special Reference to Bodawpaya's Reign. Bulletin of the Burma Historical Commission 1:117–145.

Thein Pe Myint. 1937. Tet Pongyi. Rangoon: Cyobyu Press.

——. 1943. What Happened in Burma. Allahabad: Kitabistan.

Thomas. Edward J. 1933. The History of Buddhist Thought. London: Routledge & Kegan Paul.

Tin Hla Thaw. 1959. History of Burma: A.D. 1400–1500. Journal of the Burma Research Society 42:147–148.

Tin Tut, U. 1943. The Problem of the Pongyi. In Burma File 4811/38: The Buddhist Church in Burma: Reforms and Remedy for Indiscipline. London, India Office Library and Records (mimeo).

Tinker, Hugh. 1957. The Union of Burma. London: Oxford University Press.

Tun Pe. 1949. Sun over Burma. Rangoon: Rasika Ranjani Press.

U Mya, Thiripyanchi. 1961. Votive Tablets of Burma, pts. 1–2. Rangoon: Department of Archaeological Survey of Burma.

von der Mehden, Fred R. 1963. Religion and Nationalism in Southeast Asia: Burma, Indonesia, the Philippines. Madison: University of Wisconsin Press.

Woodman, Dorothy. 1962. The Making of Burma. London: Cresset Press.

Yalman, Nur. 1962. The Ascetic Buddhist Monks of Ceylon. Ethnology 1: 315–328.

Yule, Henry. 1858. A Narrative of the Mission to the Court of Ava in 1855. London: Oxford University Press.

Newspapers and Periodicals

Bama Khit (in Burmese) (Rangoon)

Buddhism (Rangoon)

Burma (Director of Information, Rangoon)

The Burman (Rangoon)

Burma Weekly Bulletin (Director of Information, Rangoon)

Candid (in Burmese)

The Guardian (Rangoon)

Guardian Magazine (Rangoon)

Hanthawaddy (in Burmese)

Htoon (in Burmese)

International Buddhist News Forum (World Fellowship of Buddhists, Rangoon)

Journal of the Burma Research Society (Rangoon)

Light of the Dhamma (Buddha Sasana Council, Rangoon)

Mirror (in Burmese) (Rangoon)

The Nation (Rangoon)

New Burma Weekly (Rangoon)

New Light of Burma (in Burmese) (Rangoon)

New Times of Burma (Rangoon)

Pyidawsoe (in Burmese) (Rangoon)

Rangoon Gazette Weekly Bulletin (Rangoon)

Sangayana Monthly Bulletin (Buddha Sasana Council, Rangoon)

Index